*The Press Gang
in
Orkney and Shetland*

Seizing a Waterman at Tower Hill on the morning of his marriage.
Alexander Johnstone, 1815–1891.

The Orcadian [Kirkwall Press]

2011

Published by
The Orcadian [Kirkwall Press]
Hell's Half Acre
Hatston
KIRKWALL
Orkney
KW15 1DW

ISBN: 978-1-902957-45-8

© 2011 J D M Robertson
The right of John Robertson to be identified as the author of this work
has been asserted by him in accordance with sections 77 and 78 of the
Copyright, Designs and Patents Act 1988.

All rights reserved.
No. part of this publication may be reproduced or transmitted in any
form or by any means or stored in any retrieval system of any nature
without prior written permission, except for fair dealing under the
Copyright, Designs and Patents Act 1988 or in accordance with the
terms of a licence issued by the Copyright Licensing Society in respect
of photocopying or reprographic reproduction. Full acknowledgement
as to author, publisher and source must be given. Application for
permission for any other use of copyright material should be made in
writing to the publisher.

British Library Cataloguing in Publication data
A catalogue record for this book is available from the British Library

Printed and bound in Great Britain by
The Orcadian, Kirkwall and Hunter & Foulis, East Lothian

Dedicated to my wife
Norette

The nine-inch baton used by an Evie constable (see footnote p. 73).

Contents

List of Illustrations	ix
Acknowledgements	xi
Preface	xiii
The Impress Service	1
Impressment in the Northern Isles	7
HMS *Carysfort*	63
Evading and Resisting Impressment	71
Lieutenant William Wilson	119
Hiding Places	133
Women and the Press Gang	177
Whalers	199
Imprisoned on the Continent	215
Returning Islanders	223
Song and Verse	245
Tales of the Press Gang	255
The Sutherland Graeme Papers	273
Arthur Anderson and the Brazilian Navy	289
Caithness	295
Bibliography	299
List of Informants	305
Glossary	311

APPENDICES

Appendix A: Colloquy of Three Orcadian Sailors in a Spanish Prison — 317

Appendix B: James Fea's Will — 321

Appendix C: Extract from Neill's *Tour* — 323

Appendix D: Walls Session Records 1759 — 325

Appendix E: Memorial & defences for And[r] Morrison, Thomas Manson and Magnus Anderson — 327

Appendix F: List of Wills — 331

Appendix G: *Three Sisters* List of Recruits — 335

Index — 339

List of Illustrations

Dutch map of Orkney and Shetland, c.1770: *endpapers*
Seizing a Waterman at Tower Hill on the morning of his marriage: *frontispiece*

The nine-inch baton used by an Evie constable	*opposite* vii
Manning the Navy, the Press Gang of Tower Hill	*opposite* xiii
The Press-Gang, or English Liberty Displayed	3
The Press Gang, Robert Morley, 1857–1941	*opposite* 12
Exemption certificate for William Melvin	*opposite* 16
Olla Smith's challenge	22
The Tolbooth, Lerwick	24
The Tolbooth, Kirkwall	24
Army recruits 1758	*btw* 32/3
Army recruits 1757	*btw* 34/5
Receipts for remittances from *Three Sisters*, c.1770	*opposite* 43
Kirkwall Volunteers, 1807	57
Advertisement for Pike men and Fencibles, Lerwick, 1808	59
The King's Shilling or The Recruiting Party	*opposite* 75
The Press Gang, English Primitive School, depicted c.1840	*opposite* 77
The Press Gang 1772, nineteenth-century impression	*opposite* 88
Jack in the Bilboes, 1804	*opposite* 91
An Unwelcome Visit from the Press Gang	*opposite* 97
Reward Notice for a deserter	113
The Hidey Hole, Eday	*opposite* 133
Sandcroma geo, Marwick, 1975	139
Entrance to The Hole o the Head, Houton	140
Interior of The Hole o the Head, Houton	141
Paplay's Hole, Tankerness, 1969	144

List of Illustrations

View from interior of cave at Yinstay Head, Tankerness, 1969	145
Kirkwall schoolchildren in The Twenty Men Hole, Eynhallow c.1970	btw 147/152
Nine Men Hole, Eynhallow	btw 147/152
Sweyn's Cave, Eynhallow, 1972	btw 147/152
The Constable Holes, Sandwick, 1975	btw 153/156
The Halls of Garth, South Walls	opposite 156
The Covenanters Cave, Houss Ness, Burra Isle	159
Da Flegman's Hoose, Quilt Ness, Muckle Roe	161
The Orkneyman's Cave, or The Cave of The Bard, Bressay	btw 163/166
Entrance to Da Fairies Hoose, Bressay	166
Interior of Da Fairies Hoose, Bressay	166
Da Paeds Hoose, Myoness, West Isle, Skerries	167
Tammy Tyrie's Hidey Holl, West Isle, Skerries	168
Da Hoose a Heylor, Mavis Grind, Delting	btw 169/174
Da Hidey Holl, Skaw Taing, Whalsay	btw 169/174
The Liberty of the Subject – Women opposing the Press Gang	179
The Banks of the Shannon or Teddy and Patty	opposite 188
A View of the WHALE-FISHERY and the manner of KILLING-BEARS near & on the coast of Greenland	opposite 202
The Whale sea shanty	213
Nicholas Leith's Pension Certificate	opposite 230
Press Gang songs and verse	btw 245/254
Brazilian Navy Recruitment Poster	291
Brazilian Navy Terms and Conditions	292

Acknowledgements

I am grateful to my wife Norette for uncomplaining acceptance of my absences on research and writing, and for her forebearance over the not infrequent disruption to domestic life. Gratitude also to my mother for unfailing encouragement and perceptive criticism of drafts.

In preparing this volume I have received much assistance, in particular from: Ernest W Marwick, Kirkwall, a great Orcadian, helpmeet and true friend to many, for practical guidance and encouragement; Arthur Scott Robertson, Lerwick, a rare companion, for constant aid – undoubtedly a remarkable man and a musician of national renown; the ever responsive archivists Alison Fraser, Kirkwall, and Brian Smith and Angus Johnson, Lerwick; staff at the Orkney Library for making available reference books; Peter Jamieson, whose work on the Press Gang in Shetland proved valuable; Ian Robertson, John A Groat and Bruce Sandison for obtaining and recording Shetland stories and for photographing Shetland caves; Dr Charles Tait for photographing Orkney caves; George Longmuir, Lerwick, for providing Shetland documents; John Scott, Bressay, for making available the Gardie Papers; Peter K I Leith for providing information and documents concerning the five Leith brothers; The School of Scottish Studies for permission to use recordings made in 1968, 1971 and 1974; Connie Shearer and Elizabeth Dennison for typing and continued interest; R M Hall for advice on nautical matters; David Lowe for reproduction of press gang scenes and caves; Dr Alison Parkes for shrewd editing and valuable suggestions regarding structure; Drew Kennedy for his skilled pre-press work; David McLeod for endless tolerance and for providing much sound advice, constructive criticism and scrupulous guidance in layout and content; and, most especially, Marie Sutherland for undertaking detailed research over the years at the Orkney archive and for typing a voluminous correspondence and the manuscript. Without her unwavering patience and support the enterprise would have been hopelessly handicapped.

I also pay tribute to numerous people in Orkney and Shetland who over the years have contributed valuable and often unique information. Due recognition has been made in the List of Informants.

The Press Gang of Tower Hill. Engraving by Collins.
© National Maritime Museum

Preface

Various articles have been written about impressment in the Northern Isles. Some are interesting and valuable, others have been vitiated by an unhesitating acceptance of stories, a number of which are little more than legends, the passage of time having diminished the reality of events.

History should identify and concern itself with people, and the purpose of this book is to record coherently by story and document the impressment of islanders in the main, but not exclusively, from 1755 to 1815. The social background of these men is considered, as is the effect on family life when, in their absence, women and children had to cultivate the land as best they could. During these years – albeit with periods of quiescence – unfortunates were removed from kith and kin, cottage and croft, long views and familiar voes and from a frugal but essentially close family environment.

I deal mainly with ordinary, often anonymous, Orcadians and Shetlanders when the islands supplied very considerable numbers of men to serve in what were basically English wars. This was a time of such trouble and travail that the passage of two hundred years has not expunged the memory of events. In the mid-eighteenth century men were pressed into the army and the navy; thereafter islanders served mostly in the navy.

Knowledge is now rarely transmitted in an exclusively oral tradition. This was not always so and for centuries in Orkney and Shetland the normal method of communication was the spoken word – that peculiar blend of wisdom and ignorance. In the course of research I gathered a considerable number of traditional tales, many preserved by remoteness, and as these were a type of folklore they had to be examined with care and on occasion accepted with reservation. Additionally, I thought it important to identify and eliminate from an account of press gang times those myths and stories which were really part of folk imagination. This verification and subsequent intelligible committal to paper was time-consuming and sometimes seemed endless – rather like Sisyphus rolling his boulder towards an unattainable summit!

In summary, I have attempted to distil into a readable narrative a mass of homogeneous material acquired from a mélange of sources when these seemed worthwhile and true in their essentials. Some information was already in print, such as the particularly valuable *Around the Orkney Peat Fires,* some existed in manuscripts, and the remainder I obtained by personal communication and recorded for the first time. The initially ill-arranged and indigestable accumulation with which I started four decades ago has, I trust, been reduced to simple prose and communicated both naturally and logically. I hope that readers will share my understanding of a turbulent and oppressive period in the annals of Orkney and Shetland.

In endeavouring to bring together in manageable form the main threads of a fascinating part of the islands' history, I have in mind that later writers in this field may wish to build on my research.

*The Press Gang
in
Orkney and Shetland*

The Impress Service

To impress men was to force them to serve in the navy or the army. The *Encyclopaedia Britannica* refers to impressment as 'the exercise of the authority of the state to "press" or compel the service of the subject for the defense of the realm'. It was not only in this country that men were taken arbitrarily, and the Encyclopaedia continues 'armies on the continent were also made up in large part of men who had been impressed…. They had been taken from jails, snatched from taverns while drunk or kidnapped in dark streets or alleys. "Press gangs," as the military or naval parties were known, were as common in France and Prussia as they were in England. The fighting qualities of troops obtained in this manner were usually incredibly poor.'

There was a constant need for men, heightened by frequent wars with continental countries and war with the American colonies. Significant impressment occurred immediately before, at the outset of, and during the undernoted wars. The practice was discontinued only at the conclusion of the Napoleonic Wars in 1815:

- 1665–1667 Second Dutch War;
- 1672–1674 Third Dutch War;
- 1688–1697 War of the League of Augsburg;
- 1702–1714 War of the Spanish Succession;
- 1739–1748 War of Jenkin's Ear against Spain merging from 1744 with the War of Austrian Succession with France as well as Spain;
- 1756–1763 Known as the Seven Years War, this maritime and colonial conflict laid the foundations of the British Empire. England had only Prussia as an ally and faced the combined might of France, Austria, Russia, Sweden and Saxony;
- 1775–1783 War of American Independence against the rebels and also with France from 1778, Spain from 1779 and Holland from 1780;

1793–1802 French Revolutionary War;

1803–1815 Napoleonic Wars;

1812–1815 War with America.

Manning of guns and running of ships, particularly controlling the sails,[1] necessitated sizeable crews and there was great difficulty in providing full complements for an expanding navy. The demand was remorseless as the number of ships increased. In 1756 fifty thousand men were sufficient; by 1780 the number had reached ninety-two thousand and in 1802 the total was one hundred and twenty-nine thousand.[2]

From 1780 to 1815, when Britain was at the height of its maritime power, the press gang was the main means of recruiting the fleet. The action of English vessels in pressing men from American merchant ships was one of the causes that led to war in 1812 with the young American Republic. Those taken by the gang sometimes served for several years at a time, particularly during the long French Wars when vessels were at sea for extended periods.

By the late eighteenth century impressment was producing insufficient numbers. To rectify the deficit and at the same time provide some national structure for recruitment, the Quota Scheme (there were two Quota Acts) came into force in 1795. By this plan, devised by Pitt, every county and many ports had to supply a specified number of able-bodied men according to their population, and these recruits qualified for a bounty. Whether on land or sea, males under eighteen[3] and over fifty-five years of age were exempt, but they had to prove their claim with a certificate. The officer in charge of the press gang paid scant attention to the age regulation and frequently males under the age of eighteen were taken.

No man was lawfully exempt. However, from time to time exemptions were embodied in Acts of Parliament and extended and granted over the years by a reluctant Admiralty.[4] They included foreigners (although they could volunteer), crews of outward-bound merchant ships, sea apprentices who were protected for a term of three years from the date of their indenture, militia volunteers,

---

1 Nelson's flagship *Victory* had three masts and thirty-seven sails which provided a total sail area of 6,500 square yards, i.e. around four acres of sail.
2 *The Press Gang Afloat and Ashore*, J R Hutchinson, who quotes AD7.567 *Navy Progress 1756–1805*.
3 In 1779 the Justices of the Peace and Commissioners of Supply in Orkney reduced the age to sixteen. See p. 33.
4 Hutchinson, p. 80.

The Impress Service

THE PRESS-GANG, OR ENGLISH LIBERTY DISPLAYED.

Late eighteenth-century print.

certain fishermen, those employed on the Greenland whaling, particularly harpooners (although increasingly this was ignored by the Lerwick gang), and seamen involved in the coastwise coal trade. Also exempt were those sued and arrested for debt, although many such claims were fictitious.

The officer in charge of a press gang, known as the Regulating Officer, might be either a captain or a lieutenant. He organised the gang, accounted for monies expended, and was expected to ensure that recruits were fit for service. In this latter duty a doctor might be involved to make an assessment. At the gang's official headquarters, the Rendezvous, men were secured before shipment and distribution throughout the fleet. Once in the Impress Service an officer was unlikely to be considered for advancement: it may be that an appointee lacked influence or ability, but when selected for this line of duty, promotion was a remote possibility.

Desertion was prevalent at the time of the Dutch Wars, and Samuel Pepys, Secretary of the Admiralty, noted in his diary in June 1666:[1] 'Late comes Sir J Bankes to see me, and tells me that coming up from Rochester he overtook three or four hundred seamen, and he believes every day they come flocking from the fleete in like numbers; which is a sad neglect there, when it will be impossible to get others, and we have little reason to think that these will return presently again.'

Life at sea was arduous. Hard-used men were fed with poor quality, monotonous commons, not necessarily short, but often marginally fit for human consumption. The miserable quality of provisions was recorded by Sir William Laird Clowes.[2] He quoted an eighteenth-century writer: 'Seamen in the king's ships have made buttons for their jackets and trowsers with the cheese they were served with, having preferred it, by reason of its tough and durable quality, to buttons made of common metal.' This criticism may be somewhat fanciful and exaggerated, but there is no doubt that food was often impoverished and frequently affected by worms, as was water. In 1770 Dr Samuel Johnson opined: 'Being in a ship is being in a jail, with the chance of being drowned. A man in a jail has more room, better food and commonly better company.'

The harsh conditions prematurely aged seamen, whose only comforts were rum[3] and tobacco. Considerable numbers of seamen were handicapped by

---

1 *The Diary of Samuel Pepys,* ed. Henry B Wheatley FSA, Vols IV–VI, p. 305, 1893.
2 *The Royal Navy – A History,* London, 1899.
3 Rum helped to ameliorate the rigours and tedium of life at sea. It was introduced to the Royal Navy in 1655 to replace beer – a cumbersome drink in crowded ships. Stronger than the

rupture brought about by heavy work with sails and large wooden water casks. So many men were affected that trusses were provided on all ships.

Scurvy was a frequent cause of death. To counter its effects lime juice was provided in 1792, but did not become a standard issue until 1795. Yellow fever, while not a sea disease, was prevalent when ships visited or were stationed in tropical regions, particularly the East and West Indies. Typhus, often called ship fever, was also a major killer arising from overcrowding in unsanitary and filthy conditions. Other maladies induced by the dampness of ships were tuberculosis, rheumatism and bronchitis. Overall, the numbers dying from disease or accidents on board ship far outweighed those killed in action.

According to Lord Nelson the life of the man-o'-wars-man was on an average 'finished at forty five years'.[1] Furthermore, he estimated that during hostilities preceding 1803, forty-two thousand seamen deserted from the fleet and whenever a large convoy of merchant ships assembled at Portsmouth at least a thousand men absconded. Such men were easy prey for crimps who enticed them with money and drink to continue in their desertion and join the merchant service. In home ports crimps were everywhere and many ships lost men through their seductions.

Pay for seamen was meagre, honoured irregularly, often six months in arrears, and then only when the ship returned to a home port. This was to prevent desertion, the policy being 'Keep the pay, keep the man'. It was a mistaken, unsuccessful tactic.

In *The Press Gang Afloat and Ashore,* Hutchinson says 'Pay was 24 shillings a month in 1797'.[2] Roy and Lesley Adkins are more specific: At the end of 1797, when pay rates were revised after the mutinies of that year, a landsman (the lowest-paid man in the crew) earned £1 1s 6d for a month of 28 days, while an able seaman received £1 9s 6d and a sailmaker's mate £1 13s 6d.[3]

These amounts, usually in the form of a ticket and often encashed below face value, were eroded by various deductions (e.g. for the surgeon and for the hospital at Greenwich). Seamen could also draw 'slop' in the form of clothing and tobacco against their outstanding pay.

---

ordinary product, the daily tot was an eighth of a pint, and mixed 2-1 with water, became grog. The custom was abolished on 31 July 1970. At the time when medicine at sea was primitive, the spirit was administered in the treatment of various problems, including tarantula bites and scorpion stings.

1 ADM 1/580 *Memorandum on the State of the Fleet,* 1803.
2 Ibid., p. 43.
3 *Jack Tar, Life in Nelson's Navy,* p. 170.

Stark need frequently existed at home and many soldiers and sailors remitted money to their wives and parents. Of domestic importance was that by 1795 men could have money deducted from their earnings and sent to their family for accredited collection. In the Northern Isles the transactions took place at the Customs Houses in Kirkwall and Lerwick.

After the conclusion of the Napoleonic Wars in 1815, impressment was never again exercised. Nevertheless, from time to time the Crown emphasised that it retained the right to impress seamen. With the threat from the Continent having significantly diminished, the navy reduced to peace-time levels, and mastery of the seas established, the introduction of better pay and conditions for seamen made service more attractive. Accordingly, impressment became of historical interest only. In the twentieth century compulsory service in the armed forces was again brought in as Conscription and National Service.

Impressment in the Northern Isles

A Resource of Seamen

The inhabitants of Orkney and Shetland have a harsh history, enduring lifelong rigours and throughout the period of impressment they were poorly hovelled and toiled incessantly for an uncertain subsistence. Life was dull and grey in its routine and there was a shiftlessness and lack of expectation about people's attitude to seasons and soil. Illiteracy was widespread, sickness rife and men worn by fifty. For most folk life was squalid, precarious and short – a catalogue of woe, relieved only by brief periods of bodily comfort and rare moments of pleasure such as the celebration of weddings and annual festivals. Agriculture was primitive and, particularly in Shetland, only fishing raised living standards to a tolerable level. Forced recruitment on land and sea wove a strand of desperation into this fabric. Although inured to drabness and suffering, people sorrowed for those taken against their will as deeply as they mourned for loved ones who died.

During the decades about which I write the attitude of landowners inhibited community progress and individual ambition, and in many instances facilitated recruitment. Throughout the years of impressment there was little advance in social and economic conditions, and comments by various writers, including visitors to the islands, evidence the poverty in which people lived.[1]

In *The Present State of the Orkney Islands Considered* published in 1775, James Fea, a surgeon, wrote that the bulk of Orcadians had been reduced to extreme misery.[2] He deplored the lack of progress:

... I am sorry to say, that so little is Industry encouraged in our Country, that no means can be assigned, by which the lower class of people get their bread ... those who

---

[1] Impressment might be avoided by serving on Greenland and Davis Strait whalers or by service with the Hudson Bay Company. Numbers recruited for the Canadian enterprise were not inconsiderable. In an article entitled *Nor-Wasters*, Ernest Marwick states that in 1780, owing to the necessities of the war, only sixteen Orkneymen could be engaged; in 1781 the figure was forty-two, declining in 1782 to twenty-four. However, in 1799 numbers rose to sixty-three when, of the 530 servants on the company's books, 416 were Orkneymen – mostly young men and prime candidates for impressment.

[2] p. 6.

have already been so much dispirited by poverty, and sunk in sloth and ignorance, never will be industrious, or exert themselves in any degree, untill they see some prospect of attaining to a certain independence, as the reward of their Industry. While their Leases are so short, as they just now are, it is an utter inconsistency to suppose, that the Tenants will apply themselves to any thing.[1]

The Naval Log of a young surgeon Ker visiting Shetland in August 1780 is an indictment of the lairds' attitude to their tenants: '… there is no great Encouragement to Agriculture. The Landlords to render them more dependent never granting them Leases. The wretched Inhabitants holding their small Farms from year to year. The Tennants are bound to fish for their Landlords giving them all they catch above a certain Size at a stated Price. They are held in a State little better than Slavery.'[2]

At the end of the eighteenth century the Rev George Barry, minister of Shapinsay, commented on recent improvement to a part of the island by the only residing heritor,[3] and continued: 'Previous to his purchase, nothing was to be seen over its whole extent, but a dreary waste, interspersed with arable lands ill cultivated, a few miserable hovels thinly scattered over its surface, under the name of farm houses or cottages, which were not fit to shelter from the rigours of the climate a few ragged inhabitants, dirty through indolence, lean with hunger, and torpid by despair.'[4]

In 1800 the Rev Dr Kemp, Secretary of the Scottish Society for Propagating Christian Knowledge, visited Shetland and his *Observations on the Islands of Shetland, and their Inhabitants* was published the following year. He says: 'The soil in Shetland is no farther valuable in the estimation of the proprietors, than as it furnishes settlements to fishers. Out of the sea their rents are collected; and according to the number of fishers settled upon their estates, is their revenue. … It is no wonder that the farms in Shetland are ill managed when the men are almost constantly at their fishing stations (generally far from their ordinary residence), during the proper season of *labour*, which is consequently left to be carried on by women and children. But, indeed, the sea is the proper element of Shetland *men*; they are bred to it from their infancy, and acquire a hardiness and dexterity in the management of boats that can no where be excelled.'[5]

---

1 pp. 18, 121.
2 *Ker's Naval Log*, 1778–1782, National Library of Scotland, Ms 1083.
3 Proprietor or landholder.
4 *The Orkney Parishes*, p. 358.
5 Ibid., pp. 8, 10.

By 1804 the position in Shetland had not bettered and in *A Tour through some of the Islands of Orkney and Shetland*, Patrick Neill, Secretary to the Natural History Society of Edinburgh, recorded in a Preface: 'The greater part of the Shetland tenants appeared to me to be sunk into a state of the most abject poverty and misery. I found them even without bread; without any kind of food, in short, but fish and cabbage; – living, in many cases, under the same roof with their cattle, and scarcely in cleaner apartments; – their little agricultural concerns entirely neglected, owing to the men being obliged to be absent during summer at the ling and tusk fishery.'[1]

Shetland in its northern remoteness was particularly at risk of ruthless arrestment facilitated by the isolation of islands which were practically roadless. Plague-like the gang descended on district and island, refusing to be deflected. As their very existence depended on fish, Shetlanders were constantly afloat, often for days. In small boats on the open sea they had little chance against swift press gang cutters or marauding privateers. These men were prime recruits for the navy; from boyhood they were familiar with the sea, understood and respected its random moods, and were adaptable and resourceful sailors. The gangs' legacy was a litany of insecurity, fear and depredation, flagrant self-interest by landowners and heritors, and the dragooning of those with no rights at law except when the gang and naval vessels abused their powers.

Harassment by the enemies of a remote Government was an additional hazard. In the waters around the islands men and youths on coastal vessels and fishing boats risked seizure, with the possibility of death from disease or wounds, or the threat of languishing in French or Spanish prisons.

Yet a thread of hope has persisted and run through the history of Orkney and Shetland, a constant reassertion of human sentiment and the concern of persecuted people for each other. Thus, though the removal of men from home was a time of grief and insecurity, it was also a time of affection and a deep sense of community which expressed itself through help and loyalty from family and friends. Kinship in the islands was strong and reliable.

From time to time the gentlemen heritors on the islands came to an arrangement with the Naval authorities whereby quotas were set which when met obtained a general protection from unbridled impressment. Achievement of the numbers was by force or by offer of a bounty. When a bounty was paid an assessement was made on all heritors, based on their valuation. The Orkney

---

1 p. vi.

assessment for 1812 shows that the total levy for the county was £525 sterling, enough to provide a bounty of five guineas for each of the 120 seamen required.

Even a rumour of imminent recruitment to meet these quotas was sufficient for men to cease work and hide. Shetland lairds objected to fishing being affected, and used the threat of inclusion in the next quota to coerce tenants into resuming their labours and continuing in the system of truck[1] with its concomitant debt bondage.

Homecoming whalers too were taken without hesitation by cutters lurking off the coasts, and on land parties of men, armed and authorised, descended on isolated hamlet and croft to remove occupants, impervious to pleas and protests. Shetland suffered particularly, and Lerwick was the reluctant host to a Rendezvous with, at different times, Impress and Regulating Officers Walter Scott, Captain James Nicolson and Lieutenant William Wilson.

Sometimes opportunistic impressment occurred when a man-of-war lying off the coast, waiting for a favourable wind, landed a recruiting party and secured replacements for deserters, for seamen killed in action, or for those who had succumbed to the risks attendant on life at sea.

In its island activities, as elsewhere, impressment was without refinement. The demands of the gang seemed insatiable and there was general indignation, sometimes amounting to fury, against conscription and the injustice of the system. Only seamen were supposed to be taken, but severe measures were employed and scant attention was paid to the class of men obtained. Like a great fishing net, the gang caught and hauled in people of all sorts and conditions – good, bad and indifferent. No distinction was made between tradesman, crofter, labourer and seaman. Vagabonds, thieves and other petty criminals were fair game, the veritable scourings of the two counties.

The combination of overcrowded islands, a male population of noted seamen, and, in the case of Shetland, no recourse to Parliament,[2] brought about more than half a century of severe recruitment. Perpetrated on isolated communities it left an indelible mark on folk memory and generations of islanders were embittered by its effects.

Long after recruitment had ceased people remained wary of naval service. W R Duncan commented: 'The Navy was once popular, and there is said to have

---

1 Truck – to barter for goods. Fishing tenants perforce had to exchange their fish for goods at the merchant-lairds' shops, and not always on favourable terms.
2 Until the passing of the Reform Act of 1832, Shetland had no representation in Parliament.

been at one period nearly a sixth of the gross male population in that service. The system of impressment so recklessly, though perhaps necessarily, followed, had the effect of disgusting the men, and, for a long period, the Navy had been very unpopular. The authorities take no pains to induce volunteering. They send down, for the purpose of seeking seamen, some tender or sloop of war, that looks very paltry in the eyes of the Zetland youngster, familiar with the sight of dashing French and Danish frigates.'[1]

Folk associated the name *Bonaparte* with press gang times. Writing to Arthur Laurenson, Lerwick, on 9 August 1890, Thomas Mathewson, Burravoe recorded: 'An Aunt of mine, now nearly 70 years old, tells me that when she was going in 4,[2] one day she was being carried by an Aunt in a Keshie[3] in the Island of Hascosay, when they passed the ruins of the old Chapel, she said "who lives in this house." Her Aunt answered "This is a Chapel where people used to preach." My Aunt said "Was that Bonaparte people?"'[4] Mathewson adds a footnote, 'Bonaparte was used as a name to frighten children; very likely Press-gang days were in the people's memory.'[5]

The child was repeating an expression which she had heard in Shetland conversation of 1824 and associated with a threat from the outside world. The name Bonaparte, with its powerful and unsettling resonance, retained a quality of horror and doom, linked with press gang activity and the loss of the breadwinner. Repugnant to children and their elders alike, it was difficult to expunge.

Mulcting the population of breadwinners sapped island vigour and many families suffered acute hardship and privation. The *Shetland Advertiser* of 1 September 1862 gives a vivid account of the tribulation of the islanders:

The brutal and illegal atrocities [sic] of the press-gang may have been forgotten in other parts of Britain, but on the memory of Shetlanders they are burnt in as with a red-hot iron.

---

1 *Zetland Directory and Guide*, Second edition, 1861.
2 Almost four.
3 A carrying-basket made of straw.
4 Shetland Archives, D3/10/3.
5 To encourage juvenile good conduct in the early nineteenth century, the covers of children's primers sometimes bore pictures of 'Nappy' brandishing a cat-o'nine-tails or a particularly unpleasant birch rod. Nurses threatened their children, declaring that the ogre himself would arrive down the chimney. [Baby, baby, naughty baby / Hush, you squalling thing, I say/ Hush your squalling, or it may be / Bonaparte may pass this way. / Baby, baby, he's a giant, / Tall and black as Rouen steeple; / And he dines and sups, rely on 't, / Every day on naughty people.] See *Years of Victory 1802–1812*, Arthur Bryant, pp. 68–9, and an article *The Martello Towers* by L W Cowie in *History Today*, p. 604. See also the story of the deranged Deerness woman, Barbara Wick and 'Bony's coman' on p. 182 of this volume.

During the quarter of a century proceeding the peace of Vienna,[1] the British Government chose to believe that every Shetlandman was a sailor, and therefore bound to fight his country's battles at sea, and if he would not come voluntarily they thought they had a right to take him by force. During that period about 2000[2] men were impressed out of a gross population of 20,000,[3] and many of them had never trod a deck until they did so beneath a pendant. We have heard of weavers, housewrights, tailors, shoemakers, and other tradesmen being impressed into the navy, on the pretext that all the Shetlandmen followed the sea more or less. Then press-gangs used to scour the country, cutlass in hand, surround the houses in the dead of night, like African slavehunters, and drag their victims from their beds, amidst the shrieks of their wives and children. Many and varied used to be the tales that were wont to be told of hairbreadth 'scapes from, or of capture by the press-gang.

The raw edge of memory was not readily blunted and in a letter written in the 1870s the remarkable and eccentric Andrew Dishington Mathewson, schoolmaster at East Yell, referring to the first decade of the nineteenth century, recorded: 'More Men especially seamen being called for, the return of the Greenland ships were watched and the men Impressed out of them – and worse still Press Gangs sent through the Islands and men caught in Bed & taken in the night of which some strange escapes & Captures are still remembered.'[4]

That said, Britain's maritime supremacy rested on the type of seaman provided by Orkney and Shetland. In the main hardy and self-reliant, they sailed into an enforced life at sea while ahead lay excitement, strange scenes and divers dangers. It is beyond dispute that many islanders now sleeping in unknown graves have been concerned in fashioning the story of the British Isles at a time when the nation was beset by many troubles.

Eligibility and Protection

A notice discounting a rumour of an imminent Press, and probably affixed to the church door,[5] illustrates the plight of Bressay men:

---

1 The Congress of Vienna, 1815.
2 This figure is almost certainly too high, although it is now impossible to establish exactly what percentage of the male population was pressed.
3 The population of Shetland was 22,378 in 1801 and 22,915 in 1811. For Orkney the figures were 24,445 and 23,238 respectively.
4 Shetland Archives, D23/158/38/15.
5 The use of church doors for public notices was a common practice. In December 1794 Captain Alexander Graeme instructed his factor David Petrie to 'notify' at the church door (and the Ferry Inn) Holm: 'Seamen and able bodied lands men wanted for his Majesty's Ship *Glory* of 98 Guns at Portsmouth Captn Alexr Graeme commander.'

The Press Gang, Robert Morley, 1857-1941. © Gallery Oldham Uk / The Bridgeman Art Library

Advertisement[1]

Whereas the people of this Island have neglected their business for some days, & seem determined to do so longer, in consequence of a report having spread of a 'General Press'; Therefore notice is hereby given, That no general impress of men is at present intended to take place in this Country immediately, but that if such be found necessary during the Summer, a few, – & that only such as can best be spared, will be raised from this place: Wherefore, those who neglect their lawfull business of Fishing, or otherwise, will justly be reckoned careless, not only of their own Interest, but of that of all such as are connected with them; and, by so doing, take the most effectual Step they could devise for being ranked among the Number of impressed men.

Given in Bressay the Tenth day of May 1777, and warranted by Charles Sanderson.[2]

Two months earlier on 1 March 1777, a more detailed protection of certain groups had been specified by a portentous advert in *The Caledonian Mercury*. The Lords Commissioners of the Admiralty had appointed Captain Charles Napier to superintend and regulate the impress service in the north and east coasts of Scotland. Notice was given that 'he will give Protections to all Fishermen they supplying his Majesty with one man for every four men to whom protections shall be granted. He will also grant protections on the same terms to all Boat-builders, Carpenters, Caulkers, Sail-makers and men plying in passage-boats at the different ferries.' Napier hoped that those employed 'in these professions will pay due attention to this advertisement', and that they would supply without delay the necessary quota of men at the Leith or any other rendezvous. The men would be entitled to a bounty of 'Five Pounds for an able and Two Pounds Ten Shillings for an ordinary seaman.'

The advertisement expected that 'the inhabitants of the country will not lend their assistance to seamen in concealing themselves, but will, if they know of any that are lurking, give information thereof at any of the rendezvouses where they will receive a reward of Forty Shillings for every able seaman and Thirty Shillings for every ordinary seaman so discovered, upon his being apprehended.'

This brought a reply on 21 April from 'the Gentlemen of Shetland sent to The Honorable Captain Napier or Officer Superinding [sic] the Impress Service on the North & East coasts of Scotland at Leith.' The Gentlemen regretted that

---

1 Buness Estate Papers in the custody of David Edmondston, Buness, Unst.
2 Probably tacksman of the Gardie Estate, Bressay.

a tender had not been sent in early March to press men intending to join the Greenlanders. Focusing on the absentees with visceral relentlessness, they suggested that a vessel should arrive at the beginning of August to lie in wait for the returning whalers.[1] They were anxious as ever to protect their fishing interests and conveniently to satisfy the Government quota with dissidents:

… we are sorry to Acquaint, that a rumour having some time ago spead thro' this Country of a general Press being intended the young men who seem the most proper for his Majesty's Service, to the number of about 140, in order to evade being press'd, went lately to Bressay sound, where sundry Ships from London, & other parts of England bound for the Greenland Seas, were lying in need of men and many of these young men have Indented themselves as Apprentices on board these ships, and others of them have engaged for the Voyage to & from Greenland only, to be landed in Shetland in the end of July or first of August next. The Greenlanders come yearly to Bressay sound in want of men & have Annually carried away numbers, many whereof we are Informed are now in his Majesty's fleet, but more have gone off this Spring than formerly, for the reason above assigned, and therefore we would have wishd that a vessel had been sent to Bressay sound in the first of March last, whereby these young men might have been prevented from going off with the Greenlanders & had we been certain that an impress was to have taken place at all, we wd have taken that step. Youll please know further that our fishermen are only employed in Fishing in June & July, all the rest of the Year they are farmers & taken up about their farms, but the fishing is their principal Support and if they be Impeded therein during the fishing Season, it will tend to ruin their families & much hurt us besides throwing our Lands waste which they hold of us: therefore and in order that this Country may furnish a proportional quota of men for his Majesty's fleet, as was done in 1760 by an agreement w^h Lieutenant Dishington, we take the liberty to make the following Proposal to you as Superintendent of the Impress service on the North & East Coasts of Scotland, viz That you wou'd be pleased to delay sending any vessell hither untill the beginning of August next, about which time the Greenland Ships are Expected back to Bressay sound, & some of the Shetlanders will be landed from them; and then we can have an Opportunity to raise 100 men from this Country for his Majestys fleet, and which we oblige ourselves to do, without putting you or your Officers to any trouble or Expence (his Majestys bounty to the men excepted) further than receiving them at Lerwick. We shall expect your Answer & hope you will accept of our offer in which cas[e] please send us some writing to reasure our fishers who seem resolved not to venture to Sea on the fishing this sumr if we cannot certify them that they will not be impressed at sea.[2]

1 It is not known if this suggestion was successful.
2 Scroll letter, Gardie Papers 21/4/1777.

When invasion appeared imminent the need for men became acute, a hot press would take place and then protection certificates proved of no value.[1] These documents had to describe the holder with much care. William Melvin, born in Stromness on 8 February 1779, held a protection dated 10 June 1796. The exemption was for three years from 27 April 1796, the commencement of his indenture. The handwritten note at the side reads: 'Willm Melvin aged seventeen years. Brown Complexion wearing his own dark collour'd hair low of stature prety much fearn tick[2] in the face and has a scar in the inside of his left thumb.'

In pursuit of seamen, valid protections (which had to be carried at all times) were often challenged or indeed ignored, particularly at sea where there was little or no recourse for those whose rights had been set aside. Nevertheless, illegal impressment was sometimes firmly and successfully disputed.

On 17 June 1793 a Protection[3] was issued which stated:

Whereas the Inhabitants of the Islands of ORKNEY have agreed to furnish certain Number of Volunteer Seamen for His Majestys Fleet, upon condition that the Trade and Fisheries of that Country are protected; and whereas we have accepted that number for the present.

These are, therefore, to give Notice, that none of the Natives of those Islands, employed in the Fisheries there, or serving in Fishing Vessels employed in bringing Fish from thence to London or to other Markets, are to be impressed into His Majestys Service, but permitted to follow their said Employments, without any lett, hindrance, or molestation, Provided they produce a Certificate.

This commitment to furnish men had not been met, as the crew of the Brigantine *Margaret* found to their cost. In possession of a Protection for seven men and boys, in May 1798 the vessel set sail for Sunderland with kelp[4] and with the intention of loading coals for shipment to Orkney. Named on the protection certificate were:

		Age	*Complexion*
1	John Rendall Master	31	Black
2	Alexr Rendall Mate	48	Fair
3	James Rendall Seaman	22	Black

---

1 *Jack Tar, Life in Nelson's Navy*, pp. 47–8.
2 Freckled.
3 ADM 1/2740.
4 The calcined ashes of seaweed, rich in minerals such as soda and iodine.

By the Commissioners for Executing the Office of Lord High Admiral of Great Britain and Ireland, &c.

WHEREAS by an Act of Parliament passed in the 13th year of the reign of His late Majesty King George the Second, it is enacted, that the persons, under the age and circumstances therein mentioned, shall be freed and exempted from being impressed into His Majesty's service, upon due proof made before us of their respective ages and circumstances as the case shall happen: And whereas we have received testimony, that the Bearer _William Melvin_ has bound himself Apprentice to serve at sea, by indenture dated the _27 April 1796_ and that he never used the sea before that time; and he being therefore entitled to a Protection, in pursuance of the said Act of Parliament, to free and exempt him being impressed for the space of Three Years from the aforementioned date of his indenture; We do hereby require and direct all Commanders of His Majesty's ships, Press-masters, and others whom it doth or may concern, not to impress him into His Majesty's service during the said space of Three Years, provided a description of his person be inserted in the margin hereof. But in case it shall appear, that the person for whom this Protection is granted, or in whose behalf it shall be produced, is not under the aforementioned circumstances, then the Officer, to whom it shall be produced, is hereby strictly charged and required to impress such person, and immediately to send the Protection to us. Given under our hands, and the seal of the Office of Admiralty, the _tenth_ day of _June_ One thousand seven hundred and ninety-six.

To all Commanders and Officers of His Majesty's Ships, Press-masters, and all others whom it doth or may concern.

By Command of their Lordships,

Evan Nepean

Exemption certificate for William Melvin

4	George Bews do	25	Black
5	Andrew Scott do	23	Brown
6	William Smith Apprentice	16	Black
7	David Smith do	14	Brown

David Smith was left at home and of the six men who travelled, Rendall (James), Scott and Bews were pressed at Sunderland by Lieutenant William Abbs on 11 May 1798. That day Abbs wrote to Captain Evan Napean at the Admiralty, London: 'Inclosed [sic] is a Protection found on board a Brig from the Orkneys, Laden with Kelp to this Port and to load coals back. As I have no Instructions about such Protections I have Prest three men from hir [sic] till their Lordships Pleasure is Known About them.'

On 14 May a note was endorsed on Abbs' letter: 'Direct him to Retain these men for the service and to return, provided that the vessel is not thereby distressed.' A further note reads: 'It does not appear to me that the Condition is fulfilled on the part of the Island, and this detention will have the effect of bringing it into discussion and enforcing it.'

The crew of the *Margaret* were being penalised for the reluctance or inability of Orkney lairds to supply the agreed quota of 'volunteer seamen' mentioned in the 17 June 1793 Protection

Protections were highly prized: on 11 March 1811 William Dearness wrote to office bearers of the Corporation of Shoemakers thanking them for the Freeman Ticket provided to protect him from the impress service on his passage to London. On his return to Kirkwall he would 'take the earliest opportunity of being created & admitted a Freeman of said Corporation and paying the customary fees therefore.'[1]

Similarly, on 30 December 1812 the Incorporation of Hammermen acknowledged receipt of five pounds sterling 'from John Wishart, Wright in Stromness for a freedom Ticket which he received from the Incorporation to be a safeguard to him from the impress which raged in Orkney this year.'[2]

Although not able to issue Protections, Lairds sometimes obtained the release of men who had been pressed, exercising as they did a powerful influence. As a reward for gallantry in the field, Captain James Moodie of Melsetter, 8th laird, was granted the privilege of retaining one estate employee whom the gang could not press. Moodie took care never to name this man. When a Melsetter

1 Orkney Archives, D35/2/1.
2 Orkney Archives, D35/2/1.

lad was taken the Captain galloped furiously to the landing stage, identified the servant as the exempt person and had him released.[1]

In 1812 William Watt, proprietor of Skaill Estate, invited officers to dine at his mansion house. Arriving from Stromness they noticed a number of strapping young men who had been engaged as harvest hands, and the following day these workers were pressed. Watt was indignant, he protested vigorously at this violation of hospitality and the men were liberated.

Two Foula men had a different experience with their landlord. Scott, the laird of the island, known locally as 'Old Melby', imprudently pressed both these haaf[2] skippers for the Foula part of the Shetland quota and secured them overnight in his residence The Haa House whence early the following morning they were despatched to Lerwick. When their crews arrived at Ham Voe and found that the skippers had been pressed, they refused to put to sea. Old Melby was outraged but the men were adamant. In common with other Shetland landowners Scott's prosperity depended on his tenants' successful fishing. In haste the laird made for the mainland, had the men released and provided replacement recruits.

Ineligible Candidates

The church played a significant role in securing the release of an apprentice, William Smith, who had been taken by Lieutenant Wilson.[3] Smith was indentured to Christopher Grierson and apart from a voyage to Ireland in a sloop loading cargo at Hillswick, he had little experience at sea. What secured his liberation was a certificate from the church: 'We the Minister & Elders of the Parish of Northmavine do certify that the bearer William Smith (at present engaged with Mr Grierson to be an apprentice to the sea) was born in this Parish the nineteenth of April one Thousand seven hundred and Ninety two years as appears from our records. William Jack, Min[r], John Clark, Elder, Gifford Brown, Elder.'[4] As Smith was born on 19 April and had been pressed by Wilson on 4 January 1808, he was aged fifteen and therefore not liable to be taken. Supported by his apprenticeship, the church certificate was sufficient for the Sheriff to order that he 'forthwith be set at liberty' from the Tolbooth where he had been held.

---

1 It is possible that the release was effected by Major James Moodie, 9th laird of Melsetter, 1757–1820.
2 The deep sea beyond coastal waters.
3 See the Chapter on Lieutenant William Wilson, p. 119.
4 Shetland Archives, SC12/6/1808/1/1.

In August 1809 John Fleming, minister of Bressay, petitioned[1] the Sheriff Depute for the release of two men and a boy impressed in Bressay Sound by a party of marines from the frigate *Crocodile* under the charge of Captain Chamberlain. Those involved were John Williamson (his servant) and James alias Richard Morrison, both from Keldabister. The lad was Bruce Bolt, Boesetter, aged fourteen, who would have to be released on account of his age. The records cast no light on the outcome of the attempt by the Divine to have the Keldabister men released.

The support of the church was again the determining factor in securing the release of a young lad. On 4 August 1810 Samuel Fullerton, son of Arthur Fullerton, farmer on the island of Oxney, Gilbert Hawick, tenant in Burravoe, Delting, and Malcolm Smith, son of Thomas Smith, tenant in Hillswick, petitioned[2] the Sheriff for their release. They had set out in the Spring 'to prosecute the whale fishing'. On the return journey, when their vessel had 'left the ice', they were pressed by a naval vessel and put on board the sloop *Nightingale*. Transported to Bressay Sound they were there held. The petition claimed that Samuel was sixteen years of age [in fact he was fifteen].

A church certificate produced with the petition reads: 'These certify that Samuel Fulertun [sic] was born on 15th November 1794, the information extracted from the Register of Baptisms at Tingwall, this third day of August 1810.' It was signed by Thomas Jameson, Session Clerk and John Turnbull,[3] Minister. Although the records are incomplete Samuel would have been released. What happened to Malcolm Smith, who was barely eighteen, and Gilbert Hawick is unknown.

On 25 March 1778 Magnus Flett, Tenant in Ness, Gremiston, Harray, petitioned the Sheriff Substitute.[4] He alleged that he came into town on 'Saturday 21st March … about his Laufull affairs…[and] was imposed upon & Seduced ffor to be Enlisted as a Soldier by Donald Sutherland acting as Serjeant in the Company belonging to Lieutenant Donald Mudie in Lord Seaforths Rerejment

---

1 Shetland Archives, SC12/6/1809/55.
2 Shetland Archives, SC12/6/1810/52.
3 John Turnbull, a native of Jedburgh, was born in 1775 and became parish minister at Tingwall on 11 September 1806. He died in 1867 and Sir Walter Scott said of him: '…he is doing his best with patience and judgment to set a good example both in temporals and spirituals, and is generally beloved and respected by all classes. His glebe is in far the best order of any ground I saw in Zetland. He gave an excellent discourse and remarkably good prayers.' Other encounters which this minister had with the gang are recorded on p. 56 and p. 85.
4 Orkney Archives, SC11/5/1778/46.

[sic].' Flett was apprehensive that he would be carried out of the country 'Contrary to his Inclination' and asked the Sheriff for a fair trial. On 25 March the Sheriff Substitute gave Lieutenant Mudie and Sergeant Sutherland twenty four hours to respond. In the meantime he ordained that Flett should be taken into the custody of the Sheriff's Officers (presumably in the Tolbooth) until the merits of his complaints were tried. Mudie answered that no undue influence had been used to enlist Flett, who had 'taken and kept the King's money,' and that very day had received a further guinea from him 'in part of his Inlisting money.' However, Mudie continued that 'being Credibly Informed that the said Magnus Flett was troubled w^t the Epilepsy or falln sickness as he Calls it, Therefore the Respondent gives him up upon Repay^{tt} of the two Guineas he Received of Inlisting Money & paying twenty shillings of smart money.'[1] Mudie also agreed that Flett should be set at liberty after payment. Flett settled and was duly liberated 'to go about his affairs as formerly.'

Impressment as Alternative Punishment for Criminals

On 15 February 1804 Peter Robertson petitioned[2] the Sheriff Depute, Lerwick. A prisoner in the Tolbooth for three weeks, he had been confined for the alleged crime of 'his having Stole a peice of Shetland made cloath.' He did not wish to stand trial and craved to be allowed to volunteer for the Navy or failing that to 'Banish himself from this country for such space of time as your Lordship shall seem proper.' The Sheriff did indeed banish him 'from and furth Shetland for the space of twenty years', adding that if Robertson returned early he would be imprisoned and banished again until the expiry of the term. Having volunteered, he was to be sent to the fleet at the first opportunity and detained in prison till then.

Another Shetland man, Olla Smith, had the unusual distinction of being forced to serve in the navy by order of the Sheriff Depute. Born in Mousa in 1771 he moved to Cunningsburgh at an early age. A noted ruffian and troublemaker, his broiling and nefarious exploits included issuing a challenge to a duel in 1802:

> Dear Sir
> I Ola Smith chalang you & your Brother both to meet me 13th of march at half 12 o'clock on the ouns of gord or in the yard of gord man for man at fear play over a rop or over a stick[3] or any you pleas no mor bot remains your frind Oliver Smith [4]

---

1 Money paid on account of cancelling or not fulfilling a bargain or agreement.
2 Shetland Archives, SC12/6/1804/4.
3 Engage in fisticuffs separated only by a rope or stick.
4 Shetland Archives, SC12/6/1802/8/2.

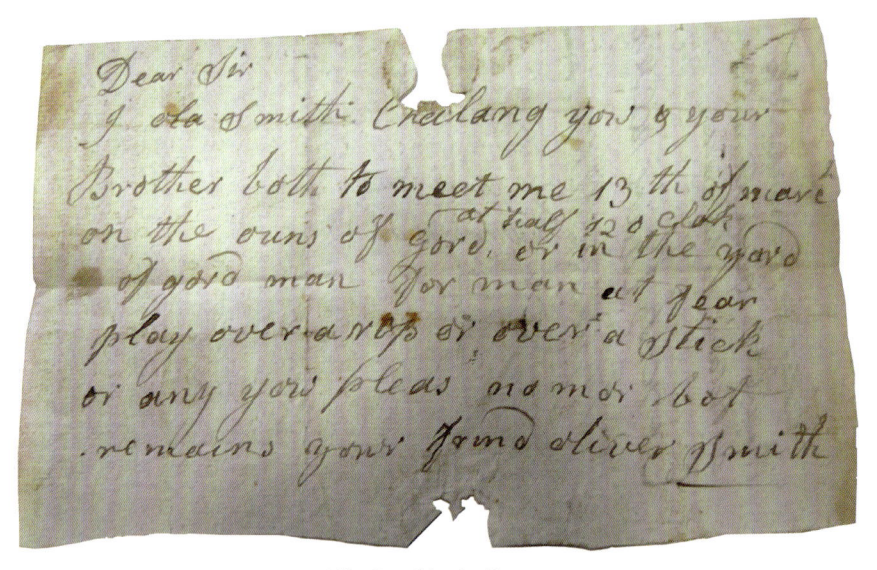

Olla Smith's challenge.

In January 1805 he was responsible for a tumult in the parish involving forty or fifty persons, as a result of which, together with several others, he was taken before the Court. The Sheriff committed him to prison 'therein to remain untill some of His Majesty's ships shall arrive at Lerwick, and adjudges him to serve in His Majesty's Navy in such Ship as the Lords Commissioners of the Ad^{my}, may appoint, and banishes him from this Jurisdiction for seven years in respect of the crimes committed by him and of his public bad character as a riotous and mischievous person having been more than once laid under Caution of Lawburrows'.[1]

On 5 October, aged thirty-four, he was taken aboard the *Mary*[2] tender and on 19 November allocated to HMS *Resistance*,[3] a fifth rate vessel, where he was classed AB indicating an experienced sailor. Not without filial affection, on 20 November he allocated half his monthly pay to his mother. Catherine received two payments, one of £3 7s 6, and another of £2 8s 6. The payments ceased on 30 July 1806[4] as he had deserted on 25 June. Recaptured on 1 February 1808 and returned to *Resistance*, on 9 February he was awarded fifty lashes. Discharged on 20 February to Haslar hospital,[5] a move presumably not unconnected with his

[1] The legal security which one man is obliged to give that he will not do any injury to another in his person or property. Shetland Archives, SC12/6/1805/8/17.
[2] ADM36/15821.
[3] ADM37/726.
[4] ADM 27/16.
[5] ADM 102/291.

flogging, on 4 April he rejoined his vessel. Smith may have transgressed again, as on 20 December he was sent back to the hospital and discharged from there and from the service on 30 December.

Returning to Shetland he was arraigned before the Sheriff Depute and on 6 March 1810 incarcerated in the Tolbooth. The following day Smith petitioned that a surgeon be allowed to visit him 'in Prison to examine the nature of his Various Complaints and to administer such medicns [sic] as he shall see proper ... and to allow him the indulgence of a fire to warm him in his present Confinement.' The Sheriff granted both these requests 'notwithstanding his indecorous and insulting conduct in Court yesterday.' Smith's medical report reads: 'At the desire of the Sheriff substitute I have enquired into the state of health of Olla Smith prisoner in the Tolbooth, & found him labouring under a chronic Rhumatism, for the relief of which he would require warm lodging & warm clothing with nourishing food, & regularity in living – given under my hand this eight day of March 1810 at Lerwick in Shetland. Lau^n Edmondston Surgeon.'[1]

On 8 March the Sheriff ordered that Smith 'shall quit the Jurisdiction within the space of one month from this date and remain absent from it during the whole period yet to run of his banishment under the penalty of Ten Pounds Sterling.' Broken in health, and exiled from Shetland, thereafter he disappears from history.[2]

Early Impressment

One of the earliest impressments took place in the summer of 1755 when two small tenders arrived off the coast of Shetland. Unaware that these were naval vessels, in accordance with time-honoured custom, two fishing boats went alongside and six men were pressed. This was the first instance of its kind in Shetland waters and resulted in a diminution of fishing activity that season.[3] This incident is recorded more fully on page 200.

The *Edinburgh Chronicle* of 5–7 July 1759 stated: '...Yesterday two ships appeared in the frith [sic] of Forth, and by their standing off and on for several hours, and hoisting Dutch colours, they gave cause to suspect they were not friends; upon which, towards the evening, the troops in the Cannongate, and

---

1 Shetland Archives, SC12/6/1805/8/15.
2 Personal communications Dr Alan M Beattie and Brian Smith, Shetland, 2010. Mr Smith is the collateral descendant of Olla Smith.
3 Shetland Archives, GD 150/2518 B2.

The Tolbooth, Lerwick, 32 Commercial Street, built in 1767. Conversion and restoration of the B-listed building was completed in 2005 to provide a new shore station for the RNLI.

The Tolbooth, Kirkwall, built 1740 and demolished 1890.

Both photographs c.1880, from the George Washington Wilson Collection, reproduced courtesy of Aberdeen University.

the companies in the castle, were put under arms in a very short time, and some cannon got ready, to march for the security of Leith. But those ships proving to be the *Swan* sloop of war, with a tender full of impressed men, under her convoy, from the Orkneys, the troops were dismissed and return'd to their quarters.' Under Captain Lobb, *Swan* had sailed from Stromness on 24 June and arrived at Leith Road on 7 July accompanied by the tender *Eagle* with the pressed men on board.

There had been much impressment in Orkney, as the same issue of *The Chronicle* recorded: 'By a Letter from Orkney, we are informed, that there has been a very hot press there; and that all the Farmers servants, without distinction, have been taken up that were judged fit for service.'

There are two references to ongoing northern impressment in the *Edinburgh Evening Courant*. On Wednesday 1 September 1779 the newspaper reported: 'On the 18th curt. sailed from Kirkwall for Leith-road, the *Oughton* tender, commanded by Lieut. Pirie, with 63 Orkney seamen and fishermen, volunteers for the navy, and raised by a contribution from the freeholders of the county. Twenty-five volunteers from Caithness were shipped in Kirkwall-road, on board said tender.' On Saturday 9 October 1779: 'We are favoured with a copy of a letter from Zetland, dated 22d of September, by which we are informed, that by the spirited aid given by some gentlemen of Lerwick, who procured him 24 volunteers, Lieutenant Hunter of the *Africa* tender, who had not then above 13 men, was enabled to take possession of the *Sally and Becky*, an American ship, now in the harbour of Leith. She is valued at 7 or 8000£ and claimed by severals, amongst whom, the Lerwick gentlemen, we hope, will not be forgot.'

The methods of the press gang throughout the country were rough and often brutal. Dr Arthur Edmondson was highly critical of its actions in Shetland during the period 1803–08: 'The mode of procuring volunteers is rather extraordinary. Immediately after a man has been impressed, he is either sent on board of a ship, or shut up in the rendezvous, and promises, threats, and privations of every kind, practised to induce him to enter. He resists for a time in the hope of being released from a conviction that he is not a seaman, but seeing his vexations daily increase, and no prospect of a termination to them, he reluctantly consents that his name shall be enrolled among the number of *volunteers* for the navy.'[1]

The Rendezvous which served as the Press Gang's headquarters was established in 1781, and was sited in the Tolbooth, Commercial Street. It is clear that

---
[1] *A View of the Ancient and Present State of the Zetland Islands,* Arthur Edmondston MD, 1809, Vol II, p. 70.

men taken forcibly who claimed exemption were held there while their liberty was being settled, usually by a petition to the Sheriff Depute. Pressed men who lost their liberty or who had volunteered were usually shipped direct to Leith for onward transmission to the Nore.[1] Sometimes the vessel put in at Kirkwall and collected more levies who had been kept in the Tolbooth situated on the Kirk Green. The conditions aboard the tenders were cramped and unhealthy.

Numbers

It is not possible to establish precisely how many men were pressed in Orkney and Shetland and how many accepted the inevitability of the situation, volunteered and obtained a bounty. In terms of numbers, Edmondston averred that compared with Orkney, Shetland was considerably disadvantaged by being the reluctant host to an Impress Service: 'The population of Orkney is greater than that of Zetland, her commerce is more extensive, and she employs in her trade twice the number of sailors. The habits and modes of life of the inhabitants of both are nearly the same, but Orkney is not scourged with an impress establishment. The farmers and fishers go annually to Greenland, and when once landed, prosecute in peace their customary occupations during the remaining months of the year. In every war, Zetland has sent twice the number of men to the navy that Orkney has done, and has paid her just proportion of every public burden.'[2]

In Shetlanders in the Royal Navy 1792–1815, Dr Alan M Beattie writes: 'The first references to the practice occurring in Shetland are in the late 1750s during the Seven Years War. At the end of that war, in 1763, 3,000 Shetland men were said to have served, and a similar total has been given for the wars of the 1770s and 80s. The figure for the French Wars of 1793–1815 is quoted as 5,000. This seems excessive, but remember: it is spread over two generations.'[3]

J W Irvine is somewhat more conservative in assessing numbers, although his figures are still very considerable: 'By 1763, at the end of the Seven Years War, there were nine hundred Shetlanders paid off from the Navy. During the American War of Independence the number in the navy rose to 2000, and by the time of the Battle of Trafalgar in 1805, the number had risen to 3000.'[4]

---

1 A naval anchorage in the Thames estuary.
2 Edmondston, p. 72.
3 *Coontin Kin*, No 7, June 1993.
4 *Lerwick; The Birth and Growth of an Island Town*, J W Irvine, 1985, p. 49.

In *The Northern Isles: Orkney & Shetland*[1] Alexander Fenton says: 'During the War of the American Revolution[2] 1200 of a peak complement of 99,831 navy men or 1.2 per cent were from Orkney, many of them pressganged into service.'

In 1800 Walter Scott of Scottshall, who was also Regulating Captain of the Impress at Lerwick, reported to Dr Kemp of the SSPCK[3] that 'since the commencement of the present hostilities [i.e. 1793] not less than a thousand sailors from this country have enlisted on board of ships of war, and ... hundreds more are employed in the Greenland whale-fishery.'[4]

Dr Arthur Edmondston, who was probably the most accurate, recorded in 1809: 'Between 1793 and 1801 the late Mr Walter Scott, regulating officer, enlisted eleven hundred men for the navy; and the whole population of Zetland did not much exceed twenty-two thousand souls. Upwards of three thousand natives of this country are at present in the navy, a proportion exceeding that of the most populous maritime county in Britain.'[5]

Early Written Records

There is a record[6] of Orkney seamen and fishermen who engaged in King William's[7] service in 1690:

KIRKWALL 1690	List of names of the seamen & fishermen who have engaged in their Maties service & received earnest accordingly –			
		£	s	d
12 Mar	James Pottinger in Deldall in Deirness	00	:14	:00
13 Mar	William Sinclare sometyme servitor to Capt. Craigie	00	:14	:00
14 Mar	Robert Paplay carp[ente]r in Kirkwall			
	George Mowat Lau[fu]ll son to Patrick			
	Mowat carp[ente]r y^r	00	:14	:00
	William Frazer Mariner	00	:14	:00
21 Mar	Magnus Work in Shapinshaw	00	:14	:00

1 1978, p. 596.
2 1775–83.
3 Scottish Society for Promoting Christian Knowledge.
4 The Rev Dr J Kemp, *Observations on Shetland*, 1800, p. 26.
5 Edmondston, 1809, II, pp. 67–8.
6 Orkney Archives, D8/1/3.
7 King William III reigned from 1689–1702.

KIRKWALL 1690	List of names of the seamen & fishermen who have engaged in their Maties service & received earnest accordingly –			
	George Rendall yr	00	:14	:00
22 Mar	Robert Aime in Stronsay	00	:14	:00
	James Flett in Netherbrugh in Harray	00	:14	:00
25 Mar	Robert Murray in Stronsay	00	:14	:00
	Oliver Scott yr	00	:14	:00
	William Wm sone in Shapinshaw	00	:14	:00
	William Simpsone in Westra	00	:14	:00
	James Skae in Stronsay	00	:14	:00
	John Rynd yor in Kirkwall	00	:14	:00
	John Begg in Sanday	00	:14	:00
31 Mar	John Meall in St. Androis	00	:14	:00
2 Ap	John Browne sone to Magnus Brown in Stromnes	00	:14	:00
9 Ap	Robert Irvine in Southronaldshay Late souldier	00	:14	:00

Kirkwall Town Council records provide evidence of island recruitment, voluntary or otherwise, and the action taken in fulfilling its obligations. On 17 March 1692 the Council met and noted that an exact list of seamen and fishermen had to be drawn up as the Privy Council wished to provide a thousand men or more for serving 'in the Fleet Royall', and that no seamen were to be pressed contrary to the freedom and the prejudice of trade. Volunteers would each be paid 'fourtie shillings stairling' and shipped to Leith. Regard would then be had to those places where seamen had voluntarily entered and the Privy Council would proceed to proportion and make up by lot 'what was wanting of the thousand men efter the volunteries are computed.' The Minute reads:

…the said lords of his maties [Majesty's] privy Council doe requyre to cause beat drumms and make intimatione upon the next mercat day after this comes to your hand for levieing and callieng on for his majesties service sutch seamen as voluntarily offer themselves within the stewartrie of Orkney and Zetland and appoint and requyre you to give ane report of what number of seamen you have so taken on with ane exact list upon oath of the wholl other seamen or fishermen within the said stewartrie of Orkney and Zetland that the councill make considder how far the thousand seamen to be furnished to his maties navy falls short yt so the seamen may be made up in ane just proportione by lott out of the said other list of seamen. And certifie and assure you that immediately upon report of sutch seamen as have voluntarily taken on for his majesties service fourtie shilling stairling for each of them shall be putt into your hands to be payed to ym befoir they mairch from home to Leith qr they are to be shipped with competent provisiones or pay in the terms of the proclamatione for their subsistence for that tyme to ther being shipped. And you are to certifie all and each of the said seamen who shall voluntary take on accordingly. And the council has resolved to have special reguard to sutch places wher seamen voluntarly offer themselves when they shall proceed to proportione and make up by lott what is wanting of the thousand men efter the volunteries are computed.

On 14 April 1709 men from Orkney were required urgently to meet the demands arising from The War of the Spanish Succession. Those volunteering as 'soldiers or marines' would be paid by the Collector of Cess 'furth of the land Tax of this Burgh.' However, the Constables and Church Wardens were enjoined 'to search for, seek, apprehend & Inbring all able bodied Idle men within the Burgh who have not suffient & honest wages how to live to the affect they may be lyfted in her Majesties service.'[1]

Unlike Lerwick, Kirkwall did not have an established press gang and Rendezvous, although the Tolbooth situated on the Kirk Green was used to hold recruits, both quota men and volunteers. Accordingly, Orkney constables fulfilled a leading role in recruitment, particularly in districts and islands, albeit sometimes reluctantly.

In June 1711 the Hudson Bay Company, having offered attractive terms for a five year engagement in the 'Nor' Wast', a group of young Orcadians enlisted and joined a Company ship at Stromness. En route to Gravesend, it was overhauled by a naval vessel and eleven Orcadians pressed. For some years thereafter recruitment in Orkney for 'The Great Company' did not prove easy.[2]

HM sloop *Shark* arrived in Stromness (Cairston Road) on 29 May 1746 and pressed three men from three vessels sheltering there. On 1 June she pressed two more men from another two vessels.[3]

Justices of the Peace and Constables

The Seven Years War with France and Spain broke out in 1756 and swingeing impressment ensued in Orkney bringing two years of travail. In 1757 and 1758 the Justices of the Peace and Commissioners of Supply set quotas for every island and parish and exhorted the constables to do their duty and meet the numbers allocated. These heavy demands in consecutive years, supported

---

1 Orkney Archives, K1/1/4.
2 *The Great Company (1667–1871)*, Beckles Willson, Vol I, p. 242, 1900.
3 ADM 51/893.

by the penalties to be visited on constables who did not or could not comply, predictably brought forth protests and requests for protection and release from those summarily arraigned. The Justices were not to be deflected by such resistance and in both years substantial numbers of men were raised for the Army. Examples are given from the incomplete records.[1]

On 3 February 1757, the Justices of Peace and Commissioners of Supply instructed constables 'to Search for all such able-Bodied men within your District who are Idlers and out of Service betwixt the years of Seventeen & forty five and not under the hight [sic] of five feet four inches in bare Soles and to bring them before the Justices at Kirkwall on or before the first day of March next. And for Every Such man So apprehended & is found fitt for Said Service you are to Receive a Reward of Twenty shillings sterling. This you'll not neglect as you will be answerable at your perill.'

That same day the Justices 'thought fitt to write to the Gentlemen of Greatest property in the respective parishes and Islands of this Country Requesting them to give their aid & assistance to the constables in their different bounds in putting the Said precepts in Execution.'

Reaction was swift and on 12 February Rev James Tyrie, Minister of Sandwick and Stromness petitioned the Justices. Two days earlier Thomas Tulloch, his ploughman, had been taken from the house of Consgarth and incarcerated in the county jail. Tyrie was the 'Tacksman of six penny King's land in the town of Hurkisgarth, parish of Sandwick and has no other servant to manage his Room[2] & hold his plow', whereas there were to be found 'stout young fellows who profess no other caring than that of the bagpipe or stroll about the country as chapmen[3] [who] are no doubt to be esteemed Idlers & who all of them may & ought to serve His Majesty.' The outcome of the appeal is unknown.

The Justices duly maintained, even increased, the pressure and on 10 March threatened all constables that if they did not obtain a list of men who could serve, a party would be sent 'for bringing in the constables themselves for their neglect of duty, and they will be sent to Edinburgh and kept in the common goal there in place of the men they should have sent until the full compliment [sic] be made out.'

Two days later David Covingtrie wrote to the Justices complaining that Magnus Dick, one of his tenants 'in Dearness had been taken up by the constables

---

1 Orkney Archives, Tait Papers D10/11.
2 Room or Roome – an arable holding.
3 Pedlars.

there in obedience to your order'. He could not 'possibly labour the labouring of Newark without him as he's obliged to perform Services when demanded, Further he's no Vagrant, Beggar or of bad fame, but has a visible way of Living so does not come under the Act of Parliament.'[1] Presumably Dick was released.

On 16 December a second draft of men was sought, and the Justices – perhaps referring to the first draft – made reference to the letter sent 'on the like occasion in February last'.

Thomas Traill, James Dinneson and William Balfour informed the Justices on 10 February 1758 that they could not find a single man in Westray fit for military service who could come under the description of the Act 'unless the Herring fishers do, and as to these, the Commissioners judged them entitled to an exemption last year.' Men had been provided in 1757 'tho' most of the men we sent were returned home as naturally unfit & others on pretence of Exemption from the service.'[2] If the Justices were determined to proceed 'it must have the effect in this place at least to lay the Lands in part Waste, or what is indeed as bad, render the Cultivating them very superficial.'

Some of the officers appointed by the Justices found the task unduly onerous. David, William and Roland Marwick, constables in Rousay demitted office on 14 March. They wrote: 'But did the Honourable Justices know the present state of our Isle through the want of servants to manure and labour the land we are of the opinion that they would have a sympathie with the labouring man, and not lay us Constables under such a weighty fine [£10 sterling] as is threatened in their second precept. For our Isle for the want of servants is almost like to lie lay. And for one instance there is a Roome called Scockness of four ploughs labouring that has not a man to hold the four ploughs save only the two tenants, and many others in the Isle is in the same state. Therefore we cannot enter on the thought to Impress a tenant nor any of the few servants when they are so much needed unless that the Justices or Landmasters name the persons that is to be apprehended, as for our part we cannot think of any. It is true there are some Fishery men in the Isle but we hear that they are protected.' They requested the Justices 'to chuse other three constables in our place as William and Roland Marwicks are two infirm men and not able nor fit to act in that business, and that David Marwick is very much and often indisposed in his health, and has other business on his hand, such as a school to teach, and a large labouring to manage.'[3]

1 Orkney Archives, Tait Papers D10/11.
2 Orkney Archives, Tait Papers D10/11.
3 Orkney Archives, Tait Papers D10/11.

The Justices appointed the following in place of the Marwicks: William Mainland in Avildshay for Sourin; James Yorston in Westness for the West Side; Hugh Marwick in Claybank for Wasbuster

On 16 March James Halkland and John Coupper, both tenants of the Breckness Estate, Sandwick, put their mark to a letter which stated that Robert Mure, a young married man who had been pressed by the Stromness constables 'had ane impediment in his knee'. This restricted his ability to work and furthermore a milln stone had crushed his side. Mure's knee was inspected by Doctor J Sutherland who attested: 'I have inspected R Mure's knee and am of opinion that he cannot walk long distances on acct of contraction and weakness of the same.'[1] Presumably Mure was freed.

The pressure was relentless and on 22 March constables were enjoined to satisfy their quota 'especially as the Officer commanding the party here has intimated that he cannot leave this place till he gets the last man of the quota laid upon Orkney.'[2]

John Traill of Elsness petitioned the Justices on 9 May on behalf of Edward Sinclair, 'Ploughman working to John Fea in Garth.' Traill wrote that on 8 May he came to Kirkwall from Stronsay taking with him Edward Sinclair as one of his boatmen. At 8 o'clock in the evening at the shore, Sinclair was 'seized by three men said to be Recruits and dragged in a most Inhuman manner to the Tolbooth at Kirkwall without any crime committed by him … and being now informed it was with intent to get him made over by your Honours as a Soldier in terms of the Recruiting Act.' The petition continued that Sinclair did not come under the description of the Act 'being bred a farmer, the principall servant and Ploughman to John Fea in Girtle who possesses a considerable farm belonging to the petitioner in the island of Stronsay which land must lye waste for want of a plowman.' Traill requested that the Justices consider 'the lawless and riotous manner in which the said Edward Sinclair was seized and dragged to Prison.' Sinclair's liberation was requested. That day the Justices met and ordained that Edward Sinclair was 'Immediately to be Set at Liberty.'[3]

Even law-abiding townsfolk were at risk. On 19 May Magnus Work, shoemaker in Kirkwall, petitioned the Justices. That day he had been 'apprehended and carried to the prison of Kirkwall' by Walter Mowat and Robert Tait, Sheriff

1 Orkney Archives, Tait Papers D10/11.
2 Orkney Archives, Tait Papers D10/11.
3 Orkney Archives, Tait Papers D10/11.

Mens Names	Date of de-livery	From Whence Imprest
34 David Harrold	15	
34 Ja.s Craigie	14 March	Parish of Deerness
35 Jo: Norrie	14 do	D.o Parish
36 David Harrold	15 do	Parish of Evie M. 1
37 Mag.s Reid	15 do	Island of Westray M. 1
38 Jno Spence	16 do	Parish of Birsay
39 Mag.s Monet	17 do	Island of S.t Ronaldshay

of Peace and Commissioners of Supply will dispense with our attendance at Kirkwall upon the Thirtieth instant being the throng[1] of Seed time.'[2] In this request they were unsuccessful.

On 30 April the Justices met the following Constables: Henry Leask and Peter Miller for Stronsay, James Shearer and Oliver Leask for Eday, George Ritch and Nicol Wishart for Orphir, William Hourston and Thomas Breck for Birsay, Thomas Sclater and David Firth for Firth, David Cromarty and James Copland for Deerness, and George Park and Arthur Esson for Burray and Flottay [sic].

With one exception all the Constables declared that they had found no suitable men. However, the Eday Constables reported: 'James Rendal resident in Eday Voluntarily entird himself for the Sea Service and expects the Bounty allowed on that account according to the determination of the Commissioners and the Officer sent here for that purpose as he is a young Man of the Age of thirty three years and is married, has a Wife and three Children and his Wife big with the fourth and expects to be maintained from this day when he entired with the Commissioners at the Kings allowance for his daily maintenance untill he is Ship'd on board one or other of his Majesties Ships of War and his Wife to have such allowance as the Law directs. And the Commissioners hereby Appoint Alexander Fraser Collector of the Cess to pay to the Constables of Eday the Sum of Twenty Shillings Stirling for their trouble and to the said James Rendal the Sum of Sixpence each day for his allowance from this day untill he shall be received By a Proper Officer.'[3] Presumably Rendal also received the bounty of three guineas.

Payment for the demanding work undertaken by constables was not always forthcoming. On 21 September 1804 five Birsay constables appealed to the Justices of the Peace asking that they be rewarded for capturing four men. The appeal was drawn up at Birsay by Justice of the Peace Hugh Moar. It certified that constables Geo Taylor, Will[m] Hervie, John Spence, Magnus Johnston and Geo Hourston 'was out part of nine days and most part of nine nights in Sut [pursuit] of men … of which we got eight – four of that was kept, and John Hervie, was laid hold of in Kirkwall which makes five. That is the Number laid on the said parish and Lieutenant Smith took one which makes six. The said Constables is received no actuity or acknowledgement as yet. Altho the work was done in risk of our lives.'[4]

1 Hectic period of bustle or activity, a busy time.
2 Orkney Archives, D/23/10/22.
3 Orkney Archives, D/23/12/1.
4 Orkney Archives, Tait Papers, D10/11.

Constables Threatened and Assaulted

Some constables took their responsibilities particularly seriously. In November 1812 a Stromness constable Alexander, and a midshipman Smith in Captain John Gourly's press gang, were in dispute over who should press a man. Alexander, active in his duties, had recently apprehended three deserters from the *Rosamund* ship of war. He was keen to offer his services, which Smith had brusquely declined. They fell to blows and the violence escalated with the brandishment of a dagger by the officer. Earlier there had been concern in Stromness about the stationing of a press gang, with 'a person being sent through the town … with a Bell Cautioning the Inhabitants from being guilty of any mobbing or riotous conduct or insulting the gang in the execution of their duty.' The fracas between constable Alexander and midshipman Smith attracted a mob, and the midshipman was assaulted by two women and some of the crowd. On Christmas Eve 1812, doubtless imbued with a spirit of reconciliation and festive goodwill, the Justices of the Peace 'having considered the Process with the Proof adduced by both parties are of opinion both have been in the fault and therefore dismissed the Present action without costs of suit to either party.'[1]

The Commissioners adjourned a further meeting upon 'the Impress Act' until 27 May when the constables who had been absent were required to report.

In March 1758 two Harray constables, both John Flett, pressed and secured James Linklater. In the execution of their duty they called for assistance from three local men. Linklater was held in a house until daybreak, when those recruited to help in his detention conspired to secure his release. The constables sought help from the County's Justices of Peace.[2] They wished to have a party sent out with the aim of securing a fit man – presumably Linklater was still the prize – and of punishing the three defecting Harray men. The outcome is not recorded.

> Harray 24March 1758
> Unto the Honourable the Justices of peace of the County of Orkney
> Sheweth

That in Obedience to the Justice of Peace Warrant datted 28th Febry last John Flett of Bea and John Flett of Mirbuster Did upon the 13th day of March last Press James Linklatter in Knarston a Very ffeeting Man to Serve his Mattie he was a Toiler[3] and Drunkard and Very ffitt Man to Serve King George we Called to our assistance William Merriman Alex Hourston and James fflett to Keep the said Linklatter Untill day Andrew Allen Piper in

---

1 Orkney Archives, JP34/5, Box 2, Box 77.
2 Orkney Archives, D24/9/105A.
3 Toil: an obsolete word for strife. Toiler: troublemaker.

Knarston Came in and that in Most rud manner ffather in Law to the said Linklatter and ther Very Rudly Treatned John fflett of Bea & said before that he should Gett the said Linklatter and that they should be Death & read Hyds [red heads] which your Petitioners will approve and Called him a Thiff & sevrall oy^r Bad Neams and Treatnings

And thereaffter Conived with William Merriman Ale^x Hourston and James Flett what way to get the said Linklatter of which they put in Execution at day Brak James Flett being Sat at the bead [bed] door to Keep in the said Linklatter let him out William Merriman threw him down before the said John Flett with Linklatters Wife upon him & Ale^x Hourston opened the doar

May it Therefore Please the Hon^{le} The Justices of Peace to send out a party to press a ffit man to Serve his Mattie & your petitioners shall and is Very willing to goe upon there head as the said Parish are Treatning and have Insulted your Petitioners before and to punish the said William Merriman & Ale^x Hourston & James fflett

> According to law & your Petitioners shall pray
> *John Flett   John Flett*
> Petition anent their being abused in the Execut^n of their office
> The Constables of Harray, *24th March 1758*

Bribery of Constables – Alleged Sword Attack

On 9 September 1790, Hary Sinclair, Pilot, and Buchanon Fotheringame, Merchant, Constables in Stromness, petitioned the Sheriff Substitute alleging that the previous day John Corrigell, carpenter in Stromness:

> ... haveing conceived a deadly hatred ill Will and Malice Against the petitioners and haveing Met the petitioner Buchanon Fotheringame in Stromness; and the Said John Corrigell haveing a necked Sword in his hand threatned to kill the Said Buchanon Fotheringame and Swore to take Out his hearts blood in the presence of severall Witnesses. And thereafter the Said John Corrigell came into the house belonging too and possessed by the Said Hary Sinclair With a necked Sword in his hand And threatned to kill him their With and make Ribbons of his guts With his Sword in presence of Severall Witnesses One of whom took the Sword from him.[1]

They accused Corrigell of 'hamesucken'[2] and eight witnesses were listed. In the petition they said that prior to this fracas the Gentlemen Proprietors in the Country of Orkney had agreed to raise one hundred men 'for His Majestys Navy incase of a War betwixt Great Britain and Spain.' It continued that 'the parish and village of Stromness' had been given an allocation to be levied by the Constables

---

1 Orkney Archives, SC11/5/1790/85.
2 A premeditated assault upon a person in his own house or dwelling place.

as a result of which Corrigell was apprehended by them and put aboard an Impress tender in the harbour. 'But having by some friends obtained his liberty' he was said to have taken revenge by assaulting Sinclair and Fotheringame in their homes.

In his Answers, Corrigell said that he had never been at sea and was unfit for that purpose: '... and therefore the officer on board the tender agreed to set him at liberty on geting another man in his place. A man was found to whom the Pursuer paid Five guineas – he also paid Two guineas to the Defenders or [to] the Press gang who went for him, and a guinea and a half to the Midshipman of the tender, upon which he obtained his liberty after having been two days and a night in the tender.'[1]

Corrigell further alleged that to avoid imprisonment and 'a high fine' he had been 'induced to enter into a compromise with them [the Constables] of the cause in consequence of which they very improperly & unjustly took from him a considerable sum of money.' The press gang sent to secure him had also benefitted financially.

The orginal documents are faded and damaged, but it seems that the Constables and the gang were not averse to bribery. Probably the dispute was settled by the repayment to Corrigell of the monies extorted from him. It is not recorded if he was subsequently pressed, but that seems unlikely as he had paid five guineas to a man who took his place. That arrangement was not uncommon.

Sympathetic Constables

A constables who felt sympathy for his quarry was Oddie from Cornquoy, Holm whose servant was sought. Oddie liked the young man and suggested that he hid at Muckle Ocklester, where he lay under a pile of heather simmonds.[2] Searching the area with a posse and realising where his servant was lying, Oddie tentatively prodded the covering with his baton. Another constable was impatient and critical of the old man's ineptitude. He thrust in his baton with such force that the fugitive grunted and is alleged to have declared, 'Man Oddie, yer pushin the stick intae thet heather as if it hed a lok o eggs in it.' The lad returned after service and remained grateful for his former master's kindness.

Thomas Firth, Mirbister, Harray owed his freedom to a compassionate constable. When pursued he ran over Greenay Hill and hid under a bank in a small valley at the Dees o' Beck. One of the constables Thomas Scott had little

1 Orkney Archives, SC11/5/1790/85.
2 A plaited rope made of heather.

relish for the task and searched the moor in a haphazard manner some distance from the rest of the party. Casually glancing down he saw the upturned face of the frightened youth who cowering and apprehensive, exclaimed fearfully 'Oh, Tammy Scott.' Scott hesitated, then, averting his eyes, moved away.

Orphir men too avoided impressment with a measure of help from a sympathetic constable. Prior to a general press he alerted those at risk by solemnly laying his baton on a table, and then sending a messenger on an apparently trifling errand to warn the neighbourhood. Men were thus given ample time to hide and the constable could not be accused of complicity.

Role of Landowners

On 21 April 1755[1] the Heritors and Freeholders in the North Isles of Orkney bound themselves to pay every able-bodied seaman one guinea, and every ordinary seaman fifteen shillings[2] who voluntarily entered for 'His Majesty's service by Sea before 20th May next'. The wives of these seamen would be given 'houses to live in for themselves & families, Gratis' while their husbands were in naval service. During the absence of their menfolk they would be employed 'in any branch of the Linen Manufacture for which they are qualified.' Pay would be 'weekly for their labour in grain or Meal at the lowest prices' and at the same time they would be allowed the highest wages for similar employment in Orkney. Excepted from this offer were all farmers and their cottars and servants employed in agriculture, as well as men already under contract with the Agents of the Society of the Free British Fishery 'for serving in the white herring Busses for the ensuing season.'

The Heritors were taking care of their interests. By obliging themselves to pay money to able-bodied seamen who enlisted, they were going some way towards meeting any quota which Orkney had to fulfil. Farmers and their cottars and farm servants were excepted, and furthermore volunteers' wives were available for labour, thus providing work people for the Heritors, although they had to make available free housing and paid employment. Additionally, the wives would give a stimulus to the linen industry.[3]

---

1 Orkney Archives, D2/47/5.
2 On production of 'a proper certificate' the amounts would be paid by Mr Thomas Mackenzie & Company, merchants in Kirkwall.
3 By the end of the century the Orkney linen industry had come to an end as it was impossible to obtain the variety of flax required. Straw plaiting was then introduced and by 1804, 150 girls were employed who could earn up to 10d per day. Not later than 1814, between 1,200 and 1,400 people, mainly girls, were employed in this industry – see P N Sutherland Graeme, *Orkney and the Last Great War*, 1915, p. 48.

Support for Those at Home

Shetland seamen appear to have been thrifty, and in 1804 Dr Arthur Edmondston wrote: 'War appears to be more beneficial to Zetland than peace. Considerable sums of money are regularly sent into it from the navy during war, which is not the case in time of peace…Money remitted by regular monthly allotments, by sailors in the navy; and money remitted from the navy by independent bills…£3500.'[1]

There are early instances of islandmen supporting relatives with remittances out of their meagre pay. Between 29 March and 2 May 1778 ninety-six Orcadians were taken aboard His Majesty's armed ship *Three Sisters*. Described as volunteers, they were almost certainly pressed and came from the number imposed on each island and district as part of the Country's quota.[2]

Remittances by some Orcadian seamen on *Three Sisters* in 1779.[3]

From whom	To whom	Relation	Where living	£	S	D
Wm Sands	Mary Halcro	Wife	Cubister, Parish of Ofer	1	11	6
Jno McKay	Janet Lanskell	Wife	Kirkwall	3	3	0
Wm Flett	Allen Mitchell	Wife	Sheepancey	1	1	0
Jno Omand	Jane Atkin	Mother	Stromness	1	11	6
Jno Petrie	Marg^t Voy	Mother	Kirkwall	1	11	6
Geo: Flaws	Allen Corston	Mother	Rossey Island	1	1	0
Thos Sandison	Kerst^n Logie	Wife	Westrey	3	3	0
Thos Harcus	Geo: Harcus	Father	N^o Parish Westrey	2	2	0
Wm Folsetter	Magnus Folsetter	Father	Rossey Island	1	1	0
Geo Flett	Cath^{ne} Linkletter	Wife	Rendall Parish	2	2	0
Wm Inkster	Mary Reed	Wife	Westrey	2	12	6
Jno Harper	Dav^d Harper	Father	Rendall Parish	1	1	0
Thos Sandison	Ja^s Sandison	Father	Saundy Island	1	1	0
Robt Hay	Marg^t Moore	Mother	Saundy D^o	1	1	0
Jno Mowat	Eliz^h Miller	Wife	Kirkwall Westrey	1	1	0
Ja^s Tulloch	Ja^s Tulloch	Father		1	1	0
				26	5	0

1 *A View of the Ancient and Present State of the Zetland Islands*, Vol II, Arthur Edmondston MD, 1809, pp. 22, 24.
2 The need for men is explained by the American War of Independence having commenced in 1775 and being followed by war with France in 1778. See Appendix G for a list of Orkney men pressed aboard *Three Sisters*.
3 Orkney Archives, D5/26/10.

A receipt (above) for the one guinea sent by each of Thomas Sandison and Robert Hay, two of the men on the list.* James Sandison and Margaret Muir made rudimentary initials to signify their acceptance of money remitted, but some recipients simply made a cross such as Janet Langskaill and Elizabeth Miller (below).

* Hay's mother's maiden name was Muir. Women then were often described (and described themselves) by their maiden names.

Some monies sent were never received due to a series of peculations by Thomas Urquhart,[1] deputy postmaster, Victoria Street, Kirkwall. Prosecuted in Edinburgh, the charges were upheld and he was hanged. The indictment included the following:

In 1794, sometime before August, James Fea, seaman, R.N., sent his father, James Fea, in Rothiesholm in Stronsay, a letter containing a guinea and a half, 'which letter never was received by the same James Fea.'

In August or later in the year 1794, 'another letter written by the said James Fea, and directed to the said James Fea, his father, containing inclosed a guinea in Gold or Bank note for that sum,' never reached Stronsay, 'the said letter, in consequence of a search made by Robert Nicolson, Esq., Sheriff-Substitute of the County of Orkney, having afterwards been discovered lying opened in the Escrutoire[2] of you, the said Thomas Urquhart.'

In January 1796, James Smith, on board H.M.S. Vengeance, then at Barbadoes, sent his father, James Smith, Breckwell, in Westray, a letter containing a bank note for five pounds. As the North Isles had then no mail service, this was addressed to the care of James Smith in Crantit. Later in the same year the dutiful son sent another five-pound note to his father, directing it this time to his brother-in-law, John Rendall, master of the sloop Anne, of Kirkwall. These letters were never delivered, and Urquhart was accused of having kept them for the money they contained.

Thomas Spence, a seaman, then confined in the Royal Hospital, Haslar, sent to his mother, Eupham Louttit, in July 1796, a letter containing a guinea. This letter, which was addressed 'To Effie Luted, in the Oald place, neare Kirkwall, Orkneys, North Brittain,' was never delivered.

William Robertson, a corporal in the North Lowland Regiment of Fencibles, quartered at Carrick-on-Shannon, sent two guineas to Isobel Millar, his wife, which never reached the poor woman. The address was somewhat elaborate, but by no means vague – 'Soldier's letter. Carrick-on-Shannon, 7th Nov. 1796. Tho. Balfour, Coll., N.L. Fencibles, to Esabellica Millar, in Kirkwall, to the care of Captant Baky, in Kirkwall, Orkney,Scotland, by North Britand.'[3]

Prudence in the form of a will encouraged men to pursue a more certain way of disposing their worldly wealth such as wages (always in arrears) and

---

1 Life in the postal service in Kirkwall at the close of the eighteenth century must have been rather dull, and doubtless by his actions Urquhart added temporary spice and flavour to his duties. It is said that for many years his ghost haunted the room in a now demolished house at 53 Victoria Street where the letters were opened.
2 A writing-desk or bureau.
3 *Kirkwall in the Orkneys*, B H Hossack, Kirkwall, 1900, pp. 336–7.

prize money. In 1812 Andrew Randall, Burravoe, Yell, then on board HM ship *Modeste*[1] put his mark to a last will and testament:

In the name of God Amen Andrew Randall being in bodily health and of sound and disposing mind and memory and considering the perils and dangers the sea and other uncertainties of this transitory life before for avoiding controversies after my decease make publish and declare this my last will and testament in manner as following … first I recommend my soul to God that gave it and my body I commit to the earth or sea as it shall please God to order and as for and concerning all my worldly estate I give bequeath and dispose thereof as followeth that is to say all my prize money that is now or may hereafter become due unto and while serving on board His Majesty's Ship Modeste as well as wages sum and sums of money lands tenements goods chattels and estate whatsoever as shall be any ways due owing or belonging unto me at the time of my decease and do give devise and bequeath the same unto Catharine Randall my beloved mother and Barbara and Elizabeth Randall all my beloved sisters now living and residing at Borovo in the Island of Yell Shetland and I do hereby nominate and appoint the said Catharine Randall Barbara Randall and Elizabeth Randall executors of this my last will and testament hereby revoking all former and other wills testaments and deeds of gift by me at and time hereafter made and I do ordain and ratify those present to stand and be for and as my only last will and testament in witness whereof to this my said will and I have put my hand and soul in the year of our Lord one thousand eight hundred and twelve Andrew Randall his mark X signed sealed published and declared in the presence of J. Coutts Crawford,[2] T.T. Lewis Senior Lieutenant, J.K. Jones Second Lieutenant, W. Venus Master.

Presumably Randall perished shortly afterwards as the document continues: 'Proved at London 28th September 1813 before the judge by the oaths of Catharine Randall widow the mother Barbara Randall and Elizabeth Randall spinsters the sisters executors to whom admin was granted having been first sworn by comon duty to administer.'[3] Randall was not alone in this regard, the practice of making wills was not unusual. See Appendix F for a list of wills made by islanders who were probably serving as pressed men.

Negotiations with the Admiralty over a Levy of Three Hundred Men

In early May 1790 an Admiralty directive was sent to Sir Thomas Dundas, Bart., Vice-Admiral of Orkney and Shetland for the procuring of men from the islands. Shortly afterwards clarification came with the demand set at three hundred.

1 A thirty-six-gun fifth rate frigate with a complement of 270, probably then in the Mediterrean.
2 James Crawford was the ship's captain.
3 The National Archives, prob 11/1548.

Although the correspondence is somewhat confused with letters crossing in the post, the Admiralty would not be deflected despite protests and compromise proposals by both counties, and a request from Shetland that it should provide only a third of the total, with the remainder recruited in Orkney.

On 19 May Patrick Hagart, Deputy Vice-Admiral for Orkney, wrote from Kirkwall to Sir Thomas thanking him for his letter of 7 May and informing him that he had communicated the content to the Commissioners of the County. He sent a copy of their subsequent resolution to Dundas in which they agreed to raise one hundred men 'which was the number they gave at the beginning of last war, although there were afterwards two levies of fifty men each.' Hagart continued that a hundred men was as much as could be raised at one time, but the Commissioners had left it to him 'to make the best bargain you can with the Admiralty who they expect will order the officers concerned in the impress Service to give the Country no disturbance.'[1]

On 20 May the Admiralty had sent a press warrant to Sir Thomas in which he was 'required and directed to cause to be taken up by your proper Officers within your vice Admiralty all Seamen and Seafaring Men fit for His Majesty's Service who shall be found lurking in those Parts.' They were to be carried on board any of His Majesty's ships, vessels or tenders at any of the sea ports or to any of the Sea Officers employed on shore in raising men. The Warrant continued, 'letting the persons who conduct them know that upon their producing Receipts to any of the Collectors of the Customs from the Sea Officers to whom such Men shall be delivered, they will be paid by such Collectors Twenty Shillings for each Seaman … and Sixpence a Mile for every Mile they respectively travel not exceeding Twenty Miles.'[2] This press warrant was be used only if the required number of men could not be obtained by volunteers who would receive a bounty.

Dundas replied on 22 May and made reference to the prior arrangements of 1755 and 1777 for a voluntary quota. He wished to ascertain from the Admiralty what 'Composition in the present instance' would be acceptable 'for not impressing any of the Inhabitants.' This was 'upon condition that the Press Warrants are not carryed into Execution and that compleat protection is granted to the Trade and Fisheries of the Isles of Orkney and Zetland.'[3] That same day he received the following response from a Mr Stephens:

[1] North Riding Record Office, ZNK/X/2/1/988.
[2] North Riding Record Office, ZNK/X/2/1/989.
[3] North Riding Record Office, ZNK/X/2/1/992.

Admiralty Office 22^d 1790

Sir

Having laid before my Lords & Commissioners of the Admiralty your Letter of this Day's date, acknowledging the Receipt of this Warrant for procuring Seaman for the Fleet in the Isles of Orkney and Zetland, representing that it has been usual for the Inhabitants of these Islands to raise a certain number of volunteer Seamen to be delivered to Office of the Navy as their Lordships may send thither for them, by way of Composition for not impressing any of the Inhabitants; and desiring to know whether their Lordships will accept of any Composition in the present instance; I am commanded by their Lordships to acquaint you that they will accept of three hundred Men as a Composition for the said Isles in the present instance.[1]

On 24 May Dundas wrote to Patrick Hagart in Kirkwall and Thomas Bolt in Lerwick, his Deputy Vice-Admirals, sending Warrants (as a precaution) and an answer from Mr Stephens of the Admiralty confirming the intention that the Gentlemen of Orkney and Shetland should furnish three hundred volunteer seamen, otherwise the Warrants would be carried into execution. In a conversation with Lord Chatham, he had stated in the strongest terms the hardship to the inhabitants that would be caused by raising so many men, but to no avail.[2]

On 19 May the Commissioners in Orkney had already met and determined:

First, that the Number to be raised be One hundred.

Secondly, That the Registered Vessels belonging to the Country furnish One Man each out of the above number.

Thirdly That One Guinea and an half shall be given, over and above His Majesty's Bounty to each Man so raised, as encouragement to Enter Voluntarily.

Fourthly, That the Gentlemen will use their best endeavours to raise the above number of Men as soon as they are advised that a Tender will be in Orkney to receive them.

Fifthly, That the Men be raised in the following Proportions, Viz, Kirkwall and Parish Six, South Ronaldshay Three, Burray Two, Flotta and Pharay Two, Holm Three, Dearness Three, St Andrews Three, Walls Three, Hoy Two, Graemsay One, Orphir & Cava Three, Stromness and Parish Eight, Sandwick Two, Birsay Three, Harray One, Firth One, Evie and Inhallow Three, Rendall

---

1 North Riding Record Office, ZNK/X/2/1/993.
2 North Riding Record Office, ZNK/X/2/1/994.

and Gairsay Three, Shapinshay One, Egilshay and Rousay Three, Westray and Papay Four, Stronsay Two, and to pay Bounty for One, Stenness Two, Sanday Three and to pay Bounty for One, Eday and Pharay Two, and North Ronaldshay One, making in all with Twenty Eight from the Shipping, One hundred Men.

Keen to protect the well-being of Orkney, the meeting requested the Preses, Thomas Balfour of Elwick, to contact Sir Thomas 'and entreat him to make the best bargain with the Lords of the Admiralty for a Protection to be granted to the Shipping and Inhabitants of the County.' A further request was that the officer regulating the Impress Service at Leith should be informed of the protection that 'has been on former occasions granted to the shipping and inhabitants of the country and the measures that are now pursuing to purchase a similar exemption from impress and to endeavour to procure the Regulating Officer's instructions for granting protections immediately.'[1]

Shetland too was anxious to reduce its allocation. The mail had taken some time to arrive and on 7 July Thomas Bolt, the Deputy Vice-Admiral laid the request for 100 men before a full meeting of Heritors whose deliberations were recorded by the Preses James Scott. They agreed to use their utmost endeavours to procure men (but as in the case of Orkney) 'upon Condition that the press Warrants are not carried into execution and that compleat protection is granted to the Trade & Fisheries of Shetland.' It was suggested that the Lords of the Admiralty should accept fifty men 'in respect that these islands in particular have been much drained of their young Inhabitants because of their seven years famine and sterility which lately afflicted the land.' Nevertheless they would 'leave their interest entirely with you good Sir and engage to furnish whatever number betwixt the fifty & hundred men you shall find proper to stipulate however distressing it may be to raise the larger number.'

The letter relied on Sir Thomas Dundas 'and the justice of the Lords of the Admiralty that we shall at no time be assessed but in proportion with Orkney that is two thirds and Zetland's one third of the whole number demanded.'[2]

The outcome of this correspondence is unknown, but it seems that a hundred men quota for Orkney was reluctantly accepted and Lieutenant Yetts and *The David* tender duly arrived in Kirkwall on 30 July. There had been considerable difficulty in raising all the men the tender had come to transport, and the excuses

1 North Riding Record Office, ZNK/X/2/1/1008.
2 North Riding Record Office, ZNK/X/2/1/1002.

as 'Deputy Post Master'.[1] The identity of the seven bounty men is unknown. Presumably they were 'volunteers', willing or otherwise. Certainly they would not have come from the ranks of the contributors.

On 22 March 1798, the Council having been asked 'for a voluntary contribution … for the defence of the country … subscribed twenty-five pounds sterling to be paid out of the funds of this Burgh.'[2]

Heightened Need

The commencement of the Napoleonic Wars in 1803 increased the demand for men. All the important and influential bodies in the County met on 8 July when it was resolved: '… to offer a Bounty of Two Guineas to every able Seaman and One Guinea to every ordinary or able Bodied Landsman belonging to or living within the precincts of the Town of Kirkwall who shall voluntarily enter himself to serve on Board the Royal Navy and appoint the Clerk furthwith to publish advertisements to that effect, … and being informed that an Officer has arrived here upon the Impress Service they appoint the Provost to wait upon the Officer and to communicate this Resolution to him, assuring him at [the] sametime that they in full expectation that no Tradesman, Landsman or Labourers are to be molested will use their utmost endeavours to discover all Sculking Seamen who may be usefull for the Navy.'[3]

On 20 August 1803 the Deputy Lieutenants, Freeholders, Justices of Peace, Commissioners of Supply, Heretors and others met in the Town Hall, Kirkwall. It was noted that following their resolutions of 8 July and 11 August 'only three men had as yet been procured.' It was therefore resolved that one hundred men be immediately recruited, all of whom would be entitled to the present bounty; that the men be levied according to the return of the population made in May 1802 by the schoolmasters of the parishes and islands; that the Heretors, Justices of Peace and principal farmers in each parish 'shall meet and fix upon and cause to be apprehended and brought before them by their Constables, such persons as they consider fittest to serve and shall either enlist them or despatch them to Kirkwall as soon as a receiving ship shall arrive. That if any of the Parishes refuses or delays to conform, Press warrants will be produced and carried into Execution.' The allocation[4] of one hundred men was:

1 Hossack, B H, *Kirkwall In The Orkneys*, 1900, p. 336.
2 Orkney Archives, K1/1/9.
3 Orkney Archives, K1/1/9.
4 Orkney Archives, Traill Dennison Papers D14/8/2.

Impressment in the Northern Isles

Place	Men
Kirkwall	6
St Olla	2
St Andrews	4
Dearness	4
Holm	4
Firth	3
Stenness	3
Orphir	4
Stromness	7
Sandwick	5
Birsay	5
Harray	3
Evie	4
Rendall & Gairsay	3
South Ronaldshay and Swunna	6
Burray	2
Walls	3
Flotta and Faira	2
Hoy	1
Graemsay	1
Weir Enhallow Rousay & Egilshay	4
Shapinshay	3
Westray & Papa	5
Stronsay	4
Eday	3
Lady Parish	3
Cross Parish Burness & N Ronaldshay	6
Total	100 Men

Indicative of the dangers besetting the nation in its 'present critical situation' a subscription[1] was also raised in 1803 at Holm 'for the defence of the country'. This was essentially for those living and working on the Graemeshall Estate – probably because the laird was Vice-Admiral Alexander Graeme. Over the years of war the parish had provided significant numbers of volunteers and pressed men. Nevertheless, the subscription raised £9, 'the money to be paid to some of the banks or banking companies in Edinburgh.'

---

1 Orkney Archives, D5/3.

Subscription for the Defence of the County, 1803.	£	Sh	d
William Craigie Senior	1	–	–
Miss Galloway in Greenwall	–	10	–
Miss Smith D°	–	10	–
James Taylor a School boy D°	–	1	–
Charles Taylor D°	–	1	–
James Bews Farmer	–	4	–
Marg^t Laughton D°	–	5	–
James Cromarty Farmer	1	0	0
Charles Langskaill D°	–	8	–
William Garioch in Cornq^y farmer	–	5	–
Peter Bews farmer	–	2	6
David Laughton weaver	–	1	6
James Laughton Skeal farmer	–	10	–
John Garioch Farmer Gorn	–	5	–
John Laughton Swartaq^y Farmer	–	2	6
John Foubister Taylor	–	2	–
Peter Pettrie Senior late farmer	–	5	–
William Odie farmer	–	2	–
John Laughton Biggins Farmer	–	10	6
Archibald Garioch farmer	–	2	6
James Garioch D°	–	5	–
Peter Garioch Cottar	–	1	6
Thomas Miller Farmer	–	10	6
James Laughton in Easterbister	–	2	–
David Langskaill Cottar	–	2	6
John Dishon Farmer	–	5	–
John Laughton farmer Breakin	–	5	–
	7	19	-
David Pettrie in Grameshall	1	1	-
	9	-	-

Liability for Expences

Quotas were more easily made than met. A special meeting of the Town Council on 14 November 1812,[1] considered a letter from the Lieutenancy of the County

1 Orkney Archives, K1/1/10.

along with a copy of Protest[1] dated 10 November from the Regulating Officer, Captain John Gourly, anent 'the deficiency of the quota' from the County.[2] Unless the men 'deficient for the Burgh' were immediately furnished the magistrates would be 'held responsible for any damage or expense to which the County may be subjected in respect of the said deficient Men.' The meeting considered the letter and enclosed Protest and decided that 'some decisive and effectual measures must be taken forthwith.' This resulted in a meeting four days later when it was reported that 'the Constables had taken and delivered over four Men being the number wanting for his Burgh, two of whom had been reported as fit for his Majestys service, and the other two would be reported to the Committee at their Meeting this day.' The Clerk was directed to communicate this information to Captain Gourly.

Captain Gourly's Protest had been addressed to the Court of Lieutenancy, Justices of the Peace, Commissioners of Supply and Heretors of Orkney concerning an agreement with the Admiralty to provide 120 men from the county of Orkney. The Agreement had been made the previous April. Gourly wrote that the failure to furnish these men had caused considerable expense 'far beyond the expence incurred to the public in any other county in raising its quota of men for the Navy.' The county was said not to have used the means at its disposal to procure the men – excepting for the exertions of a few individuals, and as a result the whole labour and expense had fallen upon him. The expense had been three times that incurred in other counties 'where I had the same Service to perform.' He stated that this would become apparent from his Accounts now before the Navy Board.

Gourly noted that there was a general dislike for the Naval Service throughout the mainland and islands of Orkney and because of this the expense involved in providing the men required was 'very great for pay and subsistence to [his] officers and men', and furthermore was 'likely to increase still more for boat hire, horse hire etc.' There would also be an expense on account of the officers and men on the ships sent to Orkney to enforce the Agreement.

Gourly protested in the name of the King that from and after the date of the document, viz. 10 November 1812, all expenses and disbursements incurred in order to procure the number of men still wanted from the county 'either by impress or otherwise shall be paid by you the said Court of Lieutenancy, Justices

1 Orkney Archives, K1/1/10.
2 A quota of 120 men which had been set in April 1811 had not been satisfied, and Kirkwall's contribution to the deficit had been determined at four.

of the Peace, Commissioners of Supply and Heritors of Orkney.' Moreover, he would render an account for his expenses and disbursements 'for each succeeding week from and after this day' for as long as he remained in Orkney for raising the number of quota men still wanted.

At this time the success of Shetland in meeting it's like quota of 100 men was used by William Mouat, Annsbrae, Bressay, as a reason for requesting release of Thomas White, one of his tenants. On 14 October 1812 he wrote to Lieutenant Hutchison, HM schooner *Pygmy*, suggesting that Hutchison might not be aware of the county having agreed to accept a quota of a hundred men, as a consequence of which impressment would cease. He continued: 'as we are in dayly expectation of Captain Gourlay with a tender to take away the men' White should be set at liberty. The following day he wrote again to Lieutenant Hutchison refuting the allegation that White was a deserter, and asserting that he had never 'belonged to HM Service.' He had served on the armed ship *Norfolk* for five years and thereafter his various duties included working in the coal trade. Since returning in Shetland in 1808 he had been employed as a farmer. White was the 'only support of an old father and mother who if he is taken from them will be immediately reduced to begging.' Mouat's plea was successful and White was liberated.[1]

Church Involvement

The Delting Kirk Session Minutes at Olnafirth on 10 August 1760 record 'Minister after sermon also Intimated that this days Collection was to be Given to the men impresed on board his Majestys Navie and Exorted them to Extend their Charity Coll. 7£ 8sh which was Delivered Accordingly.' The same Session Minutes at Scatsta on 23 September 1764 point to an even earlier impressment: 'An alistation[2] was appointed to petter Clark Bearing that Thomas Clark Sailor on Board his Majestys Ship the Lenax man of war & Died at Malina, was Lawfull son to the said petter Clark.'[3] Thomas had been pressed in 1758.

Peter's impressment has been established by Dr Alan Beattie who examined the muster of HMS *Lenox*. This records that Thomas joined the ship on 1 October 1758 from the tender *Archturus*. An ordinary seaman, he was promoted AB on 5 February 1759 and died on 5 October 1762 'killed at Malina'. During his time on board he had spent £4 14s 4d on clothes, 14s 6d on bedding and £1 3s 9d on

---
1 William Mouat's letter book 7/11/1805–16/12/1816.
2 Attestation.
3 Delting Kirk Session Minutes 1751–1811, CH2/90/2.

tobacco. Dr Beattie observed that Thomas's place of birth was not recorded, but noted that *Archturus* had also supplied *Lenox* with John Mitchell, John Cogle, James Sutherland and Magnus Ollison. He is confident that these men too were Shetlanders. Perhaps the collection of £7 8s obtained at the church service on 10 August 1760 was on behalf of these five men.

In 1758, the involvement of an Orkney minister and his wife brought about violence. On 24 March there was an affray in Hoy when the island's two constables, having made an arrest, were attacked. Malcolm Groat wrote 'Mr Sands the minister of Hoy and his wife have been the Chief formenters of this lawless & disorderly spirit among the populace & sent out this morning two of his women servants at least, they were with about 30 or 40 more most active in deforcing Ben Barnetson and William Swanson this morning when they had seized upon a young fellow one Edward Ritch who has neither house, wife or family and who was the only person most proper and best to be spared in the parish. The two constables were beat & abused with stones and otherways, particularly William Swanson who was cut in the face by old Wm Stout. I have enclosed a list of the names of those who have come to my knowledge, who were most active in this Riot.' Groat suggested to the Justices that this action should not go unpunished otherwise 'the like riotous spirit will defuse itself over the rest of the country.' Three or four soldiers should be sent to aid and enforce the constables in their duty 'and to bring all the rioters before them [the Justices], so as they may be examined and punished according to their desserts.'[1] It is not known if Rev and Mrs Sands[2] appeared before the Justices.

In 1760 six men were pressed from the district of Sandness, but after several weeks detained on a tender they were released. They gave thanks to God by adding a total of 4sh 5d to the church collection the following Sunday. The entry in the Walls Kirk Session Book is:[3]

> Kirk of Melbie, August 24th 1760 … … …
>
> The collection was £3-13Sh. occasion'd by the follwing persons giving in an extraordinary colletion [sic] on acc^{tt} of their being restor'd to their familys after having been taken and confin'd for several weeks on board a tender for impressing men for the navy. The perons forsaid are Lawrence Sinclair Junr in Melbie who gave in a shilling, George Anderson in Norbie a shilling, James

1 Orkney Archives, Tait Papers, D10/11.
2 Rev Robert Sands and his wife Jean had 22 children, of whom only four sons and three daughters were alive in 1795.
3 Shetland Archives, CH2/380/2, p. 242.

Johnson in Melbie a sixpence, Alex[r] Sinclair in the Skoes who though not press'd gave in five pence on acco[tt] of his brother Lawrence, Gabriel Cowtt in Lambtoun a shilling, and Malcom Will[m]son in Melbie a sixpence.

The Rev Hugh Mouat, minister of Evie, was much exercised by the impressment of the servant of his son-in-law William Watt. On 28 February 1771 he wrote to James Riddoch, Provost of Kirkwall, protesting that the youth had been taken aboard a tender at Kirkwall. He was not a vagrant or an idler and his aged parents depended on him to labour their part of the glebe. Two men had been impressed from the glebe during the last war and the old couple 'labourd under fearfull apprehensions that the same game would be played over again.' Mouat concludes with a PS: 'Fear would make the boy say any thing in your and the Gentlemens' presence, and as he saw he was to be impressed he might soon be prevaild on to accept of Bounty money.'[1] The outcome is unknown.

Rev John Turnbull of Tingwall is credited with obtaining the release of a Weisdale man who had been pressed and in naval custody. The story is detailed in *The Shetland Times* of 15 January 1876 in a lengthy article: *A Wild Goose Chase – Jottings of Bygone Days*. This gives an interesting if somewhat fanciful account of how three brothers from Weisdale were relentlessly pursued. After various adventures and narrow escapes two of the brothers retained their freedom but the third was secured aboard a tender at Lerwick. The captured man's wife took to horseback and sought help from Turnbull, who while endeavouring to have the man released declared: 'If her Majesty's ships must have men to keep up the fleet, take the drones, the bachelors, the non-producers, but let such men as these alone; they are at the head of agriculture, and actively ready for every good work; among the very best men in my parish and in my church.' The story continues: 'The formidable lieutenant-commander 'wilted' under the consistent blows given by this honest and sturdy servant of Jesus Christ, and he who some years previous to this time had joined these two worthy people together in God's name, now handed the loving husband to the dear weeping wife, saying "What God has joined together, let no man put asunder."'[2]

The clergy did not always so readily defend their flock against the authorities. At the time of the American War of Independence Rev John Mill, Dunrossness, Sandwick and Cunningsburgh, recorded in his diary entry of July 1777: '… the

---

1 Orkney Archives, Tait Papers, D10/9.
2 Admitted as minister at Tingwall in 1806, he died in 1867, aged ninety-one. The release of the third brother would have taken place in the early years of his ministry. See p. 85 for another exploit in which he attempted to frustrate the gang.

people being apprised that the Government had sent over a tender, with a demand of an hundred men for their service, they fled from their houses and betook themselves to their hills and skulking places, which made me take notice of this on the Sabbath from the pulpit, saying they made great haste in running away for fear of the Pressgang, who did not want to hang them or put them in prison, but only to serve their King and Countrey in the suppression of Rebells in America, who had risen up against their lawful superiors without any just grounds, and might be better employed for a year or two than at home; for when the rebellion was over, they might return again with their pockets full of money; and that they were as eager in fleeing from the wrath of a Sin avenging God, to the blood of sprinkling for pardon and cleansing etc.[1]

The Fencibles

It is beyond dispute that over the decades Orkney and Shetland made a considerable contribution to the manning of the fleet. This was in addition to those tasked with local guard duties who were volunteers or Sea Fencibles. Formed in 1798, they were briefly disbanded in 1802 following the Peace

Kirkwall Volunteers, 1807.

[1] *The Diary of the Reverend John Mill*, 1889, pp. 50–1.

of Amiens. However, in 1803 they were again assembled throughout the country to guard the coast. It was intended that they would comprise local fishermen and others who were not otherwise suitable for impressment. Included were men who worked in the coastal trade around Britain. The initiative proved difficult to implement efficiently as interpretation varied as to who might enlist. It was believed, probably correctly, that many seamen eligible for impressment had simply volunteered for the fencibles in order to avoid being pressed. In Orkney it was resolved that an offer should be made to the Government 'to raise Three Companies of Eighty Men each, viz One of Sea Fencibles in the Town of Stromness and Two Companies in Kirkwall either of Sea Fencibles or Volunteers as shall be most acceptable or Serviceable to Government to serve in the event of an Invasion in any part of the Kingdom his Majesty shall appoint.'

On 1 and 3 March 1804 at a General Meeting of the 'Principal Inhabitants of the village of Stromness' it was resolved to establish 'a corps of sea fencibles to serve without Pay and in Orkney.' Eighty-three of those present enrolled and subsequently the number reached 130. Four long nine-pounders were forthwith to be placed on the outer Holms 'as the most eligible place for the defence of the town and shipping…an account taken of all muskets, Fowling Pieces, Powder, Balls or Ammunition of any kind in both town & Parish in case of being needed for public service, and David Sinclair late a Serjeant [sic] in his Majesty's service would begin and exercise the volunteers in their marching.'[1]

By 1808 Fencibles in Shetland were being paid, and on 27 May an advertisement appeared at Lerwick 'to raise Pike men or Fescibles [sic]':[2]

>
> BRAVE SHETLANDMEN
>
> Now is your Time
>
> To shew your
>
> LOYALTY to your KING
>
> and attachment to your
>
> NATIVE ISLANDS
>
> For the sole protection of which you are now invited to embody yourselves into a corps of Sea Fencibles to be commanded by Captain James Nicolson of the Royal Navy a country man of your own, and son of the late much Revered Arthur Nicolson Esq^e of Lochend well known to you.

1 Orkney Archives, Traill Dennison Papers D14/8/2.
2 Shetland Archives, Irvine of Midbrake Papers D16/387/92.

By enrolling yourselves into this corps you will be entirely exempted from the Impress. You will only be required to meet once in each month; to be exercised at the guns and the Pike, and will receive one Shilling each time.

GOD SAVE THE KING

Lerwick 27th May, 1808

The competing demands of the volunteer and impress services came to the fore when John Laurenceson, 'a running post' having been sent to Unst, was apprehended on his return to Lerwick harbour. Aged forty-five, he was a serving

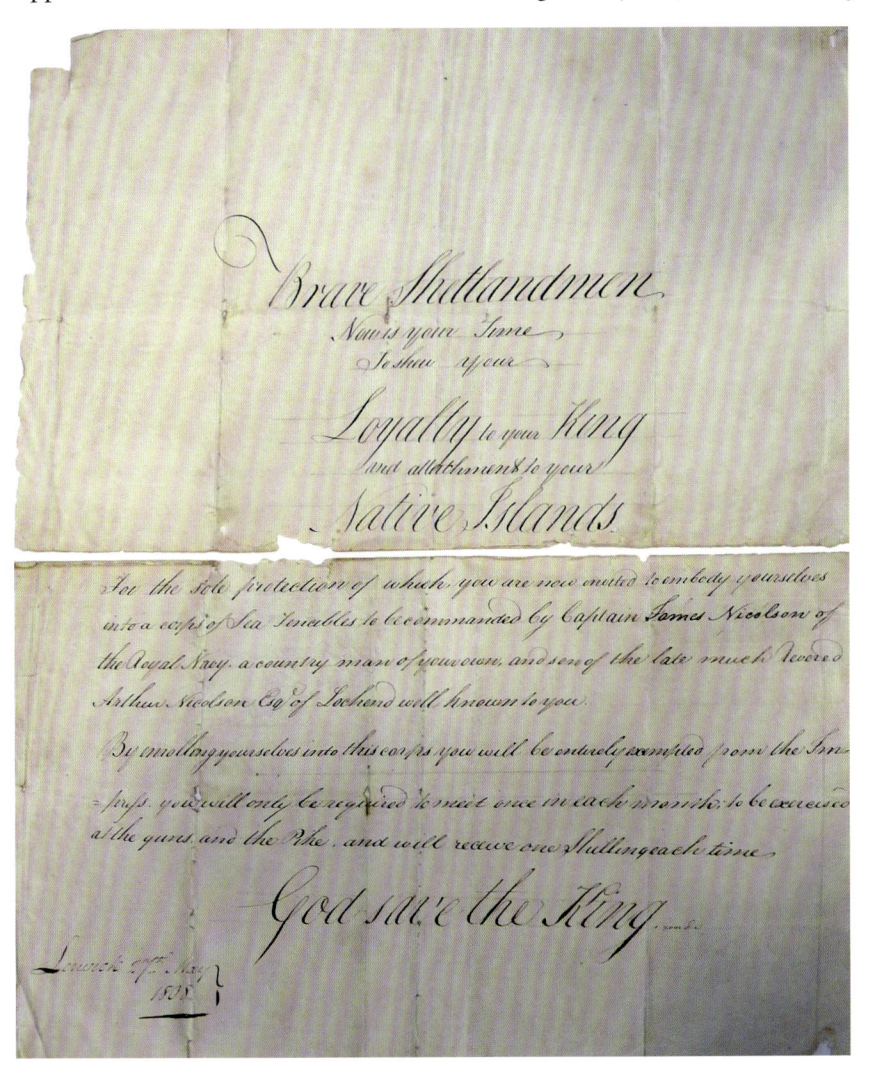

Advertisement for Pike men and Fencibles, Lerwick, 1808.

volunteer and William Mouat his employer wrote seeking his liberation: 'And altho it may be a question of courtesy between the commanding officers on the Volunteer and impress service Whether a man liable otherways to be impressed ought to be discharged from the volunteers, yet such question can never affect the man so as to render him liable to the impress till he has actually been so discharged.'[1] Presumably Laurenceson, as a serving volunteer, was protected from impressment and released.

Whenever John Goodlad, who had also enrolled as a volunteer/fencible, landed in Shetland after his Greenland voyages, he used a simple plan to retain his freedom. Once he had hidden he 'sent word quickly to his wife as to his whereabouts. Taking his volunteer uniform she would go to this hiding place and after donning the clothes Jonnie would march triumphantly to his house secure from capture on account of the trig[2] uniform he wore.'[3]

On 28 March 1809 Andrew Morrison, Thomas Manson and Magnus Anderson, privates in the corps of Lerwick volunteers, attended a volunteers muster when they were impressed by Captain Nicolson, the Regulating Officer. They appealed to the Sheriff Substitute on the basis that: 'Independent of other circumstances the Defencers apprehend that their being engaged in his majestys land service as Volunteers exeems them effectually from impress, and they were alwise taught to think so.' They added to their appeal that this was 'during one of the best fishing weeks this summer.' They were set at liberty. However, because of financial loss in their absence from the fishing and their legal expenses they then applied for indemnification. The Sheriff Substitute referred the process to the Sheriff Depute in Edinburgh who confirmed the Sheriff Substitute's decreet that the men were not impressable and ordered Captain Nicolson to pay their expenses, which he did. Nicolson appealed to 'the Supreme Court'. In a Memorial in response the men said that because of their poverty and the extravagant expense involved they were unable to defend their case without assistance and support. The Memorial lists Shetland's stormy climate, its barren soil, and the evils of impressment. The Memorial hoped that the 'Lords of Session will view the case of the Defenders … in the same light in which the Sheriff has done.' The outcome is unknown, but it seems likely that the Memorial would have been successful. It is given in Appendix E.

1 Shetland Archives, D6/171/17. Undated, early nineteenth century.
2 Neat and tidy.
3 Shetland Archives, D6/295/1. Taken from undated notes of oral traditions by E S Reid Tait, 1885–1960.

The End of Impressment

Sir John Sinclair, the noted agriculturalist, historian and philanthropist, offered a somewhat unusual scheme for abolishing impressment. His suggestion included Caithness, Orkney and Shetland as well as other areas. Sir John, perhaps the most eminent son of Caithness, produced his plan in April 1830 'For establishing a new Naval Resource, by which the necessity of impressing Seamen, unless in periods of great public danger, would be prevented.' The detail is interesting but the proposal was unreal and not pursued:

The British empire has a *resource of seamen*, in the Orkney and Shetland islands, – in the Hebrides or Western Islands, and along the northern and western coasts of Scotland and Ireland, *which no other country in Europe possesses.*

Under a proper system, and at a moderate expense, 50,000 seafaring people might be kept there, constantly ready, on the shortest notice, to enter into the public service.

A great part of this valuable resource is, at present, lost to the public; because in the Hebrides, and along the western coasts of Scotland and Ireland, the natives have but an imperfect knowledge of the English language, and in many cases speak nothing but Erse or Irish. They have a natural prejudice, therefore, against a service where they cannot make themselves understood.

But this difficulty might easily be surmounted, by promoting the acquisition of the English language in all those districts; and a plan might be formed, by which this great resource might be rendered available, and the horrid system of impressing seamen might be abolished.

Perhaps the sum necessary might be raised, by exempting all seamen from impressment, who paid a certain sum *per annum*, say £1 each. But if it were to cost the public two or three hundred thousand pounds *per annum*, should this be put in competition with the certainty of maintaining our fleets, without the necessity of impressment; and having so great a body of seafaring people always at command?[1]

---

1 *The Correspondence of The Right Honourable Sir John Sinclair*, Bart, Vol I, 1831, pp. 201–2.

HMS *Carysfort*

When men were required urgently, dispatching a man of war to Northern waters could provide substantial numbers. *Carysfort*, a 28 gun, 6th rate ship of the line, was at Shields in 1803 when war broke out. She was instructed to proceed to Shetland and impress a hundred men.

Aboard the vessel was midshipman George Vernon Jackson who had joined the navy in 1801 at the age of fourteen. He led a full, interesting life and attained the rank of Admiral in 1875 at the estimable age of eighty-eight. Captured in December 1808 at Guadalupe, in 1812 he escaped from Betche, a town in Lorraine, France at his fifth attempt.

In *The Perilous Adventures and Vicissitudes of a Naval Officer 1801–1812*, part of his memoirs, Jackson recounts what befell him in Shetland as a member of a naval recruiting party. He writes that the number of men taken was seventy, although the editor of the book says the actual number was sixty-five. Others writing about *Carysfort* correctly give the island's contribution as fifty-nine.

Most of the men are entered in the ship's musters as voluntary recruits although this is highly unlikely. There was different treatment for volunteers, and men had a financial inducement to enter as a volunteer after being taken by force.

Jackson paid a compliment to the Shetlanders: 'We were indebted to our late efforts at impressment for as fine a body of men as ever sailed in a ship. We took their average height, and it was a trifle under six feet.'

Carysfort arrived in Bressay Sound on 5 April 1803, and Jackson records: 'On one occasion, whilst prowling about in the execution of our duty, I espied a tall handsome lad coming into our vicinity unawares. On catching sight of me he fled like a deer. I was young and active too, and started off in pursuit; the race was becoming mine when he made for a house and dashed through the open doorway. I was on his heels directly, but found myself arrested by a poor, respectable-looking woman who fell upon her knees, and beseeched me, with clasped hands and tears streaming down her face, to spare her boy. Her entreaties were joined by several young girls present, all of whom were exhibiting the same tearful propensity. I gave in at once and left the spot with a queer sensation in the throat, and grumbling an incoherent anathema against the whole sex. These were strange times when a youngster of my age could lay violent hands upon almost any man he came across and lead him into bondage.'

He was affected by the dolorous scene as *Carysfort* left on 19 June: 'When the ship was on the point of leaving, it was a melancholy sight; for boatloads of women – wives, mothers, and sisters – came alongside to take leave of their kidnapped relatives. Being young at the business I was not always proof against some of the trials I encountered ashore, and often repented having made a capture when I witnessed the misery it occasioned in homes hitherto happy and undisturbed.'[1]

Reluctant Lairds

Carysfort certainly had a measure of successful recruiting, despatching boats to press men wherever they could be found – usually in the open sea or around the coast. However, by early June Captain Robert Fanshawe had not secured the required hundred men. On 2 June 1803 he sent a circular letter to Shetland's fourteen prominent proprietors: 'Understanding that you are one of the principal landowners in the Island of Shetland and have several boats employed in fishing for you which ought to begin this week, but are prevented by reason of the fear and alarm the impress has spread among the people and, as it is by no means my wish to distress the fisheries of the islands if it can be avoided, I have to propose that if the principal inhabitants will come forward and procure immediately the number of men (viz 100) between the age of 20 and 40 of strong bodies and good health … that are wanted to complete the number I came for, I shall restrain not only from impressing any fishermen but also give orders that they may be in no manner annoy'd by the boats of this ship.'

He added a threat: 'I have some intention of going to sea to cruize round the islands the beginning of next week, my proceeding with regard to pressing from the boats must be guided by the answer I receive.'

Predictably the responses were not helpful – the lairds, steadfastly self-interested, were anxious to protect their fishing revenue.

Andrew Grierson, Quendale, replied tersely: 'I have only to observe that your letter holds forth no further security for the safety of the fishermen of

---

1 pp. 27, 28.

this country than what individually attaches to you and the ship under your command.'

Thomas Bolt, Cruister, Bressay, pleaded similarly: 'I cannot doubt but that the gentlemen of Shetland would willingly and cheerfully comply with your request of raising even a hundred men for His Majesty's Navy could you give them protection for the trade and fisheries of the county; but as you can only do that for yourself, were they to comply, a like demand may be made by the first of H.M. ships that may again put in here, and every other ship of war that may follow, and still no general protection could be relied on ... I am truly sorry to give you this trouble yet I cannot help further [than] to state the calamity that the poor inhabitants of these islands now labour under from a total failure of last year's crop of corn [1802], and every Production of the earth fit for the food of man.'[1]

Gideon Gifford, Bruister, provided a different, somewhat specious answer, given that this requisition for one hundred men had been levied on Shetland. He averred that Shetland had never been deficient in furnishing its one third of the joint quota for Orkney and Shetland and that any want lay at Orkney's door:

> Orkney and this country coming at the same time from under the Crown of Denmark to that of Scotland and probably the small value of both countries and paucity of their inhabitants induced the Government to class them as one County, notwithstanding their unconnected situation, and altho' classed together, yet they are as entirely separate in interest, trade and correspondence, in fact in every respect as Cornwall and Caithness, accepting that the same Sheriff-Depute and the same Vice-Admiral preside over both countries ..... now what a pity it would be on account of Orkney not furnishing its quota, [if] this country which has no connection with Orkney (not even a vote for a Member of Parliament) and such a nursery for the Navy should be ruined and depopulated as it will be if this impress is continued. For last year these islands were afflicted with an almost total failure of their crop, and famine has only been prevented by very large imports of victuals ...

Captain Fanshawe was impervious to the troubles besetting Shetland. He refused to be deflected from recruiting and decided to leave an officer at Lerwick to pursue the work while he continued to press at sea during convoy duty to Leith, escorting a hundred men for the Army. Losing patience with the lairds' responses, on 7 June he wrote to the Secretary of the Admiralty from *Carysfort* 'then off Fair Isle':

---

1 Shetland Archives, D24/124/21. The harvest of 1803 was also exceptionally poor, leading to famine and a meal distribution in 1804.

I have to acquaint you for the information of the Lords Commissioners of the Admiralty that two recruiting parties of the 90th and 93rd Regiments being about to leave Shetland in a sloop with their recruits, (about 100), having apply'd to me to convoy them to Leith Roads, I thought it my duty to do so and have accordingly sailed with them yesterday having left the Lieutenant at the Rendezvous to enter volunteers, considering likewise I had a much better prospect of getting men at sea … the instant our people appeared the men of all descriptions fled into the mountains and bogs like goats (where it was impossible for our officers to follow and catch them) and there would remain.

On 16 June *Carysfort* returned to Lerwick. Having secured fifty-nine Shetlanders, including seven boys, and three Orkney men, on 19 June she sailed for Sheerness and duly on 18 March 1804 proceeded to the West Indies. On 23 May *Carysfort* dropped anchor in English Harbour, Antigua. Soon afterwards there was an outbreak of yellow fever[1] on board. Writing on 20 June to the Admiralty from English Harbour, the first Lieutenant, Donald Campbell, reported that since arrival ninety-three officers and men (out of a complement of 195) had been hospitalised. Amongst those who had died were Captain Fanshawe (3 June), the Surgeon, Purser, Carpenter and Captain's Clerk.[2]

The vessel returned to Deptford on 2 September 1806 when the ship's company was paid-off.[3] Of the 59 Shetlanders impressed three years earlier, fortune had favoured few and only nineteen remained to be discharged. Death from disease or accident, hospitalisation, desertion or transfer to other ships accounted for the rest. What befell the seven ship's boys is particularly poignant: three died in hospital in Antigua and Barbados, and another was discharged sick to hospital in Barbados. Three survived.

The following list comprises the Shetland men on the muster books of *Carysfort* and pressed in April, May and June 1803 (OS – ordinary seaman; AB – able bodied; LM – landman):

James Gray, 21, OS, deserted at Antigua 15 June 1804
James Johnston, 23, OS, discharged Deptford 2 September 1806
James Duncan, 24, OS, discharged Deptford 2 September 1806
William Nicholson, 20, OS, died on board HMS *Amsterdam*, 13 June 1804
James Dalziel, 23, AB, deserted Antigua Hospital, 9 June 1804
James Manson, 40, LM, discharged from merchant ship 25 August 1803
Andrew Saunderson, 19, OS, discharged Deptford 2 September 1806

1 Also known as yellow jack, it was endemic there.
2 ADM 36/16178.
3 ADM 36/16181.

HMS *Carysfort*

Magnus Tait, 20, OS, sent to Barbados Hospital 12 February 1805
John Johnson, 18, OS, discharged Deptford 2 September 1806
James Linklater, 21, carpenter's crew, died on board ship 3 April 1804
John Isbister, 20, OS, discharged Deptford 2 September 1806
William Williamson, 20, OS, discharged from HMS *Heureux* 3 June 1806
Laurence Williamson, 19, LM, discharged from Antigua Hospital (invalided) 28 October 1805
James Anderson, 19, OS, discharged Deptford 2 September 1806
Magnus Manson, 24, AB, discharged Deptford 2 September 1806
Robert Bain, 21, OS, discharged Deptford 2 September 1806
James Jamieson, 20, LM, deserted at Cork 25 March 1804
Peter Williamson, 18, OS, died at Antigua Hospital 5 June 1804
Jerh. Malcolmson, 20, OS, discharged Deptford 2 September 1806
Thomas Laurenson, 20, OS, discharged Deptford 2 September 1806
Alexander Irvin, 24, OS, invalided *Halifax* hospital ship 30 December 1804
James Lutet, 30, OS, accidentally drowned at Antigua 18 May 1805
Robert McHugheson, 24, AB, died at Antigua Hospital 12 June 1804
Magnus Ninianson, 25, OS, discharged Deptford 2 September 1806
Rasmia Anderson, 21, LM, died at Antigua Hospital 4 June 1804
James Cumming, 20, LM, discharged Deptford 2 September 1806
Charles Jeromson, 24, AB, deserted from Antigua Hospital 9 June 1804
Harry Josephson, 37, AB, discharged Deptford 2 September 1806
Ferdinand Scooner, 30, OS, deserted from Antigua Hospital 9 June 1804
John Mowatt, 22, LM, discharged Deptford 2 September 1806
Peter Thompson, 36, LM, discharged Deptford 2 September 1806
Peter Johnson, 20, OS, discharged Deptford 2 September 1806
Andrew Jamieson, 22, OS, sent to sick quarters at Madeira 27 May 1804
Walter Halcrow, 22, LM, discharged Deptford 2 September 1806
Andrew Hunter, 20, LM, died on board HMS *Amsterdam* 10 June 1804
James Manson, 24, LM, accidentally drowned 14 July 1805
Thomas Williamson, 21, LM, discharged Deptford 2 September 1806
James Tait, 30, OS, sent to Hasler Hospital 19 March 1804
Peter Halcrow, 30, LM, discharged Deptford 2 September 1806
William Kirkie, 23, LM, invalided HMS *Amsterdam*, *Halifax* hospital ship, 8 October 1804
John Cooper, 20, LM, discharged Deptford 2 September 1806
Willam Manson, 21, LM, died on board HM schooner *Mozamtrigue* 9 June 1804
Andrew Fraser, 21, LM, died on board HMS *Amsterdam* 11 June 1804
William Nicholson, 30, LM, discharged from HMS *Leyden* 4 July 1803
Thomas Tullock, 25, LM, died on hospital ship *Sussex* 11 October 1803
Thomas Gifford, 25, AB, died at Antigua Hospital 11 June 1804

Andrew Robertson, 22, OS, sent to hospital ship *Sussex* 22 October 1803

Thomas Budge, 22, AB, discharged Deptford 2 September 1806

William Rodder, 24, OS, died at Antigua Hospital 3 June 1804

Robert Patterson, 28, AB, deserted from Antigua Hospital 9 June 1804

John Anderson, 40, AB, discharged Deptford 2 September 1806

James Moncrieff, 33, OS, died on board HMS *de Ruyter* 18 June 1804

Malcolm Johnston, 19, 2nd class Ships Boy, died at Antigua Hospital 18 June 1804

Peter Henderson, 15, 3rd class Ships Boy, discharged Deptford 2 September 1806

Gavin Goudie, 19, 3rd class Ships Boy, discharged Deptford 2 September 1806

James Houry, 19, 3rd class Ships Boy, died at Barbados Hospital 17 February 1805

Robert Kirkie, 18, 3rd class Ships Boy, discharged 4 July 1803

Magnus Mowatt, 18, 3rd class Ships Boy, sent to Barbados Hospital 9 February 1805

Robert Ninianson, 16, 3rd class Ships Boy, died at Antigua Hospital 7 June 1804

The three Orkney men who appeared on *Carysfort*'s muster books on that recruiting voyage were Able Seamen Thomas Cock, twenty-three, Thomas Budge, twenty-two, and nineteen-year-old Gilbert Craigie. Cock was discharged on 7 November 1803 to *Sussex* Hospital ship. He returned to the vessel and was discharged again at Deptford on 2 September 1806 along with Budge. Concerning Craigie, there is no further information.[1]

The Ninian Brothers

Magnus and Robert Ninianson were among those pressed. The family lived at Westsandwick, Yell, and they were the youngest of Ninian Manson's four powerful sons. Under the system of shifting patronymics that prevailed in Shetland, Ninian Manson's sons used the surname Ninianson.

On 4 May 1803 Magnus and Robert sailed to Lerwick with quantities of men's half-socks, Greenland gravits,[2] yarn, wool, fresh eggs and butter. These were to be exchanged for meal. On arrival the brothers were seized by a party from *Carysfort* and Magnus, aged twenty-five, forced to enlist. Robert was allowed to return to Yell under escort with the boat and goods, and brought back to Lerwick on 15 May. He was sixteen and 'volunteered' as a boy third class.

---

1 ADM 36/16177–81.

2 A long scarf and hood combined, made of double knitted, hand-spun, home-dyed wool and much favoured by whalers. 'A three wup Greenland gravit' is still remembered in Shetland, and signified one that went three times round the neck. Gravits were often knitted in tubular form and it was common practice to slit open one end, pull it over the head in the fashion of a Balaclava and wind the rest of the gravit round the neck. This was a variation of the true hooded Greenland gravit.

HMS *Carysfort*

In a desperate effort to have her sons released, their mother rowed across Yell Sound, walked to Lerwick and hired a gig which took her to *Carysfort*. On board she pleaded tearfully but in vain for her sons' freedom. The captain replied 'Even if you were the Lord Almighty from Heaven I still would not release your sons.' He continued in an emollient vein, 'However, I will look after them and be their father from now on.'

At Westsandwick, the family was mourning their loss when a messenger arrived from the laird summoning Ninian to the North Haa. There he discovered that the gang was waiting and, with the laird's connivance, ready to press him. An exceptionally strong man, he made his escape and ran through the district shouting a general warning. Able-bodied men fled and joined Ninian in hiding[1] until *Carysfort* left Shetland waters.

In the West Indies Robert Ninianson, aged seventeen, died on 7 June 1804 at Antigua Hospital,[2] of yellow fever.[3] Magnus survived and, aged twenty-eight, was discharged at Deptford on 2 September 1806. He made a successful career at sea and became master of a merchant ship.[4]

---

1. They hid in holes, fissures and caves in the Bugarth/Whale Geo banks, three miles north of Westsandwick.
2. Another Shetlander, Malcolm Johnston, aged nineteen, boy 2nd class, died there the following day.
3. ADM 36/16178.
4. My informants in August 1975 were Mrs M J Manson, the great-great-great-granddaughter of Ninian Manson, and her son Captain Robert A Manson. The information is also contained in *The New Shetlander*, Hairst number 1975.

Evading and Resisting Impressment

Numerous press gang episodes are recorded or remembered in the Isles. The following stories in the oral tradition carry varying degrees of authenticity, although some are supported by written evidence. They all speak in one way or another to the fortitude, determination and ingenuity of both the victims and the enforcers of impressment.

Islanders were recruited into a navy in which conditions on board ship were usually poor: food was bad, discipline harsh, punishment brutal, and quarters crowded and insanitary, particularly in hot weather. Seamen had no official uniform, few rights at law, and faced the hazards of disease, shipwreck and battle.

Naval engagements often resulted in long casualty lists, and many of the injured died as a result of their wounds. Those captured by the enemy were subject to further adversity and indignities, some of their stories being recounted in the chapter Imprisoned on the Continent. Moreover, fatal accidents were frequent during the grinding daily routine aboard ship. Disease was the greatest killer and the death rate was appalling.

In addition to onerous conditions during service, forcible recruitment frequently resulted in domestic deprivation and tragedy. In the absence of the breadwinner, women and children attempted to cultivate the land, but depended on the generosity and compassion of relatives and neighbours. Elderly parents might have to fend for themselves. Islanders had to reconcile themselves to an indifferent state that simply required them to be added to the numbers essential in the prosecution of war. The agents of recruitment enjoyed much licence in the execution of their task: often cruel, they remained alert and opportunistic, especially when those they sought were most at ease.

Foreknowledge of the threat of recruitment could be put to good use, as in the summer of 1759, when on 31 July William Balfour of Trenaby, Westray, then in Edinburgh, wrote to his wife Betty: 'You'll observe that our Bairns are not to go to the Fairs.[1] Nor any Man on my Ground that wants to avoid being

---

1 Particularly the great annual Lammas Market held in Kirkwall. It commenced on the first Tuesday of August and lasted for three days 'and no longer'. There were other local markets or fairs, but Kirkwall market was the most fertile recruiting ground.

pressd, as I have reason to believe there will be a press in the County about that time.'[1]

Even the occasion of a wedding gave no protection and there are accounts of a bridegroom and his friends being arrested. In Orkney and Shetland the church ceremony and subsequent celebration were grand events, to which many people were invited. Inevitably these gatherings interested and attracted the gang.

Writing in 1809 Dr Arthur Edmondston[2] described how the appearance of an unidentified boat prompted flight from weddings and other celebrations: '… [a]nd not without reason, for often while celebrating with innocent and unsuspecting mirth, the wedding of some youthful pair, or engaged in the annual amusements of a winter night, the harmony of the scene has been rudely terminated by the sudden appearance of a press-gang, and their victims dragged, amidst tears and lamentations to the general rendezvous.'[3]

Simple misfortune could deal a fateful hand, as in the instance of the Baptist minister in Westray, the Rev William Tulloch,[4] who had spent several days proselytising in North Ronaldsay. His labours completed, there was a favourable breeze and no sight of a press cutter, so confidently he set sail for home with a crew of two old men and two youths. The wind dropped, the small boat was becalmed, and a strong tide carried it to the open sea and into the path of a naval vessel. The young men were pressed and shipped to the rendezvous in Lerwick, leaving the divine and his depleted crew to make their way to Westray as best they could.[5]

Bad luck also attended a man with the surname Archibald who lived at the now vanished croft of Starlea, Dunrossness. He was taken at the craigs,[6] sitting on a large rock called the Back Stane just below his house and never returned to Shetland.

---

1 Orkney Archives, Balfour Papers D2/18/13.
2 *A View of the Ancient and Present State of the Zetland Islands*, Volume II, 1809, p. 68.
3 This was probably the Tolbooth, Lerwick, the building separated from and immediately north of the Queens Hotel, Commercial Street. Men were incarcerated therein, transported in tenders to Leith and thence to the Nore for distribution throughout the fleet.
4 Tulloch was a native of North Ronaldsay and a cabinetmaker in Kirkwall before taking up the ministry. He formed the first dissenting church in Westray in the spring of 1803, worshipping in a large room in Noltland Castle. Subsequently in 1810 he and his followers established the Baptist Church in Westray. He was a regular visitor to neighbouring islands, this work occupying a deal of his time.
5 *Around the Orkney Peat-fires*, W R Mackintosh, 1949, pp. 218–19.
6 Fishing from rocks for coal-fish or sillocks.

The King's Shilling and Recourse to Law

The devious methods of the gang were evidenced in a ploy which on one occassion involved 'taking the King's shilling'. In Kirkwall in the early part of the nineteenth century there was a well-frequented public house known as The Ship Inn[1] at the harbour end of Bridge Street. This hostelry was a favourite resort of the gang, particularly on market days. A man was positioned at an upstairs oriel window while his fellows loitered in front of the building. When a likely-looking recruit approached the man at the window dropped a shilling. The unsuspecting victim, amazed at his good fortune, picked the coin and as he congratulated himself the gang pounced. The King's baton[2] was laid on his shoulder and he was told that, having just accepted His Majesty's shilling,[3] he had enlisted.

When a man, either voluntarily or under duress, accepted or received the King's shilling from the recruiter, he was considered to have taken the King's money and therefore was available for the King's service. By the transfer of the shilling to an individual a subtle contract between him and his sovereign was purported to have been established. From the moment the shilling found its way from a recruiting officer into his possession he was the King's man and was deemed to have enrolled.[4]

This pact was recognised by the Sheriff in the case of James Jamieson of West Newfoundland, Cunningsburgh. On 18 October 1808 Jamieson, who had aged parents and three brothers in the navy, petitioned[5] the Sheriff to be released from the Rendezvous on the basis that he had never been at sea further than in a fishing boat and was a land labourer. He declared that when the imminent approach of a man of war was rumoured, and with the risk of impressment in mind, he had come to the Rendezvous and sought to join the gang. He had accepted a shilling from Lieutenant Wilson under the impression that by this act he became a member of the gang and was thus safe from service at sea. The Sheriff sought answers from Captain James Nicolson, a Shetlander in charge of

---

1 On 12 August 1814 the innkeeper, William Scollay, was host to Sir Walter Scott.
2 A baton conferred on the holder the authority of the Justices of the Peace. The baton used by an Evie constable by the name of Yorston is in the possession of the present writer. It measures nine inches long with metal caps on each end, one marked 'GR', the initials of King George III who reigned from 1760–1820.
3 It is said that sometimes a shilling was slipped into the beer mug of an unsuspecting sailor and he was taken as soon as his lips touched the coin. Furthermore, the story continues, glass bottoms were introduced to prevent this practice.
4 *The Press Gang Afloat and Ashore,* J R Hutchinson, 1913, p. 10.
5 Shetland Archives, SC12/6/1808/84.

The King's Shilling or The Recruiting Party, Alexander Carse, 1770–1843.

the press service, and as no reply was received in the time allowed, he released Jamieson. However, Nicolson duly produced Answers, albeit two hours late. These were supported by statements from members of the gang who had been present at the Rendezvous, including Wilson, when the coin was alleged to have been passed to, and accepted by, Jamieson. The statements varied: Jamieson merely taking the shilling if Wilson would let him return home for two or three months; taking the shilling and putting it on the table in front of him; and receiving the shilling from Wilson who said that he could have five or six months liberty at home. Another witness averred that Jamieson said that he would enter if 'he was allowed to remain along with the gang and would direct them where they would get plenty of men.' The Sheriff considered all these statements, recalled his previous pronouncement of liberty and found that Jamieson had 'subjected himself to serve in the Navy.' The shilling and its alleged acceptance by Jamieson, hesitant or otherwise, had been an essential part of the bargain and the key to the resolution of the matter. It had tied him to service in the Navy.

A statement attached to the Petition and made on Jamieson's behalf, by William Ogilvy, Tacksman of the Lands and Estate of Quendale, contains the interesting comment (apart from declaring that the shilling had been imposed unfairly upon Jamieson and he did not pocket it) which cast light on the honesty of the gang's statements about the passing and acceptance of the shilling and moreover on the reputation of the press gang in Shetland: 'If a man is to be impressed and retained upon the testimony of the Gang … it is no wonder the Country is alarmed, and that the prayers of the Chourches [sic] is offered up in behalf of the oppressed and the Shielding arm of omnipotence implored to protect the distressed inhabitants of this Country from the blood & violence every Sex is exposed to from this unwarranted Gang.'

In 1805 the mate from the *Mary* tender en route to Shetland used money when he attempted to compromise the protection from impressment enjoyed by five men from Stenness and Stromness. On 23 February John Bews, John Oman, William Chalmers and George Loutit, farm labourers in Stenness, and James Anderson, ships carpenter in Stromness, were 'trepanned'[1] by a party of seamen from the *Mary*, then lying in Stromness harbour, and taken aboard the vessel.

They appealed to the Sheriff Depute on 1 March, declaring that they were landmen and not liable to be impressed. Indeed, they averred none had any

---

1 Entrapped or ensnared.

The Press Gang, English Primitive School, depicted c.1840.

connection with the sea, apart from Loutit and Chalmers who had each made one journey to Greenland, the latter 'during the last season when almost famine raged in Orkney, necessity compelled him to take a run to Greenland for a Month or two in order to earn a few Shillings for the preservation of his own and his Mothers life.'

The petition continued that on 23 February Bews and Anderson had met a Mr Davidson 'at the Bridge of Weath about two miles from Stromness' who Bews now knew to be the mate of the *Mary* tender, but who at the time had informed them that he was the mate of the *Leviathan*, a Greenland-bound whaler. Davidson had offered two pounds a month and a shilling for each butt of oil if they engaged with the vessel. The men, seemingly duped, expressed some interest and with the three others arranged to meet at the same location later that day, when they were pressed. Davidson's ploy had been to mislead the men and undermine their immunity from impressment by encouraging and receiving a declared interest in engaging for the Greenland whaling.

The five men, together with the vessel's captain, Lieutenant Laurence Smith, and his mate George Davidson, were examined by the Sheriff Depute on 3 March. After some debate, and conflicting sworn evidence, all were set free.[1]

Melancholy Endings

It is not surprising that a man would bear and risk much to evade being pressed, in a despairing choice preferring the discomfort of a remote, usually hazardous, hiding place to an uncertain dangerous life at sea from which many did not return. There are tales about avoiding impressment which are tinged with sadness and tragedy, evidenced by the story of Kirkcaldy's Sword. The incident, which took place in the early years of the nineteenth century involved Matthew Morrison, Weisdale, and a naval officer Lieutenant Kirkcaldy.

Morrison was a strong man, just the type sought by the gang, and more than once he narrowly avoided capture. One fateful morning Kirkcaldy and his party, having travelled overnight from Weisdale, arrived at Clousta in Aithsting to press John Tait, and on reconnaissance they established that Morrison too was at a nearby house. The houses were surrounded and both men captured.

Another version suggests that Morrison and Tait were in the same house and escaped through a back door. This, the more colourful account, continues that the men fled to the hills with the gang in hot pursuit. Tait purposely made his way to a

---

[1] Orkney Archives, SC11/5/1805/70.

long peat bank and with a great leap cleared the six-feet-high cutting.[1] By the time his less agile pursuers had rounded the bank Tait was running up The Hullens, where from his place of concealment he witnessed the drama unfold.

Morrison, who did not know the area well, was less fortunate in his escape route and was impeded by the small loch of Setter. Showing no hesitation, and with the gang on his heels, he waded in but made little headway on the unstable peaty bottom. Kirkcaldy followed closely, cursing and brandishing his sword. He is said to have exclaimed that if it was necessary he would pursue Morrison to hell. Despairing and at bay Morrison turned and, closing with the lieutenant, declared with chilling finality, 'We'll go there together.' The men grappled and hampered by their garments and the soft yielding moor they overbalanced, sank and drowned. The corner of the loch where the grim struggle took place is known as 'Kirkcaldy's Bight'.

Shaken, but unwilling to return empty-handed to their ship at West Burrafirth, Kirkcaldy's men went back to Clousta and pressed Tait's younger brother. Although this lad was the remaining son, the gang was so determined to take him that it required the intervention of Sir Andrew Mitchell, the Admiral Depute for Orkney and Zetland, to secure his release.

On the day following the tragedy the bodies were recovered from the loch and interred in the kirkyard at Twatt. Kirkcaldy was buried in front of the kirk door so that all who passed should tramp upon his grave. When a porch was added to this building in the 1930s workmen unearthed a thigh and a jaw bone where it is believed the lieutenant was interred.

For years Kirkcaldy's sword remained in the district. Latterly it was in the possession of a daughter of John Tait, the man who escaped. She took the weapon with her when with husband and family she emigrated to New Zealand in 1874.

There are a number of variants of the Kirkcaldy incident. One tells of a recruiting officer who accidentally fell on his sword while pursuing a Weisdale man over and along stepping stones which led to a holm at the south end of Maw Water. The place from which these stones start is known as *Da Pressgengs Point*.

Writing in the 1870s Andrew Dishington Mathewson, schoolmaster at East Yell, recalled the death of a youth fleeing from impressment. At the early age of five Mathewson could write, manage some basic arithmetic and had read Proverbs and the New Testament. A year later he was able to read so well that six

---

1 Called a three peat bank.

children living near his home at Houll, North-a-voe, Yell were instructed by him in reading from the Bible: 'They got on so well that the same six all came again in June, 1807 and might have continued. But the French War and the press gang deranged everything. My Aunt Cath's son James Jameson fleeing from the Press Gang to the Wild Rocks near the Bronga, his foot slipped on a slaunting stone and he went on the "Blue Deep" and was drowned about the year 1808.'[1]

Mathewson came to Fetlar in 1809 at the age of ten and he would have been told about the incident. Writing many years later, the old man's memory had faded and he may have persuaded himself that Jameson had been one of his young pupils and got the date wrong.

The mishap occurred in 1803 and is recorded on 1 June in the Old Parochial Register of Fetlar and North Yell: 'Died by accident say running down a precipice [sic] in the Rocks to Shelter himself from an Immaginary [sic] Runner of a press gang Landed in Fetlar, James Jameso(n) a young man. June the 1st day.'

In *Laurence Williamson of Mid Yell*, Laurence G Johnson says:[2] 'In 1801, two men, Innes Hart and James Jamieson, fled from the press gang. They went into a cave near Mongersdale, and James hurriedly misplaced his foot and fell on the sea and was drowned.'[3] This is probably the 1803 incident which was likely to have been caused by the presence of *Carysfort* in Bressay Sound.

Williamson died in the mid-1930s and left a treasure trove of notes and records, some difficult to decipher due to poor handwriting. In the 1950s and 1960s Johnson listed several episodes involving the gang's activities in Fetlar and these are given as he has made them known:

One night they came to Aith and one of them listened between the doors, that is in the byre, and heard a woman say, 'Gyud forbid at da Pressmen gangs ta da Haa[4] da night for da men is dere.' So they surrounded the Haa. The men within were aware but waited till daylight and then opened the door to try to escape. Hugh Cluness, a pretty[5] man, stepped out first. One seized his wrist at once and they shouted, 'Hold on that man, the very man we want.' Hugh drew his knife and cut his captor's wrist to the bone but was borne down by numbers. He, Tait and seven others were aboard of warmen.

They called men to the kirk and took James and Robert Donaldson, John Cluness and Murray Hunter. John Cluness escaped. His father was in the door with a staff. They

1 Shetland Archives, Andrew Dishington Mathewson Collection D23.
2 p. 157.
3 Published by *The Shetland Times*, 1971.
4 This was probably the Haa at Funzie.
5 Brave, well-made.

ran and caught him above Leagarth. They all went to the navy. Soon after peace was called. The last two returned no more.

Laurence and Andrew Murray, John Brown and Smithy Johnson lay in a cave under the cliffs upon heather plucked in Lamhoga and they saw the lights of the press gang seeking them at Tresta, but escaped. Smithy afterwards enlisted but died. Joseph Donaldson was pressed but died in a fever and his clothes came home.

The tragedy enacted in Fetlar in 1803 was almost repeated in Bressay the following year. In 1804 a young lad, Thomas Anderson, fleeing from impressment was left unaided and alone in an open boat in the dangerous Bardastrom tide race at Bressay. He was saved with considerable difficulty. John Mouat, Annsbrae, Bressay, protested vehemently on two occasions.[1]

In November 1804 in a supplement to a scroll memorandum of 21 October, Mouat expostulated about the incident and proceeded to detail the terror to which the lad had been subjected: 'The Part of the Coast of Brassay in Question is & ever will be a steep Rocky Barbarous shore projected on to the Deep Ocean. That Day & most days washed with too heavy a surff for Landing or saveing even a maned boat – And Except at the hour of still water, the tides run Rapidly about it, Particularly in the Bardastream.' A shore tide and wind had been driving the boat from the land and 'Mr Gourley left the boy alone crying at some distance from the Bard of Brassay and did not even when the danger was pointed out Either go or Send to his Relief & that the boy's life could not have been saved without axidental assistance.'

On 21 October he had contacted his fellow Lairds alleging that Captain Gourlay had 'the Preseeding night' impressed another Bressay lad James Anderson at the home of his aged, infirm parents, although he was half blind and the only child remaining with them. Mouat had sought Captain Gourlay to ask if he would find suitable employment for Anderson and release him. Instead he met Scott the Regulating Officer and asked him to add his influence 'in favour of Anderson.' The outcome is unknown. In this earlier document he addressed the serious incident involving Gourlay, Thomas Anderson and the Bressay tide race, in which he stressed the peril in which Anderson had found himself when harassed by the recruiting party. He declared 'that Coplands boats crew had rescewed [sic] the Boy and Boat out of the Bard Stream at the hazard of their lives, & that where so much cruelty was exercised that it must not pass unnotised.'

---

[1] Gardie Papers, William Mouat's letter book, 20/10/1804.

Alarm and Flight

Islanders were quickly alerted to the appearance of a warship or to the imposition of a quota and the associated arrival of a press cutter. Until the danger had passed many of those likely to be taken did not remain at home. An exception might be in severe weather when men felt a degree of confidence that recruiting parties would not be active.

In 1809 Dr Arthur Edmondston recorded the efforts of Shetland men to avoid impressment. Their outlook had hardened over the years: 'During the last and former wars,[1] great numbers entered voluntarily into the navy, for which they early evinced a strong partiality, but since a rigorous impress has been established at Lerwick, they have lost their ardour for the service, and subject themselves to the most distressing privations to avoid the chance of being forced into it.'

He stated that approximately 600[2] men went annually to the Greenland whaling. They were splendid recruits and much sought after: '… conceived to be complete seamen, they are looked upon as fair game by the impress officers, and are hunted down with remorseless perseverance. Some have perished in the rocks, in their attempts to escape from this dreaded severity, and others have had their health irrecoverably ruined by watching and exposure during inclement weather. The panic is not confined to the young and the active, its sympathetic influence extends even to old men and boys, and the appearance of a boat resembling that in the impress service, is taken as the signal for a general flight.'[3]

Outwith certain ages impressment was illegal, but in the islands these limits were not scrupulously observed and older men past their prime might be taken with as little discrimination as the young and fit. A querulous old man who grumbled about various ailments was told with asperity by an unsympathetic relative that he might yet be pressed. A finely honed persecution complex prompted the mordant reply that doubtless he would yet be good enough 'ta sock[4] a baal in.'[5]

Their consternation meant that sometimes evasive action was taken by men quite unsuitable for service, but nevertheless fearful of capture. A man Scott in

---

1 Edmondston was writing during The Napoleonic Wars 1803–15, 'The last and former wars' were The French Revolutionary Wars 1792–1801, The War of American Independence 1775–1783 and The Seven Years War 1756–63.
2 Sir Walter Scott estimated that in 1814 the number was 1,000. See *Whalers*.
3 *A View of the Ancient and Present State of the Zetland Islands*, Volume II, 1809, pp. 67–8.
4 Also *sok*, to sink in; when something is thrown with great force; to sink, as a lance into a whale; *Sockva*, to sink.
5 To stop a ball or bullet. Dr J A Hunter, Voe, personal communication 1974.

Rendall and 'a poor ting an' no worth takin' hid in a girnel[1] through the nights of a long winter. Again, although much smaller than the minimum height, John Shurie, also from Rendall, quite unnecessarily put to sea whenever he heard that a search party was in the parish. He boasted that if pursued he would take his small boat single-handed into the Burgar roost,[2] preferring that danger to impressment. An old man who lived in Stronsay, droll but harmless, caused wry amusement when the island's constables were on impress duty. At such times he would hobble to the shore, place both spindly legs across distanced rocks and, clutching a stone, declare that he would break the bones rather than be taken.

The people of Skerries,[3] islands strategically positioned to the north east of Whalsay, played an interesting and important part in warning men as they returned from the haaf fishing. When a press cutter was in the vicinity special visual signals were made. White sheets were placed in varying positions on peat stacks, the roof of a prominent house, or high ground. The number and movement of sheets indicated the location and course of the cutter. A cow tethered at a specific place also conveyed a message, and returning fishermen watched carefully for such prearranged signals. These was seen at sea not only by local men but also by fishermen from Bressay, Yell, Whalsay and Lunnasting, who used Skerries as a base.

In North Fara fishermen were informed of the presence of a cutter in nearby waters by the hoisting of flags or cloths on poles at the croft houses of Windywall and Doggerboat, buildings chosen because of their prominence.

At harvest time in Rousay horses were tethered nearby to ensure a quick escape, and women were positioned at vantage points to sound the alarm if the gang approached.

Shetland fishermen used luder[4] horns in fog and darkness to establish the relative position of their boats. These aids emitted distinctive individual sounds which when used on land in Cunningsburgh, and probably elsewhere, gave early warning to those at risk of being taken.

People lived in constant fear, and when impressment threatened, Weisdale folk would shout a warning 'da kye is i da coarn.'[5] In Sandness the kirk bell was rung to alert the neighbourhood.

---

1 A chest or barrel for holding meal.
2 A rough, boisterous area of sea, caused by the meeting of rapid tides.
3 Also known as Out Skerries.
4 Also *looder*. ON Lúdr, a trumpet.
5 The cattle are in the corn.

Peep-holes were sometimes constructed in the outside walls of houses, and enabled apprehensive occupants to identify visitors before permitting entry. A house in Victoria Street, Kirkwall, which was demolished in 1976, had this safeguard. At the upper end of The Strynd, Kirkwall, stands the attractive old cottage known to generations of school children as 'The Rocky Shop'. There is a tiny window in one of the two upstairs bedrooms which was used to give a long warning view of Broad Street, the ruins of Kirkwall castle and the sea beyond.

Men in Walls,[1] Shetland, avoided impressment with their minister's help. The kirk there was rebuilt at the end of the nineteenth century, but in its original state it had a gallery with access by a separate side door. One Sunday the gang arrived during morning service, confident that some young men would be in the congregation. Most of the lads were in the gallery and as the gang opened the front door the minister signalled a warning and those seated above escaped. They ran north to Finnigarth and reached the loch of Bardister. The water was deep with a winding path of shallows leading to a holm, but the men knew the route and found safety.

Narrow Escapes

A story with an improbable end concerns a Stromnessian who in the course of avoiding impressment eventually took to horseback. Realising that he had been marked for recruitment, the man hastened on foot towards Sandwick, closely pursued by a constable. At Consgar[2] he pled for a horse and the sympathetic farmer replied 'Tak that young staig,[3] and whin ye get whaur ye want tae be juist whip the tether tae his neck an bid him geng hame, an he'll no lose his wey.' The constable in close pursuit requisitioned a mare at the farm of Clumley, but at Quoyloo the animal refused to continue, lay down and gave birth to a foal.

With liberty at stake there was little concern for personal appearance or comfort. One night at Troall, North Unst, a young man was roused by thunderous knocking on the outer door. Pausing only to take his jupie[4] he ran naked out of the back door. Crossing fields and marshes he came to Vealie and hid in a kiln.[5] Only then did he pull on the garment and some borrowed clothes.

1 Pronounced Waas, the old, correct way to spell the word.
2 Also Coginsgair. A farm in either the Aith or Hurkisgarth tunship. For some time and until the beginning of this century it was the residence of the Sandwick parish minister. It is now named Flotterston.
3 Stallion.
4 A sleeved, pull-on garment; a woollen jerkin.
5 A conical building for drying corn.

A similar story involved one of the six sons of John Brass, udaller, of Nether Garson in the district of Northdyke, Sandwick. He surprised a recruiting party approaching his house by emerging naked and, thereafter, made for Birsay where he sought the benefits of safety and clothes.[1]

John Johnson, Weisdale, had been hiding in the hills and one night returned home for a good meal and dry clothes. He had partly undressed when the gang arrived, but without hesitation he dashed through the but[2] door of the cottage and into the barn, thence through the 'blind window'[3] to the back yard. Crawling between two skrus[4] he made his way to the kale yard and hid shivering among the stocks.[5]

A young man at the croft of Quoys, Hoy had successfully evaded the gang. For weeks he hid in the hills, until one stormy night he sought a dry bed at home. Before retiring he ventured to the outside toilet saying 'It'll be safe enough noo.' From the darkness came the terse comment 'Dinna be too shur o' that,' whereupon he was seized. Twisting out of his jacket he ran to the Glen of Quoyower on the Ward Hill. When the gang followed he rolled stones down the steep slope and, with his pursuers in disarray, escaped to the high ground beyond.

A Fetlar man Laurenson retained his freedom with a knife, although not used aggressively. He was at Sound Voe near Lerwick waiting to join a merchantman when a man-of-war dropped anchor and landed a recruiting party. Laurenson was wearing seamen's clothes with his hair in a carefully combed pigtail, and recognising an experienced sailor, they gave chase. As the Shetlander clambered over a wall one of the sailors closed sufficiently to grasp the pigtail, and in desperation Laurenson cut the hair with his sheath knife. Impressed by his dexterity and deterred by the sharp blade, the pursuit was abandoned.

When he was a young man, Sinclair Thomson, who became the first Baptist minister in Shetland, had an exciting experience with the gang. At Christmas time 1805, aged twenty-one,[6] he travelled twenty miles from Scarvister in the parish of Sandsting to play the fiddle at a Tingwall wedding. One of the gang

1 Peace's Orkney Almanac, 1879, p. 128.
2 Kitchen/living room.
3 Most barns had a back window which was called the 'blind window'. This was a wooden shutter through which corn was taken from the back yard.
4 Stacks of corn.
5 Kale stocks – cabbages.
6 Sinclair Thomson was born at Scarvister in the parish of Sandsting, Shetland in 1784 and died in 1864. The story was taken down from him verbatim on 17 September 1862.

had disclosed under oath of secrecy[1] that all young men in the company would be seized, and on his arrival Thomson warned those present. Men at risk left immediately, but when shown a safe place of concealment the fiddler agreed to remain in company with the bridegroom and best man. This hiding place was a cavity beneath the bedroom floor and capable of holding three persons.

A watch was set by those who remained – old men of no value as recruits. During the evening a heavy shower forced the sentries to leave their posts and take shelter. This enabled the gang to surround the house and force an entry. The parish minister, the Rev John Turnbull, who was dancing, gave an effusive welcome to the leader, Lieutenant Scott,[2] and tried to delay him. Thomson pushed his fiddle into the hands of a cripple lad from Scalloway and rushed to the back window[3] of the barn.[4] Finding the way barred he used a small window to gain access to the byre, but there too the gang was waiting. Attempting to climb through the byre roof he scrambled over the back of a cow, only to be frustrated again. Then he heard a woman whisper, 'Fur God's sake cum dis wye.' Guided by her he moved swiftly to the bedroom, extinguishing all the kollies[5] and leaving the barn in complete darkness. He crawled into the hole already occupied by the bridegroom and the best man, and a heavy chest was moved on top.

When order was restored, a thorough search was made of the buildings. The lid of the chest was lifted and its contents examined but the fugitives were not discovered, although they spent an uncomfortable night changing one above two in turn.

Strength and Athleticism

Some men avoided impressment with a display of strength. A Westray smack was sailing past Scarfhall Point, carrying conscripted islanders to Kirkwall for trans-shipment to the rendezvous at Leith. Suddenly a strong man braced himself across the boat, shouted 'every man fur himsel,' burst the planks and swam ashore.

---

1 At that time the gang was commanded by Lieutenants Malcolmson and Keith Scott. Malcolmson was brought up at Sandness, entering the navy at an early age, and Scott was the son of Sheriff Walter Scott of Lerwick. Among the gang members were Malcolm Smith of Seater, Sandwick, and Henry Mainland of Garthsbanks. It was Mainland who disclosed the gang's intentions.
2 The officer in charge of the Rendezvous.
3 This would have been the 'blind window'.
4 Old Shetland croft buildings usually consisted of a house, barn and byre, constructed in line, with interior access.
5 A small open lamp usually made of iron with a rush or cloth wick, in which seal or whale oil was burnt.

During transfer to a man-of-war in Kirkwall another strong man, Harcus from Tankerness, similarly shattered the sides of an old rowing boat and swam to safety. Three of the gang drowned as he took flight and escaped across the Pentland Firth never to return.[1]

Yet another strong man, Thomas Linklater from South Nesting, had to row long distances to escape from the gang. He had been sought for some months and because of his exceptional strength it was decided to employ a stratagem to effect his capture. A Tingwall man was bribed to visit him, ostensibly to purchase a cow. After the transaction was completed Linklater agreed to ferry the dealer from Vassa to Laxfirth, a distance of four and a half miles. On arrival he was surrounded in the darkness of the shore, seized, bound and taken to the House of Laxfirth. When their captive appeared to fall asleep the two guards, who had a liberal supply of whisky, drank freely. Late at night as they lay intoxicated Linklater broke the bonds, made off in his bare feet and rowed back to Vassa. Safely ashore he hurried to Garth, launched a boat and rowed a further seven miles to Whalsay where Bruce of Symbister gave him protection.

Orkney too has its story of a man whose prodigious strength saved him from impressment. A Costa man Miller known locally as 'Daddy ower the burn' lived at a croft near The Wateries. At home drinking ale, he was confronted by constables. Lifting a kirn which held ten gallons of home brew, he extended it at arm's length and invited the intruders to drink. This unlikely feat deterred and dismayed the unwelcome visitors, who withdrew.

A renowned Shetland strong man, Christie Brown, Vementry, was fishing for sillocks when the gang approached. Nonchalantly, he started picking whelks and reduced them to pulp between forefinger and thumb. His unusual strength persuaded the astonished onlookers to turn their attention elsewhere. His exploits are recorded in a rhyme written well over a hundred years later by Adam J Abernethy:

> The Press Gang came for Christie
> An Officer and six men
> Christie was pocking sillicks

[1] A similar story is told about William Carr of Blyth, Nottinghamshire, who was the first likely recruit to be met by a pressing party from a man-of-war. A huge man, standing six feet four inches and weighing twenty four stones, he was over-powered after a fierce fight. He sat quietly until the press boat was well on its way to the man-of-war. Then he positioned himself athwartships, with his back against one gunwale, his feet against the other, exerted steady pressure, burst the planking and the boat sank. Carr swam ashore and the others drowned. He resumed work in his blacksmith's shop and was not molested again.

> When the Navy body's came
> And aye he crushed the white whelks
> And threw them on his pock
> between his thumb & fore fingers
> he reduced the same to pulp
> The officer watched proceedings
> but deemed it best to quit
> he had seen enough of Christie
> to do him for a bit.

A similar story is told of a powerful man Walterson from Isbister, Whalsay, who was 'at da craigs'[1] when the gang arrived. Walterson's family feared that he had been taken with other young men, but he duly arrived home. When asked if he had seen the gang he replied casually: 'Could dat ha bin da five men at cam an stud on da bank's broo?[2] I wis just pickin lempits fae da stanes an bruckin dem doon wi me fingers fur soe,[3] an I heard wan o dem say ta da idder: "I tink at we hed better lave dis wan alane."'

John Irvine who had served for years on a man-of-war lived in retirement at The Ness, Stromness. Relaxing at a local inn, enjoying a glass of grog and the company of a friend, he was alerted to his servant's detention. Hastening to the beach, he waded in and grimly held onto the cutter. Creating a noisy scene, during which he boasted of past battles and ships boarded, he was so obdurate that the man had to be released.

Sometimes athleticism took the place of strength. Exceptional fleetness of foot enabled George Gullion, old Berriedale, Rackwick, Westray, to avoid being caught. When the gang arrived at his croft he sprinted to a safe distance then turned and taunted his pursuers. He stood on his head, whistled, clicked his heels in the air and, as the infuriated posse approached, set off again laughing derisively.[4] The gang was no match for him and fumed in frustration as he ran away over the rough open countryside, flaunting his speed and disdain. Gullion was a small man who lived to the great age of ninety-six and in his prime was so fast and possessed of such stamina that he could pursue and catch any sheep on the hill.

1 Rock fishing.
2 The brow of the sea cliffs.
3 Bait to attract sillocks.
4 My informant said that Gullion would outpace his pursuers, stop, look back between his legs, 'give a hooch' and make off again.

Weapons and Violence

If other methods of retaining their freedom failed, desperate men might resort to force, including the use of violence and weapons.

At St John's Head on the west coast of Hoy there is a headland called Bre Brough partially detached from the main cliff. The difficult approach was at one time barred by a dry stone dyke, allegedly built by Hoy men as a defence against the gang. A man from Braebuster who was cornered there stood defiantly on the narrow neck of land leading to the promontory and, brandishing a knife, dared his pursuers to advance.

Harry Clouston, known as 'Mad Harry', was a fisherman in the district of Ireland and he defended his liberty in dramatic style. Determined not to be pressed he declared that, if cornered, he would make ready use of the finely honed blubber knife which he habitually carried since returning from Davis Strait whaling. But it was to his old muzzle-loading gun that he turned when threatened. Warned by his mother that constables were approaching, he ran for the hills clutching this cumbersome but effective weapon. As his pursuers closed he stood on a small knowe, round which he had marked a circle, and vowed that he would shoot the first man who crossed the line. The threat was taken as seriously as it was meant and the would-be captors dispersed.

William Harper, also from Costa, avoided recruitment with the use of a three-toed pot. Surrounded at his croft of Row, he swung this unwieldly weapon so effectively that he scattered a party of constables and escaped to the hills.

Andrew Delday of Holland, Deerness, was a fine specimen of manhood who used his gun in repulsing what he believed was a posse. Tall, muscular and not easily imposed upon, he was a formidable quarry who made it known that he would not hesitate to use the weapon. Late one night he was awakened by what he thought was someone trying to gain entry. The furtive noises subsided and Delday relaxed, but when they resumed he threatened to shoot. This warning silenced the intruder, but when the cottar was disturbed again he fired without hesitation, aiming low to wound. On investigation Delday was aghast to discover that the nocturnal intruder was an old ewe, now lying dead against the splintered door. Embellished detail quickly spread, and though in his presence men did not refer to the incident for fear of provoking him, women were not inhibited and they teased him mercilessly.

An oak club was used by an old man to save his strapping grandson. One morning while the youth was fishing, the gang took up position at the croft on Papa Stour and the lad was pressed on his return, despite the grandfather's

The Press Gang 1772, nineteenth-century impression.

Jack in the Bilboes, 1804.

entreaties. The Shetlander dissembled, asking for permission to travel in his best clothes, and the apparently resigned grandfather was allowed to retire with him. In the ben[1] room they armed themselves with oak clubs used to kill seals on the Vee Skerries. The old man called out that his grandson had dressed, and the first man to enter was knocked unconscious. This was quite sufficient to deter the others who departed in haste carrying their dazed companion.[2]

Andrew Paplay's[3] exploits in avoiding impressment made him a hero in Deerness, and with each successful evasion the constables became more determined to catch him. One long chase began in the west of the parish and continued when Paplay launched a boat at Graemeshall, Holm and rowed to the island of Lamb Holm. There one of the oars snapped, so he sought refuge in a cave where he was captured by two constables and escorted back to Graemeshall. The Deerness man prized his liberty greatly and on landing he picked up the broken oar and swung wildly at his captors. Magnus Budge, St Andrews, was struck on the nose and laid low. Paplay was courting the sister of the other constable, William Stove, and assumed that with Budge incapacitated, escape was certain. Stove, disinterested in his sister's affections, did not scruple to do his duty and threw him to the ground. Though pressed, Paplay never saw active service as the war ended shortly afterwards. The reunion with his sweetheart, when eventually he returned to Deerness, is recorded in the chapter on Women and the Press Gang. Budge, the constable who received the severe blow, subsequently suffered from an unsightly growth on his nose. It was always referred to as 'de press gang mark' and he carried the blemish to his grave.[4]

An oar was also used by a Shetlander to rout his adversaries. Men working on their boats in Ronas Voe were threatened with impressment until a strong man, Peterson, grasping a sixareen oar in both hands, swung it in an intimidating arc and forced the gang to return to their boat.[5]

---

1 Parlour/best room.
2 Personal communication, George P S Peterson, Brae (S), 1974. Mr Peterson's grandmother who lived on Papa Stour told him the story about the oak club.
3 Born c.1788.
4 In a manuscript copy of the 1821 census a later note identifies Budge as living at Stembister. He was fifty-seven at that time. The addition reads: 'got a severe stroke on his nose from one whom he had pressed which disfigured him for afterlife.'
5 Tom Anderson, Lerwick, personal communication 1979. He obtained the information about Peterson and the sixareen oar from Willie Peterson who lived at the croft of Voe at the head of Ronas Voe. This was in 1954 when Mr Peterson was over seventy years of age.

James Smith, Fetlar, known to provide the gang with guides, was cursed by the mother of two of the men he betrayed – see Witchcraft and Curses in the chapter on Women and the Press Gang. One day his minions directed the gang to the Fordyce brothers at Mongirsdale. After stubborn resistance both were taken and leading devices clamped on their wrists. Two strong men volunteered to escort them to the ship which was anchored in the Wick of Gruting, while the remainder of the gang continued their work. But the Shetlanders were determined to escape. Their fear of service at sea transcended normal compassion and in the dialect of the district, incomprehensible to the guards, Laurence Fordyce said 'head fur da Kirn.' *The Kirn of Gula* is a large hole in the ground with a short subterranean passage to the sea – a partly concealed chasm to be approached with care. As the group neared the abyss, Laurence muttered 'Willie dinna miss, mak shur it wirks.' At the very edge they wrenched free, shouldered their captors over to a precipitate if condign end and were at liberty, exultant and unrepentant.

About a mile north of Mangaster, to the north-west of Scora Water and hard by the road, is the small loch of Stenchwater. In the east corner, the furthest from the road, there is a large boulder rising six feet above the surface. Ertie (Arthur) Hanson of Crugga, Sullom, hotly pursued by a constable, waded into the loch and climbed onto this rock. The constable followed and in the course of the ensuing fight lost his life. Some say his ghost haunts Stenchwater.

In north-east Shetland a man, aware that his animals were restive, hid in the loft of his house. When the gang burst in he climbed through the hole which served as a chimney and jumped, landing on the guard posted outside and securing him with a sheep tether. The captive's complaint that the bond was too tight elicited the laconic response 'weel fix, weel fin.'[1]

A similar story concerns a strong, athletic Fetlar man, Billy Brown. One foggy summer night a press cutter slipped into the Wick of Gruting and a party landed with specific instructions to capture him. Billy was on the alert and as the gang entered the but door, he clambered out of the ben lum and bounded across the yard. Challenged by a naval guard as he was crossing a stiggie,[2] Brown pinioned him with a tether. Asked to loosen the painfully tight binding the Shetlander replied 'ha, bridder! He that shur bins, shur fins an lauchs whin he lowses.'[3]

---

1 Well fix, well find.
2 Stile.
3 Well friend, he that securely binds, securely finds and laughs when he unties. See *Shetland Folklore*, 1899, John Spence, pp. 217–8.

Shetland Fiddlers

Perhaps the most popular diversion to alleviate long hours of tedium at sea was song and dance, which broke the monotony and raised the spirits of the ship's company. The recruitment of men with musical ability was encouraged and the impressment of Peter Sinclair, Clestrain, Orphir was a direct consequence of his skill as a piper. James Snody had been taken from a whaler off the coast of Orkney and disclosed that there was an accomplished piper aboard his vessel. It was clearly desirable to recruit such a man and Capt Gourlay, the Regulating Officer at Kirkwall, returned to the ship and pressed Sinclair in Snody's stead.

Leaving piping aside, it is not surprising that with a long tradition of fiddle playing in Shetland, there are several associated press gang stories. A Bressay fiddler George Nelson was playing at a wedding when the gang came for him, and the guests immediately lamented the removal of their only musician. To silence their protests it was agreed that if he could play for four hours without repeating a tune he would be permitted to remain with the wedding company and celebrate undisturbed. Nelson passed the test with ease and as the chastened intruders departed he laconically remarked that there was no need for them to leave as he was just warming up![1]

Another story tells of a man Shoordie.[2] He lived a few miles from Lerwick, was quite the best fiddler in the vicinity, and no wedding or jollification was complete without his presence. Fear of impressment ensured that in the early part of the nineteenth century there was little inclination, or indeed opportunity, to hold rants.[3] Despite several alarms, a whole year passed uneventfully and no-one was taken from Shoordie's district. This trouble-free period persuaded the fiddler, who was weary of living a monastic existence in 'hoidin holls', that some merry-making was overdue. Accordingly a rant was arranged. Young folk from all over the parish gathered in Shoordie's barn where the host was in superb form. As time passed frequent visits to a well-filled keg enhanced the quality of his music and quite overcame any lingering concern about the gang. The evening was at its very best – a delightful haze of conversation and melody – when one of the company chanced to see dark forms approaching. Alarmed, men fled to hiding places in the hills and on the shore. Shoordie, fortified and inspired by generous libations, and indifferent to the danger, played on and was captured.

1 George Nelson, personal communication 1973. Mr Nelson was the great-grandson of the fiddler.
2 The story of Shoordie and his fiddle is told in more detail in *Some Shetland Folk*. J J Haldane Burgess, 1902, pp. 104–113.
3 Social celebrations; happy gatherings with dancing.

Aboard a man-of-war he was required to entertain the crew. Shoordie much valued his liberty and some particularly vigorous fiddling ensured that one of the strings gave way and another soon succumbed. To the dismay of an appreciative audience the music ceased, and forthwith it was arranged that Shoordie would be put ashore under escort to effect repairs. The fiddler had schemed well. He was taken to a shop on the water front where the owner was quick to assess the situation and casually invited him into the back premises to select strings. A trap door was opened and minutes later Shoordie was hiding under the bed in a nearby house. He lay there undetected until darkness fell, then sought safety in the hills. Subsequently he took particular care that fondness for conviviality did not override a healthy respect for the gang.

Another Shetland fiddler evaded the gang for many months before he was caught and put aboard a tender. Found to be an excellent musician as well as an experienced seaman, he was a valuable prize. A fiddle was produced and he was 'set on' to play while an extra ration of grog was issued including some for the unwilling recruit, who is remembered only by his Christian name, John. The music was much appreciated and the sailors sang, danced and imbibed freely. The more they drank the better John played and 'sometime upo da middle o da night' the crew became stupified and quite incapacitated. Wearing moleskin 'breeks' and a canvas jacket, John slipped over the side and swam ashore.

Subterfuge and Disguise

Clever Ploys

At the time of impressment box beds were common in Orkney and Tom Brough, Westray, used his in an ingenious plan. He loosened some boards at the back of the recess to allow quick access to a window. When the gang arrived he obtained permission to dress in privacy, closed the bed's doors, and while his wife railed at the intruders, removed the boards and escaped.

A box bed was also used in the three-hundred-years-old farm house of Tormiston, Stenness, which was demolished in 1972. In the room which originally served as a kitchen, and just where the bed had been, there was an aperture which is firmly believed to have provided an escape route. The hole gave direct outside access and was masked by a flat stone easily pushed aside.

Local knowledge was often critical in facilitating escape. Joseph Hunter ran from his home at Scarpigarth, Weisdale, and closely pursued over Weisdale hill reached the loch of Maa Water. Access to a small island was by underwater stepping stones[1] which were placed in a straight line to a certain point, known to Hunter, where the direction altered sharply. There one of the recruiting party missed his footing and was drowned.

The small loch of Flatpund, Walls, also has an island with underwater access. A West Burrafirth man was pursued deep into the hills and his flight took him to this loch. Arriving there in haste he waded chest deep along a path of boulders positioned in the shape of a dog's leg. He had almost completed the second length when the posse came in sight and followed without hesitation. Unaware of the sudden turn in the track they got into difficulty in deep water and the Shetlander took full advantage of the situation by hurling stones at the floundering men. One was injured and had to be taken for medical attention, the gang's withdrawal enabling the fugitive to escape. When the posse returned, he watched from a safe hiding place in the hills as they negotiated the route to the island and unsuccessfully searched among the rocks and long grass.[2]

Physical Illness and Deformity

Stratagems involving mental and physical health were employed with varying success, feigned simplicity and apparent illness or disability being favoured ruses. Epileptics and the mentally deranged were safe, and during a hot press those who were handicapped with poor eyesight or a club foot considered themselves fortunate. Men who were not infirm relied on ingenuity to retain their freedom.

Thomas Tait of Culdigeo, Orphir, who had a deformed finger was brought to Kirkwall. There the abnormality ensured his release and thenceforward he took pride in a disfigurement which had served him well.

Pressed from his home in the township of Tronston, a Sandwick man affected profound deafness. After several tests it was decided that his hearing had indeed been seriously impaired as the result of a fever and he was discharged. Another Sandwick man declared that he suffered from epilepsy. Cleverly simulating the ailment he too was released.

Pursued through the town, a Kirkwall man sought refuge in a garden off Victoria Street. The houses on the west side had cultivated ground which

---

1 These underwater paths facilitated the collection of wild birds' eggs which were used for food.
2 Tom Johnston, Bridge of Walls, personal communcation 1977. He was told the story in 1930 by an old man Magnus Johnston, West Burrafirth, who said that the fugitives had lived in the house next door.

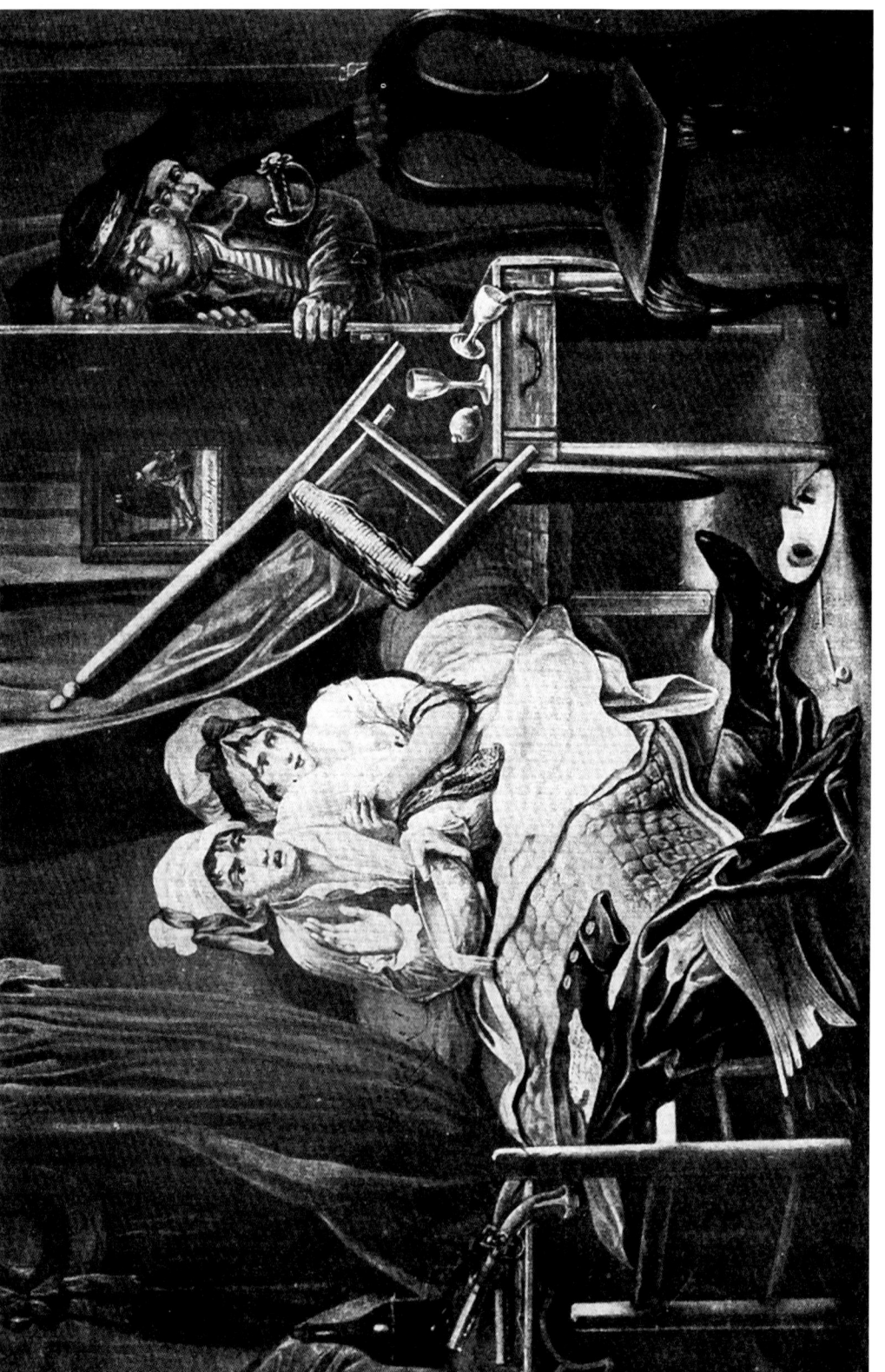

An Unwelcome Visit from the Press Gang.

stretched to the Peerie Sea, and as his pursuers closed the fugitive continued his flight into the water followed by the gang. Making his way past Grainbank and thence to Wideford hill he determined on a clever strategy. Stripping, he rolled in a bed of nettles, dressed again and allowed himself to be caught. Naturally, his captors were pleased with their success until their man protested illness and had to be taken to a doctor when his body was seen to be covered with blisters. The doctor, doubtless sympathetic, diagnosed an incurable skin disease and refused to pass him for service.

John Tait who lived in Holm was terrified of being pressed and would hide on the cupple-backs[1] of the barn and in the corn chest. Realising that he was being watched he altered his diet to make it consist almost entirely of dry, grey cuithes.[2] This spartan fare caused a skin disorder and when Tait was pressed a doctor pronounced him unfit.

A doctor also helped Magnus Goudie, a servant at Halley farm, Deerness, to regain his freedom. Goudie had no friends among the local constables and during a hot press he hid for weeks in one of the caves on the nearby coast, accompanied by four other Deerness men – William, Andrew and James Eunson from Midhouse and a man from Horrie. His absence meant that seasonal work, and in particular the sowing of bere, was much delayed. George Delday rented the farm from Kirkwall practitioner Dr Robert Groat, who examined pressed men before their despatch to the Rendezvous at Leith. On a visit to his farm, Groat found Delday toiling in the fields complaining bitterly that because of constable activity no casual labour was available. The doctor placated his tenant and encouraged contact with the fugitive, giving an assurance that if Goudie returned to work and was pressed he would certify him unfit for service. This unofficial protection persuaded the labourer to reappear. However, when the gang came for him at the cottage of his sweetheart, Jane Linklater, she threatened them with a heavy ladle, and none dared cross the threshold. She kept them at bay until Goudie trusting in the doctor's promise rode in haste to Kirkwall. There he reminded Dr Groat of his promise and duly failed his medical examination.

Whaling vessels from Dundee and Hull which called annually at Orkney and Shetland to make up crew numbers were prime targets for press cutters. When a whaler was ordered to heave to in the Pentland Firth the Captain bluffed his way out of trouble by declaring that most of his men were suffering from scurvy.

1 Cross-beams.
2 Saithe or coal fish.

Self Harm

Some men are said to have maimed themselves to avoid impressment. When the gang came for a man who was draining land in Stronsay he laid a leg across the open ditch and broke the shin bone with a stone, saying 'if you want me, you *will* want [1] me.' A woman in Rendall saved her son from impressment by breaking one of his legs with heavy fire tongs, and a Deerness man rubbed his legs with a caustic substance which so scarred and burnt the limbs that he was unfit for service.

A man with a broken or damaged leg was of no value to the navy and neither was a recruit with a mutilated hand. One evening in Shapinsay the gang surprised a convivial company of young men, while in an adjoining room their sweethearts sewed and gossiped. During the ensuing struggle one of the youths pushed his right hand under the connecting door, his betrothed mutilated several fingers with her scissors, and thus maimed he kept his liberty.

At Pierowall, Westray, conscripts were secured overnight in a thick-walled house[2] used by the laird to store rents in kind. A pressed man confined there was awakened by friends who announced that they had come with his release. Eagerly he pushed his hand under a door to take the document, whereupon a sharp chisel was used to sever fingers from his right hand. It is not certain if he was party to the arrangement.

Self-inflicted injuries during service were not unknown, and these and partial disablement in battle helped to secure a discharge and prevent future apprehension. William Moodie, a native of Lunnasting, had to leave the district because of rent arrears and came to Fetlar where he lived at the Banks of Aith. The laird of Lunnasting was a vindictive man and made contact with the gang to ensure the capture of his impecunious tenant. During an engagement at sea Moodie stabbed himself in a leg, inflicting an ugly looking but superficial wound, and was discharged a cripple in the south of England. Resolutely he set out for home using hecks[3] during the day, as would be expected of a disabled veteran, but at night he shouldered these aids and covered long distances. Reaching a port in the north of Scotland he took ship for Shetland and at Lerwick boarded a vessel bound for Fetlar, calling at Lunnasting on the way. There he was seen by the laird who fulminated, suspecting that he was fit, but with an official discharge in his possession Moodie was safe.

1 Lack.
2 The building, described in its title deeds as 'The old store', is now ruinous and directly across from the present Westray school.
3 Crutches.

Mental Illness

An ill-educated and isolated populace inevitably included a number of eccentrics and lunatics. Equally, it produced some men whose quick-witted use of an almost unintelligible dialect, allied to an unkempt appearance and faked drollery, could bemuse interrogators and persuade the most perceptive captors to classify them as unbalanced and unreliable. Walter Rossie, Stroma was on a visit to Flotta when captured. He played the fool on board ship while officers tried unsuccessfully to establish his sanity. As a last resort the Captain casually handed him a copper coin and asked what he would do with it. The malingerer pondered, then declared that it would make a fine henching stone[1] and childlike threw the penny making it skip over the waves. Delighted with his dexterity he clapped his hands in glee. He was considered a hopeless case and allowed to return to his island home in the Pentland Firth.

Faked simplicity was also used by two captured Orphir crofters, William Tait and Andrew Clouston from the district of Houton. They wandered around the ship aimless and erratic, making bizarre requests in a broad Orcadian accent. They seemed fascinated by the bright buttons on the officers uniforms and asked that they be given some for their mothers. In the galley they requested their pockets be filled with broth. On the deck they sought lengths of rope which were lying around, explaining their usefulness in tethering lambs. Told that the country was at war and they must fight, they declared no animosity towards anyone. Their maundering achieved discharge.

The strange conduct of a crofter at Cullivoe, Yell, brought about his freedom. Though persistently sought, Laurence Moar had eluded the gang. One fine voar[2] day he was carrying dung in kishies[3] from the midden to the rigs,[4] unaware of the gang's approach until he was startled by the terse statement that he could enlist peacefully or be taken by force. Moar was pliant, readily agreeing to accompany them, commenting innocently that he had heard about men being required for the navy and had wondered if he would be invited. Indeed, he was 'ower blyde'[5] to join, and they were 'bidden' to wait briefly until he changed into 'better bits o claes.' He 'rigged on claes' – the very worst he could find, and tied a length

---

1 A stone thrown by jerking the arm against the thigh.
2 Spring.
3 Also *kessi*. A carrying-basket made of straw or dried dock-stalks.
4 Strips of cultivated land.
5 Very glad.

of girse simmonds[1] round his waist. Surprised at his curious, tattered garb, the party nevertheless set out with their docile captive. Only a few steps had been taken before Moar explained that he had forgotten something and asked if he might be permitted to fetch it. This time he returned with a tekk-sye,[2] pronouncing 'dis wid shurly maw amung dem.' Moar's weird behaviour bemused the pressing party and persuaded them that he was simple-minded and unsuitable.

Feigning Death

A Whalsay man, Simpson from Skaw,[3] used exceptional nerve to regain his liberty. He was captured in a 'hoidin holl', and locked up for the night at Symbister. In the morning he seemed dead and even a finger laid on his eyelids brought no reaction. The body was put in a boat and taken to Skaw where six old men were summoned with a stretcher to carry the corpse. After the gang departed one of the bearers walking beside the dead man was startled by a painful nip on his fundament. To the onlookers' amazement the cadaver sat up and with commendable insouciance requested that food and clothing be sent 'tae da hoidin holl at da Taing,'[4] to which he departed nonchalantly.

Another version is that Simpson was taken while fishing from a sixareen.[5] The boat was escorted ashore at Symbister, where he put up a violent struggle before collapsing on the beach apparently dead. He lay motionless with his eyes shut and although his captors checked carefully, he showed no signs of life. The naval officer in charge said 'Remove this corpse, it is of no use to us.' Dolefully, the Shetlanders rowed north through Linga Sound towards Skaw. As soon as they were out of sight Simpson dumbfounded the others by standing up and saying 'I hed better tak a speel at da oars noo.'

James Lamb who lived at The Veng used a cave high on the cliff at Hoevdi Skord to achieve a remarkable escape from the gang. He told his wife Grizel and

---

1 A rope made of grass.
2 A scythe for cutting coarse thatching.
3 In 1733 there were eleven tenant families in Skaw: see *Rental of Unst, 1753*. It was a lively village, the most northerly in Unst and dependent on fishing. An apocryphal story has it that one day, as was their wont, all the men were at the haaf (middle distance fishing grounds). Squalls and poor visibility prevailed and when the weather improved those on shore saw a ship disappear over the horizon. Men and boats never returned and it was believed that the villagers had been pressed. Without the support of their men folk, increasing hardship forced the women and children to leave, and the village died.
4 The remote promontory of Skaw Taing, Whalsay.
5 A fishing boat with six oars.

one of his sisters Jeannie[1] – a tall woman who lived nearby at Grimsetter, that if a recruiting party came he would hide at Hoevdi Skord. This was a mile distant on the east side of the Bard of Bressay.[2] The following story was recounted to, and recorded by, Dr Jonathan Wills in 1968 by Tammie Laurenson who lived at the croft of Gorie and who possessed an encyclopaedic knowledge of the place names and folklore of Bressay:

> Jeemie Lamb wis liftin' airly tatties wan fine day in late August. Da Press Gang creepit up on him an he nivir saa dem atil hit wis ower late. Dey led him awa' ta da norard, whaar dir ship wis lyin at Noss Soond. Aftir a start, Jeemie says ta da sergeant: "He's a braaly warm day, sir. Wid hit be aa richt if I took aff me jaiket?" Noo da sergeant wisna da warst o' men, so he says aa richt and tellt da two marines ta had Jeemie bi da sleeves whiles he unbuttoned Jimmie's jaiket. Weel, hit wis a een o' dem lang jaikets an, as da sergeant undid da boddam button, Jeemie kneed him I'da fess[3] and jamp oot o' his jaiket and ran lik da deevil. Da marines raised dir muskets fir ta shott 'im bit da sergeant said: "Hold your fire. See where he's going, into the end of that headland with cliffs on three sides. Take your time and we'll easy get him." So dey started ta caa Jimmie inta da Bard, takkin hit aisy and walkin' slow. Bit he wis far aheid o' dem noo so dey wir a good piece ahint fan dey saa 'im jamp ower da banks at da Hoevdi Skord. Dey brak intil a run dan and fan dey cam ta da banks broo dey wir naethin ta be seen, aless Jimmie's kep flottin i'da affrug[4] twa hunder feet belaa dem. "Well," says da sergeant, "That's another one gone to the devil." An we ken he said dat becaas Jimmie heared him. He wis landed apo a peerie girsie[5] ledge, mebbe ten fit belaa da aidge and wis croagin[6] inunder da banks in a peerie hol. So dey couldna see him fae da tap o' da banks. Jimmie winderd at dey couldna hear his hert thompin. So, eftir a start da Press Gang guid nort empty-handed. Eftir dir ship sailed awa, Jimmie's wife and dowter cam weepin and wailin ta luik fir him. Dey lowered doon a ropp and up he cam ta flee anidder day.[7]

Women's Clothing

Men did not hesitate to disguise themselves in women's clothes. During a particularly hot press in Burray the use of women's clothing was so widespread that any visitor could have been forgiven for thinking that the island was inhabited

---

1 She became Mrs Ross Tait, the wife of the famous Bressay smuggler.
2 A headland whose top projects beyond its base. ON Bard, the stem of a ship.
3 Face.
4 A spent wave receeding from the shore.
5 Grassy.
6 Crouching.
7 Lamb and his family subsequently emigrated to America.

solely by females. The men who had remained, instead of going into hiding, went around heavily beshawled and petticoated.

At the farm of Langskaill, Westray, a man donned what he hoped was a fetching mutch[1] and lay in bed between two women. His attempt to avoid impressment was unsuccessful as he was betrayed by a neighbour who bore him a grudge.

A Northmavine fugitive sought refuge in a remote croft house occupied by two elderly women. He was taken in, given some of their clothes and the alibi of a visiting relative. As time passed the regular purchase of tobacco by non-smoking old ladies aroused suspicion in the neighbourhood, but recruitment was nearing an end and the refugee was never taken.

Another Shetland man dressed in women's clothes and used his skill in knitting to avoid being pressed. The story is recorded in *The Shetland Advertiser* of 1 September 1862: 'We remember to have heard a comic story of a young man who had a feminine face, and was well up in the feminine accomplishment of knitting, who evaded a press-gang by dressing in woman's clothes, and coolly knitting his stocking while they were searching the house for him.'

George Firth from Finstown had been whaling at Davis Strait. When the vessel returned to land the Orkney men, the gang was waiting near Stromness eager to secure these desirable recruits. Firth's mother was advised of the danger and immediately set out on foot. By good fortune she met her son before he was taken and dressed him as an old woman, wrapping his head in shawls. The disguise served so well that mother and son were able to reach home without being recognised.

It is said that a Regulating Officer in Shetland dealt with suspects dressed as women by throwing a small article in their direction. When he did this, women pulled their knees apart so that the object landed in their lap, while men, used to wearing trousers, drew their legs together.

The crews of returning whalers risked forcible recruitment, but Robert Miller, Kirkwall, successfully reached home one autumn and resolved to get married. Meantime, he avoided impressment by hiding in a hollowed-out peat stack. During the marriage service the gang burst in and met the full fury of the women present. They were incensed at this unseemly intrusion and the constables wisely beat a hasty retreat. The bridegroom escaped, but undaunted, returned in the evening having taken the precaution of dressing as a female. Thereafter, the clergyman performed the ceremony with, seemingly, two women

---

1   A close-fitting linen cap.

holding hands before him. Miller was never captured and in later life was the first beadle of Kirkwall Free Church.

Decoys

Those unfit or unsuitable for impressment might thwart the gang. Two Burray men, Harry Wylie and Solomon Guthrie, acted as decoys, enabling their friends to escape. They were fishing in Holm Sound when a press cutter left St Mary's village rowing at speed, on a recruitment foray. The two men put ashore on Glims Holm, turned their vessel upside down on the beach and hid underneath. The crew of the cutter noticed the boat and came ashore to investigate, whereupon the fishermen were found to be quite unsuitable as Wylie had a club foot and Guthrie a wooden leg. The cutter eventually arrived at Burray, but by then all serviceable men had disappeared.

In South Nesting, ten young men and women were hirdin[1] corn when a cutter rounded a nearby headland. Clothes were hastily exchanged in the harvest field, and the women clad in men's garb launched a boat from a nearby noust and rowed towards some small islands. They were pursued and restrained but the gang was acutely embarrassed to have captured, as they had, five girls whose male companions escaped dressed in female clothing.

The quick thinking of a Shetlander who had been disabled by war wounds enabled a friend to avoid impressment. Both were asleep at Walsta, Delting, when the gang arrived to press the man who had not already served. The discharged veteran intervened, declaring that as his companion was sickly and unlikely to live for long he would take his place. After a tedious journey on foot the party arrived at the Lerwick rendezvous where it was discovered that the 'volunteer' was unfit for service and in possession of a valid protection.

Informers and Betrayal

Sometimes even the most careful precautions were unsuccessful in avoiding impressment. Women might inform on men because of dislike or jealousy, and men sometimes informed on their fellows to prevent themselves being taken or simply out of greed.

The use of bribes to ascertain the whereabouts of suitable men was not unusual and a Shetland woman, for some unspecified reward, disclosed the location of a man she disliked. It was arranged that she would walk past his hiding place busily knitting and there drop a ball of wool.

---

1 Bringing home crops after harvesting; *Biggin* corn was building it into skrús in the yard.

On 1 October 1782 John McDonald received the sum of thirty shillings from John Bruce, Collector of Customs, Lerwick. This came about as a result of information given by McDonald to Walter Scott, then the Lieutenant of the Impress Service, whereby John Work, a seamen 'Secreting himself was Apprehended by my people.'[1] The payment certificate was dated 26 September 1782 and the money was received by McDonald on 1 October.[2]

A few months later the payment for information had increased. On 6 January 1783 the Incident Charges debursed in the Service of the Revenue by John Bruce, Collector in Zetland, for the quarter ended 5 January 1783, record: 'Paid Elizabeth Umphry, Agreeable to his Majesty's Proclamation in Council of the 21st June last for giving Information of a Seaman Secreting himself, and thereupon Apprehended and Impressed, Two Pounds.'[3]

Informers were despised and never forgiven. Long after the days of impressment bitter memories ensured that they remained pariahs. On Graemsay there was much hostility between a young crofter Tom Goldie and his devious neighbour James Mowat. Encouraged by the gang's willingness to pay a handsome sum for the capture of such a desirable recruit, Mowat betrayed Goldie. Surrounded in a hiding place[4] at the Point of Oxan he resisted bravely, but was mortally wounded. Mowat lived into old age but Graemsay folk neither forgot nor forgave the black deed. When he died, so few men offered to carry the coffin to the churchyard that it had to be transported on an ox-drawn sledge. At the graveside the minister declined to proceed with interment until there were eight men in attendance to hold the lowering cords. It required the personal intercession of the cleric to persuade labourers in nearby fields to stop work and assist. Mindful of Mowat's treachery, they performed the task reluctantly then moved away.

A District Fracas

About the year 1810 there was a disturbance between men from the districts of Stenness and Ireland. This 'tullya' was caused by impressment and in particular by the arrangement whereby a quota was levied on each parish. Much skulduggery ensued.

---

1 Shetland Archives, SC12/6/57/4682.
2 The payment by Bruce to John MacDonald appears in his account of incident charges debursed [sic] by the Collector at Lerwick for the quarter ended 10 October 1782.
3 Shetland Archives, E510/200.
4 *The Chammers o' Goldie.*

Whenever they were in danger of being pressed, Ireland men hid deep in the hills under long heather, and in such remote reaches they could remain undetected for an indefinite period among the corbies and catawhissies.[1]

The arrival of a warship at Stromness prompted the usual dispersal to hidey holes, from which a few days later they saw a man wandering on the hillside apparently trying to locate them. He was recognised as Velzian of Hoosewhee in Stenness, who when interrogated declared that there was no longer any need to hide, because of 'a neu la oot at deres no tae be ony mair pressan, gin every perish'll gree amang dersels tae gae twa men.' Furthermore, he pronounced that as two men had been obtained from Stenness, the Ireland men could now return home without risk.

Not being entirely sure of Velzian, who was said to be a 'filty leean taed,'[2] the men held a council of war and decided to send women to Stenness to verify the story. There they soon discovered that Velzian's sobriquet was justified and that the Stenness men planned to capture and offer two of their neighbours to satisfy the joint quota. Incensed, the fugitives resolved to take the initiative and at the same time to obtain a measure of revenge by pressing 'ald Velzian an' Omand o' Bigswal' – what Omand had done to merit their wrath is unknown. They armed themselves to the teeth with 'saetrees[3] an flaalsooples an han'staffs,[4] an' ald Tam Aglath teuk 'is mither's bismar.[5] Dey buist a' been a wheer leukan crood' – a band of some thirty irate men. Taking Johnston of Outbreaks with them (he was a constable and presumably added a semblance of legality to the proceedings) they unsuccessfully sought Velzian in his house: 'Dey sowt an sowt waan an oonwaan, but an ben, ap an doon, i de paetie neuk,[6] aye an even lifted de lud o de ald plowt kirn,[7] bit nae hair o'm fand dey.'

Frustrated and on their way to take Omand, someone remembered having seen Velzian's trousers at Hoosewhee, and on returning they found the miscreant hiding under the bed, 'an de ald wife api da tap o'm, sleepan bae her tale.'

Velzian was dragged forth 'piveran wi gluff',[8] handed over to the constable and, partially sated, the posse again made for Bigswell. But the incursion was no

1 Ravens and Owls.
2 Filthy lying toad.
3 Poles for carrying water-tubs.
4 Parts of a flail.
5 Traditional wooden weighing-beam.
6 Peat recess.
7 Butter churn.
8 Trembling with fright.

longer a secret and a group of armed Stenness men mustered to bar the way. The two companies confronted each other somewhere between Whys and the Dams where they 'fell teu at aince an' laid on wi' their naves[1] an' seek wapons[2] as dey hed wi' a' der poo'r.'

How the tide of battle went is not entirely clear, but when, bruised and bloodied, the sides disengaged, the Ireland men discovered that one of their number, John Clouston, had been taken prisoner while they retained Velzian. A parley was held. It was agreed that there would be no more fighting and that Velzian and Clouston would be despatched to the man-of-war the following morning. 'Dan dey skailed.'[3]

It all came right when both men were rejected as unfit for service at sea. In truth, Velzian was quite sound but duped the ship's officers by playing the fool, and Clouston proved his inadequacy in some other way. The district of Ireland paid 'twa poun' twal' to a cook off a whaler to substitute for Clouston, but how the good folk of Stenness filled their allotted place is not known.

The full vernacular account is:[4]

…Tinks du will we ever hae da days o' pressan ower again? Boy, boy, am hard me faither tellan wheer yarns aboot da ploys dey hed i' the auld times whin he waas a growan chield, an' hoo some wan aff ae wey an' some anither, bit am tinkan da best he ever telt waas aboot a tullya they hed ae night ower aboot the Dams. Id cam aboot dis wey. The Irelan' men hed hidie holes i' the hill, whar they bed for days api' en' whin dere waas ony wird o' a warship bean aboot han's. Bit id waas suerly aisy tae hide dere dan for da heather waas sae lang, min, the corbies laid amang id, an' jeust hapes o' catawhissies. Beesweel a warship cam tae da back o' the Holmes an' da Irelan' men teuk tae da hill as an' a bony piece sheu's in, an' a fine piece for hidan dere i' da burn, is id no noo? Foo bony dey could dick dem doon aboot the edges o'er.[5] Weel, ae day, whin a hale lock o' them waar lyan dere dey saa a ting they teuk tae be a man api' da tap o' the hill abeun Babylon. He waand 'is wey aboot seustu an' noos an' dans looted doon—whasacco he waas leukan for so'nting-bit aye cam narer till whar they waar hidan. Ane o' them hed a spygless an' whin he cam doon aboot da ald hoose o' Gyre, they jaloosed id waas Velzian o' Hoosewhee. Ane gaed ap till 'im an' pat speech api'm an' speered da neus. Haena ye hard, co' he, ye needna fash

---

1 Fists.
2 Such weapons.
3 Dispersed.
4 An Orcadian Battle, A Hundred Years Ago, by J T Smith Leask, in *The Orkney and Shetland Miscellany*, Volume I, pp. 61–4, edited by Alfred W Johnston and Amy Johnston.
5 How easily they could duck down around the edges of it.

hidan noo, dere's a neu la oot 'at deres no tae be ony mair pressan, gin every perish'll 'gree amang dersels tae gae twa men, sae as we're gotten twa i' Stenness 'at'll deu, ye may a' geong hame. The men waarna jeust ower seur o' Velzian as he waas said tae be a filty leean taed, sae whin he gaed awa they held a Cooncil o' war, an' t'out dey wadna be ony the waar o' sendan oot spies. They gaed dere-waas till the wives o' the Hillwhy wha waar aye gaan a hooseagettan an' gossapan onywey, an' sent them ower tae Stenness till see foo the lan' lay. The wives gaed bit seun cam hame wi' da neus 'at Velzian hed telt them a lock o' lees, an' the Stenness men waar plannan tae geong ower tae Irelan' an' press twa fae dere. Noo dis is a bit am no sae seur aboot for id seems dere waas a air o' treuth i' whit Velzian telt, else hoo could they press onybody, an' treu aneuch bit twa waas wanted. Hooever, onywey, the wives neus pat the Irelan' men jeust fair yivers, an' dey vood dey wad hae revenge upi' Velzan, whit waas amas am seur. Weel, min, dan dey hed anither cooncil an' made it ap amang derscls tae geong ower tae Stenness api the heud o' the night and press ald Velzian an' Omand o' Bigswal. I kinno whit Ornand hed deun 'at dey wanted vengeance api' 'im, bit dat waas da twa dey war gan tae hae. Dan dey ged der waas hame an' leuked oot for handy wapons, an' whin id waas dark aneuch dey met a' ermed, boy, an' seckan erms. I deuna min dem a' noo bit dere waas saetrees, an' flaal-sooples an' han'staffs, an' ald Tarn Aglath teuk 'is mither's bismar. Dey beust a' been a wheer leukan crood. I cinno min dem a', bit dere waas Tarn Aglath wi' 'is mither's bismar, min's du him? an' ald John Clouston, du'll min' o' him, he bed i' a peerie bit o' tecket hoose abeun the Burn o' Villis, an' I tink dee gutcher Smith wad been dere for dey waar aye efter 'im, an' dan dere waas me faither. I wad say dere buist a' been ower therty a' taegither. Weel, whin they met they gaed tae Ootbrecks for ald Johnstan, he waas o' the sam Johnstans 'ats i' Gear noo, an' waas whit dey ca'd the Toons Constable. Du sees buddie 'at the Johnstans aa'd Ootbrecks than-a-days.[1] I kinno gin dere waar mair nor ae Constable at a time i' the toon, bit I ken 'at Jock Smith o' the Ha' an' Jamie Smith o' Ramswhy waar Constables teu ae time or anither. Noo du buist min' on 'at id seems tae a' been la dan 'at onyane could press, I kinno foo id could a' been bit id waas the case, an' whin onyane waas pressed an' pittan i' tae the han's o' the constable he waas a' the sam as he been abeurd a man-o-war, an' could be shot for rinnan awa. Beesweel dey teuk Johnstan wi' them, an' gaed their waas ower the hill tae Hoosewhee tae tak' a ha'd o' Velzian, bit alis, alis, boy, ne'er a Velzian could dey fin' an' the ald wife waas i' her bed. Dey sowt an' sowt waan an' oonwaan, but an' ben, ap an' doon, i' the paetie neuk, aye an' even lifted the lud o' the ald plowt kirn bit nae hair o'm fand dey, sae aff they set for Bigswal tae tak' Omand onywey. Dey hedno gaen far till ane o' them

---

1 Outbrecks was sold by the Johnstons before 1799, when it was in the possession of William Velzian. None of the family ever lived there. From 1752–78 it was tenanted by James Johnston, but he was no relation of the family.

said, I'se tell ye whit id is, bairns, ald Velzian's i' the hoose, for noo whin I link api' id I saa 'is pants wi' straps api' them. Noo, du sees dat waas preuf anouch 'at he waasna far awa, sae they 'boot leg at aince, an', boy, whar tinks du dud dey get 'im – anunder the bed – an' de ald wife api da tap o'm, sleepan bae her tale. He waas dregged oot a' piveran wi' gluff an' handed ower tae the constable as a prisoner, an' aff for Bigswal they set as hard as they could pelt. A, bit, whan awhan, boy, da neus hed gotten oot ae wey or anither, Best kens hoo, an' the Stenness men gathered i' force a' ermed teu tae drive the Irelan' men hame. The twa ermies met somewhar ateen Whys an' the Dams – thu kens whar Tam o' Whys bides owerweel, am seur. Weel, dey met dere an' fell teu at aince an' laid on wi' their naves an' seek wapons as they hed wi' a' their poo'r. I kinno hoo lang the feight lested, bit i' the end baith sides ha'led aff for a rest an' air o' braith, an' dan da Irelan' men fand oot 'at the Stenness men hed taen John Clouston a prisoner, bit the Irelan' men aye hed a had o' Velzian. Boy, boy, id waas weel said id waas a blessin o' "The Best" dat John Clouston's brither Herry waasna dere dat night or dere wad a' been murder. Herry hed a gun an' car'dna for guid or bad, dog or deil. Efter restan a peerie meenit an' gettan ceuled an' the bleud rubbed aff, da twa sides hed a kind o' parly, an' id waas 'greed dat dere so'odna be ony mair feightin' dat night, an' dat da twa prisoners – Velzian an' Clouston – wad be sent tae the man-o'-war i' the mornin. Dan dey skailed. The twa waar sent abeurd bit waar baith hame again the neist day as no bean fit for sea. Velzian waas fit anouch bit played the feul sae weel dat dere waas narlans a row aboot 'is bean sent, bit I cinno min' on a' the oots an' ins o'd noo. I kinno whit the Stenness men dud, bit da Irelan' men got a cook aff a whaller for twa poun' twal, tae geong i' Velzian's piece.

Two Egilsay Pilots

Hugh Hourston, Sound, Egilsay, and William Craigie whose home was at Meaness in the south west of the island, competed for the lucrative business of piloting vessels through the dangerous and sometimes busy waters which lay to the north. Hourston had the better view of potential customers, was more successful, and Craigie became increasingly jealous.

The situation changed dramatically when Craigie was appointed a constable for Egilsay, and at once selected his rival for the quota. At the earliest opportunity Craigie and his fellow constables moved on Sound, but Hourston was prepared, having slackened a flagstone at the rear of his roof. While his sisters obstructed the constables, he climbed out and made off, delaying only to replace the covering. The posse, searching unsuccessfully, became angry and abusive. They returned several times looking for their quarry, but he remained hidden in Rousay.

Another version is that Hourston scattered his pursuers as they entered the door at Sound, by hurling a three-toed pot at them. It was an effective missile, filled as it was with potatoes cooking in boiling water.

Shortly after this incident Craigie was informed that Hourston had returned to Egilsay, so he arranged for a vessel to appear in the Westray Firth flying the pilot jack. Unsuspecting, Hourston set out to earn a fee, followed by Craigie. Too late he discovered that the frigate was a decoy. Made prisoner, he was taken to a tender which sailed to Scrabster to collect pressed Caithness men.

Robert W Marwick includes the story in notes written in 1987: 'On its return journey the ship got into difficulties. After a long beat to the windward along the north coast of Sutherland, the ship met a hurricane just before she reached Cape Wrath and had to lie to under bare poles as no sail could be carried under those conditions. She was driven eastwards on to the west coast of Orkney. The officers had no idea where they were when the Black Craig was sighted in the morning light. The Captain assembled the crew to see if any of them recognized the land. Hugh Hourston stepped forward, took charge and sailed the ship into Stromness through Hoy Mouth and anchored her in Cairston Roads. He then returned to the crew's quarters. That evening he was summoned aft to see the captain who said, "Because of what you did today in saving the ship and crew I'm giving you a day's leave. We sail the morning after that at 8 o'clock so you have to be back by then. If you are not, we will not wait for you." Hourston was put ashore and immediately set off across the West Mainland and Rousay to Egilsay, where he went back into hiding. He was never pressed again.'

Hourston was Robert Marwick's great-great-grandfather.

An article embellishing and expanding on this story appeared in *Peace's Orkney and Shetland Alamanac and County Directory*, 1875. It recounts the resistance of an Orcadian family when the press gang arrived early that century and pressed one its members:

Well, Mister Tom, it's half-past ten on Saturday night, and I've been in the boat all the week, but I'll tell you one story yet afore I turn in. It's about the Press-gang; and the sister o' the chaps told me it herself, at her own fireside. She was a widow woman then, but when the affair I'm going to tell you about happened she was a young lassie, and I think, if I mind right, there were three or four sisters o' them. Her own name was Hourston, an' she belonged to the island o' Egilshay. She had two brithers – splendid, strong fellows – an' the Press-gang were terrible anxious to nab them; an' so, one dark winter's night, eleven of them went out from Kirkwall to Egilshay, to try if they couldna take them. There were seven men-o'-war's-men an' four o' the Kirkwall gang – (there were gangs then everywhere you know – chaps belonging to the places, that kent the best men to take) – old Waas, an' black Jock Anderson, an' Willie Reid (a strong, able man), an' I don't just mind the other one's name. Any way, they got to Egilshay, an' made old Saunders Lawrence, Mr Baikie's kelp grieve, pilot them to the house where the brothers lived – the house o' Sound – the northmost house in Egilshay, I think it is, an' made him tell what sort o' a place it was too. The outer door opened into the fire-house, an' then there was a room in bye – the cellar, they ca'd it – just like any other little old house in Orkney, you know. Well, a' the lasses were sittan' aboot the fire, an' their mither an' faither, an' the fire was brunt low, when they heard men's feet outside, an' afore they kent what was up, the whole gang was in upon them. It was so dark, they didna ken even then wha they were, till one o' the fellows took the teengs[1] an' lifted a gled[2] peat oot o' the fire, an' blew on it, to see where the brithers were. Then the light flashed on the navy buttons, an' the old woman knew in a minnit what they were, an' wi' that up she jumps, an' gaes the chap's hand such a kick that it sent the teengs up to the roof, an' the gled peat to the tither side o' the hoose, wi' a dad, till the sparks stood oot aboot it like a comet. So that stopped that. Then a' the lasses raise, an' struggled wi' the Press-gang; an' one o' the gang grippit the old wife, an' was coorse on her, when Jamie (wha had been in bed in the fire-house) cried, 'If you're come for me, tak' me if you can, but don't abuse my mither.' So they fand oot where he was, an' got aboot him, but he keeped them aff; an' a' this time the lasses were no' idle, I tell you. Hughie – the ither brither – was ben in the cellar, an' tried first to get oot through the theck[3] roof, but there was nothing to stand on, an' he couldna hang by a cupple wi' one hand an' mak' a hole wi' the ither; so he dropped doon on the floor again, an took up a wappin'[4] three-taed pot that was there in baith hands, an' ran into the fire-house amang them, keepin' it gaun whirlin' aroond him; an' I'm blowed if he didn't send them to the floor just like peelin's o' onions! an' got to the door. The gang had set Willie Reid to keep the door, because he was a very strong man, but Hughie dashed him against the wa', an' made off just as he was, in his shirt an' drawers an' stockings only, an' not anither stick on him. He ran for the shore, an' hauled doon a big yawl him-self, an' pulled across the soond to Rousay; an' he was safe there, for the Press-gang were never fain o' Rousay, because a' the Rousay folk stuck oot against them to a man, an' they got very few there. The Rousay folk got clothes for him, an' sent him ower to Evie, an' he took right across the hills to Stromness, an' that very day shipped for the Straits. The gang got Jamie, though. When he couldna get oot, he cried for one o' his sisters to

1 Fire tongs.
2 Glowing, burning.
3 Thatch.
4 Weapon.

fetch his gun oot o' the barn, but his faither cried not to shoot any o' them, for God's sake, or he wad ha' done it in a minnit, for Jamie was a wild chap, an' cared for nobody when his temper was up. The gang hadna muckle to brag o', for every skin o' them got a keepsake to mind Jame by afore they mastered him. I don't mind whether they got him aboard o' a man-o'-war or no, as it's a long time since I heard the story. It was droll times in Orkney then, Mister Tom. Goodnight.

An Apprentice Betrayed

For many years Robert Mowat was a tradesman and a constable in Kirkwall. He employed a lad who served his apprenticeship faithfully, but on the last day of his term Mowat included him in the quota agreed by Orkney lairds and the Admiralty. Generations of Kirkwallians remembered this unscrupulous incident.

Deserters

To escape from harsh conditions and health hazards, and at the same time to enhance their chance of success, deserters might favour absconding in familiar territory. Dressed in sailor's clothes, in 1798 an Orkneyman John Wilson deserted at Kirkwall from a recruiting party of Fencibles. A ten guineas reward notice for his recapture was displayed in Kirkwall, and possibly in an Edinburgh weekly paper with an audience in the Northern Isles. Wilson may have remained in Orkney and sought sanctuary, or taken ship. The notice is unclear, as is the outcome.[1]

There are several recorded instances of deserters in Shetland. Thomas Mouat JP, writing from Belmont, Unst, readily used the church to promulgate his instructions. On 3 May 1812 he issued a notice to be read by the Session Clerk at service that day. The content was that in the previous August Laurence Hectorson, presumably a local man, had deserted from HMS *Cherokee* 'and has ever since skulked in this and the neighbouring Islands and has been unwarrantably protected and entertained by different persons to the prejudice of his Majestys Service and the troubling of innocent persons on his account. These are requiring that none of his Majestys Liege subjects within the Country of Shetland shall harbour or entertain the said Laurence Hectorson or further his escape out of the Island of Unst or Country of Shetland in any manner of way under the highest pains of law, but that those who know where the said Deserter now is shall immediately inform the Justice of peace subscribing thereof in order to his the said Hectorsons being apprehended and restored to his majestys service onboard the said Ship now riding at Baltasound.'[2]

1 Orkney Archives, Hugh Marwick Papers, D29/1/10
2 Gardie Papers, Copy Notice by Thomas Mouat as Justice of the Peace 3/5/1812.

Anti-press gang views were firmly held by Thomas Strong, Virkie, Dunrossness. On 31 May 1809 Captain James Nicolson, the Regulating Officer, petitioned[1] the Sheriff Substitute, stating that on 24 or 25 April two seamen belonging to the naval ship *Nyaden*, then lying in Bressay Sound, had deserted whilst on shore. 'Accordingly he losed [sic] no time in sending off into the interior of the country in quest of them.' Nicolson averred that Strong was guilty of protecting and encouraging these deserters. Seemingly, when one of the press gang, Henry Mainland, had secured the men with the aid of two constables, Strong 'came forward in a ferocious manner with a loaded gun in his hand and told Mainland that he would shoot him if he did not let them go.', The Petition continued that Mainland fortunately got hold of the gun, whereupon Strong urged and entreated the deserters to force and fight their way from Mainland, declaring that they could have his boat 'which he pointed out to them on the beech [sic] gratis to make good their escape.'

Nicolson continued, 'Mr Strong did in other respects so much entice, instigate, stimulate and aid these deserters' that it was with the utmost difficulty Mainland and the constables were able to bring them back to the ship (and to the severe punishment that doubtless awaited them).

On 9 June in his Answers to the petition Strong said that he had come upon the men at his father's house. He had challenged their identity and where they were bound. 'They very candidly asserted that they belonged to the *Ipswich* a Greenland ship who was turned leaky on her passage to Shetland'. They had 'discorded about something' with the Captain and had therefore come to Dunrossness 'for the purpose of freighting a boat to the Fair Island or Orkneys.' Strong declared that this was all he knew about the men until Mainland and the two constables appeared, until then he had never understood that the 'pretended Greenlanders were really deserters'. He denied that he had come forward in a ferocious manner with a loaded gun and threatened to shoot Mainland. He had 'happened to have an arquebuse[2] in his hand at the time', but he had said to the constables Anderson and Burgar, only in a jocular manner, that if they had come to impress him he would not allow them to do so. Strong requested the Sheriff Substitute to assoilyce[3] him from the fine requested and also to find him entitled to expenses incurred 'in this vague and unnecessary process.'

1 Shetland Archives, SC12/6/1809/42.
2 An early type of handgun.
3 To acquit, free from a charge, or prosecution.

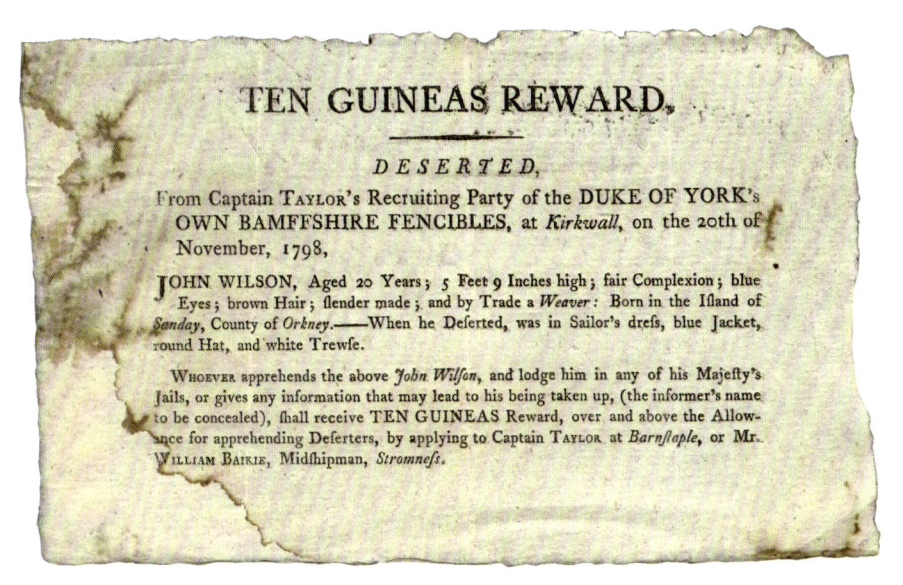

> **TEN GUINEAS REWARD.**
>
> *DESERTED,*
>
> From Captain Taylor's Recruiting Party of the DUKE OF YORK's OWN BAMFFSHIRE FENCIBLES, at *Kirkwall*, on the 20th of November, 1798,
>
> JOHN WILSON, Aged 20 Years; 5 Feet 9 Inches high; fair Complexion; blue Eyes; brown Hair; slender made; and by Trade a *Weaver*: Born in the Island of *Sanday*, County of *Orkney*.——When he Deserted, was in Sailor's dress, blue Jacket, round Hat, and white Trewse.
>
> Whoever apprehends the above *John Wilson*, and lodge him in any of his Majesty's Jails, or gives any information that may lead to his being taken up, (the informer's name to be concealed), shall receive TEN GUINEAS Reward, over and above the Allowance for apprehending Deserters, by applying to Captain Taylor at *Barnstaple*, or Mr. William Bairie, Midshipman, *Stromness*.

Reward Notice for a deserter.

In his Replies, Captain Nicolson mentioned Strong's 'ingenuity to procure credit for a studied tale' and that he would have been better simply to have made an assertion of innocence. He continued that Strong must have known that *Ipswich* was at that time 'in the Greenland seas' and that indisputably he had encouraged the deserters to make their escape.

On 3 August Henry Mainland of the press gang appeared before the Sheriff and stated that he had been sent by his Commanding Officer to search for two deserters from the *Nyaden* frigate. He had apprehended them on the fields at Wart Hill, Dunrossness, and the men had not resisted. Strong seemed very angry at the arresting party, sought sight of their warrant and said that 'if it had so been that they had come to impress him he would have blown their brains out.' Mainland continued that he had secured the gun, but released it when Strong had told him 'it was unshotted'. He concluded his evidence by confirming that Strong had declared the deserters were welcome to use his boat which was half a mile distant.

James Burgar and Robert Anderson, both constables and residents at Garth, Dunrossness, gave statements concurring with Mainland's evidence. On 20 October the Sheriff Substitute's decision was to 'assoilzie the defender, but finds no expenses due.' In his judgement the Sheriff manifestly had some sympathy for Strong despite clear evidence that the scene at Virkie had been violent and Strong had made his boat available to the men who had jumped ship.

Thomas Strong had made an unambiguous statement of his rooted aversion to impressment and its ramifications, although in this case he had chosen to defend two deserters who had no rights and were not Shetlanders.

Change of Name

The 1759 Walls Session Records contain a curious and novel method used by a Shetland man to retain his freedom. Robert Lawrenceson, then in London, was fearful of being pressed. On 6 July 1759 he wrote to his parents:

…I could not keep Clear of ye press – because Randall inform'd against me and James Henderson which we was obliged to keep our Selves up for four weeks, which we could not Show our faces in the Streets, we have Shipt our Selves both together in a Ship bound for Gibraltar, and from there to Gurie[1] which I do beleive will be a Twelve month before we return back. The Captains name is Webb and the Ships names is ye Ann Galley. I have Three Pound Ten Shillings a month. I have left wth Mrs Torrie my will and power in my Fathers name that whatever is belonging to me that he can receive it all if anything should happen [to] me in my voyage … Sic Subscribitur Robert Johnstone. P.S. I was obliged to Change my name because of the Information that Randall gave against me to the press gangs. So you must get my name Registrate in the Session books the Same that it is in this Letter, and yours Likewise, and your Sons and Daughters name the Same, for my will and power is made in your name Johnstone, and my name is the Same in the will and power.

On 27 December that year Lawrence Johnson 'shoemaker in Gruitquey,'[2] Walls, appeared before the Session, produced his son's letter and requested that: 'the Session might cause ye Same to be Insert in their Publick register, and that the desire of ye Said Letter might be Intimate from the Pulpit of this Congregation where his Said Son was born, and resided, till ye year 1757.' After due consideration the Session: 'Appoints the Sirnames of ye Said Lawrence, and the Said Robert his son, and the rest of his Children to be henceferth converted, The Fathers name from Johnson, and the Childrens from Lawrenceson into Johnstone, conform to ye Desire of the above Roberts Letter.'[3] The full entry in the Session book, including the letter from Robert to his parents, is given in Appendix D.

1 Goury on the Cherbourg Peninsula.
2 The small township of Gritquoy, pronounced Gritquee, in Walls.
3 Under the shifting patronymic system then in use in Shetland, the offspring of Lawrence Johnson automatically took the surname Lawrenceson. The agreement of the Walls Session meant that the parents changed their surname from Johnson to Johnstone, and their children, who were Lawrencesons, became Johnstones.

John Chalmers,[1] master of a small trading vessel, was pressganged on the streets of Kirkwall and taken to London. He escaped at Tilbury, altered his name to Chambers, and started work as a mast-maker on the south bank[2] of the Thames below London Bridge. There he was joined by his wife Mary Ward, also an Orcadian.

Another man who changed his name was John Fea, born at Brew, Dunrossness in 1788. Pressed in 1800 when only twelve years old he later deserted and for a time used the surname Fraser. He married, settled in Aberdeen in 1816 and was lost at sea nine years later.

In a similar vein, a Foula man who deserted and eventually reached home used bold tactics to foil a search party. A sloop dropped anchor in the island's small harbour and a cutter came ashore to be met by the fugitive, identifiable only by name to the naval men. Questioned by the posse, he suggested that the person they sought, who he acknowledged was known to him, might be cutting peats on a nearby hill. The party set off through bog and thick heather, returning empty-handed several hours later when they were directed to another peat bank. After further unsuccessful searching the dispirited sailors departed, and it is said that the deserter himself strolled to the pier and waved goodbye to the weary men.

Volunteers for Service

Some men did not try to evade impressment. There are several examples of self-abnegation.

In Shetland around 1810, at harvest time, boats were off 'shooting the haddock lines' and women were busy 'shaerin the corn' when alerted by sight of a man-of-war. The fishermen made haste for the shore and thence fled to hoidey holls in the hills 'taking their morsels of faerdin maet[3] with them.' Walter Jeemson's boat was the last to beach and he made for the Muckle Hill, where with a younger brother he hid among the heather, ferns and boulders. Nearby, two young men unwisely crept from 'behind a big roog[4] of peats.' One was a widow's son, the only support of his mother, the father having been lost at the haaf fishing. The father of the other boy had previously been pressed. The lads were seen and pursued, so Walter decided to help them. Revealing himself he

---

1 Born in Kirkwall 1775.
2 Chambers wharf still exists.
3 Ferdenmeat – food provided for a journey.
4 Heap, pile.

dashed to the loch of Gossawater knowing where stepping stones lay. He was followed by an officer brandishing his sword who, unsure of the underwater pathway, fell in and was saved from drowning by Jeemson. More Navy men continued the pursuit and one was drowned. Meanwhile, the two lads had been captured. The Shetlander made a bargain with the distressed officer that he would guide him to the bank if he would release them, and promised that he would take their place. This was agreed, and an undertaking given that no one else from the neighbourhood would be pressed. The youths were freed and that very night Walter Jeemson departed in the naval vessel. Local men searched the scene of the struggle in the loch and found the officer's sword which was given to Walter's father to keep for his son's return and to recognise that he had surrendered his liberty for two others.[1]

During a particularly hot press a man was required from the parish of Birsay. No one would volunteer and able-bodied men went into hiding. Several years earlier a vessel had been wrecked off the Birsay coast and all the crew were lost with the exception of the carpenter. He settled in the parish and folk showed him much kindness, which he repaid by volunteering.

Another version is that a vessel was wrecked on the north coast of the parish and the sole survivor was an orphan lad. He was found the following morning sheltering in the byre at Nearhouse. Years later, grateful for the care he received, he volunteered when the parish had to find a man for the quota. A rock on the northside, to the east of *Caesar o Hawn Skerry*, is named *Tammy Towie* or *Cowie* after him. It should not be overlooked that there is a hiding place in Skerries called *Tammy Tyrie's Hidey Holl*. The rock in Birsay may be an example of folk etymology.

A sailor whose ship had been wrecked at Sandwick, Orkney, also received succour and friendship. He volunteered to take the place of George Smith who was soon to be married, and for this he is said to have received forty guineas from the bridegroom. This seems an inordinate amount.

In another case of substitution, the father of a Harray lad volunteered to serve in the army in place of his son. James Sinclair, born in 1766 at Overbrough, was pressed and taken with a number of other young men to the gathering place at St Michael's Church. His father, an army veteran, was much concerned that the youth would be exposed to hardship and danger. Interested

---

1 *Da Steppin-Stanes o' Gossawater: A Tale of the Press Gang* appeared in the *New Shetlander*, No 26, Jan/Feb 1951. Written by James R Cheyne, it also features as *Walter Jeemson's Story* in Peter Jamieson's unpublished manuscript on the Press Gang.

only in numbers to satisfy the parish quota, the constables readily allowed him to take the place of his son. This incident probably occurred during the War of American Independence which ended in 1783 when James Sinclair would have been seventeen. The story was recounted by Sinclair's granddaughter, Margaret Sinclair, who died in 1948 aged ninety-four.

Temporary exemption might be sought, but in the case of a young lad, Hoseaon, was not immediately successful. On 20 October 1809 William Mouat, Annsbrae, Bressay, who had been involved in the negotiation, wrote to Captain James Nicolson RN, the Regulating Officer, pleading that his tenant's son had been pressed despite having 'agreed to enter with you upon condition of staying six months at home to finish his education.' The arrangement had not been honoured and Mouat continued 'you must be perfectly aware how great a misfortune it would be to a young man who has prospects of advancement to have his education and consequently his capability for promotion marred in such a way.' Hoseason's age, type and place of education, and the outcome of Mouat's plea are not recorded. [1]

---

1 William Mouat's letter book 7.11.1805–16.12.1816.

Lieutenant William Wilson

Wilson was commissioned Lieutenant in September 1802 when thirty-seven, and he continued to appear in the Navy list as a lieutenant until March 1819. Appointed to the Impress Service at Lerwick in 1807 in place of George Ross, he was second in command under Captain James Nicolson, the Regulating Officer, who was a Shetlander.

Wilson became notorious throughout Shetland and his name appears in a number of Sheriff Court documents. He was ruthless, abused his powers and not infrequently his actions were set aside on appeal to the Sheriff Depute. Overbearing and vindictive, at the head of a gang often comprising Shetlanders, he did not scruple to ascertain if the men and lads he apprehended were protected by reason of age, employment or infirmity. Wilson's name and exploits have resonated down the years as the personification of all that was bad about impressment.

Scrutinising some of the Lerwick Sheriff Court cases in which he featured prominently, the impression is gained that several of those in authority were prepared to contest his right to impress all and sundry. This may have been partly motivated by self-interest, since depletion of the work force would seriously effect the fishing activities on which the economy and the lairds' own wealth depended.

That Wilson and his gang were brutal is beyond dispute, and the following are some of the Petitions brought against him or matters in which he was involved.

On 20 November 1807 John Henderson, shopkeeper in Lerwick, petitioned[1] the Sheriff Depute. He alleged that on the previous night between 8 and 9 pm while serving some people in the 'shope of his Master [that he] was in an illegal and Lawless manner interrupted in the Execution of his employment by James Isbuster Junier in this town Stiling himself one of the Press gang, who in a state of intoxication entered the Shope, … … with an intention to Drag a poor Boy out that he saw in it.' He was prevented from doing so until Lieutenant Wilson arrived,

[1] Shetland Archives, SC12/6/1807/61.

as Henderson recognised no authority in any one of the gang 'without a Peace warrant to enter the Houses and Shopes of peaceable inhabitants at pleasure.' Isbuster seemed to bear a special animus against the shopkeeper as he had threatened 'to maim and wound the person of your Petitioner if ever he met him in the Street at a convenient hour for his diabolical purpose.' Henderson requested that Isbuster be put under caution as he 'dreads bodily harm, injury and oppression of the said James Isbuster,' and asked that he and all others belonging to him should be kept harmless and 'skaithless[1] in all time coming.'

On 28 November the Sheriff Depute considered the petition, and Henderson's supporting oath. Isbuster was served with a copy and ordered to find sufficient caution within twenty-four hours to keep John Henderson, his servants, family, and 'haill other dependents harmless and skaithless in their bodies, good name and reputation, goods and Effects in all time coming under the penalty of ten pounds sterling.' He also granted warrant that if caution could not be found to seize, apprehend and commit Isbuster to the Tolbooth. Lieutenant Wilson came to his rescue as cautioner 'under the penalty of £10 sterling, agreeable to a sentence of Lawburrows[2] pronounced by the Sheriff Substitute.'

Impressment of Farmers from Unst and Yell

On 10 December 1807 Magnus Nisbet, farmer, Colvadale, Unst, arrived in Lerwick to purchase some articles and was pressed by Wilson's men. In his petition[3] to the Sheriff Depute, Nisbet said that he was a farmer, head of a family and not a sailor. He sought release from the Rendezvous, damages and expenses. James Penant and James Winwick both from Muness, Unst, appeared in his defence, declared they had known him for twenty years, and that he was by profession a farmer and fisherman who had never voyaged to sea in any ship or vessel 'during the course of his life unless while he prosecuted the Ling fishing in an open fishing Boat.' The Sheriff found him 'not liable to impress and Ordains him to be furthwith set at liberty.'

When Mrs Margaret Jack left Burravoe, Yell on the forenoon of 2 March 1808, she little thought that on arrival in Lerwick at 4 o'clock, Robert Watson, by order of Wilson, would arrest and take to the Rendezvous John Williamson, master of the ship on which she had travelled. This was 'under pretence of

---

[1] Uninjured, without receiving hurt.
[2] The legal security which one man is obliged to give that he will not do any injury to another in his person or property.
[3] Shetland Archives, SC12/6/1807/62.

taking down a List of the men's names that had come in the Boat.' Her petition[1] to the Sheriff Depute stated that Williamson had a wife and three children to support and also was 'bound with a farm which he has held for several years.' Furthermore, he had left his wife 'in child-bed, and the consequences may be fatal to her if he is not immediately set at liberty.'

In his Note of 3 March Wilson declared that Williamson had been at sea for several years. Furthermore on the previous night he had offered to liberate him on receiving a letter from Mrs Jack that if upon trial Williamson was found impressable he would be returned. Wilson considered this 'a fair proposal', but it had been refused. He trusted that the Sheriff would see the 'propriety of skreening[2] a man from his Majesty's Service (who has been at sea) in the present state of the nation.' That day the Sheriff, having considered the petition and Wilson's unsigned note, found that John Williamson should not be detained and 'ordains him to be immediately set at liberty.'

The Pedlar and his Assistant

On 26 December 1807 James[3] McCra sought his liberty from the Sheriff, claiming that for four years he had been a travelling merchant and never at sea in all his life except when making passage from Scotland to Orkney or Shetland with his merchandise. He had loaded his goods and other articles on the sloop *Volunteer* of Lerwick, sailing the following day. As he made his way through the streets of Lerwick settling his affairs 'he was wantonly and maliciously, with a design to make him lose his passage, laid hold of by some of Lieutenant Wilson's gang and taken into the Rendezvous where he is now confined.' He petitioned[4] for release and damages of five hundred pounds sterling, together with expenses. Doubtless because of the imminent departure of *Volunteer*, the Sheriff instructed Wilson to appear personally within two hours to answer the petition. Both parties were present in court, Wilson did not deny the petitioner's statement 'so far as it went, but represented him as a vagrant.' McCra was liberated.

It seems that Wilson had been vindictive in this attempt at impressment, as the previous day, 25 December, McCra had petitioned[5] about the impressment of James Jameson, Olnafirth, Delting. He claimed that some time in the month of June he had employed Jameson to travel with him through the country to

1 Shetland Archives, SC12/6/1808/12.
2 Protecting.
3 His christian name was John.
4 Shetland Archives, SC12/6/1807/65/3.
5 Shetland Archives, SC12/6/1807/65.

carry his goods at 'the agreed on wages of seven shillings sterling per week.' That he had continued in this work until 5 October when Jameson, having acquired some knowledge of the business, it was proposed that if he could get credit from McCra he would travel through Shetland, sell merchandise and from time to time make payment to him. This was agreed and Jameson was given goods on credit 'to a considerable amount.' They had continued in this manner of business until that very day when Jameson came into town with the remainder of his goods and with cash resulting from sales, with a view to settling with the petitioner, who was on the eve of leaving Shetland. Jameson 'was met at the hill head of Lerwick' by the gang and taken to the Rendezvous together with goods and cash. McCra averred that Jameson was due him the sum of £24 4s 3½d and now that he was impressed this money would be lost to him, a particularly dire situation as he was on the point of leaving Shetland. Although McCra was 'no lawyer' he knew that if anyone was due a sum to the amount of £20 or more and was in the army or the navy the creditor 'could demand him back and take him out of either service.' McCra requested release for Jameson, damages of ten pounds and the expense of the process. The Sheriff sought answers from Wilson within twenty-four hours, and in the meantime forbade him from sending Jameson out of the county.

In undated Answers Wilson stated that although McCra claimed he had employed Jameson in the month of June the Agent's books in Lerwick 'shew and it is confessed by the young man himself' that he had not landed in Shetland on *Experiment* of London on its return from Greenland until 22 July. He suggested that it would have been several weeks thereafter 'before he could fall in with the petitioner.' Wilson believed that the Petition had been a fabrication. He felt it was unnecessary to 'go over the grounds advanced by McCra and follow the petitioner in the vague history of the alleged agreement twixt him and James Jameson … and does not consider it of any consequence to take notice of his rehearsal of the sale of his goods and other silly stuff advanced.' Jameson was a seaman, had confessed to being to Greenland at different times, had never been a tenant or a fisherman, but rather 'a vagrant [sic] as well as a straggling seaman.' Wilson included criticism of McCra – 'he tells your Lordship that he is a travelling merchant or in other words a Hawker Pedlar or petty Chapman without a licence,' and asked, 'is this a fit person therefore to be allowed to interfere with His Majesty's Service, certainly not except it was to accompany James Jameson to serve His King and Country?' That criticism perhaps explains why he attempted to press McCra the following day.

The Sheriff rejected McCra's petition and Jameson was retained by Wilson, with the imminent prospect of naval service.

Violence at Sandwick

Wilson was involved in an especially egregious incident involving the Sinclair family who lived at Leebitton, Sandwick. In vigorously defending their home, widow Catharine Sinclair and her daughter Ursulla Smith suffered grievously in a fracas involving Catherine's three sons.

James Greig, the Procurator Fiscal, complained[1] that assault and battery had taken place on 14 October 1808 between two and three in the morning. With a press warrant in his possession, and supported by two midshipmen and other members of the gang, Wilson had proceeded to Sandwick for the purpose of impressing John Smith and his two brothers Malcolm and James.

The posse had gone to Sandwick on the instruction of Captain Nicolson, 'Regulating Officer in Shetland, and Commander of the Impress Service at Lerwick.' He had been informed that Smith, a seaman impressed by Wilson and who had deserted, was living at Leebitton with his brothers, termed 'straggling sailors'.

The gang intended to take the three Smith brothers to Lerwick together with any other seamen who might be found in the house or in the neighbourhood. The dwelling was unlocked and the gang struck a light as they burst into the room where they hoped to find the brothers abed. This provoked a violent reaction from the occupants, one of whom, Ursulla, attempted to belabour the intruders with a stick. She was knocked to the ground by Wilson with the butt of a pistol. It was alleged that he had struck her 'when down, held her in that position while he gave her many heavy blows on her face and head, and then with an exulting exclamation left her almost senseless, wallowing in her blood.' It was further alleged that the wounds included a severe contusion on her right cheekbone and eye, and a deep cut on the left side of her upper lip. Ursulla had endeavoured to take refuge in the other end of the house, but Wilson had then struck her on the forehead with a 'naked' sword which made a large, deep wound.

The fracas continued with all the lights being extinguished by the Sinclairs and 'a severe combat took place in the dark' during which Wilson was knocked down, beaten and bruised, and one of his men, Henry Mainland, called out 'Murder'. While Wilson was on the floor, Ursulla (duly recovered) stood over him with 'a large club or stick in her hand in the very act of giving him a severe

---

1 Shetland Archives, SC12/6/1808/94/1–10.

stroke,' but was prevented by a member of the gang. She then 'attempted to strangle him by putting her hand into a red worsted neck cloth which he had on and twisting it round his throat in which she was disappointed by the knotes [sic] giving way.' She then wrested from Wilson one of the two pistols he had in a bag at his belt and attempted to shoot him, believing the weapon was loaded.

Wilson was saved by Laurence Fraser, one of the midshipmen, and other members of the gang from 'the perilous situation in which he was in from the violence and outrage of these women.' Fraser became the next gang member to be attacked, Ursulla 'aiming a stroke at his head with a large stick or peice of wood which would have in all probability have killed him outright.' Wilson had to use the butt of the remaining pistol to push her away. As a result of the violence, not only Wilson and his midshipmen, but most of the gang were 'all more or less wounded, beat, and bruised' with sticks and stones.

In the gang's defence, it was said that after Wilson and his men managed to capture Malcolm and John (James escaped), they made for Lerwick, followed to the shore by Catharine and Ursulla showering them with stones 'and otherwise maltreating them untill they came to the boat.' Then 'the said Ursulla Smith became violent, furious and perfectly outrageous' in her attempts to prevent Wilson from embarking with the men. Indeed she hurled a large stone at Wilson, 'against whom her malice was all along particularly directed,' which struck him on the thigh and disabled him. He had to thrust her away in order to defend himself.

It was suggested, somewhat maladroitly, that Ursulla received her wounds in the dark 'from her own party' as they had been armed with clubs and sticks and had put out the lights, and she might even have been hit by her mother. A further suggestion was that some of her injuries had been self-inflicted to make her story appear more 'clamant to some whose minds perhaps were not unprejudiced before.' Ursulla visited Dr Laurence Edmondston in Lerwick to have her wounds treated, and it was claimed by the defence that she asked him 'to pull out her tooth' to make her wounds more ugly, which the doctor refused to countenance. It was also averred that she 'employed herself daily in going about from door to door exposing her wounds, such as they were, in order to excite compassion.'

Wilson was sent for trial, a jury of fifteen was selected, and in his guidance the Sheriff's sympathy clearly favoured widow Sinclair and her family. Wilson was found guilty on two counts and imprisoned, but only for a fortnight, whence he emerged to continue his nefarious practices.

However, the matter did not rest there. The affray had caused considerable damage to the house contents and to an animal. An inventory was presented to the Court and the following items listed: 'Two beds, dung in bruck;[1] a large spinning wheel, dung in bruck; a table greatly damaged; a armed Shair, dung in bruck; a anker[2] Ceg, which had two heads in, dung in bruck; a anker of oatmeal, half destroyed; a large lame[3] plate, a small one, and a large ball brock; a Calf greatly hurted – expected not to live; a small chest, the lid brock; five doors greatly damaged; a hat cost 14 pounds current money, greatly hurted.'

Alexander Mouat, Malcolm Tulloch and Andrew Harper gave a qualified attestation to this catalogue: 'we have overhaled the above articles, but thinks we are not able of putting a value on it [nor on the health of the calf] as we did not see it before it was damaged.'[4] Honest men indeed!

It is not known if the request for a settlement was satisfied.

Schoolboys Impressed

On 12 November 1808, accompanied by a Shetlander, Lieutenant Fraser, Wilson forced his way into Bressay school determined to secure two boys. George Scott, the parochial schoolmaster, was outraged and on 15 December he petitioned[5] the Justices of the Peace. He alleged that about midday on Monday 12 November the scholars were prevented from escaping from the schoolhouse and Fraser 'came boldly in to the school without leave from the Master being either asked or obtained.' He told Scott that there were some lads he wanted, whereupon Wilson entered accompanied by several of the gang. He demainded to be shown Andrew Leask and James Spence, telling them that if they would enter willingly into service they would not be troubled for some time. Otherwise they would be taken by force. Both lads refused to join voluntarily and were removed. Scott was incensed, and vented his anger in the petition: 'If schoolhouses are permitted to be scenes of such transactions we may soon expect to hear of our Altar being prophaned in like manner.' The Justices ordered a copy to be served on Wilson on 7 March 1809 and instructed that he appear personally at the Sheriff Court on 2 May. On 27 April George Scott received a pusillanimous communication from William Stout, presumably on behalf of the Justices, stating that 'the time is too long delayed for Citing Mr Wilson to this Court.'[6] What became of Leask and Spense is unknown, although their age may have protected them.

1 Broken to pieces.
2 Measure of capacity, a third of a barrel, ten gallons.
3 Earthen.
4 *The Shetland Times*, 9/1/1897; also D1/135, p. 76.
5 Shetland Archives, D25/59/2.
6 Shetland Archives, D25/59/3.

Threats by Wilson

Wilson was not above intimidating individuals in the open street, using 'insulting incendiary language and threats of personal violence' and disturbing the public peace. A petition[1] on 20 September 1809 to the Sheriff Depute by James Greig, writer in Lerwick, stated that on 18 September Wilson 'unprovockedly' attacked Thomas Ogilvy, merchant, and challenged him to fight, 'applying the most scurrilous language to him because he would not.' Thereafter, Wilson 'attacked Mr Ross, Collector of Customs, who happened to be passing him on the street, who he also wanted to fight.' Wilson was heard by Robert Davidson, Tidesman, and others giving orders to one of his gang to go to Captain McPherson in Fort Charlotte and borrow pistols 'to shoot or fight Mr Ross and Mr Ogilvy.' Wilson showed the weapons to James Greig, merchant, with which he said he was to kill Mr Ogilvy. Not satisfied with these threats Wilson 'attacked and insulted' William Mouat, Advocate, challenging him to fight and 'calling him a coward because he did not agree to it.' The petitioner sought imprisonment of Wilson in the Tolbooth until he found sufficient Caution and Surety for keeping the peace. Wilson was ordered to appear personally and to admit or deny the facts stated in the Petition. The following day he appeared and accepted that some of the facts alleged are 'no doubt true' but was loath to admit to others. However, he was willing to find caution to keep the peace under such length of time and under such penalty as the court would require. The Sheriff Substitute ordered Wilson to keep the peace for eighteen months under penalty of £100 sterling and failing to find caution, gave authority to 'seek, search for, seize and apprehend' Wilson and commit him to the Tolbooth until caution could be found. This was avoided by his superior officer, Captain James Nicolson being his cautioner.

A Valid Protection for Greenland Whaler

Certain classes of men were legally exempt from impressment such as those engaged in the Greenland whale fishery. Harpooners, linesmen and boat steerers were entitled to a Protection given by a Collector of Customs, which could not be invalidated. Recipients were permitted to work onshore until required for another whaling voyage.

Such was the case of Laurence Sinclair, Liabitten, Sandwick, a line manager on *Fortitude* of London, which had been whaling at Greenland and Davis Strait. He possessed a Protection dated 23 August 1810 from the Commissioners of Customs, London on the basis that he would sail with *Fortitude* during the next

---

[1] Shetland Archives, SC12/6/1/1809/60.

whaling season. Having completed a voyage to Greenland, Sinclair had returned to London and, armed with his Protection, made his way home 'in order to pass a few of the winter months with his wife and six children at Liabitten' where they lived with his aged father and mother. His petition to the Sheriff Substitute on 21 September[1] was to the effect that no sooner had he arrived at Bressay Sound in the brig *Don* than he was pressed by Wilson, who 'obstinately refuses to liberate him notwithstanding he has seen and examined his Protection.' Sinclair strengthened his case by adding that he had proceeded unmolested to Shetland 'after undergoing particular examinations by several Impress Officers in England.' He continued that Wilson's action in impressing and detaining him, 'in the face of a legal Protection and of the Acts of Parliament upon which it proceeds seems in the petitioner's humble idea an act so unwarrantable and oppressive as to merit the severest animadversion.'[2] He sought five pounds damages as a solatium for his detention, as well as expenses, protection from being sent out of the county, and recovery of his liberty upon entering into a recognizance that he would deliver himself up if found liable to do so. The Sheriff granted Wilson twenty-four hours to lodge Answers and in the meantime prohibited him from despatching Sinclair.

In his Answers, Wilson averred that Sinclair was 'a Stragling Seaman and Supernumerary on board the brig *Don*' and attached no value to the Exemption Certificate which Sinclair had obtained, since 'as many in England do' he never intended to voyage the following season as line manager. In his Replies on 24 September Sinclair said he knew that harpooners, boat steerers and line managers were not to be pressed 'neither during their employ in the Fishery nor in the interval between each voyage'. He repeated his claim that several times he had been 'stopped by press gangs in London and Shields but instantly liberated upon showing it' (ie, the Protection). The Sheriff declared the Protection legal and valid, liberated Sinclair and found him entitled to expenses. These amounted to £2. 2s 3d.

The Apprehension of Two Miscreants

On 19 October 1810 Wilson petitioned[3] the Sheriff in respect of Laurence Halcrow, a deserter from the Navy, and James Duncan, a disturber of the peace, who were said to be 'lurking in Cunningsburgh.' He asked that a certain Robert Sinclair be made to take these two men before the Court. On 21 September a warrant

---

1 Shetland Archives, SC12/6/1810/59.
2 Criticism or censure.
3 Shetland Archives, SC12/6/1810/67.

had been issued to James Duncan, Aith, Cunningsburgh, a Constable and sheriff officer, to arrest them, but no action had been taken. Before Duncan had executed the warrant he had received a letter from Robert Sinclair, merchant in Lerwick, asking the sheriff officer not to impress James Duncan, the latter's namesake, as 'it is no part of your business and I am your faithful Friend.' Sinclair had written a second time to Duncan on the same lines. Wilson declared that this would affect the warrant because of Constable Duncan's influence 'as Tacksman of the lands which he possesses, which is a weighty matter in Shetland.' He suggested that Duncan should be liable to a penalty of one hundred pounds Sterling, but 'in the event of the said Robert Sinclair not bringing the said Laurence Halcrow and James Duncan into the Rendezvous at Lerwick for examination, to serve himself in their place over and above paying the above penalty of one hundred pounds sterling in terror to others from being the means of impeding his Majesty's Service.'

In his Answers dated 20 October, Robert Sinclair declared that the present action 'is without a doubt one of the most triffling [sic] and ill-judged that ever was brought either in this or any other court. Indeed it carries upon its very face such a frivolous, whimsical appearance that it seems more calculated for a burlesque than any thing else.' Sinclair admitted writing the two letters, but merely to warn the sheriff officer that he could not impress the men – only an Admiralty warrant gave that authority. Furthermore, Sinclair said that not only did he wish to put Duncan on his guard about the irregularity of not having a proper warrant, but also he wished to warn him that Halcrow had armed himself with two loaded pistols 'with which he was resolved to shoot the officer and his assistants upon their attempting to take him.' He continued that he had no wish 'to prevent Mr Wilson getting the men if they were liable to be taken.'

On 7 March 1811 the Sheriff Substitute dismissed Wilson's petition and found the defender Robert Sinclair entitled to his expenses which amounted to one pound seventeen shillings. Presumably the September warrant remained valid, was duly enforced, and the two men were taken to the Rendezvous where Lieutenant Wilson awaited.

A Disputed Protection

On 9 February 1811 David Greig, Master of the schooner *Eliza* of Glasgow, and Walter Fraser, land labourer in Sandness, petitioned for Fraser's release from the Rendezvous. The vessel, which had traded for some months between Shetland and Leith, belonged to John Scott of Melbie, and her crew were safeguarded by an Admiralty Protection.

The petition[1] averred that although the Protection had expired on 25 January while the vessel was lying in Bressay Sound loaded with cargo, it could not be renewed until arrival at Leith. Lieutenant William Wilson had agreed not to trouble the men and to give a Certificate to prevent impressment until a valid Protection was obtained. Wilson had sent for the crew, but on their arrival the mate and Walter Fraser were detained in the Rendezvous. 'With great reluctance,' Wilson had liberated the mate but 'positively refused giving up the other,' in which case, the Petition continued, the vessel could not sail as even with Fraser she would be one man short.

In his Answers Wilson said 'this matter is unfairly stated.' He had asked for sight of the Protection and the presence of the men 'contained in it.' If their names were either entered in or on the reverse of the Protection, Wilson would provide a Certificate of Protection. He continued that when the document and the men arrived, the names of two men did not appear on it. Everyone would have been saved much bother if their names had been inserted in the Certificate by Greig, but this 'he either studiously or stupidly did not do.' Nevertheless, 'from motives of good nature' Wilson liberated the mate but sent Fraser on board the sloop of war *Lavaret*. With unnatural generosity, Wilson offered to replace the pressed man whereby 'the vessel shall not be detained one minute for the want of Fraser; but that in place of him Mr Greig shall have one of the best seamen belonging to the Rendezvous at Lerwick to assist in bringing the said vessel to her destined Port; and if one cannot do he shall get two good seamen.'[2] Wilson hoped that this would prove 'he shall do nothing unfair in his part.' No charge for their services was requested.

The expired Protection was produced in Court. It provided exemption for five men and boys, and Mitchel Smith, mate of the *Eliza*, confirmed that the crew had consisted of four persons only, including Fraser and the Master.

Wilson's Answers did not impress the Sheriff, who ordained that Fraser be set at liberty and expenses granted against Wilson. These amounted to £2 11s.

Other Facets of Wilson's Character

Essentially ill-disciplined and unprincipled, Wilson attended to various matters and duties associated with the Rendezvous and seamen, not necessarily related to impressment.

---

1 Shetland Archives, SC12/6/1811/5.
2 Known as ticket men, or men in lieu. A ticket was a protection against subsequent impressment when the destination was reached, enabling safe return.

On 7 October 1807 he petitioned[1] the Sheriff Depute to allow the sale by public roup 'of some triffling articles of household Furniture and body cloaths' for the payment of death-bed and burial expenses of Robert Irvine, late belonging to His Majesty's Rendezvous House in Lerwick. He had died on 1 October. Presumably Irvine was a member of the gang. The sale proceeded at noon on 8 October 'for Ready money' and raised £6/12/2. Out of the proceeds Agnes Hunter was paid 16/3d for thirteen nights and days attendance and subsistence while Irvine lay ill. The auctioneer charged 7/6d and a coffin cost 10/6d. After various other costs were satisfied the residue of 7/1d was lodged with the clerk of court to be distributed to 'such of his nearest relattions as shall be found to have just title to receive the same.'

From Leith on 18 April 1808 Mrs Janet McKay wrote[2] to 'Captain Wilson, Impress Service, Lerwick.' Wilson's wife had met and encouraged Mrs McKay to detail the larceny of Thomas Abernethy, 'an Invalide Seaman who originally belongs to Higlabister, Parish of Wisdle.' Apparently, he had resided with her for five weeks and before departing had 'ransacked' her house and made away with two good new coats belonging to her husband, 'one, a fine brown cloth worth £3 with a silver wattered button.' The other was a good black coat worth £2. Mrs McKay had spoken to 'your Honour's Lady' to whom she had been introduced by Mrs Nicol, a friend. (Mrs Nicol subsequently wrote to Wilson in support of Mrs McKay.)[3] Mrs McKay hoped that Wilson would 'have the goodness to cause some of your men to wait on Abernethy and endeavour to force a confession and recover the coats.' Abernethy also owed her 20/- for board and lodgings. Another Shetland man, Lawrie Tait, had been with Abernethy but he was not implicated. Janet McKay was, she said, 'a poor helpless woman left with a family of infants to work for.' On 18 November 1808 Abernethy appeared before the Sheriff and declared that the two coats found in his possession were indeed taken out of the house of Janet McKay, lamely suggesting that the coats were offered to him by her, otherwise he would not have known of them and he would not have been tempted to take them, 'which he is now extremely sorry for.'[4] On 6 December Abernethy, by then a prisoner in the Tolbooth, petitioned the Sheriff Depute and enquired if the crime for which he had been imprisoned was 'bailable or not.' The Sheriff agreed to release him on a sufficient caution and surety

1 Shetland Archives, SC12/6/1807/55/1.
2 Shetland Archives, D25/59/1.
3 Shetland Archives, D6/179.
4 Shetland Archives, SC2/6/1808/93/3.

on condition that he would appear and stand trial within the space of six months under a penalty of 'Six Hundred Marks Scots.' Captain James Nicolson became his cautioner (perhaps with a view to recruiting him), but whether Abernethy came to trial is not known. On 26 April Wilson acknowledged receipt from the Sheriff Clerk of two 'neet bodied mens coats belonging to Mrs McKay, Leith, and stolen by Thomas Abernethy,' so presumably Mrs McKay recovered her coats. Clearly this act of kindness was occasioned by the influence of Wilson's wife.

That awareness of Wilson's disgraceful conduct was not confined to Shetland emerged as a result of James Hay, merchant in Lerwick, attempting to secure the release of an apprentice, Andrew Clark. 'Mr Wilson and his gang had impressed the lad' on the evening of 5 January 1811 and taken him on board *Strenunous* at twelve midnight. Hay's son sent Clark's indentures to Rear-Admiral Otway in an unsuccessful appeal for his release. Otway wrote on 5 February, 'Wilson was a very improper person to be the Regulating Officer at Lerwick but that no complaint had been made. The Lerwick people should address the Admiralty stating the conduct of the man, & if the matter was referred to him he would give his opinion that Wilson should be superseded & a respectable man sent in his place.'[1]

Perhaps as a result of this stricture, Wilson was removed from his post. He does not again appear in Sheriff Court documents. He departed notorious, doubtless embittered, and attended by the unalloyed resentment and enmity of Shetlanders.

---

1 National Library of Scotland, Hay of Hayfield papers, Acc 3250, Box 85, Folder 3A.

The Hidey Hole, Eday.

Hiding Places

So important was it for men to have a safe retreat that comfort was a secondary consideration. The nature of the hiding place mattered little if it was secure. A rough bed or even a recess with no bed and poor ventilation would suffice, and a fugitive was ill-advised to betray his presence by use of fire or lamp.

Islanders hid on the moors, in dry ditches, among the peat banks or in caves which were almost without exception exposed and cold. Occasionally fugitives had some comfort when a prudent man might secrete a cache of heather, straw bedding, water and dried food in the inner recesses of his chosen spot. The misery of periods of incarceration must have daunted even the bravest spirit.

Those at risk prepared holes under the floors of houses and created spaces in peat stacks and behind box beds. Men who did not thus conceal themselves sought refuge in the cliffs or roamed the hills. Whenever opportunity permitted, food and drink were taken to them, usually by women.

Soldiers and parish constables might combine to form a search party to scour the countryside. David Petrie, factor to Rear-Admiral Graeme, wrote to him from Holm on 6 October 1812: '… seeing no chance whatever of any Lads to enter for you for the Navy and having corresponded with the Regulating Capt. Gourly who has been here several weeks, I accepted of a party of Soldiers who along with the Constables of this Parish did search Houses hills & Rocks for two nights and three days and at last succeeded in Impressing 4 Young men good looking Lads all seafaring men but one a Servant Lad.'[1]

In April 1978 the present writer interviewed Mrs Jessie Alexina Craigie, Rousay, then aged ninety-nine. She had been told by her grandfather, who was born in 1808, about his boyhood recollection that whenever a strange boat was seen crossing Eynhallow Sound, 'the big hefties' fled to various hiding places in the hills. There they might stay for days while women took food to pre-arranged locations. He remembered that recruiting parties sought only fit men, disregarding 'peerie trowie tings'.[2]

1 Orkney Archives, D5/8/1812.
2 Small, sickly things.

In 1870 Alexander Marwick, Rousay, wrote in his *Reminiscences*:[1] 'About the end of the French wars Britain was so hard up for men that they had to press men for the navy and army. There was some very exciting scenes under my observation trying to avoid the press gang. There were some young men in Wasbister that had to sleep in the Haas of Gamlie[2] for safety all night. I knew a man belonging to Egilsay who slept in the middle of a stack of oats almost every night of the winter in a room which he had prepared for himself.'

Though exposed, this was probably warmer than the hiding place of a man in the district of Twatt, Shetland who slept throughout an entire winter inside a peat stack. A member of his family closed the entrance at night and released him in the morning.

In North Ronaldsay also a man found refuge in a peat stack. It happened that within reach of his hiding place a hen had chosen a secluded spot in which to lay, and daily the fugitive had cause to be grateful to the obliging bird.

James Flett, a servant at Scottie,[3] Beaquoyside, Birsay, was warned by a neighbour Mary Johnston that he was likely to be pressed. Flett hid successfully in the oatmeal kist,[4] and in the best tradition duly married the girl who had saved him from capture.

A Westray man Cooper, who lived at Noup, aware of a recruiting party surrounding his house, hid in the chimney breast. He was discovered as a result of a constable prodding the dark recess with a sharp stick, cuttting his leg which became infected: 'He hid up the lum. They bored him wi a spear an his leg bealed[5] an he hed tae come doon.' While Cooper awaited trans-shipment to Leith the wound continued to suppurate, and he was released.

A North Yell man hid, rather unusually, under the tekkin[6] and near the gavel[7] in the loft of his house which was stone built, with its gavel made of faels.[8] One day the gang, grassant, watched him enter the front door and surrounded the building. Searching more thoroughly than on previous occasions they located

---

1 *Reminisences*, Alexander Marwick of Corse, Rousay, 1801–99. He was born at Leuhoose on Fealquoy, Rousay.
2 The rocks behind Stennisgorn, an old farm in the district of Wasbister, at that time home of the author's Gibson ancestors.
3 Probably the farm now known as Quoyscottie.
4 A chest or strong box with a lid. When used for holding horses corn in a stable it was known as a cornkist.
5 Festered.
6 Thatching.
7 Gable.
8 Turf.

the fugitive, but he defied them and refused to move. At bay the man despaired, but swinging on one of the cross baaks,[1] he struck out with his feet and dislodged the faelie gavel. The turf which had been there for many years was dried and crumbling and collapsed onto those waiting outside. The fall caused 'A pooer o stoor an stjuch'[2] which blinded and confused the posse, enabling the fugitive to jump down and make for the hills.

Men at risk could expect no warning, so David Cromarty, North House, Deerness hinged the shelves in a closet to provide an immediate and easily accessible hiding place. When a recruiting party came he squeezed into this recess while his wife, unconcerned, and seemingly alone, busied herself spinning. The constables searched in vain, examining the paetie-neuk[3] and climbing onto the hallan[4] before deciding that their quarry was elsewhere. Just as they were leaving, his three year old son who had been watching, clapped his hands at their frustration, and anxious to display his knowledge in this seeming game of hide-and-seek cried 'Da's i'de press!'[5] The woman's attempts to divert attention from the child made him all the more determined to be noticed, and finally in exasperation he pointed to the cupboard. Shetland provides an almost identical story. As the gang departed following a close but unsuccessful search 'a peerie boy', the son of the house amused by their failure, shouted gleefully 'da's ahint the dresser.'

The old kirkyard in Shapinsay was reputed to be the home of spirits and ghosts. But men on the run had no great fear of spectral figures and sometimes hid among the gravestones. At a quota meeting of the island's principal landowners, William Heddle who had offended one of them, was listed. He was warned and took flight, hiding among rocks on the shore, in caves and ditches. One dark night he was making his way home for a hot meal and a sound rest when he heard the gang approaching. He found safety in the graveyard at the parish church of Lady Kirk, the superstitious constables afraid to search among the tombstones.

A ruined sheep shelter provided a hiding place for two men who lived at Clumlie, Dunrossness. One Christmas day they visited their cousin at

---

1 Beams.
2 A cloud of dust and fumes.
3 A corner, usually in the kitchen, in which the immediate supply of peats was kept.
4 An area of cross-bars below the room on which hens might roost.
5 Rev H L Mooney, Deerness, personal communication 1977. Mr Mooney could remember old people in Deerness pronouncing 'in the' as 'i'de'.

Williamsetter and while there the gang arrived. The Goudie brothers escaped through a barn window and ran until they came to their laamhus[1] at Trotta Knowe. The roof had collapsed, but they crawled under the couples and langbands[2] and concealed themselves. Shortly afterwards their pursuers arrived in the darkness. The officer thrust his sword through the tangled beams without success. At daylight the Goudies returned home and, with the remaining Clumlie men, hurried east to a cave at Ramnibanks called Da Un. There they hid for three weeks until the gang departed, their wives bringing food every night.[3]

Caves

Although the choice of hiding place varied, caves, spartan though they were, had many advantages. Known only to people in the district, they were sometimes roomy, almost always with a concealed entrance and usually difficult to reach. Resolute fugitives with food, drink and some bedding were able to remain secure for long periods in these retreats, some of which could be reached only by a combination of ropes, sure-footedness and a good head for heights.

Taking considerable risks, desperate men sought refuge in these dank holes[4] often sited in precipitous cliffs. There they listened to wind and wave and for the approach of the press gang. In little comfort and less peace of mind, fugitives were in constant fear of discovery or betrayal.

Men might row or even swim into sea caves which sometimes held sandy beaches. Food and drink could be lowered by rope and hooked in from the entrance. Such hiding places were particularly dangerous. Jessie M E Saxby writing in *Shetland Traditional Lore* wrote that one of the little islands close by Scousburgh: '… is perforated by wonderful caves … A little boat can row in one of the caves, which winds under the isle over a clear sea, until you lose the light of day … This cave – like so many others – served in ancient times to shelter men when fleeing from the press gang. Once, when two young fellows were hiding there, a great storm came on very suddenly, and the poor fugitives could not be rescued. After that doleful accident the cave was never again used for such a purpose.'[5]

---

1   Lamb House.
2   Laths.
3   *Shetland Folk Book* 1964, Vol IV, pp. 43–5. ed. T A Robertson and John J Graham; the article 'Press Gang Stories' was by E S Reid Tait. Da Un is at the Geo of Uin, Dunrossness.
4   They were called *hoidin holls* in Shetland.
5   pp. 46–7.

There are numerous press gang caves on and under the coasts of Orkney and Shetland, many now forgotten, others eroded over the years. Some were still identifiable in 1862 when *The Shetland Advertiser* of 1 September commented: 'We remember to have been shown caves at the foot of the sea-beat precipices, where men used to be hid from the press for weeks, in which they durst not have fire or light for fear of betraying themselves, and to which the women used, at great risks, to convey provisions at dead of night.'

The following are caves and other retreats known to have been used by islanders. The names of Shetland hiding places are given in the dialect.

Caves in Orkney
Deerness

There were numerous hiding places, several of which have been affected by erosion. Locations known to have a connection with impressment are: *Eunson's cave* in the cliff below Stonehall; caves in Burray Geo and Lang Geo; the peculiarly shaped *Repenting Stool* and *the Holes o the Horn* at the banks of Halley; *The Hole in the Brough* which is said to have boasted a man-made passage from old buildings at the top of the cliff; *The Smuggler's Cave* in the geo of Swinable which can only be reached by boat; *The Hidey Holes* to the east of the castle in the North banks of Halley – these were between a ledge of rock standing on legs seven feet above sea level and a natural roof which has now fallen in; *The Rivick o the Moul* at Moul Head situated behind a ledge of rock – men climbed down a fault in the rock formation and crouched on the ledge; and the *Ottar Holes* on the north side of the Brough – really two caves with a passage of some twenty feet into the larger cave. This cavern is boat-shaped and quite high, with sufficient standing room. The floor consists of sand and gravel, and is dry even at high tide, although spume is carried in during storms.

Other places which may have provided concealment are: a cave called *Anna Brettie* to the south of Lang Geo; *Maggie Cuttie's Cave* at the banks of Halley; caves on the south side of Burray Geo known as *Little John o Mirky* and *Muckle John o Mirky*; and *the Mirk Holes*, near the Point of Laber.[1]

---

1 'Round the Shores of Deerness' by Mrs R Eunson, Seaview, Deerness, *The Orcadian*, 3 and 15 September 1936.

Rousay

When danger was imminent men from the Frotoft area sought refuge in the hills of Glifter. To cover the absence of fugitives another member of the community took over the work in hand, such as ploughing.

There is a fissure some three feet wide, twelve feet long and six feet deep just to the east of Peerie Water. This unusual indentation between rock faces on the side of the hill is a quarter of a mile along the peat road from the loch. The cleavage, covered by long thick heather, provided a splendid natural refuge, and was known as the Klivvie[1] of Heshiber.

The *Cave of Skrue* or *Scroo* (also known as the *Covenanters Cave*[2]) is in the cliff west of the Knee of Faraclett. It is in the full craig and entry is possible only by rope.

Marwick

There is an unusual hiding place at Sandcroma geo. Immediately beside the geo there is a small fissure in the cliffs into which a man can squeeze, crawling through an opening at beach level. The top of the crack is packed hard with wood, forced in by wind and storm. About ten feet from the entrance the natural passage widens slightly, and at head height there is a ledge of rock on which men hid. This unnamed hidey hole, in a most unlikely place, was known only to a few, and can be passed without any thought that a man could hide inside.

Birsay

Bounded by the sea on two sides this parish has a number of suitable shore caves. *Walty Reid's Hole* is a chasm on the south-west side of the Brough. It may have been used as a hiding place, but it should be noted that Walty, Watty or Warty Reid or Red, is a legendary or semi-supernatural figure in Orkney tradition. The name was also known in Sandwick, and it was attached to a hollow on Heddle hill, Firth, and to a long-forgotten cave on the Stromness coast.

Caesar o' Haan or *Hawn Skerry* was used by a man with the Christian name Caesar who lived at the nearby house of Haan.[3] His surname is unknown.

On the Northside is *Fraasa Cave*, opposite the submerged rocks of The Bows of Fraasa. Part of the cliff has been eroded and the fissure is now exposed. This was an excellent hiding place, being difficult to enter from both sea and land. Indeed, the original cliff face would have been almost perpendicular. Two

---

1 Klivvy: a clearing.
2 There is also a Covenanters Cave in Burra Isle, Shetland: see p. 158)
3 Caesar was not an uncommon Christian name at that time.

Messrs Meadows and Taylor. Sandcroma geo, Marwick, 1975

men who hid there and had food and water lowered by rope were betrayed by a woman endeavouring to protect her son from arrest. It is said that both men died in action. This is probably the same story about a man from Flecketsquoy[1] who hid there and was betrayed by a woman from Greenhill. Many years passed, the man did not return from naval service and was presumed dead. The woman 'took thought about it,' was overwhelmed with guilt and drowned herself in Longagleeb Geo.[2]

Orphir

There are two main hiding places on the coast line. *The Cottar Hole* is at the Head of Hangaback below Gear. By 1974, the roof had fallen in but some seventy years earlier the cave was intact, providing sufficient space for five men.

The second location, known variously as *The Hole o the Head, The Hole o Houton* and *The Ingoe*,[3] is a chamber at the Head of Houton. This retreat was reached by a tunnel in the shape of a dog's leg. Searchlights were positioned in this area in 1940 as part of the Scapa Flow defence system. During site preparation the removal of several feet of rock caused a fall which partially blocked what now remains of the narrow passageway. My octogenarian informant said

---

1 Now called Doverhouse.
2 A dangerous geo with high crags on both sides and reaching more than two hundred yards inland.
3 Ingoing.

Entrance to The Hole o the Head, Houton.

that in his youth he crawled some ten yards into a small chamber six feet in diameter. Three or four fugitives from impressment could sit there, albeit with little comfort, until danger had passed. At the time of my enquiry in 1974, two men were living in the district whose great-great-grandfathers hid in this cave. Tradition claims that a cock chicken released at the entrance on New Year's

Interior of The Hole o the Head, Houton.

day negotiated a subterranean way well inland and in stygian darkness 'crawed unner the hearth stane o Naversdale' on a May morning. A similar story is told of inquisitive and itinerant fowls in both South Ronaldsay and Stronsay.

It was concerning *The Hole o Houton* that J T Smith Leask recorded: '... some boys hid in the cave at the Head of Houton. You know there is a cave there that goes from up on the Head, down under the sea. They say, but I won't vouch for the truth of it, that you can see the outer end of it at a spring tide.[1] I have heard that a number of Orphir youths stayed in it for days on end hiding from the press gang. The gang well knew that they were there and sat themselves down about the mouth of the hole till they would come out, but they never moved till the gang said they would shoot. That deceived them, and the boys came out – the fools that they were, for the law was that arms must not be used by the gang except to defend themselves with.'[2]

William Sinclair, Gerawin, and three neighbours hid in this recess, remaining for almost a fortnight. Under cover of darkness wives brought food and drink and as time passed the fugitives convinced themselves that the pressing party[3] had disbanded. They resolved to return to their families, but soon after Sinclair reached his home, constables William Garrioch and John Bews forced an entry. Dragging their man from bed, Bews placed a baton on his shoulder and solemnly intoned 'Ye are noo a King's man.' Sinclair's wife was distraught, clung to her husband and entreated the constable to have pity. Bews wavered in his resolve but Garrioch, less sympathetic, ordered him to stand aside and declared 'I'll no be lang in sindering[4] them.' The unfortunate man was taken to Kirkwall, shipped to the rendezvous at Leith and thence to the Nore.

Tankerness

The best recorded hiding place is *Paplay's Hole* or *Paplay's Cave*[5] some ten feet below the cliff edge and thirty feet above sea level. Located between Berwick

---

1 A particularly low ebb.
2 *A Peculiar People and Other Orkney Tales*, J T Smith Leask, p. 124.
3 The Orphir constables were William Garrioch, Oback, Tuskabister; Nicol Wishart, Westquoy, Kirbister; John Bews, Yarpha, Smoogro; George Flett, Heathermuir, Hobbister; and George Hutchison, Sower, Clestrain.
4 Sundering: separating.
5 Dr R P Fereday, Kirkwall personal communciation 1983. He located *Paplay's Hole* using directions and information provided in 1969 by William Spence, Cott of Ness, Tankerness. Mr Spence was then seventy six. ('Exploring Tankerness – Cannons, Caves and a Cairn', R P Fereday, *The Orcadian*, 24 July 1969.)

Head and The Ness it is named after a fugitive Paplay. Crescent-shaped, from the entrance it finds a course left (west) ending in a subterranean cleft. The headroom throughout is less than three feet, thus though there is space for four men to lie down, there is insufficient height to sit in comfort. The ledge outside the entrance has a number of initials cut into the rock face and the hole itself looks south towards nearby Hebbersgeo – a long sea cave or tunnel open at both ends. Great care must be taken when approaching Paplay's Hole as an overhang makes the cliff edge dangerous.

There is a tale that on descending to the refuge and invisible from above, Paplay struck a light. This enabled the pursuers, standing on an opposing cliff, to locate and shoot him. Details of the incident are not entirely clear and one version holds that it was a Covenanter who was shot. Another story concerning the cave is that during the long French Wars four men from the North Isles of Orkney were sustained there for eight days by Tankerness folk who lowered provisions by rope.

In *Memories of an Orkney Family*[1] Henrietta Groundwater describes a cave in which two of her relatives from the croft of Skeetquoy hid, but she is almost certainly mistaken in suggesting that it was Paplay's Hole:

When Ann[2] was about ten years old the Press Gang came to Orkney. Only Robert[3] was old enough to be taken along with his father, which would have left the family without means of support, so they hid all day in a cave at the shore, called 'Papley's Hole' if I remember correctly. This could only be entered at low tide as the entrance was completely under water at other times, but the floor of the cave shelved upwards towards the inner end so that they were quite dry and well above high water level.

Though only ten years old, Ann set out bravely every night, when it was too dark for her to be seen by any watcher, to carry bread her mother had baked and the other food she had prepared, and to leave it at a pre-determined place, where they could get it when the tide was suitable for them to come and go unseen. Ann did her duty faithfully all the time the Press Gang was in the neighbourhood, sometimes with quaking heart and trembling limbs, especially when she had reason to believe she was being followed in the dark and might be accosted, but she never met or saw anyone during her midnight visits to the place.

This unnamed cave matches one at the head of a geo immediately west of the arch at Yinstay Head. The tide reaches the entrance at high water and a storm

---

1 p. 30. The booklet was produced in 1967 when she was eighty-seven.
2 Ann Flett, Miss Groundwater's grandmother.
3 Her great-grandfather.

Paplay's Hole, Tankerness, 1969.

beach partly masks the opening which stretches back some twenty yards with sufficient headroom to stand.

In *Descriptive Notes on Orkney*,[1] George MacGregor mentions a cave which may be the one of which Henrietta Groundwater had knowledge, and also a hiding place in the rocks where a man took refuge: '… at Yenstay Head, is a small cave called *The Hall*. Close to it is an open space in the rocks, into which a man,

1 p. 87.

View from interior of cave at Yinstay Head, Tankerness, 1969.

named Peter Taylor, from the farmyard of Langskaill (situated about a quarter of a mile from the cave), made his escape at one time from a pressgang. In hiding there he would have been safe, had not his uncle informed upon him.'

South Ronaldsay

Jocky Flett's Hole, near Ham geo in the south parish, takes its name from a man who was found hiding there by Donald Tomison,[1] the constable who pressed

[1] He lived at Halcro and was a brother of William Tomison, 1739–1829, a distinguished governor of the Hudson Bay Company, who founded and endowed Tomison's Academy, South Ronaldsay.

Kirkwall schoolchildren in The Twenty Men Hole, Eynhallow *c.*1970.
Opposite, perilous entry by plank.

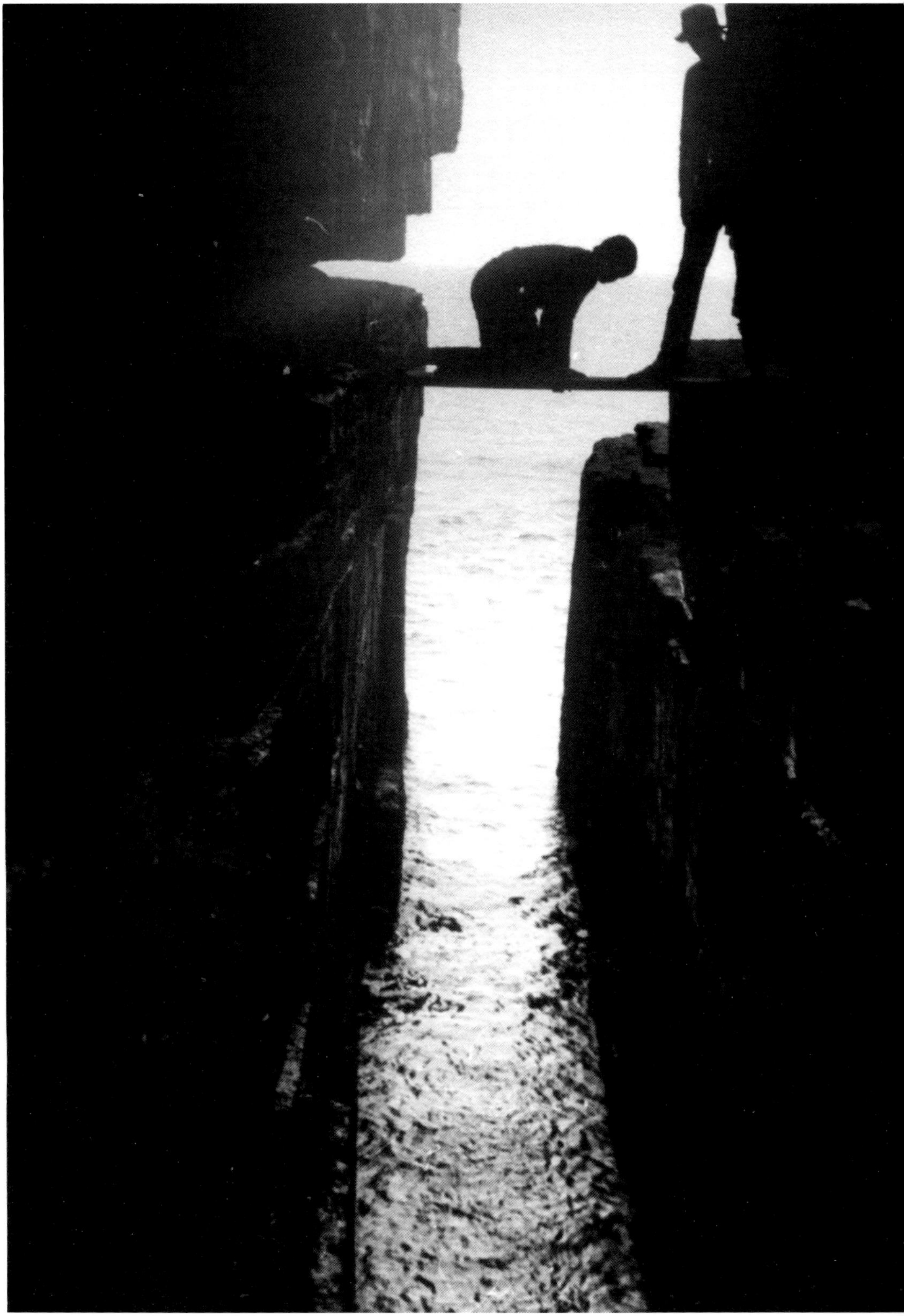

Nine Men Hole, Eynhallow.

Sweyn's Cave, Eynhallow. Susan and John Robertson with the Fereday family, August 1972.

John Mooney, the eminent Orcadian historian, held a different view. In *Eynhallow, The Holy Island of the Orkneys*, he suggests that Sweyn's cave was on Ellyar Holm, this cavern better matching the description in the Saga.[1]

Sandwick

The Constable Holes at the south side of Outshore point consist of three holes, the largest of which is about fifteen feet from the beach, with two small holes above, at an angle of some 45°, all apparently connected. The large hole recedes some fifteen feet, and provided reasonable, if cramped shelter for several men. *Rowland's Cave* in the Sandwick cliffs is named after a man who hid there.

Graemsay

A long slanting ridge of rock at the Point of Oxan has hollows or chambers weathered by wind and sea. In these Tom Goldie hid. He was betrayed by an ill-disposed neighbour, the press gang surrounded his hiding place, and after a gallant fight he was overpowered. Fatally injured in the struggle, he bled to death, and for years it was believed that the brownish red sediment on the rocks (still visible today) was soil stained with Goldie's blood. The place is known as *The Chammers[2] o Goldie*.

Holm

Three men hid in the old kirk of St Nicholas at Canniesile in the east end of the parish and had food brought to them by the beadle. His visits seemed innocent and in the course of normal church duties. The hiding place was revealed when David Spence, who bore a grudge against one of the fugitives, turned informer. Holm folk were so indignant that Spence had to leave the parish.

There is a cave called the *Hole o the Ness* at Roseness. From this recess a passage is said to lead its sunless way several hundred yards to the farmhouse of Cornquoy. The tale continues, that at the point where this route concludes, tongs rattling on the hearth of the flagstoned kitchen above could be heard. (A similar story, involving a cockerel, is told about The Hole o the Head, Orphir.)

Westray

There were two main hiding places. *The Money Box* at Aikerness could not be seen from the cliff above, and as the name implies the entrance was a narrow

---

1 p. 40.
2 Chambers.

slit in the rock. Fugitives climbed down to the recess which could hold five or six men.[1] The structure collapsed in 1982 during heavy seas. *The Gentlemen's Cave*[2] south of Noup Head is a commodious hiding place, used principally, if not solely, by North Isles Jacobite lairds in the summer of 1746, following the 1745 Rebellion. This sea cave is reached by descending a long sloping ledge.

There is also a cave at The Haa of Our Ness, to the north of the North Banks.

Costa

There is a hole in the cliff between Haafs Hellia[3] and Costa Head where men took refuge when pursued by constables. One constable more daring than the others was not deterred by height and dropped onto a ledge at the entrance to the cave. He was pushed and perished on the rocks below.

North Ronaldsay

Even its remoteness did not protect the island from impressment. Three fugitives hid on low-lying Green Skerry[4] to the north of the island, which can be reached only when the sea is calm, between half-ebb and half-flood tide. They concealed themselves on the seaward side of the skerry and remained in safety until one man indiscreetly raised his head and was seen by the search party then at a house called Sennes. With no means of escape, all were captured.

The Cellar o Himera Geo is a small cave at the west side which islanders might use, but only for a short time, since with a flood tide the recess is almost full. The rocky coastline is twenty feet high and there is no sign of a cave from above or from the sea. It is near high-water mark and a rocky outcrop masks the entrance.

In the south there is a house known locally as the Store House of Howar, which was used at one time to hold rents paid in kind. The building is now in ruins and the remains form part of the sea wall. When complete it was two-storied and pressed men were secured there pending transportation to Kirkwall. As a result of a press gang incursion John Muir, Sholtisquoy, Peter Turfus, Skelperha' and Thomas Tulloch, Garso, were held in the building and duly served in the navy. Muir was taken prisoner and died in a French gaol, Turfus was killed in a naval action, but Tulloch survived although he never returned. It was alleged that he

---

1 John Scott, Skaill, Westray personal communications 1979 and 1983. The information was obtained from William Rendall, Breck of Aikerness, Westray who was born in 1883.
2 Also known as *The Gentlemen's Ha'*.
3 Old Norse Hellir: a cave.
4 The skerry is joined to the island at low tide.

The Constable Holes, an inter-connected sequence of three caves, Sandwick, Orkney. *Opposite*, author at entrance to the largest cave, centre-foreground, 1975.

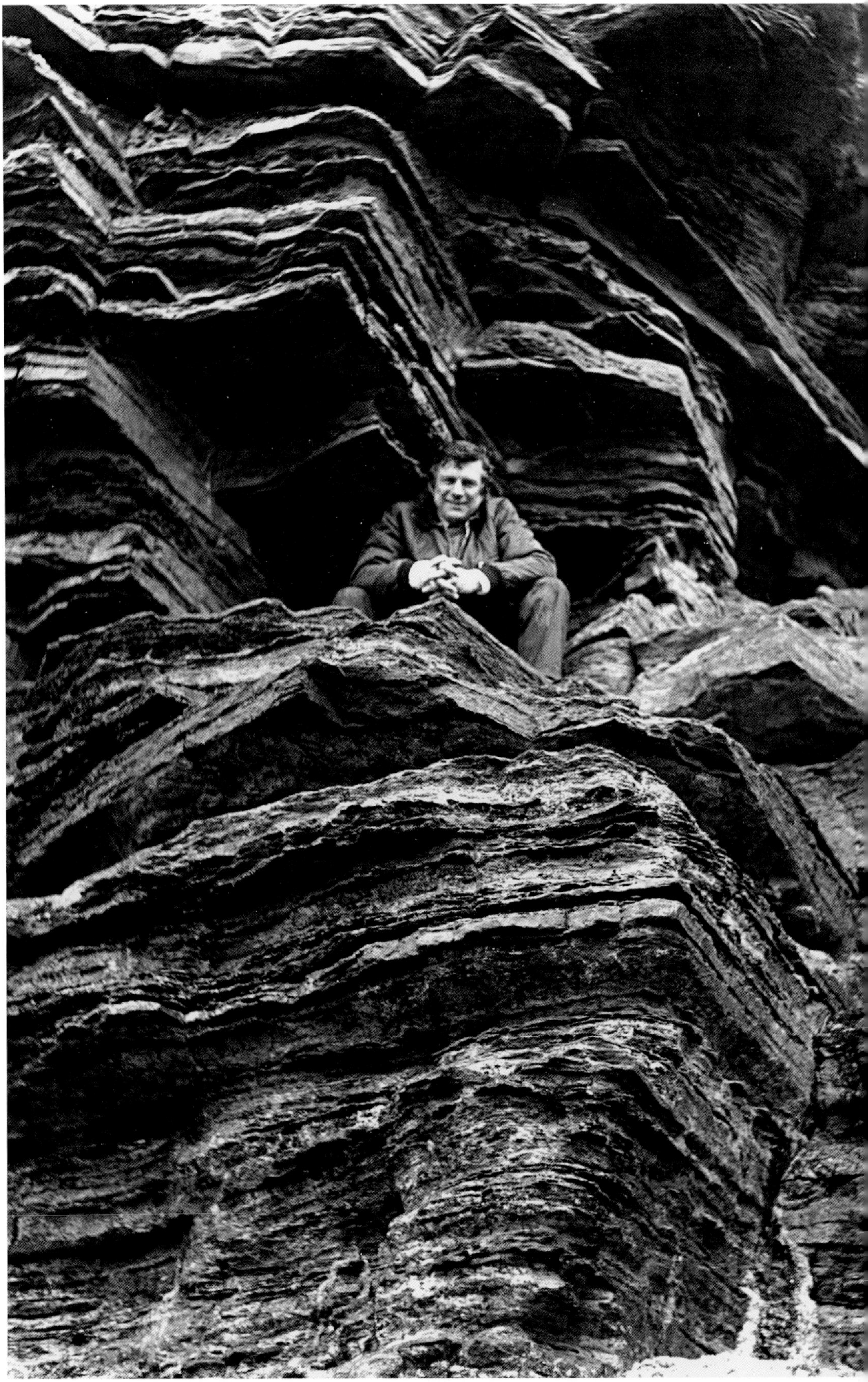

assaulted a brutal officer, deserted and quietly settled in Aberdeenshire where he became the married and prosperous Thomas Taylor.

South Walls

The Halls of Garth are two inter-connected caves a third of the way down a two hundred feet cliff at Garth Head, South Walls. The sole access is a narrow, steep track in a fissure leading to a ledge five feet wide. The smaller of the caves opens off this ledge. It is twelve to fifteen feet deep, five feet wide and six feet high, with an entrance oblong and narrow. The second cave is larger, opening off a lower ledge and is twenty feet deep, ten feet wide and six feet high. The caves, which could have held ten men, look directly south over the Pentland Firth.

Stronsay

The two caves used in Stronsay face Odin Bay. *Paets Hole*[1] near Cliva[2] is at the foot of a fifty-feet-high cliff and the entrance is well hidden by small boulders. It could take three or four men and only in an easterly gale would conditions inside be unpleasant. The other cave is midway on a cliff some sixty-feet high at the Vat of Kirbister.

The tradition in Stronsay regarding *Paets Hole* is that Patrick Fea, the owner of the farm of Airy, hid there. He was fed by Charles Goar, one of his farm servants, by whose efforts Fea successfully evaded impressment. Years later the grateful Fea family made a gift of land to the servant. By a joint will dated 21 July 1810 Helena and Barbara Fea, two of Patrick Fea's three daughters, bequeathed the farm of Hescombe to Goar. This testamentary provision was overtaken and anticipated by an *inter vivos* deed dated 17 October 1817 which conveyed ownership of the property specified in the will to Charles Goar, although reserving a life-rent. It is certainly unusual that no money passed, and the transaction may have been a gift in recognition of help given many years earlier to Patrick Fea.[3]

The disposition declares that Helena and Barbara Fea of Airy 'for the favour and regard which we have and bear to Charles Goar Tacksman[4] of Airy, and for sundry other good and onerous Causes and Considerations us hereunto moving, have Given, Granted and Disponed … All and Whole the Room and Lands of Hescome [sic] as the same are set in Tack to Charles Goar in Nebister, and presently occupied by Robert Miller, as also All and Whole the Corn Park

---

1 There is a hiding place on Skerries (S) called *Paeds Hoose*.
2 Known locally as Cliv.
3 Fea died sometime before October 1797.
4 Tenant.

Above, looking towards The Halls of Garth, South Walls, one third of the way down the cliff face, top left promontory.
Below, detail of the two caves, lower centre left.

adjoining thereto, and presently occupied by the Tenant of Airy as a part of that farm, with the whole houses Biggings, yards, parks pendicles privileges and pertinents of the same …'[1]

The spinsters did not enjoy a long life-rent: Helena died in November 1817, and Barbara departed two months later.

Caves in Shetland

Burra Isle

The *Covenanters*[2] *Cave* on the peninsula of Houss Ness, was an excellent hiding place. A Shetland lady[3] recalled that during World War I she visited the area, to the east of the Ward of Symbister, accompanied by her grandfather and others. Preparations were made to descend using stakes and ropes, but an alternative method was found of reaching the cave by sliding cautiously over the bank. Before proceeding it was decided that because of the dangerous descent the young girl should remain behind and she returned to the safety of her home. The party penetrated the cave by some six or seven yards and further progress was difficult as the opening narrowed significantly. The visitors came upon ash, which they believed was the remains of a century-old fire, and scattered around were bones and broken crockery.

Over a century earlier, women from Symbister had supplied those in hiding with baked bannocks, butter and eggs, cold meat and mutton. A creel filled with these items was lowered to the refugees, who might number as many as six. One fateful morning the gang decided to investigate. Fortunately, during the night thoughtful spiders had woven immaculate webs across the entrance and to the relief of the fugitives the pressing party assumed that the cave was empty.

Fetlar

As elsewhere, men hid in peat stacks or skrus,[4] and when required for longer periods caves were used, the entrances concealed with heather or old sails. Particularly thick brunies[5] were kept ready for an emergency departure when men had to hide. A recruiting party might approach the island in a vessel which

---

1 The document is in the possession of James D Cooper, Cleat, Stronsay.
2 Pronounced 'Coverentie' by Burra folk. Why it received its name is lost in folk memory.
3 Born in 1907.
4 Stacks of corn.
5 A thick scone or bannock made of flour or oatmeal.

The Covenanters Cave, Houss Ness, Burra Isle.

anchored in Basta Voe, Yell, and then cross to Fetlar by rowing boat, landing on Gruting beach.

There are several known hiding places of which *Da Kist a Muckle Birriers Geo* was probably the most secure, only a good climber being able to reach it, and then usually by rope. *Da Den a Crudel* near Strandabrough Ness is a large hollow above Crudels geo and not easily seen. The stones which formed two small crubs[1] in which men hid can still be seen. *Da Kist a Klonger* west of Funzie beach was another hiding place and several caves at the Head of Lambhoga were associated with press gang activity, including *Da Tieves Cave*.

Longie Geo with its overhanging ledge was a place where men frequently hid, and as there was no heather nearby, hallows[2] were used as bedding.

The hill of Stackaberg has several hiding places and was favoured by men from north and south Dale. Tresta men hid in a cave at Klifts, taking heather kows[3] for concealment and protection against the weather.

Muckle Roe

The promontory of Quilt Ness has a hiding place known as *Da Flegman's Hoose,*[4] completely hidden from the sea. In the mid-1940s the cave was still accessible to an agile climber, but part of the rock face has eroded and now ropes are required for entry. A local man's grandfather reached the cave in the 1920s where he came upon the ashes of an old fire.

Northmavine

In 1975 elderly residents recalled being told in their youth of a cave that had been discovered containing the remains of eating and cooking utensils. Alas, by then it's location had been forgotten.

Lunnasting

At Lunning Head there is a spacious, well-concealed cave with large, loose rocks scattered around the entrance. The inside is dry, and although access is difficult, a score of men could be accomodated.

Apart from local men using this cave, fugitives also came from Whalsay, Nesting and Delting. A press gang cutter was often active in Skerry Firth between Lunna Ness and Whalsay. When it was sighted, a visual warning signal was sent from the Ward of Clett in Whalsay to Kirk Ward in North Nesting, and also to Dragon Ness in Lunnasting. Men hid in the cave for long periods, and food was brought by a young girl herding cattle. Periodically she moved the cows to the vicinity of the hoidin holl, and left food and drink at a pre-arranged place.

The cave is entered by descending some four feet, and crawling through a short narrow passage which opens into a natural amphitheatre littered with

---

1 Sheep fold; a small enclosure.
2 Bundles of straw.
3 Tufted stems of heather.
4 The fugitive's house or home. Fleg: to frighten away, to flee.

Da Flegman's Hoose, Quilt Ness, Muckle Roe,
being scrutinised by Bruce Sandison.

boulders. The area, which is about ten-feet high and commodious, leads to a wall, beyond which there is an even larger space.

In former times children in the locality were warned by parents to avoid this dangerous area. A badly behaved child might be threatened with banishment to the Lunning Head hoidin holl.

Yell

At Whale Geo on the north coast a natural cavity was enlarged by quarrying rock from the cliff face, so creating *Da Press Holl*. Entry was by gradual descent over banks and dangerously along a narrow ledge above a sheer drop of a hundred feet. Men from the districts of Midbrake, Breckin and Houlland hid there, to a maximum of twelve, and in the early 1920s my informant – then a boy – several times entered the recess, now much eroded. A number of other unnamed holes, fissures and caves in the Bugarth/Whale Geo banks, three miles north of Westsandwick, were used.

There is a quaint tale of a hiding place discovered at Arisdale by a crofter searching for sheep during the great snow storm of 1917. Coming upon a ewe lying in a deep hole he descended and made a cursory examination, during which he found a heavy, rough tumbler. Later, to satisfy curiosity, he returned and closely investigated the hole, which was an underground cavern created sufficiently large to accommodate eight men. This chamber had been cut from the banks of a burn which flowed under the turf and heather. The crofter also found a brooch of thick polished glass on the front of which was carved a bunch of daisies tied with a true-love knot. It seemed to the story-teller that the tumbler had been used by fugitives and one of them had carried his sweetheart's brooch to sustain him as he hid, lonely, through cold, Shetland nights.

Bressay

A cavern on the west coast of The Bard, which is the most southerly promontory on the island, is known as the *Orkneyman's Cave* or *The Cave of The Bard*. There is a legend that a native of Orkney, closely pursued by the gang, hid in the recesses of this cavern. He had escaped from his pursuers by taking a small skiff from a Lerwick boat noust. In strong wind and dangerous conditions he managed to enter the cave, but the gang did not dare follow because of the turbulent sea. It comprises two caves and just inside the inner cave, on the right, are two accessible shelves of rock where an agile man could scramble ashore and remain safe from the rising waters. The Orkney man found safety on them until the danger passed, surviving as best he could. The story continues that his boat was smashed by the sea, leaving him stranded and later he was rescued by Bressay men who also used the cave. Its main advantage was that, once inside and on a ledge, fugitives would be invisible, even if a naval whaler entered to look for them. The entrance to the inner cave is only three metres wide at sea level.

The modern name, the Orkneyman's Cave, was noted by the Ordnance Survey in the 1970s and appears to be based on an earlier mistranslation. In 1883 Tudor[1] wrote that the Orkneyman's Cave owed its name to an Orcadian having hidden there from the press gang. But there are other opinions. According to Tudor, Sir Walter Scott, who visited Shetland in 1814, said that the cave was known as the Orkneyman's Harbour, as an Orcadian vessel had put in to avoid a French privateer. A more likely theory is that seals frequented this cave, known originally as Orknis Geo or Orkns geo – Old Norse *orkn*, a large type of seal,[2] hence the seeming link with Orkney. Bressay men who hid there had their risk of impressment heightened by the proximity of Lerwick's resident press gang, and by the island being adjacent to the main naval anchorage in Shetland.

There are several places on the east coast in which men took refuge such as the *Hellier Hol* and the *Hol of Bugars*. At the inner end of the former the opening is just wide enough to permit the entry of a Shetland four-oared skiff. Another unnamed cave was used by James Lamb, who lived at The Veng. He jumped from a cliff and landed safely on a ledge which led to a cave at Hoevdi Skord on the east side of The Bard. There he hid while the search party, looking down at his cap floating on the sea, concluded he had drowned. (Lamb's exploit is described more fully on page 100.)

To the north of Grutwick is Mirki Geo, used by men living on neighbouring crofts. They were sustained with food lowered by women ostensibly milking cows in nearby fields. At the croft of Wadbister, near Gorie, men crawled into the remains of a pre-historic underground dwelling, known as *Da Fairies Hoose* or *Da Picts Hoose*. The passage was originally some fifteen yards long, but in 1865 a length was removed to provide better access to the croft, and now six yards of tunnel lead to a stone-built circular chamber six feet across and three-and-a-half-feet high. In 1979 my informant crawled into this recess and took photographs. The chamber wall has an attractive worked oval stone built in on its side.

---

1 John R Tudor, *The Orkneys and Shetland*, 1883, p 458
2 Hugh Marwick, *Orkney Farm Names*, 1952, p. 57. Erkny (North Ronaldsay) and arkmae (Sanday). Also Jakobsen, *The Place-names of Shetland*, 1936, p. 147.

In addition to the Orkneyman's Cave on Bressay, Jakobsen mentions the Orkneyman's Stane or Skerri on Mousa. The Shetland tradition about these places is that Orkneymen were drowned or had perished there. He states that this stems from a popular attempt to explain the names of places which must be derived from ON orkn, a kind of seal. See also 'The Debunking of the Orkneyman's Cave' in *The Shetland News*, 26 May 1960. The article was by E S Reid Tait. Tait agrees with Jakobsen and he also mentions the Orkneyman's Geo, the Orkneyman's Baa and the Orkneyman's Saand.

The Orkneyman's Cave, or The Cave of The Bard, Bressay.

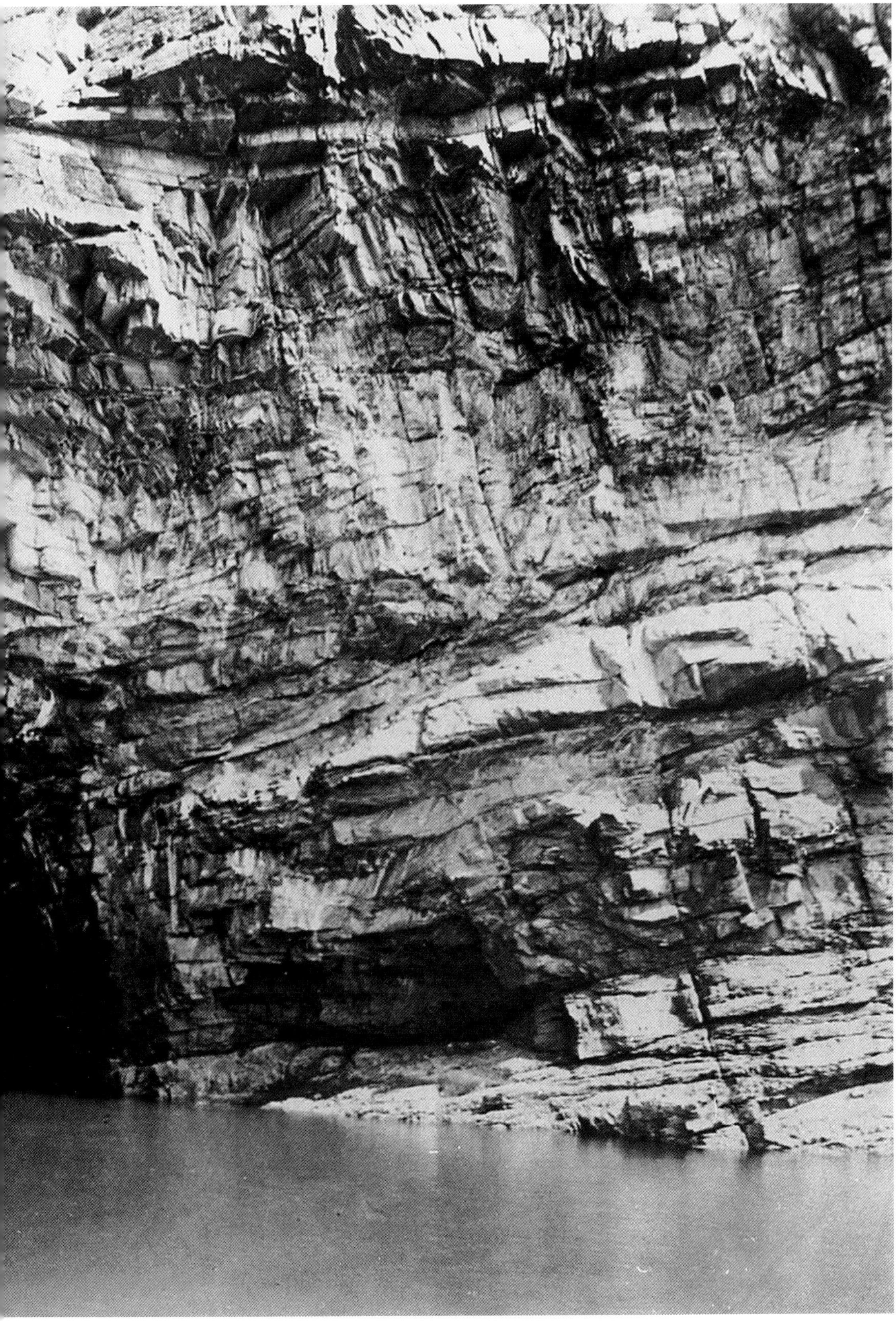

Entrance to Da Fairies Hoose, also known as Da Picts Hoose, Wadbister, Bressay. This and the interior picture below were taken in 1979 by my courteous and helpful informant, Tammie Laurenceson.

Interior of Da Fairies Hoose. Note the worked oval stone built in on its side.

Skerries

Da Paeds Hoose[1] is a large cave at Myoness on the south east end of West Isle. Access is over a grass bank and steep rocks and along a narrow ledge some three feet wide with a sheer drop of seventy feet to the sea. There is a narrow entrance passage some ten feet long into this underground cavern which can accommodate twenty men.

One day a press cutter was sighted and all the island's men hid in this cave. The landing party found only women and asked why so many fishing rods seemed to have no owners. They were told that the men were working at the far haaf[2] with lines, and the rods were used by the womenfolk for inshore fishing.

The positioning of a white cow tethered where it could be seen from the cave was the prearranged signal to those in hiding that they could safely emerge.

In *The History and Description of the Shetland Islands*, written in 1838, the Rev James Catton, for three years a Wesleyan missionary in Shetland, mentioned this cave and exaggerated its size: 'At the south end of the middle Island, there is a remarkable cave, that is said will contain a hundred men, and yet only one can enter at once; in which, men have at times, concealed themselves from the press gang.'[3]

Da Paeds Hoose, Myoness, West Isle, Skerries, end of ledge mid centre.

1 The Picts House. It should be noted that there is a *Paeds Hole* on the island of Stronsay.
2 The open sea thirty to forty miles offshore.
3 pp. 58–9. The book was withdrawn by the author shortly after publication due, perhaps somewhat unfairly, to the adverse criticism that it contained many errors.

Tammy Tyrie's Hidey Holl, West Isle, Skerries.

A small stone dyke built near the cliffs on the south side of the island is known as *Annie Elspeth's Rest*. This is reputed to have been used for shelter by an eponymous lady when carrying food to men hiding in Da Paeds Hoose.

Tammie Tyrie's Hidey Holl is on the east coast at Queyin Ness, West Isle. The name Tyrie appears in various locations in both Orkney and Shetland, e.g. Tammy Towie, who was the sole survivor of a shipwreck in Birsay and after whom a rock on the north side of that parish is named.

Fair Isle

Two of the island's many caves are particularly associated with impressment. The upper and lower *Tiefs Holls*[1] are in a 500-feet-high cliff in the south west

1 Thieves Holes.

near Malcolms Head, and *Da Holl o da Gowans* is in a cliff at Vaasetter near the Sheep Craig.

In July 1785 Prince William Henry, Duke of Clarence, later King William IV, during a summer cruise round Great Britain, visited Kirkwall and later called at Fair Isle. When the frigate *Hebe* hove-to the prince waded ashore to shoot wildfowl and the visitors are said to have remarked that the population seemed to consist only of women, children and old men. The approach of the vessel had sent all the young men into hiding.

Sir Water Scott came to Orkney and Shetland in 1814 as a guest of the Northern Lights Commissioners. On his way to Shetland he called at Fair Isle, of which he wrote: 'One lad told me only five persons had left the island since his remembrance, and of these three were pressed for the navy.'

Skeld

The bay of Silwick has a cave known as *Da Heylor a Jonaberg*, used only in good weather and accessible by small boat which has to skirt a sunken rock at the entrance. One summer it sheltered six men for six weeks until the weather broke, and throughout this time food hidden in shawls was carried by wives to a cache on the nearby hill. Cattle were moved to graze in the area so that milk was available. The fugitives were Magnus Arthurson, William Ridland, Robert Manson, Hackie Moncrieff, a man Thomson from the district of Silwick and Robbie Ridland from Scarvister who was captured subsequently and lost a leg in action.

Whalsay

There were four known hiding places. *Da Holl a Eastermuir* near Houll loch, and *Da Holl a Sneugans* in the hillside, both of which are now partly eroded. *Da Holl a Leeans*, also in the hillside, is not much more than a hollow and an old man who lived at Vevoe recalled crawling into it in 1910 when he was a boy of thirteen. In 1980 he described it as a tunnel the length of which he could not remember. He did recall that the entrance had been concealed as the area was covered in long heather. *Da Hidey Holl* at Skaw Taing is in the cliffs on the north side of the island. Twenty feet above sea level, it could be entered by crawling through a narrow passage which opened into a chamber sufficient for eight seated men. This chamber was blocked by a great gale in February 1900.

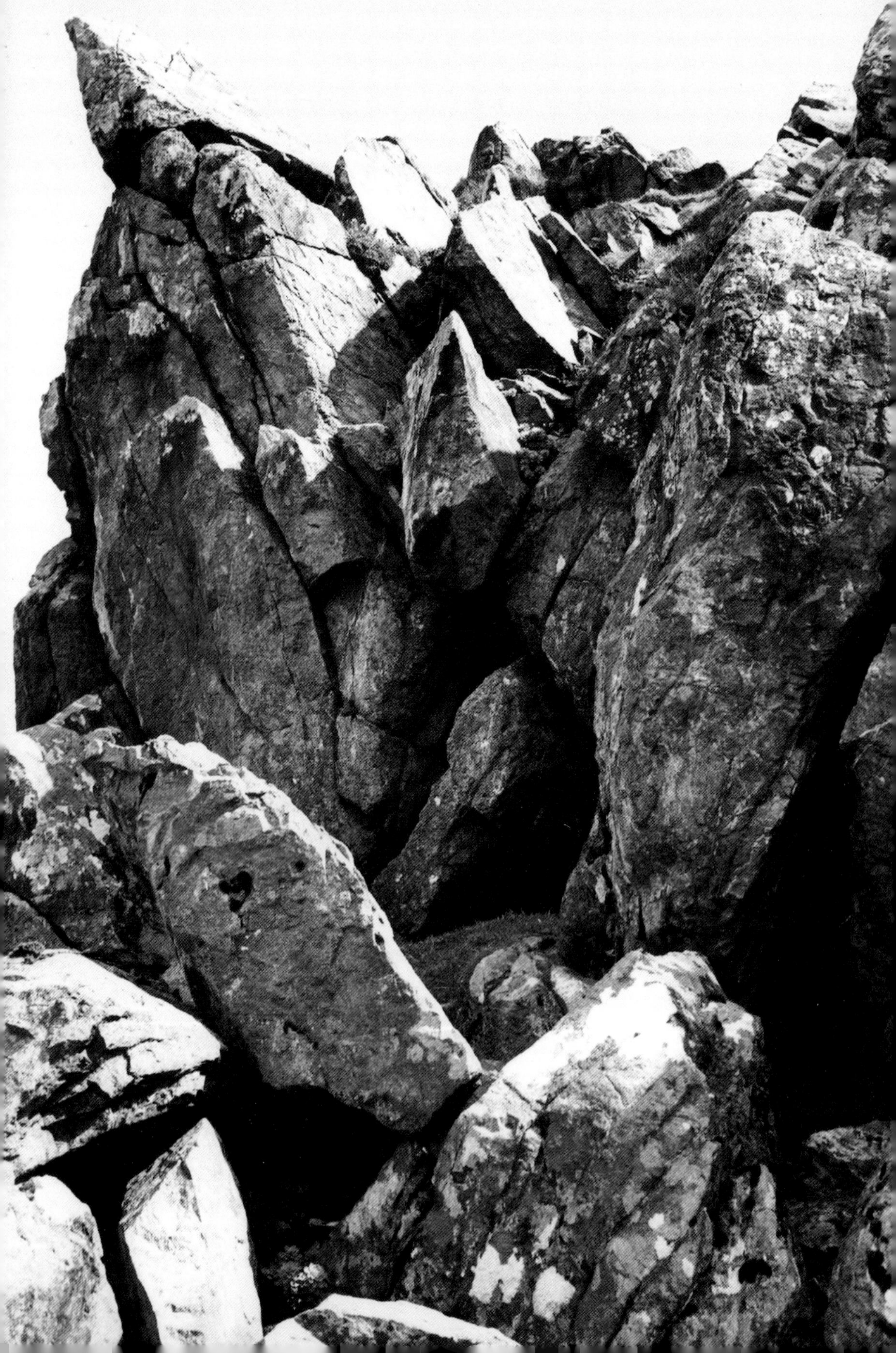

Opposite, Da Hoose a Heylor, Mavis Grind, Delting, with detail of entrance above, 1974.

Da Hidey Holl, Skaw Taing, Whalsay, with detail of entrance opposite, 1983.
Alec Hutchison in fair isle jumper and Peter Hughson looking out.

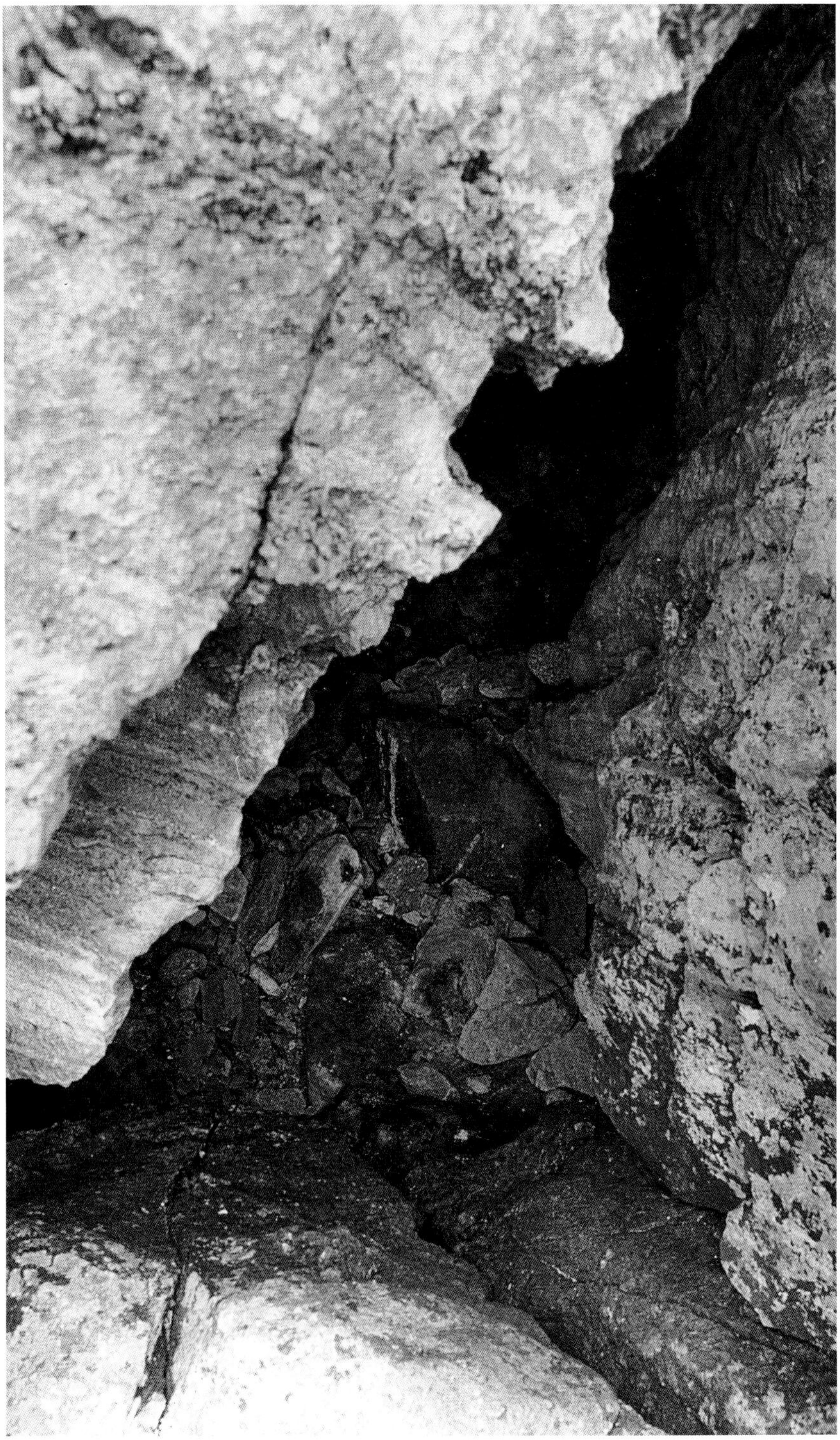

Delting

A cave at Mavis Grind is entered by a small hole, and there are two steps before access is gained to a large cave which could hold six men. It is known as *Da Hoose a Heylor*.

Foula

Two men on the run came from the mainland of Shetland and hid in a cave located on the Noup in the south of the island, only venturing forth at night to kill a sheep or steal fish hanging out to dry. They had a peat fire, and slept during the day, after they had cummelled[1] their muckle kettle[2] and doused the embers. One morning, the fire was carelessly left to smoulder. Fishermen in the vicinity saw the smoke and dismayed by the thieving, captured them. They were securely bound, but when the Foula men departed each day to fish women freed the captives, conditional on obtaining assistance in the daily work, retying the ropes before their men returned. At the first opportunity the fugitives were taken back to the mainland and to naval service. They were known as *Da Tieves a da Noup* and their hiding place *Da Tieves Holl*.

Eshaness

A large cave at Fury Geo is also known as *Da Thieves Holl*. It is hidden from above and accessible by descent on ropes or landing by boat and climbing from the foot of the cliff. Another hiding place was the *Barn of Scradda*, near the Holes of Scradda and close to the Eshaness lighthouse.

Weisdale

In Stromfirth valley[3] men hid in holes known as *Da War Hooses*. These were north of Gillaburn and consisted of cavities surrounded by rocks and camouflaged with long heather. On the top of a steep hill called *Da Face a Door* stood *Da Watch Toor* from which men kept a lookout for the approach of the gang.

Papa Stour

There are two caves known to have been used: *Da Hoose o Hirdie Geo* and *Da Hoose o Sholmack*. These hoidin-holls are in the west and north cliffs,

---

1 Turned upside down.
2 Large cooking pot.
3 Known locally as *The Valley of Dry Bones*.

respectively, and are located among boulders which have fallen from the rock face. Both contain peat ash which suggests that fugitives stayed for a period of time, and long enough to light a fire for warmth and cooking.

Trondra

Men hid on the Green Holm and other small islands which lie to the west of Scalloway. A favourite location was North Havra where they found refuge in *Da Doos Holl*.[1]

James Irvine lived at East Houll,[2] near the East Voe of Scalloway, and because of his importance as a proprietor, he was known throughout the community as 'The Laird of Houll'. He always knew when the gang planned to raid Trondra, and on being alerted he hurried to the shore and shouted across the water, 'Da press geng's coman'. The island men immediately took to the sea and rowed to safety.

Dunrossness

There are hiding places in Huepool near Spiggie, and at Ramnibanks a cave called *Da Un* was used. It was in this cave that the Goudie brothers from Clumlie hid.

Sandsting

A cave at Glisigeo was occupied from time to time by Sinclair Thomson, who became the first Baptist minister in Shetland.

Bigton

Two pillars of rock in this district are known as the *Burgi Stacks*. At the base of the larger of the two is a cave used by fugitives.

Uyea

An unusual hiding place is the *Kettlebaak*,[3] a cave at the north west corner. It takes its name from a broad beam of rock stretching just under the roof and high above the water, on the top of which men fleeing from the gang found security.

---

1 The Doves Cave.
2 Now known as *Easterhoull*.
3 A 'baak' is a bar above an open fire on which cooking implements were hung from krooks (hooks).

Unst

There is a hoiden-holl at Kidgeo, Muness. Another hole which might have attracted fugitives is described by Jessie M E Saxby in *Shetland Traditional Lore – Hadds and Hoiden-Holls:*

There was a gruesome Hoiden-holl on the summit of Vaalafiel, a short way from the track leading from Baltasound to the Westing. Its opening is on a level bit of the hill, and there was nothing to mark its dark mouth which was not conspicuous, being surrounded by long grass.

About two hundred years ago some enterprising strangers went down into that darksome pit. They were lowered by ropes. They found themselves in a large hole which had evidently been occupied at some period long gone by. There were ashes, scraps of wood and stones, also a few bones, but it was never stated whether these were human or not. There was nothing to tell who had occupied it. One can only conjecture that the hole was used by some persons hiding from foes, or by the peerie hill-men of prehistoric times.

Women and the Press Gang

There are many examples of women assisting their husbands, sons, brothers and sweethearts to resist and to frustrate the gang. Sometimes lachrymose, nevetheless their response to intrusion was usually one of smouldering resentment and seldom muted. They remonstrated with, harassed and on occasion assailed members of the gang, and the length to which women would go to assist their menfolk was remarkable. This chapter gives instances, some based on traditional stories.[1]

Guile

Merran Moad,[2] an Orcadian married to Anderson from Shetland, lived in Charlotte Lane, Lerwick, where for many years she spun hemp twine used in net making. One night, without warning, the gang made a violent entry to take her husband. Merran temporized, her comportment immaculate. Docile and respectful, she politely offered refreshments: 'da poor men wid shurly be tired an tristy[3] efter dir haard day's wark rinnin aboot da place. Wid dey no hae a coarn[4] o ale an a bannock?'[5] The intruders became tipsy, giving Merran the opportunity to slip away unobserved and assist her husband's escape through a back skylight.

The quick-wittedness of a Shetland woman foiled the gang. At the croft house of Bjurg at Kneefell Ness, Muckle Roe, a woman busied herself with the evening meal. This was a traditional dish of fish and potatoes, simmering in a large pot hung over an open central fire. Smoke eddied through the lum[6] while the men folk, waiting to eat, relaxed in the small dim room. The gang broke in, whereupon the woman overturned the pot's contents onto the smouldering

---

1 See Tales of the Press Gang, p. 255, from *A Peculiar People and Other Orkney Tales* by J T Smith Leask. This has a number of references to women helping men to avoid capture.
2 Probably Marion Mouat or Mowat.
3 Thirsty.
4 Small quantity.
5 *Lerwick During the Last Half Century*, pp. 183–4.
6 An opening on the roof ridge.

peat and driftwood. A thick cloud of ash, dust and steam arose, in which it was impossible to distinguish friend from foe. The gang retreated doorwards, and waited for the air to clear, while the Muckle Roe men took advantage of the confusion to escape through the lum.

Christina Scott from Quoycrow,[1] Sandwick, also moved quickly to help with the escape of two servants from Housbie, Beaquoyside, Birsay. In their flight on horseback the lads were pursued by two Birsay constables – George Mowat, Overabist, and a man who went by the name of 'Ingsa' from the district of Abune-the-Hill. At Quoycrow, Christina removed wooden bars which were positioned across the path at her house and allowed the youths to continue their flight, swiftly replacing them to delay the constables. Unhindered, the lads rode through the district of Tenston, past the Standing Stones of Stenness and found refuge in the hills beyond.

A formidable woman called Tytler[2] hid several young men under her box bed at the croft of Shore, Rackwick. Known as 'the queen of Rackwick' she had a considerable presence and men on the run felt reasonably safe in her cottage.

A gruesome scene was enacted by a Westray woman to frighten a constable who was seeking her husband. The woman placed a sheep's head on a smouldering peat fire. When the constable entered the primitive kitchen and asked if there was a man in the house, she pointed ominously at the grisly remains. Flanked by jaw bones, the grinning skull lay hideous in the half-light, while pungent smoke eddied from the matted strands of burning wool. The woman railed at the constable, filling the air with invective and threatened him with a similar fate. Not unnaturally he took fright and fled.

Fear of smallpox was used by a woman in a ruse to save her sons. In the late eighteenth century a strange ship dropped anchor in Widewall Bay, South Ronaldsay and a recruiting party landed to make up crew numbers thinned by sickness and death in battle. Ann Louttit lived with her family at Midtown, Herston. She watched the party come ashore and, as they approached, hid her sons under the bedsack. When the sailors entered they found her in mourning dress, intoning 'plague be here, plague be here'[3] while aimlessly tossing feathers

---

1 Now a double-storey stone house on the Sandwick road near Dounby and pronounced locally *Wheekeroo*.
2 Possibly Tyler. Jack Rendall, Rackwick, Hoy, personal communication 1974, who confirmed the story about Mrs Tytler with his aunt Miss Thomasina Thomson, then aged 86.
3 Smallpox periodically ravaged the islands.

The Liberty of the Subject. Women opposing the Press Gang, 1779. © National Maritime Museum.

in the air. Such strange behaviour allied to the threat of smallpox so shocked and frightened the men that they retreated to the ship. Believing Ann to be a witch they fired cannonballs through her thatched roof as the vessel sailed away.

In Unst, at the croft of Vealie, near Norwick, a man called Stickle[1] was on the run. The story goes: 'He cam til a toon whaur da folk wir wirkin i'da voar rig.[2] Dey wir young weeman dere. Dey got him ta lay himsel doon inta da furr,[3] dan da lasses delled him in.[4] Whan da man-a-warr 's men cam rinnin up dey fan[5] nane dere bit da weeman trang[6] at dir dellin. Dey wir nae sign a da man ava. Whan dey gud awa, da man got up oot a da muld,[7] an da lasses took him ta da hoose whaur dey gae him maet.[8] Dat wis da wye he escapit fae da press geng.'

When threatened, Shetland men might also hide in desses of hay or skroos of corn.[9] In Orkney a Westray man Rendall from Halbreck was hotly pursued and he found safety under a mass of ware[10] being spread on the fields by women.

Grizel Thomason lived with her husband Magnus and their five children at a croft on the island of Uyea, to the south of Unst. Returning from fishing one evening, the presence of a warship forced several men to hide. Taking sustenance to the fugitives was made impossible as the gang set a strict watch. Women on the move suffered the indignity of being closely searched and any secreted provisions were confiscated. This brought about the surrender of several hungry

1 Fredamann Christopher Stickle from Upper Saxony is said to have jumped ship at Baltasound, Unst, and there, shortly after 1766, he married a widow at the farm of Cliff. His grandson Fredamann (Freddie) was born in 1794 and he became a famous Shetland fiddler and composer of folk music. A number of his compositions survive in Shetland, as does the name Stickle. Another version of the story is that the original Stickle was shipwrecked on Unst, where he was cast ashore clinging to a spar and clutching his fiddle.

   Yet another version is that Christopher Fredamann Von Stiegel jumped ship at Burrafirth in 1743. He married a Henderson from Pettister in Unst and his son Fredamann Stickle became a fiddler of note and was the composer of the popular melody Air From Unst.
2 Spring land.
3 Furrow.
4 Covered him with earth.
5 Found.
6 Busy.
7 Top soil.
8 Food.
9 Stacks of hay or corn.
10 Ware (0) or Waar (S): The large broad-leaved seaweed which grows under water. It was then, and for many years subsequently, widely used as manure – 'the very backbone of the old husbandry.' In 1793 the parish minister of Westray the Rev James Izat wrote: 'The only manure here is sea-weed or ware, with the help of what house-dung they can produce.' When men were in hiding or absent at the fishing, carrying ware and much other heavy work on the croft had to be undertaken by women.

men. But food and drink was never found on Grizel. It is said that for two weeks, until the gang departed, she sustained Magnus with her own milk, while her recently born fifth child was fed by a cow.

Strength and Determination

Women were often raucous and sometimes aggressive when confronting the gang. In the part of Yell known as The Herra[1] lived a family renowned for physical strength.[2] Consequently the men were much sought after for naval service. Arriving at the croft house one morning a recruiting party came upon the mother outside washing clothes. They demanded to know the whereabouts of her sons and attempted to force their way into the house. But strength was not confined to the male line. The bold matron, inveighing against the intruders, laid hands on their leader, upended him and 'dookit' his head in the tub full of hot water and washing soda.[3]

Another powerful Shetland woman, Porteous by name, lived at Colloquey, Ollaberry, with her foster son Arthur or 'Yarta', to whom she was devoted. She was in the hill cutting peats when the gang seized the youth, securing him in an outhouse while they sought more recruits. On her return she was furious, but concealing her wrath asked to be allowed a farewell embrace. The request was granted although as a precaution two of the gang accompanied her to the outhouse and secured Yarta while she consoled him. The woman lamented and feigned to put her arms round the lad's neck, but instead took both guards by the throat. Squeezing relentlessly she shouted, 'Run, Yarta, run.' This he did and escaped.[4]

On the island of Swona, the brothers Allan – Stewart, John, William and James – were sought by the press gang and despite their mother Catherine attacking the party with a large baton, the men were pressed and taken to Kirkwall. John, advanced by merit to the rank of Captain, was taken prisoner and died in France.

---

1 At Whalefirth Voe.
2 The name of the family was either Smollet or Spence.
3 There is not a fund of press gang stories in Yell, and most of what does exist are fragments. The reason is probably the 1881 fishing disaster which eliminated much earlier lore. The references to impressment which do exist are mainly to be found in South Yell where the impact of the tragedy was less.
4 J Ratter, Kingland, Ollaberry personal communication 1981. The story regarding Mrs Porteous appeared in *The Shetland News* of 23 December 1948 under the heading 'Da Helly Rod – A Powerful Woman'.

Using the ruse of signalling for a pilot, a large vessel hove-to off the Moul Head, Deerness, and its cutter lying on the offside tried to capture four fishermen who had rowed out to offer their services. The Deerness men quickly put about and, closely pursued, made a landing west of Newark Bay, to take refuge in a cave with which they were familiar. Watching anxiously from the cliffs, Barbara Wick,[1] the sweetheart of one of the men, effectively halted the gang with a shower of stones as the fishermen scrambled to safety. Alas, the girl's lover duly married another woman, and his faithlessness so upset his one-time sweetheart and saviour that in her distressed mind she linked the national enemy Bonaparte with her misfortune. Henceforward, desolate and dependent on Deerness folk for food and shelter, she wandered about the parish, shouting occasionally in insane terror: 'Bony's coman, Bony's coman, wae a hunder an fifty black men. He'll cut ane's throat an drink his bleud; hid'll need nae boilan, nae boilan!'

Sunday, sacred day as it was regarded, gave no protection and, as he left the Orphir church, Peter Tait, Howar, Clestrain, was seized by a constable, John Bews. The women of the congregation were angry and rushed to his aid, calling down imprecations on the constable's head. During the melée they cursed impressment in all its wretched aspects. Their intervention was as unexpected as it was dramatically violent and in the general commotion Tait escaped.

When determined constables forced their way into a Kirkwall wedding ceremony, the women present displayed such fury at this unseemly interruption of a special occasion that the intruders retreated. However, the resistance of women was not always so successful. There is a poignant tale about a newly married couple, recorded in *The Shetland Times* of 20 February 1892. Signed 'A Lerwegian', it was written by a person who had witnessed the incident seventy-seven years earlier. The letter is given as an example of ruthless impressment in Shetland, although in this case the bridegroom regained his freedom:

Perhaps a short account of the last of the pressgang days in Shetland would be found interesting to most of your readers. I was an eye-witness of the following incident, which happened in Lerwick one day towards the end of 1815.[2]

On my way to school one morning, in passing the house which stood at the foot of the lane leading up to Fort Charlotte, and which was then occupied by Mr Robert Henry, I noticed a group of men and women gathered together. There were about half-a-dozen men and three women, and while the men were gesticulating and apparently quarrelling,

---

1 In her efforts she was assisted by another young woman, Barbara Dinnie.
2 As Napoleon was finally defeated in mid-1815, the year given is inaccurate. Nevertheless, impressment was legally permissible well into the nineteenth century.

the women were crying. I stopped and on enquiring the cause of this strange occurrence, was informed that it was the press-gang at work. It seemed that a war vessel had come into Bressay Sound that morning, and the commander noticing a boat crossing from Bressay to Lerwick with two men and three women aboard, had ordered a boat's crew from his ship to go on shore, press the men and bring them on board; and they were engaged carrying out their orders when I came on the scene. It was explained to the officer in charge of the pressing party that the two men were a bridegroom and his grooms man, and the women a bride and two bride's maids. Tears and entreaties were alike in vain, however, his instructions were to press the men, and he must perform his duty. As a last resource the females of the party approached the wife of the commander of the Fort [Charlotte], and they succeeded in rousing her sympathy in their cause. She at once made intercession on their behalf, applying to the Commander of the war brig for the release of the pressed men. Although he could not see his way to give up both the men, he allowed the bridegroom to regain his liberty, but he kept the other man, and sailed away with him on board.

Sandwick women could be particularly belligerent and one of them, while assisting a young man to escape, attacked a constable with a shearing hook and wounded him. Other Sandwick women wielding ware picks[1] are alleged to have attacked a pressing party which was threatening their husbands.

The stories about the attacks in Sandwick are probably an echo of the disturbance which actually took place there on 3 October 1812. The following day William Watt, Skaill, principal landowner in the district, wrote to John Mitchell, Writer in Kirkwall, regarding the Skaill proportion of the thousand guineas bounty money levied on the county. In his letter Watt also commented on what must have been a formidable display of female fury:

I have been most unfortunate in my endeavours to get men for this parish. Yesterday I sent a party of Constables and after getting a serjeant and ten men from Captn McNeil they were so opposed by a mob of women that they made nothing of it. If these women are not punishable and immediately punished for what they did it will be in vain for me to make another attempt as I have got two of my servants hurt and one of the Constables was knocked down by a stone. The Crop is perishing upon the ground and something should be done immediately to remove the alarm that people may return to the necessary work of the season.[2]

This was harvest time and the impressment of servants would have been particularly unpopular.

1 This implement, used in winter for dragging seaweed from the sea, resembled a strong hay fork and had two prongs set rake fashion at right angles to the shaft.
2 Orkney Archives, Taylor Papers D9/10.

A few days later there was a related incident in Sandwick, again involving women, when several constables were attacked. Hary Crukshank [sic], Stromness, wrote to William Watt on 7 October:

'I am truly sorry to inform you that Davd Kirknes Mags Garson George Marwick and John Spence are all desperately [sic] wounded, they say, by the family of George Irvine of Brackness, for attempting to impress one of his servants, your presence will be needfull as soon as possible. Kirkness, had a Corn hook stuck in his belly, but Jaffray thinks it will not be mortall.'[1]

The sequel was a letter on 20 October from the Regulating Officer, Captain Gourly, to William Watt:

I have just rec[d] yours of this date I shall do every thing in my power to prosecute the persons who have wounded the Constables. I mean to apply to the Sheriff and the Committee respecting this abominable outrage – With regard to my giving any of the Men now in my possession for your Parish I am sorry to say it is out of my power … continue the labours of the harvest peaceably and perhaps something effectual will be done to relief [sic] your parish in the course of a few days.[2]

What happened to the women involved in these affrays is not known.

Clemmie o Huxter, a redoubtable Shetland woman endowed with an amplitude of frame could 'maa girse an cast paets'[3] to match any man. Belligerent by nature, and with independent views pungently expressed, she could be a formidable adversary. It was certainly not her intention that anything untoward should happen to her brothers and nephews and on one occasion, alone, she defied the gang. One of the Johnston family, Clemmie lived at Weisdale, where for months her men were pursued relentlessly, but had found safety in the lang kames.[4] Finally, furtive and starving, they made their way home. Approaching the house they became aware that the gang was in pursuit, so they ran to the nearest eela boat[5] with the intention of rowing to the Voe of Weisdale, where they could land on either side or make for the isles. Clemmie helped to launch the boat. As soon as it was afloat she moved swiftly to the next noust, removed the nile[6] of the remaining boat 'an balled[7] it i'pa da sea.' This done she took 'aa

1 Apparently, Watt had asked that some of the men already pressed and under the control of Captain Gourly should be credited to the parish of Sandwick.
2 Orkney Archives, Watt Papers D3/358.
3 Mow grass and cut peats.
4 The collective name for the series of hills between Tingwall and Delting.
5 An inshore fishing boat. 'Going to the eela' – inshore fly fishing for sillocks.
6 A plug that fits into a hole where bilge is run off.
7 Threw.

da oars an cabes[1] an balled dem i'pa da sea.' Finally, as the officer advanced she stood her ground, aggressive and abusive, brandishing a helm and defying him to pass.

Sentinels

The efforts and resolution of women had varied success. Frequently they acted as sentinels when their men were working. In Evie a young man cut peats while his sweetheart took up a warning position on a nearby hill. For hours she was vigilant then left her post for a short time to bring food. On returning she was aghast to find that in her absence the constables had closed in and captured the man she was safeguarding.

The plea of another Orcadian woman on behalf of her nephew succeeded only in forcing her husband to withdraw from the pressing party. One morning the South Ronaldsay constables, on a recruiting drive, assembled at the house of their leader Donald Tomison, Halcro. His wife asked who was to be taken and her husband confided that they sought her nephew, a lad Rosie who worked on a neighbouring farm. Pointing a minatory finger at him, her uncompromising reply was 'Donald Tomison, that young lad's father is dead and his only living relative is his mother. I swear by all I hold dear that if you take him, one blanket will never cover us again.' Faced with this dire threat, Tomison perforce instructed the others to proceed without him. Young Rosie saw the men approach and fled to Quarral geo in the south of the island, a gloup[2] stretching about thirty yards inland. In his terror the boy slid into the chasm and swam along the channel towards the sea. Among the men waiting at the entrance was his uncle from the farm of Gossigar. The story goes that when he reached open water the lad called out in despair 'Uncle whaur can I go?' and the man replied with pious duplicity, 'Come tae me boy an I will save you.' The lad obeyed and was pressed.

A woman and her husband lived with their two young sons at the croft of Howar,[3] Evie, and when the gang took the man there was no one to provide for the family. Food was scarce and the woman despaired. One night she dreamed that there were fish in Solgeo, Costa. In the morning, hungry but hopeful, she trudged to the shore and discovered with joy a large turbot stranded in a small

---

1 Single-stemmed rowlocks.
2 A rock cavern whose roof has collapsed well inland from its mouth, leaving a yawning chasm upon which one comes entirely unawares.
3 This croft in the district of Costa has now disappeared. The land has been incorporated into the farm of Midhouse, two fields of which are called Lower Howar and Upper Howar.

inlet on the west side. The fish sustained the family in its extremity. Later, the woman had another dream in which she saw more fish in the same waters and this time beneficent nature provided a shoal of herring.

Although fear of poverty was always present in the minds of women, when John, the only child and support of widow Hourston from the farm of Hozen,[1] was captured, in a mort of despair she begged unavailingly 'Tak me only coo, bit laeve me son.'

It was not unknown for men to be warned by the wife of the person planning impressment. In the first decade of the nineteenth century Bailie James Shearer was a merchant and ship's chandler in Kirkwall. He was also a Justice of the Peace whose duties included satisfying the quota imposed on the district of Kirkwall and St Ola. His wife Ann was a strong character who disapproved of her husband's involvement in impressment and took positive steps to counteract this activity. She would arrange a bolster in her bed to resemble a recumbent figure, then, while the town slumbered, hurried in the darkness to inform likely recruits of the fate that had been planned for them. In the words of one who knew the story, 'she fleed roond tae waarn the lads tae get oot o' sight.' The young men hid in crevices on the water-front or in derelict boats.[2]

Mrs Ritch, The Kitchen, Deerness, was a kind-hearted woman whose husband William was a constable. Whenever she heard plans being made to press some of the local lads, she sent one of her sons to give warning, so that all serviceable men had time to run for the cliffs.

Constable Magnus Isbister of Ingsay, Birsay, had a number of daughters who eavesdropped on their father's plans, and frustrated them by warning the young men who had been listed.[3]

Harvest Time

Despite fear of impressment the crop had to be harvested, and perforce men risked being seen and taken. Women too worked in the harvest field, and when constables or a recruiting party appeared they might become aggressive and threatening. Their favourite weapon was the readily available corn hook.

1 Or Hosen – a farm adjacent to Dounby.
2 Mrs G Cuthbertson, Edinburgh, personal communication 1972. Mrs Cuthbertson, a great-grand-niece of Mrs Shearer who warned the men when impressment threatened, supplied the information when she was eighty-seven.
3 Dr W J Isbister, Orphir, personal communication 1970. Dr Isbister was ninety when he recorded this story. Eighty years earlier he heard it from a ninety-year-old grand-aunt (b. 1800) who was one of the daughters of constable Isbister.

One fine September morning Thomas Sinclair, who occupied a small croft, Fingerow, Scapa, decided to risk cutting his bere. He was in the harvest field when a signal was shouted that the gang was approaching. Having no time to reach his usual hiding place in the cliffs he decided to lie quietly in the uncut crop. Constables Peter Wick and Joseph Tait searched the croft house, followed by Sinclair's sister Kirsty who was brandishing a rusty shearing hook. The woman was a noted termagant with a sharp tongue, but her implacable hostility and derisive remarks only encouraged Wick and Tait in their search and in due course they found their man. A strong, coarse fellow, Sinclair struck out wildly with a heavy baton, knocking Tait unconscious, but Wick grappled with him and won the ensuing brawl. Believing that her brother was mortally injured, Kirsty, her face suffused with anger, rushed at the constable and dealt him a blow on the back of his head with a corn hook. Sudden though it was the attack was ineffective. She was thrown to the ground and left lying in the crop with her injured brother, while the constables sought reinforcements from a warship anchored in Kirkwall Bay.

That night Sinclair was dragged from his bed. Exhausted, he collapsed several times on the way to Kirkwall and was beaten vigorously with a rattan.[1] On examination the next day his weals and other injuries persuaded the authorities that he was unfit for service. It is said that as he had resisted the constables in the discharge of their duties and moreover had attacked them with a stave, Sinclair's only cow should be forfeit and made over to Tait as compensation for his injuries. Kirsty, always an unbalanced person, was further deranged by the whole affair and shortly afterwards she killed a child, for which she was hanged in Edinburgh.

Impressment in Graemsay was made difficult by the turbulent waters around the island. Whenever the press cutter approached, threatened men rowed to a dangerous tideway where the gang did not dare to follow. But one harvest day the cutter arrived unnoticed. The alarm was given and men ran to the boat noust[2] at Vaevil. They were almost afloat when the foremost pursuer grasped the gunwale. One of the Graemsay women who had accompanied their men, a Sinclair from Dean, seeing that capture was imminent, seized the nave[3] of an oar and struck the restraining hand such a fierce blow that it had to be amputated.[4]

---

1 A short cane or stick used in the naval punishment of *Starting*.
2 A landing-place for a boat.
3 Hand grip.
4 For over a hundred years the nave of an oar was kept in a cupboard under the pulpit of the island's church. Its authenticity was doubted, and around 1950 it disappeared without trace.

The men launched their boat unhindered and rowed to the safety of the roost[1] of Milbunas.

One clear night Annie Taederson, Norwick, North Unst successfully used her stentorian voice to give warning when the gang was active in the district. Her remarkable alert carried a quarter of a mile from the Norwick houses on the south to Vaelye on the north side.

Love, Loyalty and Betrayal

Even after long years of separation, often with no communication, most women remained faithful to their men folk. John Garrioch from Holm was plighted to a constable's daughter who warned him that he was to be pressed that very night. Garrioch sought refuge in a neighbour's house, departing under cover of darkness. The following day, disguised in women's clothing and wearing a shawl, he hid in a field of cut oats, but his furtive movements aroused attention and he was arrested. As the wedding day was close, his capture caused much anger among women in the district, and he received more than the usual measure of sympathy. Escorted to Kirkwall, he was followed along the post road by several women, including his sweetheart, who upbraided the constables. During the journey the company stopped to rest and the sweethearts took a last opportunity to renew their pledge. On his discharge several years later Garrioch returned to Holm where his betrothed's affection had not wavered and they were married.

A Birsay woman also remained true to her sweetheart after his impressment. The jovial proceedings of a New Year party in the farm house at The Earls Palace were interrupted by the approach of constables. Without hesitation John Johnston (known as 'Johnny o Smerchants'[2]) and Sandy Comloquoy, the men who were sought, made off. Comloquoy, fleet of foot, escaped but Johnston was caught at the North side of the parish. Passing The Palace under escort he met his sweetheart Kitty Comloquoy who, distracted, murmelted[3] that an unkind fate had thus decreed their separation – felt the more keenly at the festive season. As Johnston was led away she handed him a farewell present of bread and cheese, promising to remain constant. Tradition maintains that he retained the food through years of active service, carrying it as a reminder of his abiding affection for Kitty, who he wed on discharge.

1 Roose, rose or roust – tumultuous waters caused by the meeting of rapid tides. An area of rough, irregular and dangerous waves. The roost of Mulbunas became less turbulent after block ships were sunk there in World War I.
2 Smerchants was a small croft on the North side of the parish, now a ruin.
3 Lamented.

The Banks of the Shannon or Teddy and Patty

But, woe is me ! the press-gang came,
And forc'd my love away
Just when we named next morning fair
To be our wedding day.
"My love," he cried, "they force me hence,
"But still my heart is thine;
"All peace be yours, my gentle Pat,
"While war and toil be mine:
"With riches I'll return to thee."
I sobbed out words of thanks,
And then he vowed eternal truth,
On Shannon's flowry banks.

Some men were betrayed by women they trusted. In 1850, when elderly, Andrew Paplay of Deerness recounted how for several years he avoided being taken. When eventually pressed he blamed his sweetheart, along with one of her relations,[1] and felt much animosity towards them. Returning at last to Deerness, he resolved to have nothing further to do with the girl. However, he was out walking one day and met her face to face. He described the experience thus: 'I thought "will I spik or will I no?" an than cheust whan I cam up tae her I glamsed[2] at her an said "peerie cuttack[3] whar du gaun?" An she said, "Muckle man, muckle man, why grups[4] thu me?"' The former lovers were reconciled, and soon afterwards became man and wife.[5]

A man in Leveneap in the district of Lunnasting jilted the girl he had been courting and she informed on him. For four years he served on a man-of-war, until one day in a gale off the coast of Denmark the yard-arm became detached from the main mast. The young Shetlander volunteered to fasten it on condition that he be freed if the risky task proved successful. Showing both courage and skill, he climbed the ratlings, secured the spar and obtained a discharge on return to port. He came home to Leveneap, but nothing is known of the young woman whose unrequited love had constrained her to betray him.

Impressment with its inevitable long absences could severely disrupt family life, and in one instance brought about a charge of incest and church involvement. Intimacy was alleged between a woman and her brother-in-law, then deemed a serious breach of the law. It seems that long years of naval service by Laurence Smith had weakened the faithfulness of his wife Elspeth Halcrew, who lived at Blosta in the parish of Cunningsburgh. A fracturing of morals invited questioning, and following unsuccessful church investigation, on 5 April 1811 James Greig, Procurator Fiscal, petitioned the Sheriff Depute.[6] In a resumé of previous events he stated that last summer 'the Elders of his Session reported to the Rev[d] Mr Duncan, Minister of Dunrossness, that Elspeth Halcrew in

---

1   Shortly after Andrew Paplay was pressed, the informer's cart was removed one night from his home at Cutpool, pushed over nearby banks and destroyed. Paplay lived at either Howes or Barebreck.
2   Glamse – to make a sudden dive; to snatch; to grab.
3   A term of endearment addressed to a pleasant young girl, and perhaps derived from cuttack, a vole.
4   Grasps.
5   Rev H L Mooney, Deerness, personal communication 1972. The story about Andrew Paplay and his sweetheart was told to Rev Mooney in 1930 by James Foubister, Waterfield, Deerness, who was born in 1843.
6   Shetland Archives, SC12/6/1811/19.

the parish of Cunningsburgh the wife of Laurence Smith, sailor in the Royal Navy (who had been for several years back in the service and still is so) was with child.' The Divine and his Session summoned her to appear before them. Interrogated, she confessed that she was pregnant, declaring somewhat ingenuously, and almost certainly mendaciously, that 'she did not know who was the Father of her Child, or any thing about him further than that he was a man belonging to some Ship or other which happened to be in Bressay Sound, the name of which she did not know, whom she met accidentally at the hill head of Lerwick one evening.'

The Session was incredulous and the matter advanced by a Summons to the next meeting of the Presbytery of Zetland where her statement was 'adhered to in all respects'. The Presbytery debated and disbelieved her story, but declared that nothing more could be done through the Church Courts. The Fiscal's petition continued that Adam Smith, also in Blosta, her husband's 'Brother German [sic]', and a widower, might be the father of the child. Adam next sought to marry Elizabeth Halcrew, who was Elspeth's sister, but the minister refused to sanction this request 'untill Smith should clear himself of the crime so publicly laid to his charge.' Elizabeth too was with child.

Various witnesses averred significantly that Adam and Elspeth had slept together on the night of 19 January 1810 and that she 'was delivered of a child on 17 October following.' Others had seen them abed, but Elspeth protested that they had slept in the same room only when there was a corpse in the house, and beds were scarce. Further, that they had been so together when she was 'comforting him under his affliction for his wife's death.' His bereavement does not seem to have prevented Adam from being something of a lothario. The Petitioner, Mr Greig, sought 'to have these facts and circumstances investigated, because if they are true as suspected, the crime committed by the said parties, is no less than that of incest.'

On 11 April 1811 the Sheriff Substitute having considered various statements by witnesses consigned Adam Smith and Elspeth Halcrew to the Tolbooth 'therein to remain untill they are tried for the crime alleged against them or otherwise liberated in due course of law.' Unfortunately the records then become silent. It is not known if the couple went to trial, what happened to the cuckolded Laurence Smith, and if he ever returned to Shetland. At the time of the alleged crime he had been absent for seven years.

An unprincipled Orkney woman was anxious to marry and used fear of impressment to further her plans. She warned a friend that the gang was coming to take him, so he hid in her house and was fed and looked after until the alleged danger had passed. He married her out of gratitude, but on discovering that his wife had invented the story, he became embittered and never again spoke to her.

Kate Huntly

History is sometimes reflected in legends, albeit in a simplified form, often overlaid and distorted by mistaken theories which linger on at popular level. An example is the story of Kate Huntly who was determined to save her son from impressment. A widow living at Millburn, Birsay, she became aware that her only child, a mentally retarded youth, was in danger of being taken. So mother and son moved from the district and built a rude hut in the remote peat moss of Sandwick, on the border of Birsay and Harray. For sustenance the lad trudged as far as the Rendall shore to catch fish and gather ebb-meat[1] which, with a few sheep, enabled mother and son to eke out a precarious living. Thus they lived in a measure of secure isolation which was to prove temporary.

An informer, who lived at Rantan, Birsay, led constables to the hiding place. Though greatly dismayed, Kate kept her nerve and explained that her son was in the hills but would accompany them on his return. She encouraged the men to indulge in libations of her strong heather ale[2] and the gang drank freely. Time passed, discussion turned to argument, fighting ensued and in the mélée clothes were torn and injuries sustained.

The fracas caused a stir in the county. The crestfallen posse, discredited and derided, improbably accused her of attacking them, and Kate was summoned to Kirkwall where she was charged with causing an affray. Impenitent, she conducted a vigorous defence in a curious local dialect: 'Stoon fa me, thei set tew at a low tut-mut; afteran thei gaed a heich cullya shearg, at a nun's bark thei ware at a heich cullya whumlie.'[3]

1 Shellfish.
2 Kate brewed several kinds of ale, as is illustrated in the jingle:
    Twenty pints o stale (sic) gool (sic) ale,
    Twenty pints o plooman's drink,
    Twenty pints o hink-skyink,
    Twenty pints o clitter-clatter,
    Twenty pints waur or water.
  The jingle concerning Kate Huntly's various types of ale is contained in a letter to *The Orcadian* of 11 December 1924 and signed 'Legend Lover'.
3 'So help me, they set to without much serious argument, afterwards they were shouting and yelling, and at a dog's bark they were at each other's throats.' A lengthy version appears in *Around the Orkney Peat Fires*, p 254.

The manifestly unjust charge was deserted, but the indomitable Kate died shortly afterwards.[1] Without his mother's protection the son was pressed and subsequently perished at sea.

A mixture of tradition, rationalisation and misconception have helped to create the tale of Kate Huntly. The legend is complex and contains the Kate Corrigall[2] story, the troll or Ket Huntlins[3] connotation, a second press gang tale,[4] and mistaken ideas based on the existence of steps which were actually built by herdie boys.[5]

Witchcraft and Curses

James Smith owned[6] a shop and a fish-curing business near the Kist of Klonga, Fetlar and he was also agent for ships engaged in impressment. Paid for providing information about able-bodied men on the island, Smith and his family suffered grievously by betraying the two sons of widow Marion Jeromsdaughter.[7] Jerome and James were captured, secured in the bod[8] at Funzie and sustained overnight with a skol[9] of burstin[10] and two crooks[11] of Dutch gin.

---

1 She is supposed to be buried in the south-west corner of the churchyard at The Palace, Birsay.
2 It was probably her son who was pressed.
3 The name of the hill where the drama took place – Ket Huntlins, almost certainly derives from the Old Norse words ketta, a cat and hyndla, a dog, hence a monster or troll. Jakobsen records that Ketthuntlin in the Shetland Norn meant a fabulous or mythical being, something between a cat and a dog. It was also used as a general name for a troll or fairy. In the Norn, Keddhontla was a kind of ogress probably belonging to a certain class of troll. There is little doubt that the name Ket Huntlins goes back to the 17th century and probably much earlier. The burn of Kithuntlins rises in the Bog of Surtan and flows south-west to join the burn of Rush.
4 In this version of the story Kate, after supplying copious quantities of heather ale, dislodged the 'main tree' of her house, trapping under the fallen roof the drunken Harray men who had come to take her son.
5 Young lads who kept animals from straying onto growing crops, in the days before fields were fenced.
6 If Smith did own the shop this was unusual. Property normally belonged to the landlord.
7 She married James Anderson but reverted to her maiden name when her husband perished in the fishing disaster of June 1791. Her sons' surname was Jamesson, in accordance with the system of shifting patronymics then in general use.
8 Also called a *booth* it contained all necessary items of fishing gear and household goods. The landlord did not permit another shop on his land and tenants were expected to deal only at his booth. There was an annual reckoning between landlord and tenant. Bods or booths are not to be confused with the lodges which fishermen used as bases when at work. These were constructed of stones and turf and thatched with feals and straw.
9 A wooden bowl.
10 Corn dried in a pot over a fire.
11 Also *crock*: an earthenware vessel.

Marion's plea to visit her sons was refused and her distress turned to anger. Impelled by a desire to take vengeance, she knelt, and abasing herself before God sought help. She shook down her hair[1] and in a voice thick with hate invoked mellishon[2] on Smith. The words of doom, as rendered in English, were: '…you cheat me of my husband's earnings and now you do me this evil – deprive me of my sons and only hope. This is your fate – every root branch will die a premature death – some will lose their reason – your fine house will become a ruin and the sun, moon and stars will look down on the roofless, derelict building. The birds of the air will nest in the walls, and the beasts of the field will make the place a dunghill.'

The curse succeeded. Several members of the family died shortly afterwards, James Smith being buried within two days of a daughter. Despite their mother's supernatural powers Jerome and James Jamesson did not return to Shetland.

A version of the curse was recorded in the adjacent island of Yell, with an opening comment 'da curse o' da poor is faain apo[3] da habitation o' da rich.' This tells of a woman at Hubie, Fetlar, who had hidden an adult son in her bed. He was discovered and pressed, whereupon she prayed to The Almighty for retribution, asking that two of those associated with her son's betrayal might die: 'Shu prayed da Almighty wid grant da wiyt[4] o' it, an twa might follow i'ta da kirk yard. An so it cam ta pass. James Smith an his daughter died, wan at da bod o' Funzie an da idder died at Bayanne, an wis brought ta Funzie. An whin wan companion[5] [sic] wis crossin da burn o' Pober da idder wis comin doon da gaet[6] o' Leagarth.'

There is a third version of the story. Marion Jamieson was known as a 'witchie' woman well practised in the black arts. When her sons were taken she intoned 'vengeance is mine, I will repay.' She sat down, let her hair fall loose and fasted for several days while she worked her vengeance on the Smiths. The curse itself varies little. In this account she portended that the entire Smith family would die in quick succession, ten coffins being required for the funerary proceedings.

The Smiths, reputedly from Deerness, Orkney, undertook fish curing for Sir John Mitchell.[7] In due course James Smith started his own business and died a

1 A preliminary to cursing and employed when a witch was particularly furious.
2 A Shetland form of *malison*: in archaic English and Scots usage – a malediction or curse.
3 Fallen upon.
4 Blame.
5 Company.
6 Path.
7 Sir John Mitchell of Westshore, 1734–83.

rich man. The burial of a notable person required a heavy oak coffin, and a sixareen[1] was dispatched to transport one from Lerwick. But a man of importance merited not only a special coffin but also two ministers to keep vigil during the wake[2] preceding the interment. In late evening the clerics moved to the south room of the Haa of Funzie, while the body lay in an open coffin under a shroud in the north room. At midnight knocking was heard and on investigation the startled ministers beheld the corpse sitting upright. Smith declared that because of misdeeds for which he had not previously repented, he could find no rest for his soul. He sought a benison[3] and, furthermore, asked if God would forgive him 'at dis late oor.' When given an assurance on the matter, he admitted evicting a crofter, and that in purchasing a fat cow from a man who 'couldna coont English coin', he had cheated him of thirteen shillings. He also confessed to betraying the two sons of widow Marion Jeromsdaughter. These sins revealed, he again enquired about forgiveness. The senior divine reaffirmed that all things were possible with God – although he could have 'axed sooner.'[4] A comforted James Smith then murmured 'on dat assurance I lay me doon again in peace.'

The ministers recounted their weird experience at a Presbytery meeting in Tingwall. After due consideration the Moderator was of the opinion that if two men in full possession of their 'sight and senses' told an identical story it should be accepted 'and the day of miracles is not past.'

It is possible that when James Smith was streekit,[5] he was in a coma and that during the funeral proceedings knocking did come from the coffin. This story may have been borrowed from an incident when a Fetlar woman does indeed seem to have been buried alive.

Another curse associated with impressment was uttered at Lochend, Lunnasting. A young man spurned the unattractive daughter of a local witch, who took revenge by betraying him to a recruiting party. His grandmother, not without her own powers, cursed the witch, declaring that never again would she be able to disadvantage anyone by her diabolism. On his return from service at sea the man – who still showed no interest in the unlovely girl – was attacked by the witch in the form of a pig. By good fortune he was carrying a strong oak staff, and straddling the animal he belaboured it vigorously. The beast scuttled home

---

1 A six-oared open fishing boat. Also *sixern*.
2 A watch or vigil held over the body during the night before burial.
3 A blessing.
4 Asked sooner.
5 Laid out on a bier; prepared for burial.

and attempted to revert to human form. But the curse could not be undone and the transmogrification was only partly successful. With upper-half human and lower-half pig the creature perished.

The originator of an unusual curse was a deserter given refuge by an old woman in a croft house at Ronas Voe. Times were hard and she had no means of supplementing her meagre store of food, which was soon exhausted. Reluctantly, the man was asked to leave, whereupon he was captured. Despite the weeks of refuge the ungrateful fugitive was aggrieved and he cursed the woman and her holding, declaring that misfortune would befall future tenants. Successive occupants have indeed suffered calamities, and it is believed that the curse persists to this day.

Hapless women cursed those responsible for the capture and impressment of their loved ones, calling down the wrath of God on the betrayers. However, on 11 October 1761, when the Walls Kirk Session met at the Kirk of Papa on the island of Papa Stour, clergy would not countenance involving the Almighty. During the summer of 1760 two local men had been pressed, and a group of people, including four women, were accused of 'imprecations[1] such as God might scatter the families of such as by authority had given y^r assistance in taking and sending to Lerwick two young men their freinds[2] [sic].' The Session disapproved of this entreaty and Katharine Chyne, whose brother was one of those pressed, bore the brunt of the church's displeasure. The entries in the Session Book[3] are:

> Kirk of Papa, Octo^r 11th 1761. After Prayer
>
> Sederunt The Mod^r, Elders and Deacons of Papa &c.
>
> This day compeard John Muffeat ruling elder in Papa and aquainted the Session that some people in this place about the time of the press last year had been guilty of imprecations such as God might scatter the families of such as by authority had given y^r assistance in taking and sending to Lerwick two young men their freinds, being interrogate who these persons were, he answered it was Katharine Chyne James Clerk and his wife and his mother in law and his own mother, being further ask'd if he had any witnesses, he gave in Nicol Henderson factor in Papa and his wife, Thomas Will^{m}son in Uphouse and his wife, and Mrs Greig in Northhouse. The Session appointed the officer to cite both the parties and witnesses to their nixt meeting at Sandness.

1 The action of invoking evil upon someone; cursing.
2 Relatives.
3 Shetland Archives, CH2/380/2, pp. 273–4.

Kirk of Papa, Nov 1st 1761.

… This day Katharine Chyne who was summond apud Acta[1] in the Kirk of Sandness Oct 18 last bypast being three times calld at the Kirk door, and not compearing nor any relevant excuse offered, for her absence, the Session declares her contumacious to discipline and appoints the officer to cite her before the Pb^y[2] who are to meet at Lerwick Wednesday nixt, reserving power to y^m selves to sist the process provided the said Katharine Chyne shall twixt and that time satisfy any two elders of Papa that she had any relevant reason for her absence this day, and if she has then she is to appear before the Session at Sandness nixt Lords day.

Kirk of Sandness, Novr 8th 1761.

… This day according to appointment compear'd Katharine Chyne in Papa and having given in relevant reasons for her not attending on the Session when first cited before y^m at y^r meeting in Sandness, the Session thought proper to examine into ye complaint given in against her by John Muffeat ruling elder in Papa, and the said Katharine being examind as to ye truth y^r of, she confess'd that she did not doubt but she might have imprecate but being so overcome wth sorrow for her brother that was press'd – she therefore was not sensible what she said, but she was willing to submitt herself to the Session. The Session upon inquiry both from ye elders and Nicol Henderson then present as to the truth of what she had said, they acquiec'd in ye same whereupon the Session appointed the said Katharine to appear before the congregation the nixt Lords day that sermon shall be in Papa to be publickly rebuk'd & to converse privatly wth the Min^r twixt and that time.

Kirk of Papa, Decr 5th 1761.
This day Katharine Chyne in Papa appear'd before the congregation and being publickly rebukd was dissmiss'd from discipline.

A Westray woman who had a premonition about imminent impressment was accused of communication with the devil. Three islanders were preparing to fish when the sweetheart of a man Harcus, darkly prescient and filled with foreboding, begged him to stay on land. He discounted her warning, but at the fishing grounds a cutter pressed him and another of the crew, leaving a simpleton to

---

1 According to the Act.
2 Presbytery.

return to Pierowall. The bereft families, distraught and ignorant, accused the girl of evil practices. She was hurried to Kirkwall and 'pitten in the Hole in the auld Kirk.' This was *Marwick's Hole*[1] in St Magnus Cathedral where miscreants who gave offence to an often blinkered ecclesiastical authority were incarcerated.

The story had a happy ending. The vessel with Harcus aboard subsequently put into Kirkwall, he escaped, rescued[2] his betrothed and together they established a successful business in Manchester.

---

[1] Situated beneath the strong room, the dungeon was used until the last decade of the eighteenth century.

[2] It is possible that the woman was imprisoned in the Tolbooth on the Kirk Green, from where her release would have been more readily contrived.

Whalers

Shetland lairds were apprehensive of community progress and individual initiative and they suffered financially from any shortage of tenant labour caused by fishermen joining vessels bound for Greenland and Davis Strait.[1] Vigorously discouraging service on whalers, landowners argued rather speciously that the absence of young men had a debilitating effect on the county's economy. This entrenched attitude and the thrall in which tenants were held is recorded by Neill in *A Tour through some of the Islands of Orkney and Shetland* which took place in the summer of 1804:

… in Shetland, some of the most salutary laws of Britain are unknown, or do not operate, so detached and overlooked are these islands. … Every tenant, or at least every cottar-tenant, is expected to fish during summer. And as a striking proof of the subjection in which the Shetland cottars are held, I may mention as an undoubted fact, that for every lad who goes to the Greenland whale-fishery for the summer, the cottar-family to which he belongs must pay to the landlord *one guinea* of fine. This is an exaction which the landlords who practise it, may well wish to slur over: but if the fine be not levied avowedly on that ground, we have been credibly informed that a guinea is always added to that year's rent, and that the reason of the addition is perfectly understood by both parties.[2]

In November 1805 Neill gave further details of what he termed the 'Whale-fishing exaction'[3] imposed on cottar families, noting that since his visit to Shetland the fine had been increased: '… *advertisements* were, last spring (1805), affixed to some of the parish-church doors of Shetland, informing the poor Shetlanders belonging to particular estates, that no permission would henceforth be granted them to go to the whale-fishery, under *three guineas,* instead of one.'

---

1 In 1808, six hundred Shetlanders were employed aboard whaling vessels: see James R Nicolson, *Shetland*, p. 169. According to Sir Walter Scott, writing in his journal, by 1811 the number of Shetlanders recruited had risen to 1000. This figure is probably exaggerated.
2 Published in 1806, pp. 97–9.
3 Ibid., pp. 111–12. His comments are given in Appendix C.

Ships from Hull and Whitby, and latterly Peterhead and Dundee, bound for Greenland came annually to recruit and provision at Lerwick. Lairds and merchants wished to protect their fishing revenue and also to punish those tenants who planned to avoid working on locally based boats. In August 1756, resentful and vindictive, they submitted a Memorial[1] to the Earl of Morton which addressed both these matters, particularly requesting a Protection for the fishermen who served their interests. They recommended that a tender should arrive in early March[2] to press those tenants who planned to join Greenland ships. The Memorial commences:

As not only the whole Wealth but the chief Subsistence of the whole People in these Islands arises from and depends on the Success of the Fishing Trade, they cannot miss to have the strongest Apprehensions of every thing that may in the least give any Stop or Interuption thereto, & should of Consequence take such Measures as appear most prudent for preventing thereof, And for having the Fishery protected in the Prosecution of their Business. In the present Time of War,[3] they cannot with any Reason expect an Exemption from his Majestie's Service, or from being brought into the same by those compulsitory [sic] Methods all his other Subjects are liable to; And although the Service cannot in all probability ever be much benefited by any Attempts to press the Fisher Men, yet the Fishing Trade which is the most important Interest of this Countrey must be utterly ruined by such Attempts. This appeared very evidently in Summer 1755, when two small tenders in his Majestie's Service arriving on the Coast, two ffishing Boats, According to their usual Custom on seing Vessells, went onboard one of them, And had Six Men pressed from them, the first instance of the Kind that ever happened on this Coast, Which gave such an Alarm that though these Tenders hovered during the remaining Part of the Fishing Season, it never was in their Power to catch another Man; for the Fishery through the whole Countrey became so intimidated that none of them would venture to Sea again during that Season, So that the Fish caught that whole Year did not exceed One half of what might have been with the greatest Probability expected.

The Memorialists are highly Sensible that it is their Dutie to contribute all in their power to his Majestie's Service upon all Occasions, and more especially in the present Juncture of Affairs.

The Memorial continues:

[1] Memorial for the Right honourable The Earl of Morton on Behalf of the Gentlemen Heritors Merchants and other Inhabitants of the Islands of Zetland. Dated 14 August 1756. Shetland Archives, GD 150/2518 B2.
[2] The whaling season was gradually extended, some vessels arriving as early as mid-February and delaying their return until August when forced south by ice.
[3] The Seven Years War with France and Spain broke out in 1756.

It is a matter of ffact that the Countrey is very thinly peopled And stands in Need of nothing more than a greater Number of Hands for cultivating the Ground, as well as carrying on the Fishing, ffor there go annually a very considerable Number of the most spirited young ffellows out of the Countrey onboard Vessells casually coming there.

The Memorialists … are willing and ready to give all the Aid in their Power for pressing into the King's Service as many Hands as they possibly can; And towards the doing of this they stand in Need not only of Warrands but a Posse; And the Season for doing it with the greatest Probability of Success is about the Time, or a little before the Greenland Ships arrive on this Coast which is about the Beginning of March, At which Time should a Tender arrive, it is to be hoped that with the Aid of her Crew, Fourty or Fifty Hands might be Secured …

The Memorial concludes:

But at the same Time, should such a Number be got at Once, So many could not be looked for again in ffive Succeeding Years during which Time, if the Protection to the ffishers was continued, the Countrey might be enabled at the End thereof to do something more considerable for the Service.

[signed] Mitchell, John Bruce Stewart, Ja^s Henderson, John Leslie, J Cumming, J^{on} Fraser, Robert Scott, James Scott, Jas Craigie …

A naval surgeon, Lieutenant Ker, visited Lerwick in 1780. His diary entry of 22 August is a chilling account of how seven men who had returned from Greenland whaling were incarcerated in the Tolbooth, and, mere chattels, languished there in miserable conditions:

Now in Time of War when contrary to the Will of their Tyrants they go in the Greenland Fishery they are sure on their Return to be impressed. Of this We have an Instance in seven poor Fellows whom upon my Representation Capt Perry has taken on b^d.[1] These poor Wretches as soon as they arrived at their Homes from the Greenland Service were immediately hurried to Goal where when We arrived they were laying on the bare Boards without any thing to cover or defend them from the Severity of the Weather in a small Room. An Iron Grate admitted the Light but not a Pane of Glass to exclude the cold Wind.[2]

Such sentiments regarding the impressment of returning whalers were not restricted to Shetland. David Petrie, factor to the Graemeshall Estate, Holm, in a letter[3] of 14 August 1812 to Rear-Admiral Graeme said: 'Gourly the Regulating Capt. is at present here. The Davis Straits & Greenland Ships have only a few of

1 Presumably to add to the ship's complement.
2 *Ker's Naval Log 1778–1782*, National Library of Scotland, Ms 1083, p. 92.
3 Orkney Archives, D5/8/1812.

them yet arrived. It is thought by every one that these men ought to serve. But it will be difficult to lay hold on them if once they get on shore.'

In July 1804 *Catherine*, nine miles out from Bressay Head was boarded by the brig cutter *Osnaburgh* commanded by Lieutenant Ginsty, and twelve Shetland men were pressed. The ship was returning from Greenland with 'between 70 and 80 seals and 5 whale fish, 2 of them size 7 foot and the other 9 foot which filld us 70 butts of blubber.'

The *Catherine*'s captain, Joseph Gibson, wrote to James Hay,[1] merchant, complaining about this action, having remonstrated with the Lieutenant '… but without effect in so doing and on the great hardship and cruelty in taking those poor men and so near their own homes after having endured such severe weather and other circumstances that naturally attend a Greenland voyage. He answered me with great civility and in a very gentleman like manner and declared that upon his word and honour which I could not bring into doubt or question that his orders were absolute and positive from the Admiralty to take all Shetland men and others that were not legally protected.' Gibson listed the debt owed to him for slops:[2]

	£	s	d
Peter Frazer	1	0	6
Mitchel Reed	0	15	6
Andrew Mowatt	3	1	10
Lawrance Murray	1	12	4
Peter Ancaster	0	16	10
Donald Williamson	0	12	10
Nicholas Peterson	1	18	6
Lawrance Mowatt	1	11	6
John Reed	0	7	0
Magness Mowatt	0	3	4
Thos. Johnson	0	3	6
John Sanderson	0	3	4
	12	7	0

Presumably Hay would have deducted the amounts from any monies due to the men and forwarded the balance to their families.

1 Letter by Joseph Gibson to James Hay, July 1804, Duncan MacMillan Collection, 08.012/5/56, Trent University Archives, Ontario. Transcript by Angus Johnson, Shetland Museum and Archives.
2 Sailors ready-made clothing and other furnishings such as bedding issued from the ship's store.

Engraved for Millthons Complete System of Geography

A View of the WHALE-FISHERY, and the manner of KILLING-BEARS near Jon the Coast of Greenland.

Whalers were also at risk of impressment during their long homeward voyage. A convoy of three ships returning from Davis Strait was sighted by a press cutter when off the coast of Ireland. As the whalers lumbered on, several small boats put off filled with desperate men. They were captured and among their number was James Matches from Holm. During the journey to port, the Straitsmen[1] overpowered their guards and battened down the hatches. Anchoring in a remote Irish bay the pressed men quickly dispersed. During the arduous journey home Matches was often famished and dispirited, and on one dire occasion sold his neckerchief to purchase a bannock. It took several months to reach Holm where, duly recovered from his privations, he lived to a great age.

Crews nearing Orkney came to know from bitter experience that press cutters usually lay to the east. Captains were wary and sometimes sailed their weather-beaten ships west, landing Orkneymen near Cape Wrath, Sutherland. From there the men rowed home in open boats along the Caithness coast and across the dangerous waters of the Pentland Firth.

David Vedder, a famous son of Deerness born in 1790, went to sea as a cabin boy. In March 1812 he sailed from Stromness on a whaling trip which was to last almost five months. Towards the end of the voyage a frigate bore down on his ship then off Cape Wrath, and in his journal, he describes the resultant consternation, his feelings about impressment and what happened to the crew:

During the homeward passage, we were daily employed in cleaning the ship, scrubbing the boats, dressing bear skins, repairing the sails, and looking sharp out for Yankee privateers; but dreading our own cruisers a thousand times more than all Jonathan's navy.[2] The impress—that blot on our national escutcheon—terrified those who had no protections; and I am convinced that two-thirds of our people would much sooner have been carried into the Chesapeake than into Plymouth Sound. On the 11th of August, being then off Cape Wrath, the frigate hove in sight; all was confusion and insubordination. Some stowed themselves away in the hold among the 'shakes',[3] others swallowed tobacco juice and shammed sick; while a third party, more ingenious than either, wrapped themselves in the top-gallant studding-sails in the fore and main tops. The frigate's 'black cutter' was alongside in a trice, and a general rummage commenced. To the query 'Where are all

---

1 Men engaged in whaling at Davis Strait.
2 An American privateersman, Captain Jonathan Haraden. One of the ablest sea fighters of his generation, he is alleged to have captured one thousand British cannon afloat.
3 Cracks in timber caused by wind or frost.

your men?' the captain responded that they had taken one of the boats the preceding day. The boats were then counted, and one was found missing, being that which was stove by the whale as mentioned above; but even this would not satisfy the scruples of the lieutenant; and five or six miserables were dragged out of the hold, more like the aborigines of New Holland than natives of Yorkshire and Durham.

By the stratagem of the studding sail, I escaped the general scrutiny, landed next day on one of the jetties of Stromness, and bade adieu to whales, Esquimaux, and frigates, for ever.[1]

In the early 1800s a vessel was intercepted ninety miles off Cape Wrath and in the darkness eight Orcadians hurriedly took to a dinghy. They intended to return to their ship when the danger had passed, but fog descended on this hazardous stretch of sea and the whaler could not be located. With no food and little water the small boat drifted for a week before making landfall in Shetland. Three of the men belonged to the parish of Orphir – John Wilson, William Groundwater and William Isbister.

About the same time a Davis Strait whaler approaching Orkney was ordered to heave-to by a British man-of-war, but crowding on canvas she increased speed until a cannon shot underlined the demand. Two further balls, which carried away the wheel and part of the foremast, crippled the vessel, but the crew were not to be taken easily. A boarding party was repulsed by resolute seamen who lined the sides armed with blubber knives. Only with reinforcements was the deck gained and eighteen Orcadians pressed.

There is a similar Shetland story, although the home-coming whalers avoided capture. A Hull vessel had anchored in Busta Voe when a man-of-war's boat was seen coming from Olna Firth. There was confusion on board the whaler. A hurried consultation resulted in the officers setting off for Roe Sound ostensibly on a shooting expedition, while the men stayed behind. As the naval party came alongside, the entire crew appeared menacingly from behind the bulwark armed with whale-lances. Gauging the strength and determination of resistance, the naval men withdrew and the Shetlanders quickly departed homewards. When the matter was investigated, the officers, having been absent, were able to plead ignorance.

Around the year 1800 a whaler on a five-year voyage anchored off Yell in order to make up crew numbers depleted by impressment. John Clunies-Ross was one of two brothers who signed on. After becoming a captain, Ross settled

---

1 'Nautical Reminiscences' in *Poems, Lyrics and Sketches*, pp. 327–8.

in the Cocos Islands in 1824 and founded a unique and highly successful community which was controlled into the mid-twentieth century by his remarkable descendants.[1]

Two Dunrossness brothers – experienced Greenlandmen – were told that whaling skippers from vessels which had anchored in Tofts Voe to avoid the gang were making their way south recruiting en route. Keen to obtain employment they set out accompanied by a younger brother. Reaching Fladdabister and fearful of impressment, they instructed the boy to build them into a peat stack. This done, the lad sat at the roadside and waited for the Greenland masters. When the captains arrived the boy bargained, saying he would bring two splendid seamen, but only if he too was engaged. They demurred, thinking that though spirited, he would not be able to withstand the rigours of Arctic voyage and work. But the lad was adamant and they agreed. Released from the stack the brothers were unhappy at the arrangement made by the intrepid youth, but the bargain had been struck and was kept.

A whimsical story describes an incident between a whaler and the gang. Contained in *Longhope Lore* by J Stirling Mitchell, it indicates the real risk of forcible recruitment from homeward-bound whaling vessels:

> During the early years of last century there was much stir and excitement. ... The pressgang kept a close eye upon Longhope. Its shipping, above all its splendid seamen, drew the gang. They could not exploit such harbours as Dundee and Aberdeen, where men were protected, so they waited at Longhope to press Orcadians into durance vile. One of their frigates caught a tartar, in the form of a whaler. The frigate 'set French colours' to deceive the Orcadians. But the whaler had a letter o' mark (that is, to fight as long as he could). So the whaler fired, and with the first shot broke the wheel and killed two men on the frigate. This was more than the pressgang bargained for. Still there was more to follow. The whaler kept on firing until the frigate hauled down the French colours and hoisted British. Then the pressgang surrendered to the whaler. The captain of the frigate and his crew got short shrift at Longhope.[2]

Two returning Greenland whalers, George Bichan from the croft of Peerie Grindigarth, Deerness and a parish friend were put ashore one night on a quiet beach at Longhope. Delighted with their successful avoidance of recruitment

---

1 *Kings of the Cocos*, by John Scott Hughes, 1950, pp. 25, 31. The atoll of Keeling-Cocos lies in the Indian Ocean midway between Ceylon and Australia. Impressment was again to touch the life of John Clunies-Ross – he met his wife to be, Elizabeth Dymoke, when evading a London press gang 'by darting into the house of one Samuel Dymoke.'
2 1932, pp. 35–7.

they were carousing at a nearby ale house when pressed. Both men were sent to join the fleet, but the war ended and they saw no active service.[1]

Poverty forced many young Shetlanders to sail north on Greenland whalers, but John Nicolson, born at Queensetter, Aithsting in 1790 chose to travel south and enlist in the army. Drafted into the Royal Artillery he became a bombardier. It is believed that he took part in the battle of Waterloo in 1815, and subsequently served as an orderly to a general who helped to educate him. In 1819 Nicolson returned to Shetland as a lay preacher and in 1822 was responsible for the establishment of Methodism in the islands.

Armed Resistance by Greenland Men

In October 1805 men returning from Greenland whale fishing, having determined to avoid impressment and reach their homes, formed an armed band. News of the assembly and its hostile intentions alarmed the authorities. A party comprising soldiers from Fort Charlotte, sailors from the tender *Mary*, and members of the Scalloway press gang was assembled and sent to control and arraign them. During the confused attempt to disarm and apprehend the whalers, firearms were discharged, but there was much dispute about the source of the order to fire. After debate and recrimination the constable in charge of the foray was found guilty and sentenced to one month in jail, stripped of his post and fined £20. In court the witnesses disagreed about his guilt, and furthermore, it is not known if the Greenlanders' attempt to avoid capture and reach their homes was successful. However, in the end, the poor of Weisdale parish benefited to the extent of £10. The following are excerpts from the various documents and give a flavour of the proceedings.

On 14 October Walter Scott, Scotshall, a Justice of the Peace, reported[2] receipt of information that a party of Greenland seamen had assembled at the Scord of Weisdale 'in the house called Huckster and other houses adjacent thereto, armed with Knives, Whale launces [sic] and other offensive weapons under the pretence that they meant to defend themselves against the impress gang of the *Mary* tender under the command of Lieut Smith'. A blacksmith, Magnus Jameson, living in Sound, Weisdale had made some of the offensive weapons which were lodged in the house of John Erasmuson, Huckster. Erasmuson was said to be the leader of the men, who he encouraged to defend themselves with

---

[1] Steven Bichan, Denwick, Deerness, personal communication 1980, the great-great-grandson of George Bichan.
[2] Shetland Archives, SC12/6/1805/69/3.

these 'mortal weapons against all persons whatsoever whether civil or military.' Scott continued that the whalers had effectively broken the peace and it was 'absolutely necessary at least to disperse these armed men if they could not be apprehended.' He made application to the officer commanding Fort Charlotte for an officers party to assist Lieutenant Smith in his sortie. A warrant was granted to constables with their assistants to accompany the assembly of soldiers, sailors and some gang men from Scalloway, all under the command of constable Henry Peterson. It was a special instruction that nobody but the Greenland seamen and those who might come to their aid would be apprehended, and that no hurt or harsh treatment would be given to any person except in the event of what might be occasioned in personal defence, or should the party be attacked 'with mortal weapons' and in no other case whatsoever. Scott granted a warrant for bringing before him any of the Greenlanders who were apprehended or those in whose house custody 'the said mortal weapons may be found' and this was addressed to Andrew and Henry Peterson, Constables, and other officers of the law.

In a Complaint[1] of 20 December Andrew Duncan, Procurator Fiscal of the Court said that by the laws of the land 'firing upon the Lieges with loaded arms or the ordering soldiers to fire upon unarmed people without just cause is a crime of a heinous nature and severely punishable'. He complained that Henry Peterson, South Laxfirth, Tingwall, had committed that offence on 16 October when he had under his command 'as a Constable or civil magistrate' a certain body of soldiers belonging to the Sixth Royal Garrison Battalion. He said that Peterson 'did order one or other of the whole of said soldiers to load their muskets and to fire upon certain inhabitants of Weisdale Voe.' Duncan asked the Sheriff to consider the matter, and if proved to imprison Peterson. At the end of the Complaint he listed ten witnesses 'to be adduced for proving the above Complaint.'

In a Judicial Declaration[2] on 20 December Henry Peterson said that Scott gave him verbal instructions that he should go along with the armed party to three places on Weisdale Voe where the men were assembled. When he arrived there he was to 'show his batton', ask the men to keep the peace and then take them into custody. In the event of refusal they were to be surrounded and detained. Should the Greenlanders open fire or throw knives or other deadly weapons at his party then he could give orders to Ensign McDonald 'to fire upon them.' The party proceeded to the head of Weisdale Voe and consisted of 'twenty soldiers from

1 Shetland Archives, SC12/6/1805/69/1.
2 Shetland Archives, SC12/6/1805/69/2.

Whalers

the garrison, about the same number from the *Mary* tender and ten men from Scallaway [sic] nine of whom were of the press gang there.' They arrived the following night. The next day there was considerable confusion. At one stage men ran to the beach to detain Greenlanders who were now attempting to escape by boat and who previously had dispersed to the hills. Two seamen who left their house near Sound and 'began to screw corn'[1] were apprehended. The turmoil continued and some Greenlanders who made off by boat were fired upon randomly. Peterson declared that during the whole of that day he 'did not give orders to any soldier either to load his piece or to fire,' but that in coming from the hill several soldiers 'discharged their guns in the air by way of emptying them.'

Peterson was incarcerated in the Tolbooth and petitioned the Sheriff on 20 December. He had been committed by a warrant for an alleged breach of his duty, but he had been for some time in a poor state of health and was apprehensive that confinement in a damp room would be injurious. He asked for liberation on bail. This the Sheriff granted on his finding Caution for £20. Walter Scott, Scotshall, stood security and gave a Bond to that effect.

Nine soldiers were called as witnesses and in their testimony several views of the events emerged. All said that orders were given to fire. Some thought that Peterson had given the order. Others agreed that shots had been fired but did not know who gave the order. One Scalloway man of the press gang said that Mark Smith gave the order to load and fire. On 23 December, despite the conflicting evidence, the Sheriff Depute found the complaint proved. He upbraided Peterson, declaring him 'to be unworthy of the office of Constable and recommends to the Justices of Peace to dismiss him from the office and never after to employ him in any such situation.' Peterson was to be carried 'to the Jail of Lerwick and there to be detained for the space of one calendar month.' He was ordained to pay to the Procurator Fiscal a fine of ten pounds sterling to be applied by him to the poor of the parish of Weisdale, and detained in prison until the fine was paid. Patently, the Sheriff was disinclined to show clemency.

It does seem that Peterson was somewhat harshly dealt with and that any order to fire (although no one was killed or injured) may have come from Lieutenant Mark Smith. Perhaps the Scottish verdict of 'Not Proven' would have been appropriate.

On 23 January 1806, his sentence having expired that day, Peterson requested 'that altho he had not ready cash to pay the Fine imposed upon him in whole, yet

---

1 Build a corn stack.

that he had value in account for cattle delivered by the Sheriff Substitute's order equal to the extent thereof.' This sufficed, the keeper of the jail was instructed to set him free and the Procurator Fiscal directed 'to write a letter addressed to the Heritors and Kirk Session at Weisdale desiring them to furnish him with a list of proper objects to whose relief the said fine should be applied so that it may be immediately paid to them.'

The Nature of Whalers

It may be of interest to record something about the men so sought after for naval service. It is beyond dispute that many were wild; drinking and broiling were their chief pleasures and the riotous behaviour of whalers at Lerwick sometimes necessitated the enrolment of fifty special constables.[1] Indeed, the presence of outward-bound whalers made the town virtually lawless. This was from late-February to mid-March, when 'Greenland weather' prevailed, i.e. a time of wild winds and wild men – a term familiar to older Shetlanders.

An indication of the problem and the action taken to contain it is given in a letter of 4 April 1812 from Sheriff Andrew Duncan to James Greig, Procurator Fiscal:

> Dr Sir,
> I have engaged a Sergt's Party from Major Fortye to patrol the Streets a little after nine oclock in order to lay hold of and lodge in the guard room every sailor that may be then on shore without some probable and excusable cause.[2]

On 8 August 1814 Sir Walter Scott, aboard the Trinity ship *Pharos* then at Lerwick, wrote a rhyming letter to Charles, Duke of Buccleuch. He commented on the behaviour of visiting crews:

> Here too the Greenland tar – a fiercer guest –
> Claims a brief hour of riot not of rest
> Proves each wild frolic that in wine has birth
> And wakes the land with brawls and boisterous mirth[3]

Scott's diary of 'The Voyage in the Lighthouse Yacht to Nova Zembla, and the Lord knows where'[4] also refers to the unruly conduct of men who manned the Greenland whalers:

1 *The Arctic Whalers*, Lubbock, p. 9.
2 *The Hjaltland* Miscellany, E S Reid Tait, Vol, pp. 71–3.
3 *The Letters of Sir Walter Scott, 1811–1814*, ed. H J C Grierson, p. 483.
4 *Memoirs of Sir Walter Scott*, J H Lockhart, Vol II, p. 338.

4th August – Harbour of Lerwick … The streets full of drunken riotous sailors, from the whale-vessels. It seems these ships take about 1000 sailors from Zetland every year, and return them as they come back from the fishery. Each sailor may gain from £20 to £30, which is paid by the merchants of Lerwick, who have agencies from the owners of the whalers in England. The whole return may be between £25,000 and £30,000. These Zetlanders, as they get a part of this pay on landing, make a point of treating their English messmates, who get drunk of course, and are very riotous. The Zetlanders themselves do not get drunk, but go straight home to their houses, and reserve their hilarity for the winter season, when they spend their wages in dancing and drinking.[1]

William Erskine, Sheriff of Orkney and Shetland, who became Lord Kinneder in 1822, was one of the party on the voyage, and on 5 August Scott's diary entry reads, '… Erskine trying the rioters – notwithstanding which, a great deal of rioting still in the town. The Greenlanders, however, only quarrelled among themselves, and the Zetland sailors seemed to exert themselves in keeping peace …'

Not all whaling men were wild and rough. A man-of-war lay at anchor at Bressay Sound when one October day a weatherbeaten ship from Davis Strait arrived. A tall, unusually powerful man John Hunter, from Burrafiord was pressed and put to work aboard the warship. At the end of the first day, fiddles were produced, music made and the crew began to drink and dance. John's religious beliefs were such that he was constrained to rebuke their behaviour. In the language of the psalmist he intoned: 'The plowers plowed upon my back and long their furrows drew; but the righteous Lord will cut the cords of this ungodly crew.'[2] Profane and unrepentant the roisterers gibed that the marks on his back would be caused by the lash, and dismissed the possibility that the cords that bound him would be cut.[3] The Shetlander was a tireless worker and held in awe because of his extraordinary strength. Indeed, the officers were so uneasy about his presence that the Captain came to an accommodation with John's landlord, Andrew Grierson of Quendale, to procure his tenant's liberation. On landing, John doffed his cap and thanked the laird for 'this heaven sent deliverance.' The psalmist's prophecy was fulfilled. The day after he was released the ship sailed north, ran onto a rock off Unst and was lost with all hands.

1 Ibid., p. 344.
2 Metrical Psalm 129, verses 3 and 4:
    The plowers plow'd upon my back;
    they long their furrows drew.
    The righteous Lord did cut the cords
    of the ungodly crew.
3 Verse 4 explains the words allegedly used by the sailors as they mocked John.

There is another story about the same religious John Hunter. Hull men and Shetlanders worked well together, and islanders preferred to sail with Hull and Whitby ships, aboard which food, working conditions and treatment were generally superior to those on London and Scottish vessels. When men were being recruited for the Hull convoy, an old shipmate asked 'Whit ship dis year John?', to which the powerful man replied, 'I am juist shipped in da Cumberine.' This was the local pronunciation for the *Cumbrian*. Hunter was famous among whalers as champion fighter of the Arctic fleet.[1] His strength was prodigious, his courage undoubted, and armed only with a boat axe he is reputed to have killed a Greenland bear. He died in the early 1880s at the age of ninety-three.

Stromness, with its magnificent harbour, was for many years a whaling port of call – particularly for Hull masters – where crews were completed and fresh water and provisions obtained before sails were set for the Arctic. Alexander Peterkin, appointed Sheriff Substitute of Orkney and Zetland in 1814, mentions this connection in *Notes on Orkney and Zetland*: 'It is no uncommon thing, in the spring months, to see in these harbours 50 large vessels on their way to the whale fishery at Davis Straits and Greenland, exclusively of other casual visits – so that property worth half a million at least is frequently afloat in the harbours of Stromness.'[2]

The men who risked life and limb on a dangerous calling in the far North were reliable, hard-working seamen, and when pressed they proved splendid recruits for the Navy. Although the crew were busy and often toil-worn on the long voyages, they sang sea shanties while working or passing the time making carvings from whales teeth and whale bone. One such shanty is 'The Whale', which mentions Stromness,[3] and the opening stanza is reproduced opposite. Another ditty which makes reference to the town and whaling, entitled 'Farewell to Stromness', was much sung by Orkneymen to the accompaniment of heels drumming on sea chests: [4]

> The mountains and valleys
> Of Orkney farewell;
> If ever I do return again
> There's no one can tell.

1 *The Arctic Whalers*, pp. 54–5.
2 *Notes on Orkney and Zetland*, Alexander Peterkin, Vol I, 1822, p. 16.
3 This song refers to 2 June 1794, but it was usual for whalers to depart in March for Greenland and Davis Strait.
4 Both 'The Whale' and 'Farewell to Stromness' are taken from Captain W B Whall's *Sea Songs and Shanties*.

'The Whale'

O, t'was in the ye-ar of nine-ty four, and of June the se-cond day, That our gal-lant ship her an-chor weighed, and from Strom-ness bore a way, brave boys! And from Strom-ness bore a way!

And you pretty fair maids,
How happy you live here,
While away on the ocean,
My course I must steer.

Farewell to Stromness,
Since I must away;
I leave my best wishes
To one who there stays;
May fortune protect her
And with her remain
May she never want a friend
Till I see her again.

Adieu to all pleasure,
Adieu for a while;
When winter is over
Sweet summer will smile.
Wherever I wander
By land or by sea,
I will always remember
Your kind company.

Let us drink and be merry,
Drown care in a glass;
Here's health to each lad
And his darling sweet lass:
I've read in a proverb,
And I find it is true,
'That true love is better
Than the gold of Peru.'

So farewell to Stromness
Since I must away,
I bid you farewell
For many a long day.
May fortune protect her,
That's loyal and true,
Here's a health, peace and plenty,
Farewell and adieu.

Imprisoned on the Continent

During the course of hostilities Orcadians and Shetlanders might be captured at sea and languish for years in French and Spanish prisons. Contact with their families was infrequent and letters, of which a number survive, could take months to reach their destination.

Charles Garrick from Holm was for several years a prisoner of war in France. A brother of Admiral Graeme of Graemeshall's manservant John, he had been made a midshipman on Graeme's recommendation. On 6 July 1809 he should have been serving on *Le Bonne Citoyenne* when she captured the French vessel *Furieuse* in the West Indies, the crew thereby qualifying for prize money. Unfortunately for Garrick he had been put on board a prize ship which was retaken by the French on 21 February 1809 and he was imprisoned at Arras.

On 10 November 1809 John Garrick[1] wrote to his mother, Mrs Christiana Garrick, *at Banks, Holm, Near Kirkwall, Orkney, N.B.* He refers to a letter from Charles, which presumably had been sent to her and which David Petrie, factor to the Graemeshall Estate, had passed to John. Written in the stilted fashion of the time, he recounts in quaint terms what had befallen Charles:

I feel for [his] unluckiness, and I sympathize with you as a Mother on this trying occasion. But let me now offer my sentiments of comfort and consolation, altho' poor Charles's fate has been truly hard and unkind, have not you and myself great reason to thank God that in the dispensation of his providence, that he has made the fate of Charles no worse than it is; Suppose for a moment he had been left to himself to have committed great crimes in the Eyes of God and man such as Murder, Robbery, Thievish dishonest forgery, and the like, Committed to jail as a Criminal and punished as the Laws of God and his Country directs; Now dear Mother candidly say whether you would not under such circumstances have felt sorrow considerably more than you do on the present occasion, Charles's destiny is what the Prince and so down to the meanest subject in all Ages has experienced and I say to be taken Captive while in defence of one's King and Native Country however distressing is highly honorable, it is the fate of War and the distribution

---

1 Orkney Archives, D5/8/1809.

of Gods providence. You must my dear Mother acknowledge this case to be widely different from a Criminal confined in prison, to be a Captive or prisoner of War is honourable both in the sight of God and man and we have no reason to be ashamed of it, but to be a Criminal Prisoner we had great cause to blush both in the face of the Almighty and likewise in the face of our fellow men … I am told our prisoners in France are better treated than they were formerly, I would indulge a hope that before long we shall see Charles either on account of Peace or an exchange of Prisoners. I do not know whether Charles's Half pay will or not be stopped but if it is you can write me, you have at least for a time lost in Chas a generous and an attentive son, and so far as I am enabled I shall endeavour to supply his place …

Writing again to his mother from Arras on 29 March 1810, awaiting a reply to two earlier letters, Charles mentioned the presence of another Orcadian prisoner, James Gaddie. He gives his own experience of being a prisoner of war:[1]

Dear Mother

I take the oppertunity of informing you that I am verry well in health at present, thank God, hopping this few Lines will find you in the same condition; dear Mother. I was captured in a Prise belonging to the Le Bonne Citoyenne in the British Channel the 21st Feby 1809 and has wrote you two Letters since and has never had any answer from you; which makes me doubt of your well being; I have sent you home a Certifficat of Life; in purpose that you may receive my half Pay; about a month ago I sent a Letter to James, for some monney and I hope at the same time that you will remember it to him. remember me to William and his wife and all enquiring freinds; Please to send a not to Buchannan Fotheringham in Stromness and Let him know that his Son in Law James Gaddie is here and well in health and desires to be rememberd to him. Longs to hear of him. write as soon as this comes to your hand and Direct to Charles Garrick Prissoner of War at Arras, France; no more at present but remains your Affectionat Son, Charles Garrick.

Charles survived his imprisonment and on 21 December 1815 John Garrick wrote to David Petrie Junior:[2]

In answer to your kind questions respecting my brother Charles, I can only say, that on his arrival in Britain out of French Prison he Volunteer'd into the Alpheus Frigate to sail to the East Indies: and it is more than a year since I heard by his own pen, what He is about, or what he is doing or what situation he is in: – but I saw in the Newspaper's about a Month ago that the Alpheus was in the China Seas and you know that it will take a considerable time for Accounts to come from the East Indies.

1 Orkney Archives, D5/3/1.
2 Orkney Archives, D5/8/1815.

Prisoners of war were in constant need of funds to supplement their fare. On 1 August 1805 John Tilloch [presumably Tulloch] and William Tilloch, both from Kirkwall, John Linak, Stromness, William Hercus, Papa Westray, and William Michall, Shapanshay [sic], sent a letter, probably by another hand, addressed to James Riddoch, Collector, Customs House, Kirkwall. Held in the Citadel of Valenciennes, France, they refer to an earlier letter requesting help to which no reply had been received, and continue: 'We implore your goodness should this come safe to hand to take our disagreeable situation into Consideration and Contribute but a little to our relief. We only address you in the like manner that our fellow sufferers has done, [to] the different places of Scotland they belong to which they have not failed by their several petitions to raise Subscriptions for the relief according to the number belonging thereto, viz Edin^h, Lieth, Dunde.'[1] Any money raised was to be sent to a London agent for onforwarding to a banker in Valenciennes.

In the letter quoted earlier, Charles Garrick had asked for money, and probably some assistance was available from his half pay. But there were cases when neither the prisoner nor his friends had any resources, and the parish might then attempt to relieve the unfortunate man's needs.

In 1808 there was a subscription for John Laughton, presumably from Holm, a prisoner in Valenciennes. This amounted to £4.12.10 and a statement in the Graemeshall papers shows that the money took ten months to reach him:[2]

> Rec^d p Subscription for behoof of John Laughton
> prisoner in Valenciennes France … … …   £4.12.10
> 1808 Decr 16th Wrote Capt. Foubister to pay
> into the hands of Messrs Chester & Co. Charlotte
> Row near the Mansion house London for to be
> Remitted to the said Jno Laughton … … …   4.10
>   2.10

1809 Septr 13 Capt. Foubister wrote me that he had not forwarded this £4.10/ owing to his being in Jamaica when my order arriv'd at London. I wrote him again of the 17th Octo^r 1809 to get the same Remitted to France thro' the hands of the same Gentlemen. Afterwards had a Letter from Lieu^t W Garioch informing of Capt Foubister's having made the Sum out £5 & given it to Mr Garioch who paid it to the Gentlemen and since that time had a Letter from John Laughton acknowledging the receit of the money.

1 Orkney Archives, D10/9.
2 Orkney Archives, D5/3/1.

Another Orcadian at Valenciennes was James Fea[1] and there, on 8 March 1806, he signed a will[2] wherein he bequeathed 'to my said beloved friends Will Gun and Peter Sutherland all such worldly affairs as I am at present possessed of, or may afterwards appear to be possessed of.' Almost certainly Gun and Sutherland were Orcadians and it is probable that James Robertson, one of the witnesses to Fea's signature, came from the north. The document was drawn up in an educated hand and is given in Appendix B.

Capture in coastal waters by privateers, or other enemy vessels, was a danger risked by fishermen. Thomas Moar, Barnhouse, Birsay and some neighbours were off Marwick Head in 1803 when made prisoner by a French sloop. Their fate was unknown until three years later when they were released and returned to Orkney. They declared that in bleak and comfortless conditions a recurring problem was lice, at that time a scourge in the armies and prisons of Europe.

Abraham Fraser born in Papa Stour in 1789 was also imprisoned by the French. One hairst[3] day in 1812 he was working in a rig[4] when a large vessel appeared at the entrance to Hoosa Voe, flagging for a pilot. Together with two older men Fraser rowed out expecting a commission. Beckoning the young man the captain had him seized. The Shetlander discovered that he was on a Danish vessel and had been taken to make up crew numbers. When crossing the North Sea the Dane was intercepted and sunk by an English ship, whereupon Fraser, to his dismay, was pressed. Shortly afterwards the English vessel was engaged and sunk by a French frigate. Captured and incarcerated for more than a year, he whiled away the long hours playing a fiddle provided by a sympathetic gaoler. When peace came he journeyed home and was greeted as though he had returned from the dead.[5]

Illness was frequent due to meagre or unsuitable food and lack of hygiene. An Orcadian prisoner suffering from jaundice was cured by an old French woman who used medicine made from a mixture of herb juices, and the patient learned the ingredients of the preparation. On returning to Burray he successfully treated several cases, but never divulged the contents of the potion, known locally as 'The French cure for jaundice'.

1 It is probable that he came from South Ronaldsay or Swona.
2 Orkney Archives.
3 Autumn.
4 Field.
5 George P S Peterson, Brae (S), personal communication 1974 – the great-great-grandson of Abraham Fraser.

J T Smith Leask's *A Peculiar People and Other Orkney Tales*[1] contains a chapter Tales of the Press Gang in which reference is made to a young Orcadian imprisoned in Egypt: 'John was taken by the French and kept in prison in Alexandria two or three years, until he took scurvy[2] and was a poor thing to the end of his days.'

Successful escape from a continental prison was rare, but there is a Deerness tale of how William Delday and some companions skirting the French coast reached the English Channel in a small open boat. With little food or drink for the voyage and only tobacco as a comfort, their luck held and they were picked up by a friendly vessel.

Accounts of privation filtered through to Orkney in various forms, and sometimes assumed the quality of folklore. One such story, told at weddings by a well-known minister himself an Orcadian, was *Colloquy of Three Orcadian Sailors in a Spanish Prison*. The dungeon conversation about their plight was related to him by one of the men, apparently the sole survivor. A few excerpts from this reported discussion by the men bring out the flavour of such tales. The period was the War of the Spanish Succession (1702–14) and the islanders had been at sea for two weeks when their ship was captured.

The storyteller communicates an air of deep despondency in the utterances of the first man. Indeed the poor fellow wished he had drowned: 'An they're stappid[3] is i this filt'y hol' tae dee lik breuts.[4] I wiss I hed luppid[5] i' the sea afore I leut the Spanish ruffians tak' me'. Concerned in which direction he would be laid when he died 'i' this heathenish land', he doubted if the immemorial custom of burying a corpse facing east[6] would be observed – 'an' wha kens bit they'll lay wur feet tae

---

1 p. 129.
2 Bonaparte's expedition sailed from Toulon about 21 May 1798 and, with a ten day stop at Malta, arrived off Egypt on 29 June. It is likely that such a large fleet would have taken some prizes during its passage through the Mediterranean. Prisoners were kept at the walled city of Alexandria until its surrender some three years later. The British had to starve out the French and there is little doubt that with short rations prisoners would have suffered from scurvy.
3 Crammed.
4 Brutes.
5 Jumped.
6 In the direction of Jerusalem – in most, if not all, of the old cemeteries in Orkney and Shetland, bodies were orientated when laid to rest. People were buried facing east to signify that they died in hope of the Resurrection. E Cobham Brewer LLD, ed., *Dictionary of Phrase and Fable*, 1901, p. 401.
  Perhaps the custom of burying the dead facing East was an echo of an earlier past – see G M Nelson, *The Story of Tingwall Kirk*, 1965, p. 1: 'Many things, done in the sun's way in Shetland and attributed to the worship of Odin, go further back than that: they go back to the days of

the wast!' He was sure that he would never rest in his grave 'gin they lay me i' this withifo[1] land.'

The second man did not think that his companion would have benefited by drowning 'fur there's no' muckle pace[2] there aither fur deed or livin' folk.' He was sure that his 'auld creukid mooth'd aunty Maggie, vild witchy jad,'[3] had put a curse on him for 'stealin' her darnin' needle. He had seen 'the auld sinner' at the ship's foretop on the day they were captured, blowing wind in the enemy's sails and preventing the breeze from reaching them. He longed to return to Sanday and 'haul keuthes[4] a' me days.'

The third sailor, the only married man, pined for his family, but he had gone to sea for good reason. In the words of his wife 'I deu no' bleem thee fur ga'n tae sea, fur hid's only black starvation tae stey' – a bleak reflection on social conditions in Orkney.

The dialogue, made familiar by the old storytellers, captured the imagination of folklorist Walter Traill Dennison in *The Orcadian Sketch-Book*,[5] and his vernacular version is given in Appendix A.

Experiences in continental prisons were not entirely detrimental to health and morale, and men acquired habits and interests which they brought back to the islands. Words and phrases with a foreign provenance had a brief local currency, and one Shetland cottage was given its name as a result of time spent in a French prison. Three men from Quarff returning from Greenland whaling were pressed by an English frigate which was subsequently wrecked on the French coast. The men, a Eunson and two Johnson brothers from a croft called Purgatory in Wester Quarff, were kept for several years in a dungeon where though often hungry they were otherwise well treated. When the war ended the men returned to Shetland – the Johnsons to their croft and Eunson to build

---

the Druids, who worshipped the great spirit, the giver of all life, who dwelt in that life-giving element, the sun. Around this very church of Tingwall, we still bury our dead the Druids' way, facing the east, although the ground has a distinct slope to the west.' In a letter to Arthur Laurenson, Lerwick, dated 9 August 1890, Thomas Mathewson, Burravoe, Yell (S) wrote: 'What, you say, was told to you by the old woman at the Kirk of Ness is indeed very interesting to me. It seems to me that ritual could not have been very distasteful to the old people, seeing how particular they were in observing the Calendar, and also the care they took in burying the body to face the East.'

1 Wicked.
2 Much peace.
3 Vile, witchlike jade.
4 Fish for saithe.
5 pp. 54–5.

a house at East Voe, Easter Quarff. Shortly after this house was completed he called to a passing friend 'come on in an tell me whit du tinks o dis cachot.'[1] From that time the house was known as Cachot, now spelt Casho.

A Napoleonic veteran, William Mitchell, died in 1865 on the island of Shapinsay where he had been born ninety years earlier. He was captured at sea and spent ten years in a French prison, enabling him, even in old age, to speak the language fluently. His was an interesting story, alas known only in part, and *The Orkney Herald* of 8 August 1865 reported: 'Mitchell originally joined the service to relieve his brother who had been pressed, and who had no great ambition to distinguish himself as a naval hero. The deceased was a man of quiet and retired habits, shewing no special desire to boast of the exploits and hardships of his earlier years.'

A man at Castlehill, Harray was recruited in the early years of the French Revolutionary War which commenced in 1793. He returned after nineteen years in a French prison and was not recognised by his relatives, who were Johnstons and lived at Brettaville. To have been imprisoned in France for that length of time seems remarkable. If indeed he was absent for almost two decades (the Napoleonic Wars ended in 1815) the unknown Orcadian may have lingered in England before booking a passage home. Doubtless his appearance over the years would have changed dramatically.

A native of Sandwick, impressed on return from whaling, was captured and imprisoned for seven years by the French. A proficient shoemaker, he busied himself making footwear for his captors and the money so earned bought extra food.

There are several instances of men on their way to imprisonment on the continent recapturing their vessel from enemy privateers,[2] mostly featuring strong drink. One Saturday afternoon *Seagull* sailed from Lerwick to fish for ling. The crew of six men and a boy, enjoying pleasant weather, were startled by a cannon shot followed quickly by another. These came from *Jeanette*, a French privateer, and *Seagull* was forced to heave to. Skipper Manson and four men were transferred to the enemy vessel and replaced by Frenchmen. The task of sailing to France in company with the privateer was given to Magnus Bolt and a lad Jamie Ross. The boarding party discovered and broached a cask of rum, in due course becoming drunk. While the inebriated Frenchmen were below deck, Bolt battened down the covers and in the darkness altered course for Lerwick. *Seagull* was some distance from land when a fierce cannonade was heard coming from

---
1 Dungeon.
2 These were also known as *picaroons* or *pickaroons*, from the Spanish picarón – a pirate.

behind a bank of fog. The following morning when the thick haze cleared, Bolt and Ross were delighted to discover that *Jeanette* had been captured and shortly afterwards the Shetlanders were reunited.

Arthur Deerness, South Ronaldsay was homeward bound when his vessel was captured in the English Channel by the French and a prize crew put on board. The ship was well-stocked with drink and before long the Frenchmen became intoxicated. Three remained on deck and Deerness took the first opportunity to throw two overboard. The third man staggered below for safety where he and his remaining comrades were secured by the Orcadian. It is said that aided only by a boy, Deerness navigated safely to the Downs in the south of England.

In *The Arctic Whalers*[1] Lubbock mentions several cases of recapture. *Chaser* of London, anxious to avoid the English Channel, came north about and was taken off Orkney on 19 July 1794 by an eighteen-gun privateer. She arrived at Peterhead eight days later, having been retaken from her prize crew by the second mate and three boys.

Also in 1794 *Raith* was seized by a privateer when off Shetland and returning to Hull from Greenland whaling. A prize crew of sixteen Frenchmen was put on board and her crew removed with the exception of the mate and a seaman. After a carousal the nine men who formed the first watch clambered into one of the whale boats and fell asleep. With commendably quick thinking the mate and the seamen cut the ropes and the boat was cast adrift. They battened the remaining seven men below deck and successfully sailed the vessel to Lerwick complete with its cargo of spik.[2]

---

1 Ibid., p. 135.
2 Whale blubber.

Returning Islanders

Impressment was a miserable business: insensitive and indiscriminate, with recruits subjected to absences of indefinite length. Loyal and efficient service did, however, enable some pressed men to obtain promotion in a navy at war, in which opportunities were created by sickness and the long casualty lists that inevitably followed any major engagement.

Sometimes these men returned unexpected and in unusual circumstances. When a man-of-war put into Unst for supplies, the usual flotilla of small boats came out with produce to barter.[1] Fish and poultry were exchanged for rum, tobacco and brandy, and the chaffering was as usual concluded over a drink. On this occasion the ritual was interrupted by a pronouncement from the Captain's cabin: 'Give Robbie Gray a *good* drink.' After many years of service, a press-ganged Unst youth had risen to a command, and recognised a boyhood companion, Gray, amongst the locals involved in the bartering.

Few conscripts were literate and for years there might be no contact with pressed men, anxious relatives fearing that loved ones had perished from disease or in action. It was as though they had been effaced from the ken of their families and those who did survive had to return as best they could. Not lacking in fortitude, they travelled long distances often in difficult conditions.

Alexander Greig was pressed in South Nesting and served for years before being discharged at Portsmouth. Doggedly, he walked to Aberdeen and boarded a schooner bound for Shetland, completing the entire journey in some three months.

A similar story is told about Edward Groundwater, farmer in Tankerness, captured and taken by a frigate. A resourceful man, he deserted in the south of England and moved inland avoiding ports and main roads. He acquired a reaping hook, obtained work as an itinerant harvest hand and, thus employed, journeyed

---

1 Many sailing vessels called at Shetland for repairs, or to obtain water and provisions. Fresh fish, eggs and chickens were purchased, or salt beef, pork, biscuit, cotton handkerchiefs and other articles of apparel were offered in exchange.

northwards using by-ways, sleeping rough and finding chance employment. Apprehended on the Meikle ferry at Tain, Ross-shire, and subsequently interrogated in the Burgh Court there, he declared that he was Edward Smith, a farmer from Ireland, visiting his brother in Wick, Caithness. This story was accepted and eventually, in mid-October he reached the Pentland Firth. Wary of using the mail boat, he persuaded a fisherman to convey him to Orphir where he landed penniless and ill-clothed.

Hugh Cormack was pressed when fishing off the Calf of Eday. The transfer in a heavy swell to a naval vessel was difficult and his leg was crushed between the two boats. He was transferred to a captured Spanish man-of-war, the *Salvador del Munor*, and after only a month discharged disabled on 20 June 1814. The enabling certificate, reproduced in a privately printed book,[1] was signed by W V Hull, the ship's captain: 'Hugh Cormick [sic] is five Feet four Inches high, is of a fresh complexion, and aged twenty-six years. He, having been surveyed and found unfit for His Majesty's Service by reason of an ulcerated leg, is this day discharged unserviceable.' The port is unknown. Cormack made the long journey to Eday, recovered his health and lived at Quoyfaulds to the great age of ninety-six. He was regarded as an authority on Napoleon, about whom he readily recounted stories which doubtless became embroidered with the passage of time.

William Johnson and a lad Ratter, both from Northmavine, were engrossed in guddling[2] trout in a local burn when taken. Johnson's father John Jarmson[3] who lived at Feal, Ronas Voe, hastened to the tender which was anchored at Ollaberry and pled without success for the youths release. Ratter never came back, but years later Johnson did return with two daughters and one arm. After his impressment he had come to enjoy naval life, in the course of which he married at Chatham. Later he transferred to the army, served with Sir John Moore at Corunna in 1809 and six years later lost an arm at Waterloo.

Another pressed Shetlander who readily adapted to service life and who also fought at Waterloo remained in France for six years. *The Shetland Times* of 13

---

1 *The Cormacks of Eday, Orkney Islands, Scotland*, Maribelle Cormack, 1969.
2 Catching fish by groping under stones or banks.
3 The shifting patronymic system of surnames was in common use at that time in Shetland, and in some families existed well into the 19th century. James Manson, one of the last Shetlanders with a patronymic surname, died in 1875 and his father was Magnus Olason. Arthur Anderson who died in 1855 was the son of Andrew Robertson, and as late as 1910 some older people whose parents had patronymic surnames experienced difficulty in proving their age and the right to a State pension.

March 1909 reported: 'In our obituary column to-day, we publish a notice of the death of Miss Catherine Gray,[1] which took place at Billister, North Nesting, on Friday of last week. It may be interesting to state that the deceased's father was present at the battle of Waterloo, and resided in France for six years after. He was first pressed into service, and then escaped, but subsequently joined the ranks voluntarily.'

The crofters and cottars of Westness, Rousay were served notice to quit in 1848 by the laird George William Traill. Nevertheless, he may have felt a tincture of compassion for one crofter who had served in the wartime navy. W P L Thomson in *The Little General and the Rousay Crofters*,[2] writes: 'Only one croft, the little holding of Magnus Mass Hill, was allowed to exist for a further nine years. The laird may have felt a special responsibility for the tenant, James Kent,[3] a navy pensioner and veteran of the Napoleonic Wars.

What happened to a lad Spence from Gorn, Grimeston, typifies the experience of some islanders. Betrayed by a neighbour and caught in bed, he realised the futility of resistance, stoically accepted his fate, dressed and prepared to leave. There was a poignant scene at the cottage door as his stepmother, tearful and distraught, handed the youth a toom piece[4] to sustain him as he went moagsan[5] over the muddy rutted track to Kirkwall. Melancholy, he departed wondering if this might be his last meal of home fare and contemplating the bleak prospect of indefinite service at sea. Years later Spence, then a hardened veteran, did return and quickly sought revenge on the informer. A fight took place at the Slap of Araquoy in the township of Netherbrough, Harray and, in the best tradition, Spence left the villain unconscious on the ground.

There was also trouble on the island of Westray following the return of a pressed man Harcus from the district of Lochend. Prior to being taken he was in surly disagreement with the laird, James Stewart of Brough and Cleat, who took an early opportunity of selecting him for the quota. A press gang officer arrived to escort him to Kirkwall, whereupon Harcus volunteered, saying 'Stewart is never to send me, I'm enlisting of my own free will.' Thus he obtained bounty

---

1 Catherine Gray died on 5 March 1909 aged eighty-five, and was registered as 'pauper (formerly knitter)'. Her father Robert Gray, a crofter, probably died before compulsory registration commenced in 1855. Her mother Margaret Gray died on 24 April 1883, aged ninety-three.
2 p. 49.
3 Allegedly Nelson's cabin boy; see p. 239.
4 Also thoomb piece: a piece of bread, bannock or oatcake spread with butter, the thumb being used as a spreader.
5 Trudging.

money and ensured that the cantankerous laird had to find another man. The Orcadian served for eleven years and on discharge resumed his island way of life, although no longer resident on the estate. On his way home one summer evening from peat cutting at Skelwick, he was confronted by the laird who remonstrated, stating that only tenants were permitted to take fuel.[1] Harcus was furious and threatened him with a flail, declaring 'I'll tak the paets I want, I fought lang fur you an your moss, anither word an I'll stretch you.' Stewart hurriedly departed and never again interfered with his erstwhile tenant. Harcus had been partially incapacitated by a wound and apparently received an annual pension of £4. He collected the instalments in Kirkwall where an accommodating woman helped to spend the money. After each visit he returned penniless but contented, to continue the teaching duties he assumed in his later years.

A Shetland prisoner called Work had an unusual reunion on his release and return to this country. Captured at sea when a youth and imprisoned for years in France, he had a memorable meeting in Newcastle with a brother from whom he had been long separated. This took place in 1814 and was reported that year in the *Edinburgh Annual Register*[2] of 20 September. *The Shetland News* of 27 February 1909 reprinted the article and commented:

Many Shetland seamen served in the Royal Navy at that time, enduring all the hardships and viscissitudes of fortune incidental to the King's service, and a good many of them, as well as merchant sailors, had the misfortune to be taken as prisoners of war and confined in the French prisons. The young man referred to in this narrative had probably been taken off a merchant ship, seeing that the capture had been made by a French privateer, and had been liberated at the termination of the war on Napoleon's first abdication in 1814.

The *Register's* report of 1814 details the Work brothers reunion:

INTERESTING OCCURENCE — The captain of the Don schooner, from Gottenburg, while delivering a cargo of deals and iron to Messrs Head and Co. of Newcastle, a few days ago, was accosted by a miserable-looking young man, just returned from a French prison, beseeching a little employment. The captain, in reply, said he was sorry that he was not in want of any additional hands, as his crew was fully adequate

---

1 Sir John Sinclair, *The Orkney Parishes*, p. 349. In 1793 the Rev James Izat, minister in Westray, recorded: 'There is only one peat moss in the island of Westray, and none other in the parish; this is the exclusive property of one heritor, who a few years ago has prohibited almost all the inhabitants from the benefit of this moss, excepting his own tenants … This is a most distressing consideration to a great number of the inhabitants of Westray.'
2 It was also contained in the 13 September 1814 issue of *Flindell's Western Luminary*, printed in Exeter.

to discharge the cargo. The young man, in return, expressed his regret, but urged the captain to suffer him to work only for his meat, as he was literally starving for want of food. Commiserating his unhappy situation, the captain complied with the condition, and the young man went cheerfully to work in the hold among the crew. Observing, on the second day, the assiduity of the stranger to discharge his duty, the captain asked him of what place he was a native; 'Lerwick,' he replied. 'Lerwick— Lerwick!' rejoined the captain, 'and what is your name ?' 'James Work,' replied the youth. [1] Palpitating with eager anxiety, and afraid he might be mistaken, the captain immediately enquired if he had a brother. 'I had [said he] but it is a long time since I saw him.' 'What is his name—his name?' almost breathlessly enquired the master. 'Laurence Work,' replied the youth. 'Then you must have had letters from your brother?' says the captain. 'Oh yes, sir.' 'Come, come, come along with me,' said the captain, hastily, and immediately hurried him into the cabin. 'Have you any objections to shew me those letters from your brother?' asked the captain. 'Certainly not,' said he, and immediately produced them. The captain, assured then almost to a certainty who the young man was, produced corresponding letters to himself, and upon the mutual correspondence being laid upon the table, each exclaimed 'brother!' and they instantaneously rushed into each other's arms, and for several minutes their feelings were so overpowered, with the warmth of their affections, that neither of them could speak till tears came to their relief. To explain the cause of the brothers being unacquainted with each other's countenance at first sight, it is only necessary to state, that the younger brother, when a perfect youth, was captured in the early part of the war, by a French privateer, and had grown into manhood in a French prison.

Ned Shearer of Clett, Whalsay, failed to return to his home, and with the passage of years was presumed dead. One fine voar morning his father was gazing out to sea when a small boat with one occupant grounded at the noust below the croft. Looking intently the old man became animated and exclaimed that had he not known his son was dead, the seafarer could have been Ned 'bi da shape o his boady an da hard hat at he's wearin.' It was indeed Ned, returned safely as from the dead, after much voyaging and many adventures. He had served for twelve years and in 1817 married Catherine Rendall. They had five children all born in Whalsay, the last in 1830, and the family later moved to Lerwick where his wife died in 1877 aged 85.

---

1   He was Jeremiah Work, a native of Whalsay and an apprentice on board a Newcastle collier when the vessel was captured by a French privateer. Imprisoned for nine years at Arras and at Valenciennes, he became reasonably fluent in French. He also obtained some knowledge of navigation from fellow prisoners, and furthemore developed a skill in bookbinding.

The Press Gang in Orkney and Shetland

Sent to Lerwick to collect goods and supplies, a noted fiddler, David Gray, was apprehended. Aged twenty-eight, he was pressed by HMS *Quebec* on 16 November 1806 together with five other Shetlanders. He soon returned home, being discharged on 14 June 1807 following intercession by Thomas Bolt, representative of the Earl of Zetland. Gray resumed working for the Edmondston family of Buness,[1] Unst, playing at balls and social occasions in the laird's house. During his enforced short service at sea his ability to play the fiddle was discovered. Indeed he was required to play frequently, in particular the Captain's favourite tune Lord Kelly's Reel, and his expertise earned him welcome respite from more arduous duties.

Gray was also noted for his strength. One day he was gazing with interest at kegs of Spanish dollars which had been taken from a merchantman. A somewhat supercilious officer came by, looked at Gray and said, 'You're big enough and ugly enough, but *you're* not the man.' The Unst man accepted the challenge, lifted a full keg to his knee, then raising it above his head said 'Do du dat sir.' In 1971 the School of Scottish Studies[2] recorded another version of the story with Gilbert and Annie Gray, Unst. The following dialect transcription was prepared by Angus Johnson, Shetland Archives:

Weel, Dauvid Gray, he wis another relation of ours, he played da fiddle too. An hit wis ida years, I forgit how many years ago now, bit hit wis idaa years whin, you're heard aboot whin da pressgang wis going on, pressin men ta take dem away from here.

Weel, hit wis in dat times. Bit anyway he wis goin away … He wis a servant at Buness … an he played at dir balls and he gud Freideman Stickle[3] ta help him an he hed da best bow haund. An he wis doon in Lerook, an errand ta Edmondston whin two men cam, wan on every side o him and took him, an he wis goin ta throw dem both an he lookit ower his shooder an dere dey wir anidder two so he could mak no more o it. An took [and] pressed him, an he wis upon a ship an he played, dey fan oot at he could play da fiddle an he played an dey keepit him at it. An he cutted da strings whin he got da chance as he wis played dat often. An, of coorse, he got his freedom whin dey wir nae strings upo da fiddle. An he wis walkin aroond ship wan day an wir, dey hed kigs o … Chinese dollars. An he wis lookin at dem an da mate cam by an he says, you're big an ugly enough bit you're not da man an he took dis kig an he lifted it as faur as his knee, an said, do you that sir? An da officer went away an said nothing. An Edmondston he couldn't do

---

1 It may have been the Edmonston family who wrote to the Admiralty and requested his release.
2 SA1971/221.
3 His father was also a noted Unst fiddler. For further details about the Stickle family see footnote on p. 182.

withoot his servant an he wrot ta da Admiralty an told tem, asked fur da man back. An da Admiralty said at dey didna tink at day wir a man in Shetland at could pen such a letter. An he got Dauvid Gray off. An dat wis da end o Dauvid Gray.

Experience was often the sole reward of discharged seamen whose years of hard, dangerous service, and sometimes impaired health, were not always recognised by a pension. *The Shetland Advertiser* of 1 September 1862 stated:

After the nation had made the utmost use of the slaves it captured it generally turned them adrift, to depend on parochial relief when unfit for labour. We give the simple story of an old Trafalgar man, as taken down from his own lips:

'Robert Robertson, aged 76, born in Nesting, first went to sea in 1804, pressed in same year on coming home from Greenland by the Cutlow sloop-of-war. Served in the Agatnetanon, 64, until she was wrecked in South America in Maldonada bay in 1809. Was in three actions – 22d July 1805, under Sir Robert Calder; 21st October 1805, Trafalgar; 6th February 1806, St Domingo, under Admiral Cochrane. Was at Copenhagen in 1807. After being wrecked in the Agatmemon, joined the Elizabeth, 74, Captain Edward Leveson Gower, and served in her till 1814 when he was invalided from the Mediterranean station for an asthmatic complaint, and was discharged at Portsmouth. Went to sea occasionally until the year 1835. Is now unfit to support himself; and must apply for parochial relief. Has applied for a pension, but never got any answer.

'There is an end for an "old Agatnetanon." Should such be the closing scene of the life of one of those to whom Britain owes the supremacy of the seas. The great and rich, the glorious and free British nation, robs one of its free-born sons of his birthright of freedom, forces him to serve for less than he could earn by honest labour, pushes him forward into the front of battle, and then, when he is old and worn out, says, let him go to the parish …

'…We think that the British nation ought to acknowledge that they committed a great and grievous sin, or rather that their fathers committed a great and grievous sin, in having recourse to the impressments of seamen; they ought to insist on the right of impressments being once and for ever renounced by the crown; and by way of partial restitution, and to remove a foul stain from the British escutcheon, they ought to search out every sailor, now living, who was ever impressed, and settle on him a pension, equivalent to a deferred annuity which might have been purchased by a sum equal to the amount of wages received by him while in service.'

Five Stenness Brothers

The lives of the Leith brothers from Nether Onston, Stenness, provide an insight into life below deck during the Napoleonic Wars. What makes their story so interesting is that they were literate at a time when literacy among seamen was unusual. William, Peter, Nicol, James and Charles were all pressed at some time in their naval careers. Over twenty letters, now lodged in the National Library of Scotland and dating from 1801–10, were mostly addressed to their father William Leith. They give details of a hard life at sea and the demanding conditions under which these Orkneymen served in foreign climes.

William, born in 1760, joined the merchant navy. In 1804 he was pressed and sent to HMS *Illustrious* where he became a quarter gunner.[1] There he was joined by his brother Nicol. Aged fifty he died of cholera in the Indian Ocean during an expedition to attack Mauritius.

Peter, born in 1772, went to sea at an early age and became a ship's carpenter. Pressed in 1804 he was released later that year. To avoid the gang who were being troublesome he shipped aboard a vessel bound for Malta. Following William's death, he was requested to return home and in 1815 served aboard a Customs vessel at Stromness before returning to sea as a ship's carpenter. He died in 1861.

Nicol, born in 1775, was a Straitsman.[2] In January 1801 he was pressed at Longhope from a fishing boat by HMS *Lynx*. He too was promoted to quarter gunner on *Illustrious*, served in 1809 at the Basque Roads engagement off the west coast of France and received prize money for taking part in the action. In 1811, discharged as unserviceable due to consumption, he was thirty-six, but his discharge papers give his age as fifty. Recruits sometimes gave a false age as older seamen did not have to face the perils of duties aloft. The fresh Orkney air cured Nicol's tuberculosis and he lived to the age of ninety-seven or, according to his pension papers, 109. Awarded prize money and a pension of £23/12d for life, in his later years it was collected by his son Peter from the Customs Officer in Kirkwall. On one occasion, probably riled by the long period of pension payments, the Officer declared 'Is that old devil not dead yet!' He was the only member of the family who married (1820). On return to Stenness, Nicol spent his time fishing and whaling and bought two farms adjacent to Nether Onston. These were Greavas (now known as Grieve House) and Appiehouse. This latter farm has remained in the ownership of the Leith family.

Between 17 September 1810 and 3 February 1811, Nicol kept a diary detailing the voyage of *Illustrious* from Calicut, now Kozhiriode in south west India, on expedition to Mauritius, having embarked a regiment of foot soldiers. Shortly after the fleet sailed, cholera broke out and Nicol's diary is composed largely of

1 Petty Officer with the responsible position of maintaining and furnishing four cannon.
2 Davis Strait whaler.

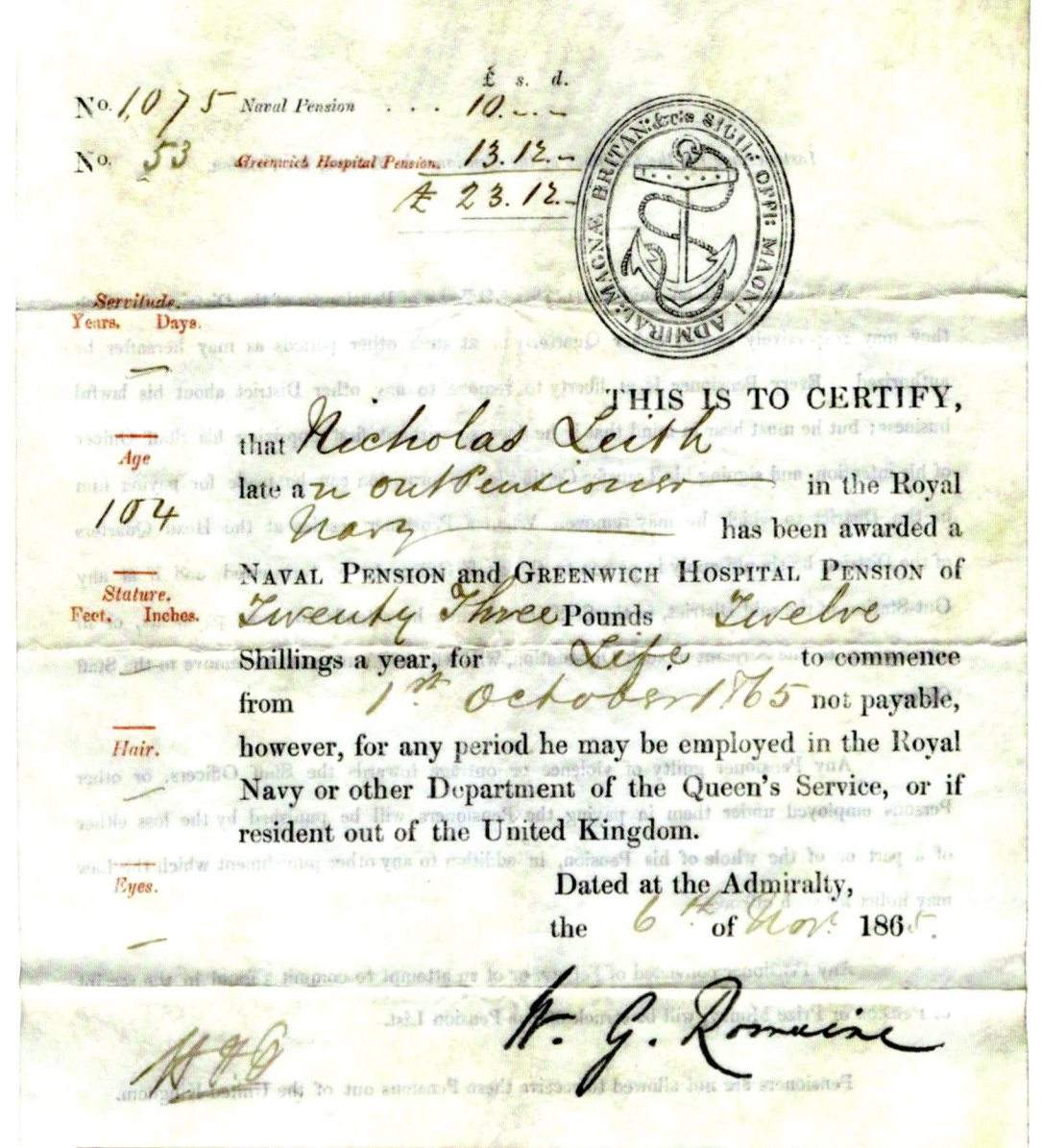

No. 1075   Naval Pension ... 10. — —
No. 53   Greenwich Hospital Pension 13. 12. —
              £ 23. 12. —

Servitude.
Years.   Days.

THIS IS TO CERTIFY,
that *Nicholas Leith*
late an *out Pensioner* in the Royal
Navy has been awarded a
NAVAL PENSION and GREENWICH HOSPITAL PENSION of
Twenty Three Pounds *Twelve*
Shillings a year, for *Life* to commence
from *1st October 1865* not payable,
however, for any period he may be employed in the Royal
Navy or other Department of the Queen's Service, or if
resident out of the United Kingdom.

Dated at the Admiralty,
the *6th* of *Nov.* 186*5*.

W. G. Romaine

Age
104

Stature.
Feet.   Inches.

Hair.

Eyes.

N.B.—The personating or falsely assuming the name or character of a Naval Pensioner in order to obtain his Pension Money, or procuring any other to do the same, is made FELONY, by Act of Parliament.
This Ticket is not transferable, and is no security for Debt.
The Pensioner is desired to attend to the Instructions on the other side hereof.

Nicholas Leith's Pension Certificate.

names of those who died. On 29 November 1810 the diary entry reads 'came to anchor close to the Isle of France. Landed all our troops without the least opposition, not as much as a musket being fired.' There was no abatement in the cholera outbreak and two days later '60 or 70 of the ships company were sent to sick Quarters ashore.' On 2 December conditions improved with 'fresh beef served and a few hours liberty ashore for the benefit of our health.' The diary is a rarity as usually such records were kept by officers.

James Leith was born in 1778. In 1804 he is mentioned as being on board *Polyphemus* and in September that year on *Leydn*. In 1805 he returned to the former vessel and saw action at Trafalgar.[1] In 1806 he wrote that he was due a great deal of prize money. He was in Quebec in February 1820 and then Cork (bound for Jamaica) from where he communicated that he was unwell. Thereafter nothing more was heard from him.

Charles, born in 1782, became a merchant seaman. Pressed onto *Rose* in 1805, in 1809 he wrote that his ship was bound for the Baltic and he was suffering from scurvy. He died during the voyage.

Tall Tales

Although people living in remote island communities little understood or appreciated the great events creating history in the outside world, veterans returning from the French Revolutionary and Napoleonic Wars nevertheless commanded much respect, amounting almost to awe. As the years passed, tales recounted by these old campaigners were always interesting, often colourful, and at times significantly improbable.

'Lang Willie' Hoseason of Gloup, North Yell, had been pressed into the army and served with Wellington at Waterloo. When discharged he came back to his island home, lived to a great age, and over the years delighted in revealing just how the decision to join battle was taken. Slowly, savouring every moment of the unfolding drama, he recalled lighting his pipe and strolling across the wet ground to Wellington's tent. Greetings were exchanged and when each was sufficiently assured that the other had breakfasted adequately, the Duke solemnly pronounced: 'In that case, Willie, we had better make a start.'[2] In later years, perhaps

---

1 His Trafalgar medal remains in the possession of the Leith family.
2 A similar story was told by an Orcadian, Willie Newlands, on his return from the Crimean War. It goes that on the morning of battle, after the British and French regiments had formed up, the Commander-in-Chief galloped along the line and enquired anxiously of Newlands' Colonel 'Is William Newlands in the ranks?' On being assured that indeed he was, the General confidently proclaimed 'In that case, let battle commence.'

stimulated by libations of smuggled Dutch gin, Willie would confide how at the height of the conflict one of Napoleon's veterans was heard to exclaim: 'There's Lang Willie Hoseason o' Gloup, shoot the b-!'[1]

James Henderson, Lea, Whalsay also had a story to tell. Captured at his croft he was taken aboard a tender where an obnoxious officer insulted him. The infuriated crofter seized the offender 'bi da scruff o da neck an da saet o da breeks and balled[2] him ower da side.' The lieutenant pitched into the inhospitable waters of Lerwick harbour on which the tails of his jacket lay spread like a 'young craw's wings.' The Shetlander was punished severely, being beaten with a cat of nine tails and secured in irons. Subsequently, in a great sea battle he served as a powder monkey, and on returning to Whalsay, when asked about the extent of his involvement, Henderson declared 'I kerried pooder lik be damned.'

Some pressed men appeared briefly at home while in service. Theodore Anderson from Skerries was taken when picking limpets for bait. Several years after his capture a man-of-war's boat landed and the party went directly to a well where they filled casks. It was assumed that Anderson was one of the sailors as no stranger could have known where to draw fresh water.

Several Birsay boats were fishing off the Brough when a man-of-war bore down and took the men aboard. The captain escorted Robert Comloquoy to the privacy of his cabin where the two were closeted for some time. On deck the captain freed all the fishermen and the vessel stood off. Comloquoy was reticent about what had transpired, though it was generally accepted in the parish that the men were brothers. Not only was there a family resemblance, but it was recalled that some years earlier an elder brother had left Orkney to seek his fortune. It was thought that the captain had given Robert a sum of money and this belief was supported by the family's subsequent affluence.

A curious tale is told about a Whalsay man who had some ability with the fiddle. In resisting impressment he killed two members of the gang and fled from Shetland. One winter's night years later his aged parents were sitting by the fireside when they heard the strains of fiddle music. Fearful but curious, they opened the door of the adjoining room, where at the sight of their long-departed

---

1 This story may have been confused with that concerning Captain 'Lang' Willie Henderson born in the Haa House, Gloup, North Yell. At the Battle of Waterloo Captain Willie was on horseback and had the heel of one foot removed by a cannonball which killed his steed. He survived and was eventually buried in Edinburgh. When the Haa House was renovated in 1909 a cannonball was found by one of the workmen. It has always been believed that this was the missile which damaged the Yell man's heel and killed his horse.
2 Threw.

son they exclaimed 'Jack's alive!' The tune which the returned exile had been playing was thereafter known as *Jack's Alive* and remains in traditional folk music to this day.[1]

Another version of the story tells of a fiddler called Jack who was pressed at sea along with the rest of a fishing boat's crew and no-one knew what had befallen them. He served in the navy for five years and when discharged set out for home. Travel to the North was slow and arduous, and to while away the long hours he composed a fiddle tune. Eventually he reached Shetland and the story continues:

> Whin he got to da hoose it wid dark, an whin he guid in his midder tocht he was a feyness.[2] Hooever, shu saw it wis real an made him a cup o' tae. Whin he'd finished his tae he rekked[3] doon da fiddle it was hangin' upa da wa' an efter he'd gotten her tuned he played a tun. His midder wha kent aa da tuns at dat time said, 'Boy, I'm never heard yon-een afore; what's yun?' Jack said, 'Yun's een I made up as I wis maakin fir hame an I caa him "Jack is Yet Alive".'[4]

John Paul Jones and the Mousa Men

In late August 1779 three Mousa men – John Adamson, James Smith and James Bain – were fishing inshore from a small boat when a strange vessel flying a pilot flag bore down and took them and their boat on board. Questioned about the number of warships anchored in Lerwick their answer, inspired to prevent attack on the defenceless town, was that there were two. Replying to a further enquiry about the size of the vessels they said 'dey hae twa muckle masts afore an a peerie wan ahint.'[5] This sufficed to divert the captain, who was none other than the illustrious John Paul Jones. Born a Scotsman, his dramatic exploits in

---

1 Arthur Scott Robertson, personal communication 1991. He was a distinguished Shetland fiddler of national fame. His mother, who was born in Whalsay in 1880, heard Jack's Alive and the associated story in her youth. Jack was said to be a Whalsay man.
2 Spirit, ghost.
3 Reached.
4 *Haand Me Doon Da Fiddle*, Tom Anderson and Pam Swing, 1979, p. 40. Additionally, Tom Anderson, Lerwick personal communication 1979. Jack's Alive was one of the first tunes learnt by him. When aged 10 he heard it played by his grandfather Thomas Anderson, Hamnavoe, Eshaness, then a man of 78 (in 1920). Curious to know the background to the title Jack Is Yet Alive, Mr Anderson, who was a noted fiddler, investigated the matter and, with only minor variations, obtained the same story from different sources. It should however be noted that an Irish Air Jack's Alive appears in Hamilton's *Universal Tune-Book* published in 1844. The two tunes have certain similarities.
5 *The Shetland Times*, 19 January 1889.

the American War of Independence have made him a legendary naval hero.[1] Employing brilliant tactics, he attacked British men-of-war and struck at the mainland itself in a series of daring raids.

Any hope of early release for the captives was dashed by concern that they might alert the imaginary men-of-war. Sailing south, Jones took a number of prizes, but his attempt to attack the port of Leith was frustrated by contrary winds. Eventually off Scarborough on 23 September his ship *Bon Homme Richard* encountered and engaged the British man-of-war *Serapis*. For several hours the vessels fought yardarm to yardarm, and finally *Serapis* struck – on fire and boarded by the crew of the sinking *Bon Homme Richard*. So great was the carnage that Jones wrote 'no action before was ever, in all respects, so bloody, so severe and so lasting.'

The prisoners had been confined under hatches in a foetid hold. As *Bon Homme Richard* foundered their attempts to break out were frustrated by a guard on the hatchway who with rifle cocked and menacing bayonet exclaimed 'prenez garde.'[2] The water level rose rapidly and John Adamson in desperation rushed the sentinel, tumbling him headlong into the hold[3] whence only 'a muckle groan' was heard. The captives broke out, gained the lower deck and scrambled aboard the surrendered *Serapis* which then sailed to The Texel.

The battle between these vessels is one of the best known naval engagements on record. So heavy was the cannonade that James Bain, one of the Mousa men, when subsequently asked what he recollected of the encounter replied vehemently 'I heard naethin bit cannicks roarin.' Thereafter he was always known as 'Old Cannicks'.[4]

Only in December did the three Mousa men obtain passage to Shetland on a Dutch smuggler, arriving there on Christmas Eve,[5] to the great joy and surprise of their friends who thought them dead. Adamson, the skipper, had with him the sail of his skiff, having carried it throughout the hazardous journey.

---

1 His remains are interred in the crypt of the United States Naval Academy at Annapolis and the inscription reads: 'He gave our navy its earliest traditions of heroism and victory.'
2 'Beware'. *The Shetland Times*, 19 January 1889.
3 As they planned how best to overpower the guard, Adamson whispered 'Whin I set my fit apo dye upper ledder dan haeve him ida howld.' Whereupon they did so.
4 Another version used the word *canoks*. See *Old Lore Miscellany*, Vol III, pp. 67–9 and *The Shetland Times*, 26 January 1889.
5 5 January 1780. Old Christmas and Yule Day was then 6 January (and sometimes 7 January depending on the district).

There is a tradition that the local landowner, John Bruce[1] of Sumburgh, granted them land rent-free in South Cunningsburgh as a reward for saving Lerwick from bombardment by their quick-witted reply alleging a British naval presence.

Further evidence of the involvement of Mousa men with John Paul Jones and the beneficial consequences to Lerwick is contained in information offered to the Crofters, Commission sitting at Cunningsburgh in 1889. Reporting the proceedings, *The Shetland News* of 9 November under the heading 'The famous Paul Jones and the rent of a croft', prints a statement read to the Court on behalf of Charlotte Adamson, great-grand-daughter of John Adamson:

My greatgrandfather, while at the fishing, was forcibly taken by the famous Paul Jones who wanted a pilot to guide him into Lerwick-harbour. But my greatgrandfather made him believe that an English fleet was lying there, and the pirate sailed away, and Lerwick escaped. My grandfather, his son, probably on account of this, got the Gill (my husband's present croft) free of rent from the laird of Sumburgh. He lived to be an old man. I cared for him in his last years. At his death I went to the late Mr Bruce about the bit croft. He told me to keep it. The march stones show the boundaries.

She stated that her grandfather was granted The Gill from Bruce of Sumburgh, but there is little doubt that it was in fact her great-grandfather John Adamson who in 1783 was given the right to break out[2] The Blett.

The incident with the Mousa men and their protection of Lerwick may have occurred during the Napoleonic Wars and, after years of repetition, become merged in the mosaic of anecdotes about John Paul Jones and his famous earlier expedition round the coast of Britain. However, Tudor records:[3] 'The women clad in red wadmell petticoats, coming in to market on the Knab, are said to have frightened away Paul Jones when he intended, as was his wont, making the Lerwegians "bail up" as they say in Australia.' He does however comment that the man who took the *Serapis* was hardly likely to be frightened by women, however attired. (A similar story exists in Cornwall regarding a vessel from the Armada.)

1 Collector of Customs at Lerwick – first named as Collector in Zetland in the quarter ended 10 October 1778. He died on 17 October 1788, and although named as Collector in the quarter ended 5 January 1789, this was presumably because a replacement had not been appointed. E S Reid Tait's statement in *The Hjaltland Miscellany*, Vol I, p. 66, that Bruce was not connected with any branch of the Bruce family in Shetland is incorrect.
2 When men were allowed to break out (cultivate) holdings it was normal practice (presumably based on the economics of the matter) that for the first few years the land was enjoyed rent-free. The land granted to and broken out by Adamson and Smith, who were brothers-in-law, was The Blett.
3 *The Orkneys and Shetland*, 1883, John R Tudor, p. 453.

Belated Revenge

Although he did not return in person to Orkney a Holm man showed patience and originality in eventually revenging himself on the person responsible for his impressment.

Constable Garrioch, who lived at Upper Bu, had received instructions to secure a recruit. Correctly suspecting that he was at risk, his neighbour at Lower Bu hid in a field of uncut corn, but was discovered. After discharge he never returned to Orkney, but many years later a bulky package arrived for Garrioch. In those days sometimes carriage was paid[1] by the addressee and initially, because of the amount involved, the constable was reluctant to settle. But curiosity prevailed, he paid the carrier and took possession. The contents were cleverly assembled and numerous thick layers of wrapping had to be undone before Garrioch found in the centre a neatly folded, unsigned, handwritten note:

> Who wrote this message you cannot tell,
> The grass is green the sea is blue,
> The devil's deceitful and so are you.
> Who wrote this message you cannot tell,
> But pay the carriage and go to hell.

The pressed man had achieved a measure of revenge.

Orkney Memories of Nelson and Napoleon

Returning veterans from wars with France and Spain had tales to tell of momentous times. Some accounts were true, others less so, and all were repeated and embellished in folk memory. An enterprising few brought back souvenirs.

John Tulloch, Senness, North Ronaldsay, found his way into the Infantry during the American War of Independence, 1775–83. It is not known if he was pressed, but he lived to an old age and in recognition of war service his three sons were each given the tenancy of a croft. John is said to have returned with sixpence in his pocket and an American clock under his oxter. He may have been the first man pressed on North Ronaldsay.

It is not known if Swan (a Swanney from Claypows, North Ronaldsay) was pressed on the island or taken off a ship, but he rose through the ranks to become

---

1 The Post Office Acts of that time did not specify an upper limit of weight, but normally only letters and light packages were carried by the service. However, 'common carriers' were involved in the transportation of heavier items, and they exercised their discretion regarding payment. The carrier who took the parcel to Orkney may have been an individual undertaking the work for personal profit.

a Master-at-Arms and is credited with having accumulated £300 by the time he returned.[1] His tombstone records that he died in 1836 aged eighty-two.

Ernest Marwick, author, folklorist and historian recounted in a broadcast in the mid-1960s what befell some of the soldiers and sailors, mostly pressed men, who served in the long French Wars of 1792–1815. His account contains fascinating memories, fragments of which exist to this day:[2]

I spent some months, as a very little boy, in the cottage of a maiden aunt. Her parlour was also her spare bedroom, and it had a cavernous box bed, closed during the day by a set of panelled doors. From this recess, vast but comfortable, the last thing my eyes rested on, ill lit as it was by a flickering oil lamp, was a huge coloured print of the Death of Nelson.

It wasn't the famous painting by Davis, but a far cruder thing, showing the scene on the deck of the Victory at Trafalgar just after Nelson fell. Its somewhat lurid colouring disturbed me as much as its subject matter. And I simply couldn't get away from it: it occupied in its dull gilt frame the greater part of the wall. The stricken Nelson was undoubtedly a noble figure, but there were nasty splotches of blood, and some of the sailors seemed villainous. I suppose the artist meant them to appear heart broken, yet determined to pay out the French, I don't know if they frightened the Frenchmen, but as Wellington would have said, they terrified me.

I discovered later on that the print was extremely popular in the Orkney Islands, having the place of honour in many a home. You might wonder why its subject made such an appeal in isolated islands on the outermost fringe of Britain, until I tell you that these islands played a vital part in the Napoleonic wars, providing out of their small population perhaps two thousand men for the Navy, something like a twelfth of the total population. So the picture which scared me told a story which had been related familiarly by more than one Orkneyman. It was almost a piece of family history.

In one home in Kirkwall, our chief town, it was regarded more as a family portrait, for to every visitor the woman of the house would point out a shadowy figure, a man named Cooper, who helped to carry the dying Admiral into the Victory's cockpit. He was her father. Had I known things like that as a child, I might have identified some of the other sailors who scared me, with families and places with which I was entirely familiar.

Among them would be James Leith of Stenness, a gunner, whose Trafalgar medal I saw only the other day. James valued his medal, as his descendants still do, so he did not throw it overboard like other sailors did when they found that the medals were made of

---

1 Probably the same Quartermaster William Swanney serving on *Rochefort* in Marwick's account; see p. 242.
2 Orkney Archives, D31/68/4.

pewter instead of silver. Between decks on the *Victory* James contracted tuberculosis. He came home to his native island to die, but the strong northern air restored him and he lived to be a bane and portent to the pension officer. He died at the age of ninetyfour, but he had added ten years to his age on joining the Navy. Thus to the officials he seemed to be going strong when well past a hundred. They paid his pension with grudging and awe.

Somewhere on the *Victory*'s deck would also have been John Gaudie of Birsay and George Gaudie of North Ronaldsay. All I know about John Gaudie is that he came back to the moorland farm of Surtadale, from which an improving landlord evicted him. George Gaudie had an even harsher fate. He had taken part in nearly all of Nelson's battles. Most of the time he was a quarter-master belonging to Nelson's barge. Lady Hamilton declared that he was the finest looking fellow in a crew of picked men.

George served in the Navy until the peace of 1815. When he left the sea he had saved over a thousand pounds. With a job assured at the Portsmouth dockyard, he married a pretty, apparently pious girl, and was happy until she, having obtained control of his money, silently disappeared. The shock quite unbalanced the quiet red-haired Orkneyman. Back home in Orkney, he took to wandering all over the islands. With his troubled blue eyes, the man in the Scotch bonnet and brown monkey jacket was known everywhere. He slept in the fields in summer, in barns in winter, eating when and how he could. He was completely harmless and inoffensive, but one thing angered him – the offer of money. He loathed the sight of it.

You will notice that I have spoken of these simple island men who shared Nelson's glory as if it all happened yesterday. So it seems, for local memory is long. Another Nelson touch which came my way recently was in the island of Rousay. A lady there was telling me about her great-grandmother, a wise and imaginative woman, whose stories of the past left an indelible impression on her mind.

One man, with the surname of Kent[1] (fairly common, as it happens, in Orkney) came striding purposefully out of the remembered tales. A taciturn crofter he was, who remembered every few months that he had once been a seaman. He would go quickly past with an empty spirit keg on his back. Over the water in Kirkwall he would get it filled,[2] and collect his pension.

Who was he? I asked.

My ignorance could be excused in one not born on that island. My friend explained patiently, 'He was Nelson's cabin boy,' and she went on to say 'He was with Nelson in the West Indies when Nelson took very ill with a fever. He thought he was dying, and so did

---

1 He lived at Riverside and had been pressed.
2 Rum was his choice, known by sailors as 'Nelson's blood'.

everyone else, so he ordered his coffin to be made. Shortly after it was delivered Nelson got better, but he liked the coffin so much that always afterwards he kept it in his cabin. One of the cabin boy's jobs was to keep it spruce and clean and polish the handles.'

Probably that Orkney cabin boy saw Nelson laid at last in his coffin – not the shining one which had stood in the cabin, but a chest of lead, later to be broken in pieces and sold as souvenirs.

From the Orkney Islands had gone these hundreds of ordinary sailors to fight alongside Nelson. With them was a sixty-year-old Orkney admiral, Alexander Graeme. As Commander-in-chief at the Nore he became intimate with Nelson, who wrote once to his 'dearest Emma', 'Today I dined with Admiral Graeme, who has also lost his right arm (Nelson had lost his at Santa Cruz); and as the commander of troops has lost his leg, I expect we shall be caricatured as the lame defenders of England.' The Orkney admiral described Nelson after Trafalgar as the most extraordinary man this country ever produced.

To look around in the islands for stories of Nelson is to find ones of Napoleon. Two extremely interesting links with Napoleon have rewarded me. I had heard of a teacher in one of our country schools, dead for over a decade, who used to preface his history lessons on the Napoleonic Wars with this preamble: 'The great Napoleon made his final surrender to James Tait of this parish, and his great-grand-daughter is sitting among you.' Somewhat heady stuff for an imaginative girl.

Alas, this piece of 'history' was only partly true. But the schoolmaster could hardly be blamed, for the encounter between Quarter-master James Tait,[1] of Deerness, and Bonaparte acquired over the years so much impressive detail and seemingly authentic dialogue that none but a historian would have questioned it. It was eventually written down by the local poet, a man who once sat with his neck in splints for three weeks, believing he had broken it, and on another occasion declared his intention of marrying a mermaid who was repeatedly seen off the coast. Little wonder if his history of James Tait was partly fabulous.

Tait, the story went, was ashore at Rochefort for water with part of the crew of the *Bellerophon*, when Napoleon came up to him and Introduced himself. Tait gave the salute due to a superior officer.

---

[1] The muster books of the *Bellerophon* do not record a James Tait. Only two Orcadians are listed. Some years before, Magnus Wood from the parish of Rendall was pressed and left behind a young wife and baby boy. Feigning deafness he was eventually discharged. His son was also pressed when seventeen and with a fellow islander he served on *Bellerophon*, the muster books recording 'John Wood, twenty-one, and William Rusland, thirty-eight, both ordinary seamen' (1 July to 13 September 1815, ADM 37/5032). Allegedly he was in the party sent ashore at Rochefort to bring off Napoleon at the commencement of his journey to St Helena (*Around the Orkney Peat Fires*, pp. 217–18).

But Napoleon said, 'I see you are a courteous man, but you are to be my superior officer now; here is my sword, for I surrender unconditionally and must obey your orders now.' To which Tait replied, 'Well, my orders are that you keep your sword until we come to Captain Maitland, and then hand it over to him.'

There is much more dialogue, but I think some of it must be true. At any rate it deserves to be true. Listen to this: 'What is the reason,' asked Napoleon, 'that you all treat me so kindly and look on me, an enemy, in such a kindly and respectful manner?'

'Do you remember,' asked Tait, 'one time when you sent an English sailor over the Straits of Dover because he attempted to escape from France in a queer little boat?'

Napoleon said, 'I remember the queer little craft and the brave man who attempted to cross to England in such a wherry.' And then the great Napoleon laughed like a boy at the remembrance, and the kindly sparkle of his eye transformed his usually stern countenance as he gazed at the men who thus acknowledged their admiration of a kindly action performed by him when he had such power as few men ever had.

So much for the local poet's account. What I believe really happened is that Quartermaster Tait was in command of the barge which went out from the *Bellerophon* to take Napoleon and his suite off the French brig, which had taken them from Aix roads, thus Tait would have been the first to make contact with the Emperor. On the slow journey to England with its many delays Napoleon spoke much with officers and crew, so that Tait brought back with him to Orkney memories of several conversations. He also took back a more tangible token of the Emperor's regard – a great-coat which Napoleon gave him. If it had been today, that great-coat would have been put in the museum in Kirkwall; but James Tait wore it year after year through the cold island winters for the excellent purpose of keeping himself warm. Our Orkney farms, after centuries of a most primitive agriculture, were then in process of improvement, and Tait had to build walls and dig drains, often donning Napoleon's great-coat. No one knows whether coat or quartermaster survived the longer.

By an amazing coincidence another relic of Napoleon came to Orkney, also brought home by a quartermaster. But let me tell you the story, as I have heard it several times, of Napoleon's window.

It began on the battlefield of Waterloo, after Napoleon had fled, abandoning his private carriage. That, by the way, is the subject of another well known picture, by Ernest Crofts, which is owned by the Walker Art Gallery in Liverpool. In it you can see Napoleon just stepping from his carriage to take possession of a spirited white horse held by one of his officers.

The picture is a dramatic one: a horse drawn field gun thunders by on the left; on the right soldiers of the famous Old Guard stand with their faces towards the advancing

Prussians, all around are wounded or dying men. And there in the centre of the picture, in the middle distance, stands the abandoned carriage with its door wide open, and in the upper part of the door a square window; and it is about that window that my story tells.

In the advance which followed Napoleon's defeat a young British soldier fell shot through the knee. Darkness came on without any appearance of rescuers, so he dragged himself to the Emperor's carriage and spent the night on its comfortable cushions. He felt better in the morning, and determined to provide himself with a souvenir. The only thing that seemed accessible and portable was one of the thick panes of glass that formed the windows. These had in the centre a plain Roman N, Napoleon's monogram.

With his bayonet the wounded man prised the piece of glass from its mountings, and placed it later in the wooden box with which soldiers were then issued.

Soon afterwards he was found by the ambulance corps, who put him on board the Rochefort for transportation to England. He became very ill during the voyage, his wound having become septic. It was soon obvious that he could not recover.

With other badly wounded men he was put under the charge of the Quartermaster, William Swanney, who came from the little Orkney island of North Ronaldsay, Swanney did what he could to ease the lad's misery. As a gesture of gratitude the dying soldier gave Swanney his field-box and its contents.

This was Swanney's last trip: after Waterloo he was paid off. Although he could have obtained another berth, his wife, who had travelled all the way from Orkney to Portsmouth in search of him, persuaded him to return home. She is still remembered in the island as a masterful woman, whose nickname was 'muslin Meg' (I don't know what it meant, but it sounds rather ominous anyhow). Swanney went back with her to North Ronaldsay, with a pocket full of prize money and the box containing Napoleon's window.

In his native island he built himself a new house. Because he was a careful man, who didn't like to waste anything, he used the pane of glass for a skylight. There it remained during his own lifetime and that of his wife.

By the 1870s the house was in the possession of another man, who had a visit one day from a friendly but persuasive American who had heard of Napoleon's window. He saw the piece of glass, now stained by weather and encrusted at the edges with lichen. But it was completely authenticated by the deeply etched Roman N. He coveted the souvenir greatly, and the easy-going islandman let him have it. Indeed, out of the goodness of his heart he constructed a strong box out of driftwood and provided the straw in which Napoleon's window was carefully packed for its long journey to America.

It was on display in the editorial rooms of the *San Francisco Examiner* in 1887. Perhaps somewhere in America this Orkney link with Napoleon still exists.

In 1974 the present writer corresponded with the *Examiner*. The then editor could not confirm that the window had ever been in its possession, although the relic might have been housed in a building pulled down in the 1880s. A subsequent *Examiner* office was destroyed in the 1906 earthquake and fire, so we will never know the truth of this colourful, but by no means improbable, story.

Song and Verse

The activities of the gang are recorded in song and verse, a valuable component of the islands oral traditon. The ballads evidence the effect that the actions of the gang, and the dolorous stories about conditions on board naval vessels, continued to have on the minds of an apprehensive populace. The dread of impressment and service at sea lingered on.

Andrew Ross, The British Sailor

This ballad can still be heard in Orkney. Although not specifically about impressment, it illustrates the fear of life at sea in an exaggerated way. Written several decades after impressment had ceased, it recounts the fate which befell an Orkney man and was sung as a terrible example of what could happen to a seaman at the mercy of sadistic officers. There is a tradition that Ross belonged to either Stronsay or Stromness. *The Orcadian* of 1 September 1857 reported 'Execution of Captain Henry Rodgers, late captain of the *Martha Jane*, for the murder of Andrew Ross, an able-bodied seaman on board the vessel, took place in front of Kirkdale Gaol, Liverpool.'

> Come all you seamen and give attention
> And listen for a while to me
> While I relate of a dreadful murder
> Which happened on the briny sea
>
> Andrew Ross, an Orkney Sailor
> Whose sufferings now I will explain
> While on a voyage from Barbado
> On board the vessel *Martha Jane*
>
> Oh think of what a cruel treatment
> Without a friend to interpose
> They whipped and mangled, gagged and strangled
> The Orkney sailor, Andrew Ross

The mate and captain daily flogged him
With whips and ropes, I'll tell you true
While on Andrew Ross' bleeding body
    Water mixed with salt they threw

For twenty days thus ill they used him
Oh think, what sorrow, grief and shame
    Was suffered by this gallant sailor
    On board the vessel *Martha Jane*

The captain trained his dogs to bite him
    While Ross for mercy he did pray
And on the deck, his flesh in mouthfuls
    Torn by the dogs they lay

Then in a water tank they put him
For twelve long hours they kept him there
While Ross for mercy he was pleading
The captain swore none should go near

    The captain ordered him to swallow
    A thing thereof I shall not name
    The sailors all grew sick with horror
    On board the vessel *Martha Jane*

When nearly dead they did release him
    And on the deck they did him fling
    In the midst of pain and suffering
    'Let us be joyful,' Ross did say

The captain swore he'd make him sorry
    He chained him with an iron bar
    Was that not a cruel treatment
    For an honest British tar

A timber hitch the captain ordered
    All on a rope to be prepared
And Andrew Ross' bleeding body
    Was then suspended in the air

    Justice then did overtake them
    Into Liverpool they came
And there found guilty of the murder
    Committed on the briny main

Oh think of what were the captain's feelings
When both his mates they were released
To think that he alone should suffer
He could not for a while believe

'Oh God,' he cries, 'Is there no mercy
Must my poor wife and children dear
Be hounded out by public scorn
It nearly drives me to despair'

Soon after that an hour arrived
Captain Rodgers had to die
To satisfy offended justice
And hangs on yonder gallows high

I hope his fate will be a warning
To all such tyrants who may suppose
Who would treat an Orkney sailor
As what was done to Andrew Ross

The Nightingale and Billy Taylor

These two ballads are not special to Orkney, but the former was recorded there in 1968 by Dr Alan Bruford from The School of Scottish Studies.[1] The recording was by Mr and Mrs David Budge, Grahamston, South Ronaldsay, and Mr Budge's tune, with its unusual cross-rhythms, was thought to be a superior version of a press gang ballad from Yorkshire.[2]

My love he was a rich farmer's son
When first my tender heart he won
His love to me he did reveal
When I little thought of the *Nightingale*

The eighteenth day of September last
The wind did blow a bitter blast
Tremendous gales my love was in
To the bottom went with the *Nightingale*

The very night that my love was lost
Appeared to me his deadly ghost
In sailor's clothing, his visage pale;
I'll bemoan his fate on the *Nightingale*

1 SA 1968/198B4.
2 *Journal of the Folk Song Society,* Vol III, p. 226. A fuller text is in Greig's *Folk-Song of the North-East,* article 8.

Oh cruel father, oh mother dear
It's unto me you've proved severe
My true love William was pressed away
And his body's sinking in the sea

My father's dwellings I shall forsake
Some lonesome valley myself I'll take
Some lonesome valley, some hill or dale
Where I will not think of the *Nightingale*

The Nightingale

Two years later, Dr Bruford recorded James Henderson and Jock Dass in Burray singing *Billy Taylor,* which they did with great gusto, although apparently not in complete agreement as to the words, refrain, vocables or tune. The result was that the recording had to be edited. James Henderson heard the song from his mother.

Billy Taylor was a sailor
Billy Taylor stout and gay
Instead of Billy getting married
He was pressed and sent to sea

CHORUS:
FolandtherolandtherolandIdo
FolandtherolandtherolIday

She dressed herself in seaman's clothing
She dipped her hands in pitch and tar
Then like a seaman bounded forward
And marched aboard the man-of-war

On this vessel was a wrestle
She sprang up amongst the rest
A silver button sprang from her waistcoat
And the Captain spied her snow white breast

Song and Verse

O my fair my upright lady
What misfortune brought you here
I'm in search of my true lover
Who was pressed, this seven long year

O my fair my upright lady
Come tell to me your true love's name
Some do call him Billy Taylor
But William Taylor is his name

O my fair my upright lady
Come on deck at the break of day
And I shall show you Billy Taylor
Walking with his true love gay

Early, early the next morning
Just before the break of day
There she spied young Billy Taylor
Walking with his true love gay

Gun and powder she commanded
Gun and powder at her command
And there she shot young Billy Taylor
With his bride at his right hand

O my fair my upright lady
What misfortune have you done
I have shot young Billy Taylor
With a double-barrelled gun

Take you that you false deceiver
Take you that you false young man
Seven long months I've searchéd for you
All on board the *Mary Ann*

Billy Taylor

249

True Lovers

This ballad was still being sung in Orkney districts after the First World War and is similar to seaport ditties all over the British Isles. However, the opening verse of the Orkney lay is different, as is the melody.[1]

A fairer pair was never seen
True lovers they had ever been
Ere sun rose on their wedding day
The Press Gang bore her true love away

'Oh father dear build me a boat
That on the waters I may float
And every vessel I pass by
I will enquire for my sailor boy'

She voyaged near she voyaged far
Till she met in with a man o' war
'Please tell me Captain' she implored
'Have you my sailor boy on board?'

'What colour is your sailor's hair
What kind of clothes does your sailor wear?'
'His hair is yellow. His heart is true
He wears the bell-bottomed navy blue'.

'I fear, my dear, your boy's not here
I fear he's lost on yonder bier
D'ye mind last night when the wind loud roared?
We lost a young sailor overboard'.

She wrung her hands, she tore her hair
She beat her breast in wild despair
The watching sailors saw her die
Had heard her last sad appealing cry:

'Oh dig my grave both wide and deep
Put a marble cross at my head and feet
And on my breast place a turtle dove
To let the world know I died in love'.

---

[1] Gilbert Voy, an Orcadian living in Glasgow, personal communication 1975. He first heard this song in St Ola in 1921.

True Lovers

Da Lad at wis ta'en in Voar

In 1889 James Stout Angus wrote about a lass whose Shetland lad was pressed by an armed party, stealing him away from family and friends. Two local men are in love with her, both with houses, farms, boats and sheep, but she does not respond to their advances because of her abiding love for the absent man. At the end of the poem she implores those who sail the oceans, if ever they meet her loved one, to pass a message that she lives still in hope of seeing him.

Dr T M Y Manson set the piece to music in 1973.

> O sailors at sail da sea,
> Far nort at da Labrador,
> Or oot whaar da icy barbers[1] flee,
> Aboot Greenland's frozen shore;
> O tell me, and tell me true –
> Bit A'm no tinking ye wid lee –
> Ir ye ever seen ocht o my boannie young laad
> At wis hustled awa frae me?
>
> Hit wis i'da first o da Voar
> Wi da towe[2] o da hidmist snaa,
> Whin a ship cam sailin in ta wir shore
> Frae some place far awa;
> I sat at da window da day,
> An I stöd i'da open door,
> An I heard da rinklee o her iron shain,
> Shö anchored dat near da shore;
>
> An shö sent a boat ashore –
> Dey laanded doon at da Hwi –
> An every man hed a glitterin gun,
> an a swird apon his tigh;

1 A freezing mist rising from the surface of the sea.
2 Thaw.

An dey took my laad awa
Frae his faeder an midder an me,
An da dey hystit der sheenin sails
An sailed awa ta da sea.

O sailors at sail da sea,
Far sooth whaar da sun is high,
Ye shörely see mony a boannie laand
Whin ye geng sailin by.
O tell me, an tell me true,
Whinever ye göd ta da shore,
Saw ye onything dere o my boannie young laad,
At wis taen i da first o da Voar?

O sailors at sail da sea,
Far aest at da world's rim,
Or up trowe some unkan midland sea,
Or wast at da dayset dim,
O tell me, an tell me true,
If ever ye happen ta see
Or meet wi, ta spaek til, my boannie young laad,
Will ye tell him dis wird frae me:
At A'm livin, an lippenin[1], an still hae a hoop
At A'll see him afore I dee.

Da Lad at wis ta'en in Voar.

1 Expecting or looking forward to.

Da Press-gang Sang

Another Shetlander, Bobby Tulloch (1929–96), penned this song:

De wir hunted on da hillsides, dey wir ta'en fae da crofts
Dey wir forced ta feed da cannon, dey wir made ta clim aloft.
Wives an midders left aweepin, what can da future bring?
Dir men impressed be force inta da navy o' da king
Dir men impressed be force inta da navy o' da king

Da harvest mon wis shinin on da toonships doon below,
Her golden face reflectin in da waters o' da voe,
Da sons o' Shetland rested fae da labours o' da day,
Whan silently a man o' war cam sailin in da bay
Whan silently a man o' war cam sailin in da bay

Why, oh why, can't dey lave da islands be?
Wir men fight hard enough to get dir livin fae da sea.
Will da day never dawn whan dir freedom is secure?
Dirs wan law fur da rich man an anidder fur da poor.

A whispered order giv'n, an a boat wi muffled oar,
Five an twenty bluecoats put silently ashore.
Along da banks in single file an through da stooks o' coarn,
Anidder five will join da ranks afore da day is born.
Anidder five will join da ranks afore da day is born.

Why, oh why, must da poor man always pay?
Why must he fight da battles when he has so little say?
He dusna hate da Spaniard, he kens na what is right,
Lat dem dat mak da quarrels be da eens ta stand an fight.

Da crashin o' da musket butt upon a crofters door,
A greetin wife an a faider beaten ta da earten floor,
A sullen son in manacles is hustled ta da shore,
Five men less in Kirkatoon ta wirk anidder voar,
Five men less apo da haaf ta haul upon an oar.

De wir hunted on da hillsides, dey wir ta'en fae da crofts
Dey wir forced ta feed da cannon, dey wir made ta clim aloft.
Wives an midders left aweepin, what can da future bring?
Dir men impressed be force inta da navy o' da king
Dir men impressed be force inta da navy o' da king

Da Press-gang Sang.

Tales of the Press Gang

J T Smith Leask's *A Peculiar People and Other Orkney Tales*[1]

These stories, written for The Glasgow Orkney and Shetland Literary and Scientific Association, were part of a series of essays gathered and published in 1931 in the twilight of his life by an Orcadian, J T Smith Leask, who practised law in that city.

The quaint tales give in anecdotal form details of hiding places and subterfuges used to evade and frustrate the gang. Although somewhat exaggerated, the stories, leavened with humour as well as astute and leery sayings, provide some understanding of conditions in Orkney at the time. In addition to being a valuable record of dialect, they illustrate what an isolated community living in Napoleonic times felt about impressment, and how people reacted to the social and domestic pressures it brought.

An English version, following the original as closely as possible, is given for those who might have difficulty with the dialect.

---

[1] pp. 123–38.

Da Pressgang is id thu're speeran aboot? Blide wad I be buddie
tae tell dee aboot id, bit du sees A'm no jeust saw young as I aince waar, an'
A'm stootly trowie an' sairly fashed wi' da watter-traa, an' I hae sic a
stoond i' me breest. Och, min, A'm jeust hingan taegither. Me mind's
gaen sairly teu, deed A'm no wirt a pension o' grottybuckies,
bit I'se deu me best till ableege dee, a'to' A'm no on da lay O'd.
Min, id maks me tink a hape o' lang tae discoorse aboot ald times, cis dem 'at
telt me o' dem ar' a' awa – pace be wi' dem. Aye, aye!

A'm leeded tae a nantie o' wheer whasays i' me time aboot id gin I could
bit mind dem on. Du sees over dis wey was sairly hinted
is da men-o'-war aye lay at da back o' da Holmes. Hid
was peetifu' times dan, aye waas hid. A' da folk waar skaired is
nane kent whan da gang wad be aboot, or wha wad be taen neist, an' a'bothy
kens nane waas i' a hurry tae be taaken. Miny's da time A'm hard me
ald faither tellan o' foo dey deud, an' whar dey bed, an' droll pieces
de waar teu. Da hill waas da great piece for da boys i' dis gate-en'
tae tak till. Dey hockid hidie-holes i' da Burn o' Burrallie – dere's ane o'
dem aye tae da fore, but sheu's no aisy fund. Du geongs intill 'er anunder
a bit o' facey abeun da 'Tree Burns'. Sheu's biggid o' runckly stanes like a peerie
hoosiekin. Da aesiest wey tae find 'er is da wey wir Willie deud – 'e fell trou
da tap o' 'er an' narlins breuk 'is tirrlin bane.

Dan dere waas da 'Holes o' Cupsermung', bit dey waar dangerous, oh
vera. A hantle o' folk's faan i' dem an' no been hard o' again.
Da heather waas dat lang 'at da taps o' da Holes waar a' groun ower,
an' id leukid jeust da sam is da apen veallience. ….

Weel, dan, some boys hed i' da cave at da Head o' Houtan. Du kens dere's
a cave dere 'at geongs fae ap api' da Hade, doon annunder da sea. Dey say,
bit I winna vooch for da treuth o' id, 'at du can see da oooter en' o'
'er at a spoot ebb, A'm hard 'at a swad o' Orphir childers bed I' 'er
for days api en' hidan fae da Pressgang. Da gang kent fine 'at dey
waar dere an' sat deir waas doon aboot da mooth o' da hole till dey
wad come oot, bit dey niver mudged fill da gang said dey wad sheut.
Dat gocked dem, an' da boys cam oot – da gluffices dat dey waar, for
id waas da laa dat airms buistna be eused bae da gang bit tae keep aff deirsels wi'.

Ither anes kent o' hidie holes i' da White Breest, ower by dere i' Hoy.
Dey hed boats lyan at da Skerries o' Clestrain, an' is seun is dey waar awaar
'at da gang waas aboot de boys teur for da boats an' rowed ower till Hoy.

Tales of the Press Gang

The press gang is it you are asking about? I would be pleased friend to tell you about it, but you see I am not just so young as I once was, and I am very poorly and sadly troubled with heartburn, and I have such palpitations in my breast. Ah, man, I am just hanging together. My memory has gone sadly too, and indeed I am not worth a pension of grottiebuckies,[1] but I will do my best to oblige you, although I am not in the mood for it. Man, it gives me a lonely feeling to talk about old times, because they that told me about them are all away – peace be with them. Aye, aye!

I have listened to a lot of queer tales in my time about it, if I could but remember them. You see this neighbourhood was thoroughly searched because the men of war always lay at the back of the Holms.[2] It was sad times then, indeed it was. All the people were scared because none knew when the gang would be about, or who would be taken next, and anybody knows that no-one was in a hurry to be taken. Many a time I have heard my old father telling what they did, and where they stayed, and strange places they were too. The hill was the great place for the boys in this neighbourhood to take to. They dug hiding holes in the Burn of Burrallie – there is one of them still in existence, but it is not easily found. You go in to it under a little bank above the 'three burns'. It is built of rough stones like a little house. The easiest way to find it is the way our Willie did – he fell through the top of it and nearly broke his collar bone.

Then there were the 'Holes of Cupsermung',[3] but they were dangerous, oh very. A number of folk have fallen in them and not been heard of again. The heather was so long that the tops of the holes were all overgrown, and it looked just the same as the open plain. …

Well, then, some boys hid in the cave at the Head of Houton. You know there is a cave there that goes from up on the Head, down under the sea. They say, but I wont vouch for the truth of it, that you can see the outer end of it at a spring tide.[4] I have heard that a number of Orphir youths stayed in it for days on end hiding from the press gang. The gang well knew that they were there and sat themselves down about the mouth of the hole till they would come out, but they never moved till the gang said they would shoot. That deceived them, and the boys came out – the fools that they were, for the law was that arms must not be used by the gang except to defend themselves with.

Others knew of hiding places in the White Breast, over there in Hoy. They had boats lying at the Skerries of Clestrain, and as soon as they were aware that the gang was around the boys ran for the boats and rowed over to Hoy.

1 Small cowrie shells.
2 Small islands off Stromness.
3 *Cupstermung.*
4 A particularly low ebb.

A'm hard me ald faither tellan o' foo dey aye keepid deir horse
nar dem whin dey waar wirkan. Ae day whin Mm an' me Uncle Tam waar
putheran aboot deir rig at Skithiwee, dey hed deir horse
tethered or huppid at da en' o' da rig is eusual, Dey keepid deir wather
eyes liftin an' whin dey saa da ald wife o' Fea stanan waivan 'er ald
white mutch for a' sheu waas wirt, bony kent dey 'at so'nting waas i' da
wind, an' whin dey leukid dey saa da gang coman abeun Breckan. Dey
haved doon deir etches, luppid api deir horse, an' reed for da Skerries at
a spunder. …

Weel, is I waas tellan dee aboot da Pressgang – folk waar aye api
da leukoot for dem, bit nooes an' dans dey wan ower nar afore dey
waar spied. Dan da boys tried droll weys o' winnan awa. Dere was ane
fae hereaboots 'at saa 'e wad be taen, sae, boy, whit tinks du dued 'e – 'e
cuist o' 'is clais is fest is 'e could an' rowed 'imsel' ower an' ower,
mither naked, i' a roo o' nettles. Hid wad made 'im swee, aye wad hid.
Dan e' pat on 'is clais an' lit 'imsel be taen. Hid waasna lang
fill 'e waas afore da doctor apin a man-o'-war at da back o' da Holmes. Hid waas
a black shame o' dem, bit dey seun made 'im cast o' 'is clais tae da ceuvie
afore da doctor tae see gin 'e waas a' right an' fit tae feight. Boy, hid waas
a splor whin da doctor saa da man's skin, he hookid id 'imsel
an' yowled tae dem 'at waas aboot hans tae haive da man ower, is
'e hed a awfu' bad trouble. Dan, boy, dere waas a cataclue
is dey a' made for da deck like mad. Da man waas pittan intae a boat an'
waas fain tae geong ashore 'imsel – nane wad geong wi' 'im. He rowed
ashore and keepid da boat. Seustu, noo – hid waas guid mains api dem, bit ever
hard du o' seekan a pleunkie to win awa? Hid wad taen 'im a peerie
while tae ceul, bit A'm seur 'e madena ony molligrant ower da sweean.

Noo, lit me tink, whar'll I tell du o' neist. Oh yea, dere waas me
mither's gutcher. Whin 'e waas a peerie bit o' nappy boy o' ten, ae bony
hairst e'enin', 'e waas oot at da Skerries o' Clestrain wi' 'is faither and
twa-r-tree neebors at da sillicks. A cutter fae a warsman
cam' by, an dey hard a offisher sayan, "We'll tak dat peerie fair-
haired boy," sae da cutter rowed ower an teuk da bit o' bairn fae aside 'is
ain faither, an' rowed awa. Whin dey hed gaen a peerie bit, John telt
da men 'e hed forgotten 'is knife api da thaft o' da boat. He buist
a'been weel aff tae haen a knife o' 'is ain dan-a-day, bit hid
wad been a tullie an' no a eusless ting o' a penknife is da bairns
hae noo. Oh, co dey, "Wees geong back for dee knife, for du'll
hae aneuch tae cut wi' 'im," sae back dey rowed, an' John teuk 'is knife
an' baad guid-day till 'is faither an' da tither anes, an' gaed awa is croos
is du likes wi' da gang. He deudna mak a main an' greet is miny a peerie ane
wad deun – na, deed. …

Tales of the Press Gang

I have heard my old father telling of how they always kept their horses near them when they were working. One day when he and my Uncle Tam were leisurely working in their fields at Skithquoy,[1] they had their horses tethered or hobbled at the end of the rig as usual. They kept their weather eyes lifting and when they saw the old woman of Fea standing waving her old white mutch for all she was worth, they well knew that something was in the wind, and when they looked they saw the gang coming above Breckan. They threw down their hoes, leaped on their horses, and rode for the skerries at a gallop. ….

Well, as I was telling you about the press gang – folk were always on the look out for them, but now and then they came too near before they were spied. Then the boys tried droll ways of getting away. There was one from here who saw he would be taken, so, boy, what do you think he did – he threw off his clothes as fast as he could and rolled himself over and over, mother naked, in a clump of nettles. It would make him smart, aye would it. Then he put on his clothes and let himself be taken. It wasn't long till he was before the doctor on a man of war at the back of the Holms. It was a black shame of them, but they soon made him cast off his clothes to the skin before the doctor to see if he was all right and fit to fight. Boy, there was consternation when the doctor saw the man's skin, he ran off himself and yelled to those who were nearest him to throw the man overboard, because he had an awfully bad trouble. Then, boy, there was panic as they all made for the deck like mad. The man was put into a boat and was obliged to go ashore himself – nobody would go with him. He rowed ashore and kept the boat. Look you, now – it served them right, but did you ever hear of such a trick to get clear? It would have taken him a little while to cool, but I am sure he made no complaint over the smarting.

Now, let me think, who will I tell you about next. Oh yes, there was my mother's grandfather. When he was a little sturdy boy of ten, one bonnie harvest evening, he was out at the Skerries of Clestrain with his father and two or three neighbours fishing for sillocks. A cutter from a warship came past, and they heard an officer saying, 'We'll take that little fair haired boy', so the cutter rowed over and took the child from beside his own father, and rowed away. When they had gone a short distance, John told the men that he had forgotten his knife on the thwart of the boat. He must have been well off to have a knife of his own in those days, but it would have been a large knife and not a useless penknife such as the children have now. 'Oh,' said they, 'We will go back for your knife, for you will have enough to cut with it,' so they rowed back, and John took his knife and bade good-day to his father and the others, and went away as happy as you like with the gang. He didn't moan and cry as many a small child would have done – no, indeed. …

---

1 Now part of the farm of Seattersquoy.

I kinna foo lang John waas i' da Navy, bit id buist abeen a guid
feu year, cis whin 'e left, hid waas t'out 'e waas wirt a pension, bit a'
da sam 'e got id no. Da countra waas ma'be jeust is hard up dan is ids
noo, sae i' piece o' a pension dey gaed 'im a Public Hoose Leeshance for a'
time, wi' po'er tae set ap i' ony pairt o' da Kingdom bit twa toons 'at
I dinna min' on da names o'. Weel, hame 'e cam wi' 'is leeshance i' 'is
pooch and begood a public hoose here i' Ireland, an' 'id waas carried on bae 'is
mither fill sheu dee'd an' dan bae 'is weedoo fill sheu dee'd, miny's da day – I
wad say forty year – efter 'im. I'm afen whizzened, bit nane seems
tae ken, waas dere miny leeshances o' dat kind gaen. Da wey I speered waas
cis whin me faither married 'is first wife, dere waar hale
seevan publics i' Stenness. Boy, dat buist a'been fine times. …

Haen been i'da Navy, John waas aye trang trokan wi' da ships,
sae whin 'e waas a ald man o' seeventy 'e waas oot at da ships ae day is eusual
an' saa a bit o' boy 'at hed been pressed, greetan aneuch tae brak id's bit o' hert.
Haen waded da watter 'imsel, he teuk peety api da puir ting an' helped 'im tae rin
awa. Whit tinks du, boy, illwhinnered neebors o' 'is ain waar illfain
o' 'im for ha'in sae muckle siller, an' kennan whit 'e hed deun, dey couldna
hail id, bit telt api ald John an' 'e waas pressed ower again is a punishment.
A'm seur id waas a sin, for 'e waas stootly hoved i' 'is ald days, bit 'e waas
litten aff. Min, bid's ceurious foo dat neebors waar aye tellpies fae
da first o' dem fill dis very day. Hid seurly rins i' da bleud like
crewals or widden legs.

John hed a swad o' bairns – ten or a dizzen – bit ane or twa cam till
onyting, atween ae misanter an' anither. Ane fell trow da reuf o' da
deuckyhoose an' waas killed ae Sunday whin da folk waar at da kirk.
Dat waas jeust a jeudgment for braakin da fort comman'ment -'e sood abeen
at da kirk or reedan a guid beuk, an' no climmeran aboot on da Lord's
Day. 'Is son John waas taaken bae da French and keepid i' prison i' Alexandria
twa-r-tree year, fill 'e teuk scurvey an' waas a puir ting tae da end o' 'is
days, Tam gaed doon wi' Herry Cloustan aff Cantik Hade da herrins. His
eldest daughter – a unco strong and weel far'd lass sheu was teu – de'ed
twa-r-tree weeks afore sheu waas tae been merried. Anither daighter
merried a ald man an' de'ed young teu, an' A'm dootan sheu waas rightly blide tae
geong, for ald Tam, 'er man, waas bad till 'er. He waas aye shargan at 'er an'
sairly mittled 'er a hantle o' times, an' ae time i' 'is maddrum 'e narlins drooned

I don't know how long John was in the Navy, but it must have been a good few years, for when he left, it was thought he was worth a pension, but all the same he didn't get it. The country was maybe just as hard up then as it is now, so in place of a pension they gave him a public house licence for all time, with power to set up in any part of the kingdom except two towns that I don't remember the names of. Well, he came home with his licence in his pocket and began a public house here in Ireland, and it was carried on by his mother until she died and then by his widow till she died, many a day – I would say forty years – after him.[1] I have often enquired, but no-one seems to know, were many licences of that kind given. The reason I asked, was because when my father married his first wife, there were no less than seven public houses in Stenness. Boy, these must have been fine times. …

Having been in the Navy, John was always busy bartering with the ships, so when he was an old man of 70 he was out at the ships one day as usual and saw a boy who had been pressed, crying as though to break his heart. Having been a sailor, he took pity on the poor thing and helped him to run away. What do you think, boy, awkward neighbours of his own were jealous of him for having so much money, and knowing what he had done, they couldn't conceal it, but told on old John and he was pressed again as a punishment. I am sure it was a sin, for he was very swollen in his old days, but he was let off. Man, it's strange how these neighbours were always telling tales from the first of them till this very day. It surely runs in the blood like tubercular glands or wooden legs.

John had a squad of children – ten or a dozen – but only one or two came to anything, between one mischance and another. One fell through the roof of the ducks' house and was killed one Sunday when the family were at the church. That was just a judgement for breaking the fourth commandment – he should have been at the church or reading a good book, and not climbing about on the Lord's Day. His son John was taken by the French and kept in prison in Alexandria two or three years, until he took scurvy and was a poor thing to the end of his days. Tom drowned with Harry Clouston off Cantick Head at the herrings. His eldest daughter – a very strong and well favoured girl she was too – died two or three weeks before she was to have been married. Another daughter married an old man and died young too, and I think she was very glad to go, for old Tom, her man, was bad to her. He was always nagging at her and sorely injured her several times, and once in his madness he nearly drowned

---

1 He had married late in life. The story goes: 'Then he came home again and married Jeannie Hay of Breckan, a girl of 15. The old fool was old enough to be her grandfather. They were right affectionate too, but she kept him in order…'

'er i' da graith tub, da illhivered, dirty ald scoot 'at 'e
waas. Bit ane o' John's bairns leeved tae be ony age ava, an' 'e waas
bit fower score an' fower whin dathe ca'ad api 'im. 'E gaed bae da eet-
name o' Billy-pent-dee-whistle.

Billy waas a Straitsman, an' I'se wirran dee, gaed tae da Straits
da best pairt o' forty year. He teuk efter 'is mither an' deud a bit o'
smugglin teu. For a lang while 'e waas harpooner an' dan spiksoneer.
Miny a teulya hed 'ewi da Pressgang an' rancelmen, an' t'o
dey narlins hed 'im miny a time, 'e aye slippid trow deir fingers
ae wey or anither. He waas ane o' da Ireland men 'at waas i' da tetilya
at da Dams ower bye i' Stenness 'at A'm telled dee o' afore.

Ae year dere waas aboot a dizzen o' young men fae hereaboots i' ae ship
at da Straits, an' Billy waas ane o' da crood. Da sam illwhinnered folk 'at
telt api' 'is faither helpan da boy tae win aff, telt da gang o' dis lock
o' men an' whit ship dey waar apin an' whin dey waar lippened name. A man-
o'-war waas pitten Nort tae meet dem. Seurly da ship waas langer awa nor sheu
sood abeen, cis da man-o'-war hed tae geong a guid bit farder Nort
nor sheu t'out she wad needed tae. At da lang an' da lent sheu cam api da
Straits-ship an' da meenit da Straitsmen saa 'er, bony kent dey 'er
errand. Da Capin steud aff bit da man-o'-war fired a shot afore
'er an' dat seun brou't dem ap. Da Capin ca'ad da men eft an' telt dem
gin dey wissed tae geong 'e widna be able tae hinder dem, an' a' da time
'e waas noddin' till a boat hingan i' da davits. Hid's said 'at a wink's is guid
is a nod tae a blin' horse ony day, sae it waasna miny meenits fill da boat
waas i' da watter ower da side fardest awa fae da man-o'-war. Da men
ran an' buckled ap twa-r-tree tings i' deir bans 'at dey might need afore
dey wan hame, an' while dey waar doon, da Capin fummelled aboot, an' wi'
'is ain han' pat a peerie kag o' watter an' a feu biscuits i' a poke, i' da
boat, an' whin dey waar peulan awa, 'e haved a compass tae dem. Hid waas
rael guid o' da, Capin, 'e buist abeen a Christian gin ever dere waas
ane, an' dan 'is dey waar peulan awa he ca'd tae dem tae poo fair
i'da wind's e'e. Du sees, buddie, gin dey deud dat, da man-o'-war wad

her in a tub of urine,[1] the bad tempered, dirty old scoundrel that he was. Only one of John's children lived to be any age at all, and he was but four score and four when death called upon him. He went by the nickname of Billy Paint-your-Whistle.[2]

Billy was a Straitsman,[3] and I'll warrant you, went to the Straits the best part of forty years. He took after his mother and did a bit of smuggling too. For a long time he was harpooner and then head harpooner.[4] Many a quarrel he had with the press gang and the Excisemen, and although they nearly had him many a time, he always slipped through their fingers one way or another. He was one of the Ireland men who were at the set-to at the Dams over in Stenness that I have told you about before.

One year there were about a dozen young men from hereabouts in one ship at the Straits, and Billy was one of the crowd. The same spiteful folk that told about his father helping the boy to escape, told the gang of this lot of men and what ship they were on and when they were expected home. A man of war was put north to meet them. Surely the ship was longer away than she should have been, because the man of war had to go a good bit further north than she thought she would have needed to. At long last she came upon this Straits ship and the minute the Straitsmen saw her, they well knew her business. The captain stood off but the man of war fired a shot in front of her and they soon hove to. The captain called the men aft and told them if they wished to go he would not be able to hinder them, and all the time he was nodding to a boat hanging in the davits. It's said that a wink is as good as a nod to a blind horse any day, so it wasn't many minutes until the boat was in the water over the side furthest away from the man of war. The men ran and wrapped up a few things in their hands that they might need before they got home, and while they were down, the captain fumbled about, and with his own hand put a small keg of water and a few biscuits in a bag, in the boat, and when they were pulling away, he threw a compass to them. It was very good of the captain, who must have been a Christian if ever there was one, and then as they were pulling away he called them to pull straight into the wind. You see, friend, if they did that, the man of war would

---

1 At one time a *graith* or *strang* tub was to be found in every Orkney cottage. Urine was collected for several purposes: it was used domestically as a disinfectant; during an outbreak of scarlet fever in Stenness c.1850 the blankets of infected children were soaked in cow urine; about the same time in the parish of Harray human urine was used as a hair wash for vermin control. It was also utilised in the treatment of newly woven cloth, for scouring yarn and in dressing leather.
2 Lazy; shiftless.
3 Went to Davis Strait whaling.
4 Possibly from the Dutch word *specksnyder* – chief harpooner. He had charge of all whaling gear and directed the processes of flenching and making blubber. See also the German word *speckschneider*, a man described as being 'directly below the mate and commands the cutting of the whale … When on ships's duty, he must also understand navigation…' SND: spik – blubber.

hae tae tack sae muckle 'at sheu wad niver catch ap wi' dem. Dey pat
oot eight oars an' laid dem till id wi' a' deir birr. Dey waarna
miny strokes awa fill da man-o'-war dreu straes whit waas ap
an' lenched a boat an' efter dem. Baith boats rowed an' rowed an' better rowed, bit
da warsmen couldna mak ap api da tither anes. Dan dey begood tae
sheut, bit a' da shots gaed glide, an' dan da warship fired a shot tellan
deir boat tae come hame again. On deir wey back, dey gaed abeurd da
Straits-ship, an' dey waar dat mad at lossan sic guid men, dey teuk
da cook an' da kebinboy, haddan oot dat dey waar naither offishers nor
printices. Du sees id waas against da laa tae lay han's api offishers or
printices.

Da boat wi' da Straitsmen waas i' Stromness eight days afore deir ship.
I kinno foo lang dey waar api da wey, bit whin dey cam ahint
Stromness dey waar a' fair faemished. Dere dey fand a man oot fishan,
an' dey spak till 'im an' telt 'im dey waar fantin. He telt id 'imsel efter
'at 'e hed bit twa bere bannocks an' a peerie sap o'
milk, an' 'e gaed dem id, bit id waas jeust a bite an' a sook apiece.
Da men waar tankfu' for id, peerie is id waas, an' dey aye minded on da ald man
fill 'is deean day. Hid waas da best day's fishan ever 'e deud, cis du sees
dey t'out dey waar behaddan tae fim. Aye min, id jeust shaws da treuth
o' whit da Beuk says o' whit'll befa' dee gin due casts dee bread
api da watter.

Whit, anither? Dorrin api thee, thu're ill tae plase. A'm tinkan A'm
gabbed aneuch for ae day. Weel, weel, A'll be fain tae ableedge dee wi'
jeust anither. Bit hover-dee-a-blink fill I tink.

Oh, aye, i' da ald days, du'll ken dere waas twa hooses o' Cumminness an'
dey gaed bae da names o' Nether an' Iver Cunndnness. Herrie Cloustan
bed i' Iver Cumminness wi' 'is mither fill 'e waas lost. A'm seur du'll
mind o' 'is brither Johnnie 'at bed i' Approo abeun da Burn o' Villice
'at played api da fiddle an' cairted api a sheummid ox. Oh yae, I t'out dat,
da bairns afen gaed in bye tae hae a teun is dey cam fae da scheul. Ever hard
du 'im playan da teun 'at 'e telt folk 'is ox danced tae i' 'is
beuild an' da ither ane 'at 'e gaed a bottle o' da Ald Kirk for?
Some heud oot 'at 'e kent bit pairt o' ae teun a'taegeither.
Johnnie waas ane o' da twa 9at waas taen a had o' bae da Pressgang i' da teullya
atween da Ireland an' Stenness men ower dere at da Dams a hunder
year sin …

have to tack so much that she would never catch up with them. They put
out eight oars and plied them with all their strength. They weren't
many strokes away until the man of war became suspicious of what was up
and launched a boat and followed them. Both boats rowed and rowed, but
the naval men couldn't catch up with the other ones. Then they began to
shoot, but all the shots went astray, and then the warship fired a shot telling
their boat to come back again. On their way back, they went aboard the
Straits ship, and they were so angry at losing such good men, they took
the cook and the cabin-boy, claiming that they were neither officers nor
apprentices. You see it was against the law to lay hands upon officers or
apprentices.

The boat with the Straitsmen was in Stromness eight days before their ship.
I don't know how long they were on the way, but when they arrived at the back
of Stromness they were all quite famished. There they found a man out fishing,
and they spoke to him and told him they were starving. He himself told afterwards that he had only two bere bannocks[1] and a small sup of
milk, which he gave them, but it was just a bite and a swallow each. The men
were thankful for it, small as it was, and they were always good to the old man
until his dying day. It was the best day's fishing he ever did, because you see
they thought they were indebted to him. Yes man, it just shows the truth
of what the Book says about what will happen to you if you cast your bread
upon the water.

What, another? Bad luck to you, you're ill to please. I think I've
gabbled enough for one day. Well, well, I'll have to oblige you with just
one other. But wait a minute while I think.

Oh, yes, in the old days, you know there were two houses at Cumminess and
they went by the names of Nether and Over Cumminess. Harry Clouston
stayed in Over Cumminess with his mother until he was drowned. I'm sure you
remember his brother Johnnie who stayed in Approo above the Burn of Villice
who played the fiddle and carted with a white-faced ox. Oh yes, I thought so,
the children often went in to hear a tune as they came from school. Did you
ever hear him playing the tune that he told folk his ox danced to in its
stall and the other one that he gave a bottle of the Auld Kirk[2] for?
Some people claimed that he knew only part of one tune and no more.
Johnnie was one of the two who were taken by the press gang in the set-to
between the Ireland and the Stenness men over there at the Dams a hundred
years ago. …

---

1 Barley scones.
2 Whisky.

He waas a muckle ravsay whalp o' a chap an' could rin like da
ald chiel, for t'o 'e waas owergrovm 'e waasna a clurt, an' t'o da
Pressgang gaed lang an' afen efter 'im dey niver minaged tae lay a finger
apin 'im. Dey seurly t'out 'e waas a frag or dey waar illfain o' iim,
cis min, he waas hinted is gin 'e'd "been a wild ting an' no a man ava,
bit haith, boy, 'e gaed is muckle is 'e got, aye deud 'e. A' da sam, alt'o
dey deudna jeust get deir cleuks api' fim, dey narlins nabb'd 'ira twa-r-tree times. …

Beesweel, ae bony foreneun i' hairst a hale swad o' wives waar layan
deir withs leithfilly, shairin' an' kempan at Curaminness an'
id leuks as gin Herrie waas hame aboot dat year teu. Ma' be he wad gaen tae
da herrins atween nans. Whin id waas kent 'at da Pressgang waar oot, da
doors waar a savandidly boolted whin folk waar at deir grain o' mate an'
ither times teu. Veel, dis day whin da folk o' Cumminness gaed in tae deir
twal 'oors, da door waas made fest is eusual, an' a guid job id waas, teu, cis
boy, if da middle o' deir mate da Pressgang chappid at da door, an baad
dem apen i' da King's name. Bit haith, dem 'at waas in, waarna I' ony
hurry apinin', dey gaedna i' da shakkers, na giddeed. Dey caredna a preen
for da King's name. He wad been bit ane o' da Geordies onywey. Bit, alt'o
dey deudna rin an' apen at aince, dey warna idle. Herrie's mither, a
boosam body sheu waas, bit a muckle scow o' a wife a' da sam, waas api' 'er feet
i' twa-twas tae pit tings i' boona for siccan oncan veesitors. Dere waasna ony
chingley stanes i' da clay sheu waas made o', an' t'o sheu waas illhivered dere was
nane o' da hallit aboot 'er, bit sheu wad gae Herrie a luggit i' da bygan for
iddlin' wi' Sibbie Gorie, an' sma' winder, for Sibbie waas a slesterin'
pell, is 'er oys an' eerie oys waar efter 'er, t'o I
waadna cast it ap tae dem. Dey waar a' wives dat waar if da noose, a' bit
Herrie, sae sheu made dem intae a kind o' whit du wad caf a gu.erd o' honour
tae 'im. Sheu pat dem i' pooster i' twa raws in fae da door, an gaed dem a heuk
or ane o' Herrie's exes apiece, an' pat Herrie at da ironist end wi' is airms
falded. Bae dis time da gang waar maakin' a bony murgis dunderan an' brogan
at da ald door, aneuch tae ding 'er in. Whin Herrie's mither hed gotten a' tings
tae 'er mind, an' castan aff her ald brattoo an' pitten on a clean claith bootack, sheu
waaled a exe, an' wi' hid i' ae han' sheu apened da door wi' da tither.

Da gang buist abeen fair stundered whin dey saa da swad o'
wives a' ermed wi' Herrie linan ahint da back, snikkerin an'
laichan, wi' 'is erms api 'is breest. Da ald wife speered da gang in is
ceevally is sheu kent foo, bit shairan 'er teeth an' shaftan 'er exe at dem,
sheu telt dem wi' a golder sheu wad spelt apen da harnpan o' da
first ane 'at darkened 'er doorstane. An' fegs, hid waas weel said, sheu wad
deun id teu. Da leuk sheu gaed dem waas seurly aneuch, hid stowed dem
onywey, an' boy, dey sleued an' spraited awa, an' deudna speer Herrie tae geong wi' dem.

Tales of the Press Gang

He was a big coarse brute of a chap and could ran like the devil, for although he was overgrown he wasn't clumsy, and although the press gang went long and often after him they never managed to lay a finger on him. They surely thought he was a prize or they took a dislike to him, because man, he was hunted as if he had been a wild thing and not a man at all, but faith, boy, he gave as much as he got, aye did he. All the same, although they didn't quite get their clutches on him, they nearly nabbed him a few times. …

However, one fine forenoon in harvest a whole crowd of women were working hard and faithfully, shearing and competing with each other at Cumminess, and it seems that Harry was at home that year too. Perhaps he would have gone to the herrings at intervals. When it was known that the press gang was out, the doors were all securely bolted when the folk were at their bite of food and at other times too. Well, this day when the folk of Cumminess went in to their dinner, the door was made fast as usual, and a good thing it was, too, because boy, in the middle of their food the press gang knocked on the door, and bade them open in the King's name. But faith, those who were in, weren't in any hurry opening, they didn't get in a panic, no indeed. They didn't care a pin for the King's name. He would have been one of the Georges anyway. But, although they didn't run and open at once, they weren't idle. Harry's mother, an active person she was, but a great gaunt woman all the same, was on her feet in an instant to put things in readiness for such strange visitors. She was made of stern stuff, and though she was bad tempered there was nothing flighty about her, but she would give Harry a slap in the passing for getting mixed up with Sibbie Gorie, and small wonder, for Sibbie was an untidy slut, as her grandchildren and great-grandchildren were after her, though I wouldn't blame them for it. It was all women who were in the house, all but Harry, so she made them into a kind of what you would call a guard of honour for him. She positioned them in two rows from the door, and gave them a hook or one of Harry's axes apiece, and put Harry in the inmost end with his arms folded. By this time the gang were making a fine noise knocking and pushing on the old door, enough to burst it in. When Harry's mother had got everything to her liking, throwing off her old apron and putting on a clean stole, she chose an axe, and with it in one hand she opened the door with the other.

The gang must have been completely astonished when they saw the crowd of women all armed with Harry leaning against the fireplace,[1] jeering and laughing, with folded arms. The old woman invited the gang in as civilly as she knew how, but grinding her teeth and shaking her axe at them, she told them with a loud voice she would split open the skull of the first one that darkened her doorstep. And faith, it is well said, she would have done it too. The look she gave them was surely enough, it silenced them anyway, and boy, they turned and sprinted away and didn't ask Harry to go with them.

---

1 The small wall in the middle of the room against which the fire was built.

Anither time Herrie waas i' da hoose 'is leevan lane whin da gang cam till da
door, bit sheu waas fest again. I' waan o' da gang, Herrie haed gotten a
gun an' a footh o' pooder an' ladedraps, sae 'e waas i' nae hurry an'
deudna pit 'imsel aboot whin da gang chappid an' baad 'im apen. Da taed i'
chairge waasna jeust ower weelbred, for 'e gaed an' gan'd in trow ane o' da
windicks. Dan-a-day dere waasna miny windoos i' ony hoose, an' whit
waas, waas peerie, peerie a'cis o' da deuty api' wid an' gless, an' nane
ava apened.

Hid waas ma'be jeust is weel, an' A'm no sayan bit hid wad be a
Guid's blessin' gin dey waar a' da sam noo. Hid wad keep da moniment
tings o' boys oot onywey. Whin da of fisher leukid in, dere waas Herrie
concordidly takin' 'is gun aff da twartbacks an' loadin' 'er. 'E pat
in a guld air mair nor da eusual chairge of baith pooder an' ladedraps, an' dan
rammed dem weel hame. Hid waas a ald flinty, an' Herrie waas unco parteeclar
aboot pittan a corn o' pooder right i' da pan. Dan, whin 'e t'out a' ting waas is id sood be, 'e
gaed a reult an' gaed is waas tae da door an' hailed back da bar. Whin 'e apened
da door, 'e pat 'is gun till 'is shoother an' teuk emm at da offisher wi'
's finger api da trickker. He waas rightly iltafoo an' a' piveran wi' madrum,
but lendie ken I whit 'e said, bit I'se wirran dee hid waasna oot o' da
Beuk, an' A'm seur 'e deudna traa wi' dem. Hid seurly waas aneuch t'o,
cis da ontakin offisher an' a' 'is men gaed backlins fill dey fell
i' a brulyoo, dan dey ap an' teur awa, an' deudna leuk ahint fill
dey waar a' fair bursin. Hid waas coorly for sae miny tae rin fae ae
man, bit ma'be da gun fleggid dem, wha kens.

Ae een'in i' da grimlins Herrie waas haddan for hame fae da hill wi'
'is tuskar anunder 'is oxter an' 'is hans i' 'is bickets. He'd
been gaen some puir bothy a day's pate shairin, ma'be ane
'e waas behadden tae, wha kens. Da Pressgang met 'im, bit whin dey made
tae lay hans apin 'im fe eused da tuskar wi' a' fis birr api
dem an' keepid da hale swad at erm's lent, fill he wan name pooran o'
sweat. 'E gaed ane or twa a guid cloor. Whin 'e wan in,
da door waas made fest, an' A'm seur du wadna guess i' a'
thee days whitna droll waapan waas prepared. 'E waas fairly fantin,
sae while 'e gleapid a sap o' loots an' burstin, a muckle pat
waas pittan api da fire fill ids boddam waas rade hate, an' dan, whin ony o'
da gang shawed 'is face, Herrie fairly yivers dabbid da hate pat apin
id. Trath, boy, sheu waas a coorse waapan, bit haith, sheu deud fine, sheu
raffled dem.

Another time Harry was in the house all alone when the gang came to the door, but it was shut fast again. Expecting the gang, Harry had obtained a gun and a plentiful supply of powder and shot, so he was in no hurry and he didn't worry himself when the gang knocked and bade him open. The rascal in charge wasn't too well-bred, for he went and stared in through one of the windows. In those days there weren't many windows in any house, and those that were, were small, small because of the duty on wood and glass, and none of them opened.

It was perhaps just as well, and I'm not saying but what it would be a God's blessing if they were all the same now. It would keep the mischievious things of boys out anyway. When the officer looked in, there was Harry deliberately taking his gun from the rafters and loading it. He put in a good deal more than the usual charge of both powder and shot, and then rammed them well home. It was an old flintlock, and Harry was very particular about priming it. Then, when he thought everything was as it should be, he gave a shrug and went to the door and hauled back the bar. When he opened the door, he put his gun to his shoulder and took aim at the officer with his finger on the trigger. He was rightly insensed and all shaking with anger, but little know I what he said, but I'll warrant you it wasn't out of the Book,[1] and I'm sure he didn't bother with them. It surely was enough though, because the officer in charge and all his men went backwards till they fell in confusion, then they got up and tore away, and didn't look behind till they were all quite exhausted. It was cowardly for so many to run from one man, but maybe the gun frightened them, who knows.

One evening in the twilight Harry was making for home from the hill with his peat-cutting spade under his arm and his hands in his pockets. He had been helping some poor person with a day's peat-cutting, perhaps somebody he was beholden to, who knows. The press gang met him, but when they were about to lay hands on him he used the spade with all his strength against them and kept the whole squad at arm's length, until he got home sweating profusely. He gave one or two of them a hard knock. When he got inside the house, the door was made fast, and I'm sure you wouldn't guess in all your days what a queer weapon was prepared. He was quite starving, so while he swallowed a mouthful of sour milk and burstin,[2] a large pot was put on the fire until its bottom was red-hot, and then when any one of the gang showed his face, Harry thoroughly angry, thrust the hot pot towards it. Truth, boy, it was a rude weapon, but faith, it did the trick, for it defeated them.

---

1 Bible.
2 Bere dried in a pot over a fire (instead of being dried in a kiln) and ground down like meal.

Anither e'enin' Herrie an' 'is mither an' twa-r-tree gossips waar
sittan coorin ower da fire crackin like pen guns, no lippinin
onyting, whin a' at aince da gang pramed in withoot chappin. Seurly
da gang hedna been scroongin' aboot for a while afore da door waas left
api da sneck, or someane hed misglimed id. Beesweel, in dey cam, an'
sal hid leukid is gin Herrie wad be nabbed noo, for 'e hedna a
waapan handy, forbye, dere waas siccan a crood dat nae o'nar bothy wad
t'out id wirt 'is while maakin for da door. I'se wirran dee dat
da offisher waas is prood is a dog wi' twa tails an' smoored an' leuch till
'imsel whin 'e saa, is 'e t'out, 'at Herrie waas i' 'is po'er at da lang an' da lent.

Bit haith, da great gomeril gin 'e waaned dat Herrie waas da muckle vaal till
gae in wi'oot a teullya for id, fe waas sair mistaen. Dere waas a muckle
pot rampin' an' boilin' i'da cruick, an' jeust is gin sheu'd been da waapan
'e hed i' 'is e'e 'e niver said kirnaou, bit i' 'is madrum 'e grippid a had o' 'e bae da
bools wi baith hans, suized 'er aff da fire an' swyin' 'er roond 'is
hade, 'e made da gang stan till a side an' lit lim geong i' da name o'
da Best. Gin da pot hed hittan ane, hid wad dung lim doon
an' scadded fim teu. Whin 'e wan oot 'e klashed da pot i' rinnick
foment da door an' slestered dem 'at waas efter 'im 'a ower wi'
iper, dan fe telt dem tae geong tae da bad piece, an' wi' a
flink spraited for da hill, Peinty ane could catch 'im dan, sae 'e wan
awa. Bae me sal, hid waas a prettikin teu, an' da iper wad
left a bony waaf wi' dem, bit id waas guid mains api da rugfis moniment
o' a offisher for no haean mainers aneuch till chap at da door.

Another evening Harry and his mother with two or three cronies were sitting huddled over the fire cracking away like pen guns,[1] not expecting anything, when all at once the gang crowded in without knocking. Surely the gang had not been lurking around for some time as the door was left on the latch, or somebody had neglected it. However, in they came, and upon my soul it looked as if Harry would be taken now, for he hadn't a weapon handy, besides, there was such a crowd that no ordinary person would have thought it worth his while to make for the door. I'll warrant you that the officer was as proud as a dog with two tails and chuckled and laughed to himself when he saw, as he thought, that Harry was in his power at last.

But faith, the great fool if he expected that Harry was a great dolt who would give in without a struggle, he was sorely mistaken. There was a large pot boiling furiously on the crook,[2] and just as if it had been the weapon he had in mind he said nothing, but in his frenzy he grasped it by the handles with both hands, whizzed it off the fire and swung it round his head, he made the gang stand to one side and let him go in the name of the Lord. If the pot had hit one of them, it would have knocked him down and scalded him as well. When he got outside he threw the pot in a drain before the door and bespattered those who were after him all over with foul liquid from the byre, then he told them to go to Hell, and with a dash he ran for the hill. Never a one could catch him then, so he got away. On my soul, it was quite a feat and the foul liquid would have left a nasty odour with them, but it was good return on the rude fool of an officer for not having manners enough to knock at the door.

---

1 A child's pop-gun made out of the wing bone of a goose.
2 An iron hook and chain on which pots and kettles were hung over the fire.

The Sutherland Graeme Papers

The second son of Mungo Graeme, 4th of Graemeshall, Alexander joined the navy at an early age. In 1760 he received his commission as a lieutenant and served for years in the West Indies and American stations. Promoted Captain in 1776, five years later he took part in a battle with the Dutch fleet off the Dogger Bank where he lost his right arm. In 1786 he succeeded his brother to the family estate, becoming 6th of Graemeshall. Appointed to command HMS *Glory* in 1793, in June that year he obtained flag rank as Rear-Admiral. He became Vice-Admiral in 1799 and was appointed Commander-in-Chief at the Nore. Graeme was promoted to full Admiral in 1804.

These accounts of impressment and recruitment, in the main extracts from correspondence[1] between Alexander Graeme[2] and his factor, the assiduous David Petrie, cover the period 1790–1812 and evidence the amount of recruiting which took place in Orkney. Graeme was anxious to obtain men for the 98-gun *Glory* and additionally, as a laird, he had to satisfy a share of the Admiralty quota levied from time to time on the county. While some of the historical context and references remain uncertain, the correspondence highlights the involvement of a laird absent at sea in fufilling his duties with regard to recruitment through instructions to Petrie. The exchanges show that Graeme had to make available his share of bounty money to help raise the parish quota of men, although this did not always result in sufficient volunteers. Both parties had slightly different concerns for local men: Graeme hoped that locals would come forward to serve on his ship; Petrie disliked having to press men and was conscious of the effect of naval recruitment and other seafaring employment on the local labour force which had been 'drain'ed of men'.

1 The original letters from Alexander Graeme are in the Orkney Archives, D5/7 and D5/8. David Petrie's letters were destroyed but fortunately he retained copies from which information in the following pages has been taken. The correspondence is contained in *Orkney and the Last Great War*, P N Sutherland Graeme, 1915.
2 1741–1818.

David Petrie to Captain Graeme – Graemeshall, 22 May 1790

... If men are demanded from Orkney I suppose the Gentlemen here will agree to levy some in order to protect the Trade, In that event I fancy you will be willing to give a Bounty to encourage men to enter for your Estate in proportion with the other Gentlemen ...

Captain Graeme to David Petrie – Edinburgh, 6 June 1790

... when I was in London there was great appearance of a rupture with spain and Sir Tho[s] Dundas[1] told me that the Press warrants as usewall wer sent to M[r] Hagarth[2] but that as soon as the Gentlemen had had a meeting and would give into him a proposal to raise men the Admiralty had assured him that they should be protected as usewall which by this time I suppose is done as I saw M[r] Craigie the other day at Sir Georg Home's the Regulating Cap[tn] here who said that the County wer willing to raise 100 men. Sir George said that he had no directions about it but in the mean time they might rest satisfied that he would send no Tenders there. When the Bounty is fixed upon you will give for me the highest that is given by any Gentlemen and endeavour to get the young men that can best be spared from the parish and tell them that in case I go to sea I shall endeavour to get them with me. When I was in London I asked for a 74 Gun ship if we have war shall get one ...

David Petrie to Captain Graeme – Graemeshall, 11 October 1790

... I could not get a third Lad to enter voluntarily and as the Tender would not wait I were obliged much against my inclination to raise a party of our Men and Impress one. They fell in with one Peter Eunson a very Stout Lad [who] when brought to me cried & was very much averse to go but after many arguments used with him Entered upon which I gave him the same bounty as the two you saw. Lieu[t] Yetts[3] was very ill to please with Lads. There were two young Lads who offered to Enter with me but upon presenting them He would not accept of them. One of them belonged to Holm and after Lieu[t] Yetts was gone another Tender came from Shetland who cheerfully accepted of the Lad who indeed was very likely. He served for one of the Kirk[ll] vessels. There are several of the Gentlemen who have not yet delivered their Quotas of men but I did not chuse that your Quota should be among the Last ...

---

1 1741–1820. Elevated to the peerage as Baron Dundas of Aske, 1784.
2 Patrick Hagart, factor to the Earldom Estate.
3 The Naval Recruiting Officer.

Captain Graeme to David Petrie – Edinburgh, 6 December 1790
… You did very right to get my quota of seamen at any rate it would have looked ill to have had mine among the last the Gentlemen of Orkney have behaved shamefully and broke their compact with the Admiralty I dare say that had there been war there would have been a Press in the country …

Captain Graeme to David Petrie – Edinburgh, 11 April 1791
… You will have heard of the Bounty and Press but I think we shall have no war and the present armament is only to give weight to the King of Prussia and Bully the Empress of Russia into a Peace, the ministry are much blamed for it, there is no Regulating Cap^{tn} appointed yet at Leith and probably will not …

Captain Graeme to David Petrie – Edinburgh, 25 April 1791
… I have likewise your letter by Jno Garrioch his men will be very safe at present they only press from homeward bound ships and they have orders not to press on land …

Captain Graeme to David Petrie – Edinburgh, 3 July 1791
… the Pressing for seamen is now over and the rendesvouse here broke up. I never looked upon it as any thing seriouse nor did I think they would take men from Orkney as no place gave a Bounty …

Captain Graeme to David Petrie – Edinburgh, 16 February 1793
… we have long been threatend with war the French Convention has commenced hostilities and we have issued orders to make capturs as yet no Press for Seamen but great bounties no doubt a demand will be made on Orkney for men Sir Geo^r the Regulating Cap^{tn} has no directions as yet he is not much pleased with their last conduct all I can say is that you will always give for me the highest Bounty that is given by any Gentlemen in the Country …

David Petrie to Captain Graeme – Graemeshall, 13 March 1793
… There has no intelligence arrived here yet whether a demand is to be made for men on Orkney, or not. The Gentlemen it appears to me are not unanimous as some of them thinks raising of men are very troublesome and thinks Orkney may be nothing the worse to be on the same footing with the rest of Scotland. While others think that paying of men & being protected is much better. The last Lieutent^t that was here Mr Yets was very ill to please otherwise he might have

got a greater number and in shorter time. He refused Lads from me which were cheerfully accepted of by others a week or two afterwards and answered very well.

Jean Graeme[1] to David Petrie – Edinburgh, 30 March 1793
… Cap[tn] Sutherland will be in Orkney before this he Carried down Press Warrants with him …

Jean Traill[2] to David Petrie – Moredun, 30 May 1793
… You are all growen very loyal folks in Orkney and going to rais Fencibles, as bad a thing as can be done the Country but I hope it won't take place, the Women that has taken such an active part in it, I think should be obliged to serve themselves but I suppose they would act in that as in other things out of character …

Captain Graeme to David Petrie – Edinburgh, 6 July 1793
… As to the War it is more likely to continew than ever and the expence on the Continent will be very great, what have you done about the reasing [of] seamen. I hope the Fencibles take no men from the parish it will only make them idle …

David Petrie to Captain Graeme — Graemeshall, 18 July 1793
… The 100 men for the Navy was delivered Some time ago. I could get none to enter from Holm save W[m] Wood my own Servant. The Bounty was Two Guineas each and was paid by each Gentleman according to his proportion of Cess. Your proportion came to 6 Guineas and as I were at Some more extra Expences in going to Kirkwall several times & in procuring the men & not willing to Charge you with any thing but the real Bounty I laid on the Extra Expences upon the young men in the parish which they paid me. This was a method taken Several times before on like occasions.

But if you think there is the least fault in it I shall not do so on any future occasion. I likewise raised a feu Shillings from the Small Heritors in Holm proportionable to their Cess which I have put to your Acco[t]. I endeavoured to dissuade our young men from entering with the Fencibles and None has gone from the Parish and rather than be under the disagreeable necessity of raising a party & Impressing I offered more than the Bounty to any one who would enter from

---

1 Alexander Graeme's mother.
2 Daughter to Patrick Traill of Kirkness and niece of Gilbert Meason.

other parishes as at this time every one was at liberty to enter men where they could be got, accordingly I got three more … There were no young men from this parish that entered in the Fencibles.

David Petrie to Captain Graeme – Graemeshall, 23 April 1794
… I have in the Course of the winter got Kelp men engaged for the ensuing Season But they are much worse to be got than formerly partly I suppose owing to so many having engaged in the Fencibles …

Captain Graeme to David Petrie – Edinburgh, 31 May 1794
… I dare say you will be distressed for want of men every place is drained for recruits and no saying when or where the war will end but it is better having war abroad than Rebellion at home.

Captain Graeme to David Petrie – Edinburgh, 20 November 1794
… I see Ld Dundas has advertised a meeting and perhaps some plans of defence will be proposed such as inrolling as Constables or kind of Malitia which will be better than reasing more fencibles, the War goes on badly, God knows how it will end …

Captain Graeme to David Petrie – London, 3 December 1794
… I have been with Lord Chatham who has promised me the Command of his Maj^{ys} ship Glory of 98 Guns she is just now paying off to be new copperd when she will be one of the finest ships in his Majestys service and will be ready for me in about three weeks time and Lord Chatham has promised me to have any men that enter for me, make my Compliments to Mr Richan and tell him I will be obliged to him if he will enter any men that offer for the Glory at Portsmouth where she probably will be the greatest part of winter and you may notify it at the Church[1] door and Ferry Inn.[2] Seamen and able bodied lands men wanted

---
1 The parish church of St Nicholas, which now stands empty.
2 The Ferry Inn is still inhabited in the village of St Mary's. It stands where the ferry boat carrying passengers and mail left for Caithness. During his tour through Orkney in July 1760 Richard Pococke, Bishop of Meath, wrote: 'The post comes over from Ratter [Caithness] every Tuesday when the weather permits, lands at South Ronaldsha, crosses to the North End of it, ferrys over to Burra, then goes North and embarks for Gromshall Ferry house, and so goes to Kirkwall, from which place the bag is sent to Stromness and the letters are dispersed to the different places. And a boat on Monday takes the bag at the Ferry house and so it goes in the same manner to be conveyed to Ratter by the boat that brings over the letters.'

for his Majesty's Ship Glory of 98 Guns at Portsmouth Captn Alexr Graeme commander ...

Eupham Sutherland[1] to David Petrie – Edinburgh, 6 December 1794
... he [Captain Graeme] is in high Spirits having got his bussiness done directly as he is just to be appointed to the Command of the Glory a 98 Gun ship and all his martial Glory and ardor burns out afresh upon the Occasion as he Says he hopes to be the Leading Ship in Lord Hows Fleet but the news that pleases Mrs Graeme the best is that she is not to go to Sea this Winter wanting some repairs & to be Coppered & new Mannd no doubt the Cap^{tn} will write to you & his Friends to Enter what Men they can for him but as he Says the Grass grows not under his Feet he has so many things to do he therefore desired me to write you To get what men you can for him & Lord Chatham told him that whatever men entered for the Glory Cap^n Graeme he should be sure to get and if you will send them up to Sir George Home the Regulating Cap^{tn} (and the Cap^{tns} intimate Friend) they will be taken care of & Sent to him I dont supose he means to give any Bounty himself as it would be quite impossible in a Ship where there are so many Men and he will be at a great expence besides in fitting her out. I supose the good Parish of Holm will be prity well draind by this time tho I dare say they have found out before now that the Sea Service is as lucrative to the private men as any Fencible Corps in the Kingdom ...

David Petrie to Captain Graeme – Graemeshall, 24 December 1794
... I am made extremely happy to be informed of your being appointed to the Command of His Majestys Ship Glory of 98 Guns at present Coppering & fitting out at Portsmouth. May Heaven grant you health to enjoy it to your wish. I presented your Compliments to Mr Richan[2] who says He shall do his utmost to get any men who may offer to him, to Enter for the Glory. I have also spoke to Mr John Gordon at Stromness and to Mr Riddoch[3] who both promises me their Endeavours to the same purpose ... I have Advertised in Your Parish also for men whether Success may attend any of these applications I cannot yet say. Miss Sutherland also wrote me to the same purport with your last which I have answered by this post ... This Country was never so much drain'd of men as it

1 Daughter of Dr Hugh Sutherland, and Margaret, daughter of Patrick Graeme, 3rd of Graemeshall. For some years she was a companion to Alexendar Graeme's mother.
2 Lieutenant William Richan RN.
3 Son of Sheriff-Substitute John Riddoch.

is at present. Mr Balfour[1] is now straining every Nerve and is well advanced in raising a Regiment to Serve in Great Britain or Ireland and is appointed Colonel. He has got a good number of the Orkney & Zetland Fencibles to enlist for that Regiment and has just now Recruiting parties thro' every Island in Orkney Some in the Highlands of Scotland and I hear some in England. He went himself the other day by Ferrys for Caithness or elsewhere. So great and many inducements have lately been given to young men both for the merchant & Land Service that few or none has staid by the farmers who are very much straitened for hands all over this Country. It is with difficulty I have procured hands for the Kelp for next Summer. Not one person has Entered from this parish for the Fencibles or other Land Service my best Endeavours shall not be wanting to get some Lads to Enter for you. But I have but little prospect of Success owing to the above Causes …

Gilbert Meason[2] to David Petrie – Edinburgh, 10 January 1795
… I now have the pleasure of telling you that he has gott his Commission to the Glory of 98 Guns & will now be at Portsmouth as I am writing this I have a Letter from him & he was to leave London on Sunday if you can gett any Sailors to enter for him do it but I hardly think it worth while to enter Land men … Mrs Graeme tells me the Cap^{tn} had wrote you about raising Men for him. Lieut Yeats went to Shetland lately with a Tender, in case he calls att Orkney he will take any Volunteers that offer & promised me he would do his utmost to gett Men for the Glory & he had Sir George Homes desire to do it likeways.

Captain Graeme to David Petrie – Glory at Portsmouth, 26 January 1795
… I am very much pleased with my Ship in Dock and cannot be ready in less than a month by that time I hope the severity of the winter I hope will be over at presend it is very bad. I have letters from Lieu^t Scott[3] in Lerwick saying that he has sent 33 men for the Glory and I have applyed to the Admiralty for them there is sometimes difficulty in getting them if any enter for me in Orkney tell Mr Richan that he should put for Cap Graeme as well as for the Glory and the men may be instructed so as to refuse going to any other ship and after they

---

1 Thomas Balfour of Elwick, 1752–99. Married in 1770 Francis, daughter of Field-Marshal Earl Ligonier.
2 1725–1808. Alexander Graeme's friend and a leading merchant in Leith. Son of Magnus Meason, merchant in Kirkwall.
3 Charles Scott, Royal Marines, b. July 1760. Afterwards landwaiter [officer] in the Customs at Lerwick. Son of James Scott, merchant in Scalloway.

arrive at the Nore tell them to write to me and I will be obliged to Mr Richan if will send me lists of their names by Post saying what ship or tender they are put on board & that I may instantly write to the Admiralty, as yet the only Orkney man I have is Mr Jas Stewart …

David Petrie to Jean Graeme – Graemeshall, 10 March 1795
I beg leave to trouble you with this Letter tho I have nothing very particular to Communicate only wish to inform you how small matters go on here as I would not wish to trouble Cap[t] Graeme at present with triffles except something worth notice was transacting. I had a Letter from him of 28th Jan[y] Discharging my Annual Acco[t] and giving me directions in the event of any Men entering for him here. I have done every thing in that respect that I could except force. Mr Richan has exerted himself very much as had young W[m] Baikie with a piper & Drummer thro all the South Isles & Mainland beating up & has himself been thro' all the North Isles in very bad weather he has got in all Twenty Young Lads and has wrote to the Admiralty concerning them and asking liberty to go up to the Nore with with them himself when he would make sure Cap[t] Graeme would get them. I believe he has also wrote Sir Geo: Hume. We expected that Some more might have Entered but Sunday last Capt. Sutherland issued out Advertisem[t] offering £20 Ster. Bounty to every seaman & £10 Ster. to every Land man who would Enter with him. To what purpose he is to apply them is not known here but it is surmised that they are to Clear for some fishing Smacks with which he is concerned. That Bounty being much more than can be offered for Capt. Graeme will operate as a Bar to our geting any more as also the new levy of Seamen and Landmen now proposed by Parliam[t] when each County & Parish must furnish their quota – Mr Richan has given 30/- per man over his Majestys Bounty to those who have entered and he tells me has been endeavouring Among All those who He considered as Capt Graemes friends to bring forward a Subscription but can get none to take an active part in it. Only M[r] Laing[1] who wishes to Subscribe Something & Cap[t] Suth[d] who said if the matter was brought forward would Subscribe something for L[d] Dundas and himself. I have had Several conferences with M[r] Richan on the Subject and mean to speak to him in a few days again but it stands at present as I have described it …

---

[1] Robert Laing, provost of Kirkwall, merchant and agriculturalist. Father of Malcolm, Scottish historian and Member of Parliament for Orkney and Shetland, and Samuel, provost of Kirkwall and translator of the *Heimskringla*.

David Petrie to Gilbert Meason – Graemeshall, 10 March 1795
… I fancy the Glory is by this time ready for Sea. There are 20 Men entered for him with Lieu^t Wm Richan & waits a Tender to take them away. Capt Suth^d is now offering £20 bounty for seamen & £10 for Landsmen it is supposed to clear for Fishing smacks which will be a Bar to our geting any more men for Capt Graeme …

Gilbert Meason to David Petrie – Edinburgh, 4 April 1795
… I dare say Cap Graeme will not gett any of the Men that is entered for him. I gott 30 odd entered in Shetland for him not one of whome he gott & he wrote me he would give himself no further trouble since he would not gett them when they were entered for him & now by the Bounty that is given you need not trouble yourself about it …

David Petrie to Gilbert Meason – Graemeshall, 14 April 1795
… Mr Richan has 30 men on hand just now who have all Entered for Capt Graeme I dare say few or none of them are able Seamen and as He did not get the Zetlanders you made Interest for I shall take the less concern here. Let things take its course. If the Admiralty finds it necessary to send the Glory to Sea They will certainly man the Ship …

David Petrie to Rear-Admiral Graeme – Graemeshall, 1 September 1795
… When the demand came lately for men from this County I got two men to Enter for the Parish of Holm & your Lands in St Olla which makes you clear in that respect the bounty agreed by a meeting of the Gentlemen was 10 Guineas to each man. Some of the Gentlemen paid the volunteers the 10 guineas in hand, others only 1/3 thereof agreeable to the late Act and lodged the other 2/3 in the hands of the Collector of Cess. I paid the two Lads for you 1/3 of their bounty viz. £7. and Subsistence from the time of their Entry to their being taken off by a Tender £2/. I have not yet lodged the Remainder with the Collector as I know the whole will not fall to your Share and the Gentlemen have not yet proportioned it on their different Lands as they have not got the number of men compleated. There has been 56 delivered 12 is yet wanted …

Rear-Admiral Graeme to David Petrie – Edinburgh, 10 October 1795
… I approve of every thing you have been doing about the reasing of men … when you see Mr Richan tell him I am very sencible of the pains he took to procure men for me tho they did not join before I left the ship …

David Petrie to Rear-Admiral Graeme – Graemeshall, 1 November 1796
… Inclosed also you have my Acco^t with you for 1 year to 1st Septr 1796. I have no observes to make on it only the Cess of last year to 1st March 96 is not in it. The Collector of Cess Mr A Fraser is making out for all the Gentlemen of this Country their due proportion of the Bounty paid to the last quota of men raised for the Navy and is when ready to settle with each for their Cess accordingly when yours will be done also … I am Sorry to See by a Letter I had last Post from one James Voy belonging to this place that he has been troubling you to use your Interest in procuring his Discharge from the Navy. It seems he was Invalided lately at Spithead for Harbour Duty and was to have been sent on board of a Gun boat, if it had not been for the Interposition of a Surgeon Sempill of the Puissant. This Voy was two years a Servant to me before his going to Sea. I were very well pleased with him and he left a little money with me to bestow upon his mother I have no further connexion with him. I had not heard from him these three years and I wonder how he could think of troubling you. But I suppose he has been advised by Surgn Sempill or some other person in the Ship to make this application. I do not wish you to give yourself any trouble about him …

Rear-Admiral Graeme to David Petrie – Edinburgh, 19 November 1796
… I had a letter from Jas Voy and I wrot to Capt Hotchkis of the Puissant about him he answerd my letter from London and said when he went to Portsmouth he would see what could be done … I see little prospect of Peace there is new Levy of men to be laid on the County I think some of the men who have returned from Hudson bay this year might serve.

David Petrie to Rear-Admiral Graeme – Graemeshall, 25 January 1797
… We have just begun to issue advertisements and a Bounty of 10 Guineas for each man who will enter for the present quota of men But they do not seem to come forward. There has only 4 entred out of the whole yet. I dare say we shall be difficulted to procure them more so than upon any former occasion.

David Petrie to Rear-Admiral Graeme – Graemeshall, 22 February 1797
… I wrote you that four only of the present Quota of men for the Navy had Entered. Not one has Entered in all this Country since. I am not Yet Sure what Resolution the Gentlemen may take but I think none will be got unless they are Impressed …

Rear-Admiral Graeme to David Petrie – Edinburgh, 25 February 1797
… I dare say you will find great difficulty about raising men …

David Petrie to Rear-Admiral Graeme – Graemeshall, 25 April 1797
… As I could prevail upon none of the Lads of this Parish to enter for this Quota for the Navy I applyed to Mr Richan who very obligingly let me have one to answer for your property in Orkney. I find him very obliging at all times whenever your Interest is in question.

David Petrie to Rear-Admiral Graeme – Graemeshall, 13 December 1797
… The Fencibles were Disbanded & paid off two days ago. There is much ill blood between their officers and Some of the other Gentlemen of this Country who they suspect of making bad Representations and being at the bottom of their being dismissed …

Vice-Admiral Graeme to David Petrie – Sheerness, 16 July 1801
… we are short of Seamen so that all the men have been lent from the Zealand to other Ships among the rest Ja^s Johnstone was sent to the Aeolus but I expect him to return, when he went he gave Capt Mitchel of the Zealand Ten Pounds sterling which he sent to me by a verbal message to send to you. I suppose he has or will write you about it, I have got Robt Graham a grandson of Brakeness[1] made Gunner of the Arrow a fine sloop of 30 Guns …

Vice-Admiral Graeme to David Petrie – Sheerness, 5 July 1802
As I have reason to believe that I shall not be many more days here as all the Ships are payed off and the men departed quietly to their homes I would not have you write me here …

Vice-Admiral Graeme to David Petrie – Edinburgh, 22 April 1803
… I have not heard of any compromise having been made for men from Orkney but as Lord Armadale is in London he will see Lord Dundas and take care of it …

Vice-Admiral Graeme to David Petrie – Edinburgh, 22 July 1803
I find the Gentlemen of Orkney have had a meeting to offer a Bounty of two Gineas for every Able Seaman and one for ordinary & which I think a very

---

1 Possibly a son of Patrick Graham of Breckness.

right thing, you will acquaint Mr Fotheringham by letter that I concur in their Resolution – I fancey we must do much more and all encouragement ought to be given. You will see by the newspapers what resolves are going on here. You will at all times Subscribe for me a[s] high as any Gentleman in Orkney does. I can as well as a single man afford it besides my Rank requires it …

David Petrie to Vice-Admiral Graeme – Graemeshall, 7 September 1803
… The Gentlemen of Orkney finding that their first offer'd Bounty of two Guineas had no effect in bringing forward any Volunteers for the Navy have now offered 5 Guineas to Seamen & 3 to Landmen there has about 18 Entered only yet out of 100 proposed to be sent from the Country, 4 is the proportion laid on Holm, In order to encourage Lads to come forward I sent thro' this parish for a Voluantary Subscription from among the Single Lads from 17 years and upwards. I find they have offered £2 for each of the first 4 Lads who may enter for the Parish in addition to the Country bounty, this was only two days ago I have got none yet. If Constables & a party shall be raised in the Parishes where men don't enter, to Impress from amongst themselves no doubt I will be under the necessity to do the Same. But this is a method I by no means like as in cases of that nature they go to it with very much reluctancy & awquardness and the Lads are much more averse to be taken by their own people than by a regular Gang authorised by Goverm^t. However I shall on my part conduct it in the best manner I can …

David Petrie to Vice-Admiral Graeme – Graemeshall, 15 September 1803
Mr Graeme with his cutter is just now in Kirk^{ll} Road with 26 Volunteers from Zetland for the Navy, he will also take what is ready here, I suppose about 20. I have yet of this date only one for Holm, the Lads are very slow in coming forward in Orkney, I presume they must be impressed, this for my own part I much wish to avoid …

Vice-Admiral Graeme to David Petrie – Edinburgh, 7 October 1803
… I see that notwithstanding the high Bountys it will be a difficult matter to raise 100 men in Orkney but the people will see the necessity and as the County is freed from finding men for the Malitia and Army of reserve the Gentlemen are bound to produce men for the Navy and a part must go to protect the others and I wish there was a Kings Officer on the spot …

David Petrie to Vice-Admiral Graeme – Graemeshall, 24 November 1803
… By this time you will have seen Mr M. Laing who went up to Leith with Capt. Graeme's cutter going with a Division of the 100 men for the Navy, and by whom I sent for you an Anker[1] of Butter, he will give you the Orkney news. I got one man from Kirkwall and three Sailors from Stromness to enter as Substitutes for Holm they were paid the County bounty & the young people in Holm paid the extra expence for procuring them. The Town & parish of Stromness, Flotta, Gremsy & some more places also procured Sailors from the Shipping as Substitutes …

Vice-Admiral Graeme to David Petrie – Edinburgh, 9 December 1803
… I find all the men are not yet raised in Orkney tho a Lieut^t went down in the cutter and probably little more will be done this winter but extra expence you may charge against my Account …

David Petrie to Admiral Graeme – Graemeshall, 14 March 1805
… I dare say it will be very difficult this year to get hands to burn the Kelp through Orkney there is so great a demand for men to Davis Straits & Greenland, a great number of ships & giving high wages … This world is always growing worse …

Admiral Graeme to David Petrie – Edinburgh, 4 October 1805
… When in London I had an opportunity of writing Admiral Dacres and strongly recommended J^{no} Laughton to him to be made a gunner which I dare say he will do if the captain of the Centaur gives him a good character …

Admiral Graeme to David Petrie – Edinburgh, 9 March 1810
… the Ardent was here before Christmas. I saw your Son Archibald and was much pleased with him. Capt Honyman gave him a most excellent Character he writes under his Clerk who he says is a very good one and he thinks will soon make him capable of taking charge of the ships Books …

David Petrie to Admiral Graeme – Graemeshall, 14 August 1812
… The Gentlemen of Orkney have offered a bounty of Five Guineas to each Seaman & Three to each Landman who might enter for the Navy but none have yet come forward. I suppose it will land in Impressing them which is very

---

1 A cask or keg.

disagreeable to be done by ourselves but the 120 men I believe must be delivered in the course of next month. Gourly the Regulating Capt. is at present here. The Davis Straits & Greenland Ships have only a few of them yet arrived. It is thought by every one that these men ought to serve. But it will be difficult to lay hold on them if once they get on shore.

David Petrie to Admiral Graeme – Graemeshall, 15 September 1812
… Letter of 14 Aug that the Gentlemen of Orkney had offered a Bounty of 5 Guineas to each Man for the Navy, this not having any effect at a Subsequent meeting they have voted 1000 Guineas for the County which will make 10 Guineas a Man. Only 6 or 7 Men have yet come forward to take it. I made out a Subscription paper lately for our parish when 40 Guin. was placed in my hands from the young men & others for an additional bounty which would make 20 Guins for each man for the Parish of Holm, None have yet come forward. An additional bounty something similar has also been offered in other Parishes but without effect. As the time for delivering the men is limited to 1st Octo^r something must soon be done …

David Petrie to Admiral Graeme – Graemeshall, 6 October 1812
…seeing no chance whatever of any Lads to enter for you for the Navy and having corresponded with the Regulating Capt. Gourly who has been here several weeks, I accepted of a party of Soldiers who along with the Constables of this parish did search Houses hills & Rocks for two nights and three days and at last succeeded in Impressing 4 Young men good looking Lads all seafaring men but one a Servant Lad.[1]

With much entreaty they all entered here before being sent to Kirk^{ll}. The Ferret (Bg) Capt. Halliday is in Kir^{kll} Road receiving the men. The rest of the Country have not yet succeeded so well altho using Similar Means. They have not yet got half the Number. This 4 men with the one I formerly delivered makes out the quota laid by the Gentlemen upon this Parish so you are clear for this time. Your proportion of the public Bounty which I settle with M^r J Mitchell the Gentlemen's Collector, comes to £21.17.10. Besides this I were obliged to bestow victuals & spirits upon the Party & Constables from myself which I cannot state to the public Acco^{ts}. I am happy it is over. It is not a popular measure here to take the Tennants Sons from them by force. I have found Capt Gourly very ready to serve me as far as it was consistent with his duty …

1 See Hiding Places, p. 133.

David Petrie to Admiral Graeme – Graemeshall, 14 December 1813

… I had a letter lately from a John Laughton collector of the Pier dues & keeper of the Meal Market at Kirk[ll] setting forth that he has a son Wm Laughton at present a midshipman on board HM Ship Duncan that his servitude is nearly out and praying that I would write to you to use your influence in getting him made Lieut[t]. I have told him that it was with difficulty often that such things could be obtained & that I did not like to trouble you with things in which you were not interested but that I should barely mention it.

Altho' the Lad was born in this parish when his Father was a Tennant I know very little about him, he was Impress'd from a Davis straits ship & he has an uncle living in London a Lieut[t] in the Navy a W[m] Garioch who put him in midshipman but who I suppose can do little for him …

The Factor's Account Book [1]

This has entries concerning bounty and subsistence money to volunteers, Graeme's proportion of the county assessment, and the composition and expenses of a recruiting party. Bounty money was used as an enticement to enlist and the amount varied from time to time.

		£	Sh	d
1793 Ap[l] 19	By paid to M Ja Riddoch to Acco of the proportion upon the Cess for the Parishes of Holm & St. Olla laid on by a Sederunt of the Gentlemen of Orkney in order to furnish a Bounty for raising 100 Volunteers for the Navy Receit	6	3	–
Sept[r] 1	To Re[d] from the Small Udalers in the Parish of Holm towards payment of the Bounty to the Seamen raised this Spring	–	6	1½
1795 Sept[r] 1	By paid to John Clett Volunteer for the Navy to Serve for Admiral Graeme's Lands in Holm the 1/3 of 10 Guineas the agreed bounty £3 10/- as also Subsistence money for 56 days preceeding the 21st July 95 at 9[d] per day £2. 2/- is	–	5	12

1 Orkney Archives, D5/33/8.

		£	Sh	d
Septr 1	By paid to Mag{s} Robertson Volunteer for the Navy to serve for Holm & St Olla the 1/3 of 10 Guineas £3 10/- and Subsistence for 21 days preceeding the 21st July 1795 at 9d per day 15/9{d} is	4	5	9
1797 Septr 1	By paid Mr Richan for a Man to Serve in the Navy for Admiral Graeme's Lands last levy paid from Orkney	10	10	–
1806 Feby 1	By paid Patrick Fotheringhame Adm{l} Graemes proportion of 500 Guineas assessed on the County of Orkney for raising Volunteers for the Navy per Rec{t}	10	9	1
1812 Octor 10	By paid to Mr J Mitchell Adm Graemes prop{n} of Assessment of 1000 Guineas for 120 Men for the Navy Per Accor{t}	21	17	10
1813 Jan 18	By expences of Victuals & spirits to a party consisting of a Serjeant 5 Privates & 6 Constables for 3 days & nights employed in Impressing Adm{l} Graeme's quota of men for the Navy	2	–	–

Arthur Anderson and the Brazilian Navy

Arthur Anderson, founder of the Peninsular & Oriental Shipping Company and one of Shetland's most famous sons, was born in February 1792. In 1804 he became message boy, then boatman and later clerk to Thomas Bolt, Cruister, Bressay, a landowner and general merchant who was also factor for Lord Dundas. Three years later he was seized by a press gang from the office of the fish booth at Cruister, but released on Bolt's remonstrance and on an assurance that at a proper age his employee would volunteer to join the navy.

In 1808 Anderson did indeed sail from Lerwick as a sixteen-year-old volunteer and at an affectionate leave-taking Bolt exhorted him to 'Do weel and persevere', now the motto of Anderson High School, Lerwick.

Until his discharge in 1815 Anderson's service included a period in the Baltic aboard the sixty-four-gun *Ardent*, latterly as midshipman, and five years as a clerk on the ten-gun sloop *Bermuda*. A highly successful career in the world of shipping ensued.

An attempt was made in 1836 to obtain seamen from Orkney and Shetland for Brazilian whaling, and recruits were offered good rates of pay on a three year contract with the Marquis of Barbacena. Seamen were also required for the Brazilian Navy. Furthermore, there was a suggestion that a colony of Shetland people should be settled on the coast of Brazil, where the islanders would farm and fish.

The terms and conditions[1] on which islanders were to be 'engaged and employed in Brazil' is reproduced in this chapter, as is the 'Wanted for the Brazilian Navy' notice displayed in Kirkwall on 9 April 1836.[2] The events are

---

1 In a footnote, Anderson stated that the Marquis 'is possessed of very extensive estates in Brazil.' Though the Marquis was a rich man and the proprietor of mines he was not an estate owner. Sailors and other immigrants were to be recruited for official service and colonisation, not for work on the Marquis's lands. The intention was that the sailors would serve in the Brazilian navy in the state of Para.
2 The *Wanted for Brazilian Navy* and *Terms and Conditions* documents are reproduced with the permission of the National Maritime Museum, photograph nos. B4215 and B4214, respectively.

recorded in issues one to five of *The Shetland Journal*,[1] Shetland's first newspaper. Founded by Anderson it was printed in London and sent north for distribution.

In the first issue an editorial stated that the Government had invoked the Foreign Enlistment Act to prevent men in Orkney and Shetland being engaged for naval service in Brazil. Anderson was furious and in this issue he published a letter dated 12 May 1836 addressed 'To the Shetland men who have come forward to engage in the Brazilian employ.' He referred to the representation that had been made by some parties in Shetland which resulted in the Government prohibiting[2] the employment of Shetlanders in Brazil. He informed his fellow Islanders that they had to submit to this decision 'harsh and unjust though it be.' He would help those who wished to enter 'the Merchant Service at London' by advancing money for a passage south, providing a place to lodge and 'assistance to get a ship in a good employ.' Also in this issue was a petition to King William IV which described the poverty in which Shetlanders lived and asked for permission to accept the offer of employment in Brazil.

In the second issue of the *Journal* dated 10 September 1836, Anderson mentioned that three hundred Shetland fishermen had signed the petition.

Ninety men and lads left Shetland as a result of Anderson's offer. They were given free passage to London and pocket money, and were lodged and boarded at the expense of his shipping firm Uillcox & Anderson. Sixty-eight obtained employment on various ships, either by their own efforts or with assistance from the company; sixteen found jobs in Aberdeen and were given money to help them make a start; one was sent home; two absented themselves and a further three were kept by Anderson in a sailors' home until they obtained employment.

Nearly four hundred men were engaged in Hamburg and Bremen for service

---

1 In 1838 it became *The Orkney and Shetland Journal*.
2 In FO 13/131 there was correspondence between the Foreign Office and the Brazilian Ambassador concerning the Marquis of Barbacena's policy of recruitment. A note signed by Lord Palmerston and dated 6 May 1836 stated 'H.M. Gov[t] have been informed that certain persons in the employment of the Marquis de Barbacena are engaged in enlisting men in the Islands of Orkney & Shetland for the service of the Brazilian Navy; and as the enlistment of H.M. Subjects for the military or naval service of foreign States, without permission from the Crown is a breach of the Laws of this Country … the local Authorities will be directed to take legal measures against the Agents concerned in these transactions.' Ambassador Galvao agreed to stop recruitment, but in November that year he requested permission to recruit 160 men for the Brazilian service and the Government agreed.

WANTED

FOR THE BRAZILIAN NAVY

From 200 to 300 able bodied Seamen, ordinary Seamen, and Landsmen, natives of the Orkney Islands.

Liberal Wages will be given, considerably above the ordinary rates.

Distribution of Prize Money, Pensions for Hurts, Provisions and Victualling the same as in the British Navy.

The term of engagement will be for 3 years, upon the expiration of which, such men as may desire to leave the service will be provided with a passage home to England at the expence of the Brazilian Government.

The pay will commence on the embarkation of the men at the port where they are raised, and **TWO MONTHS PAY** will be paid in advance on embarkation, to be employed so far as required in supplying the men with the necessary clothing which they will have the means of doing at the London Cost Prices.

The men will have the necessary facilities afforded them for remitting such proportion of their pay as they may think proper to their wives or relatives at home as in the British Navy.

A large Vessel fitted up with every regard to the comfort of the men with cooking and mess utensils, hammocks, bedding, stores and provisions for the voyage outwards, will be provided.

Steady well behaved men may look forward to promotion as petty and warrant Officers.

Farther particulars will be expressed in a future advertisement. In the meantime application may be made to Mr William Banks, Jr. at Melsetter, Walls; or to Mr A. M. Garrioch, Post Office Kirkwall.

Kirkwall, 9th April, 1836.

Recruitment Poster.

The following paper has been circulated in Shetland, where men are eagerly availing themselves of the offer to engage in the proposed employ. Through the intervention of some Gentlemen connected with Orkney, the highly respectable House in London, which has the management of the business, has been induced to give the opportunity of engaging in it to Orkneymen also, as it is considered that the same disastrous circumstances which have prevented the fitting out of a number of Whalers, this season, must deprive a great many Orkneymen as well as Shetlandmen of their usual employ. The number of men which can be taken here, can only be decided, on the return from Shetland, of Mr. King, the gentleman who has just arrived from London on this business, as it will necessarily depend upon the number which have already been engaged by the Agent at Lerwick.

TERMS AND CONDITIONS
Upon which British Seamen will be engaged and employed in Brazil.

1. The term of service is three years; at the end of which term, any men who may desire to quit the service will be provided with a free passage to England.

2. The rates of pay are as follows, viz.:—
   For able Seamen .... 45 shillings per month.
   For ordinary ditto .... 40 ditto
   For Landsmen .... 32/6 per month.

The pay of such men as may be promoted to be *Officers* will increase in the same proportion to that of able-seamen as it does in the British employ.

Able-bodied men of from twenty to about forty-five years of age, free from bodily infirmity, and who have been two or three voyages in the whale-fisheries, or have otherwise qualified themselves so as to be able to hand, reef, and steer, will be considered as able-seamen.

Men who have been at least one voyage in the whale-fishery, will be considered ordinary seamen.

A certain number of men, not under eighteen years of age, will be also engaged as landsmen.

3. Men desiring to engage in this service, must apply, in the first instance, to Messrs. Willcox and Anderson's Agent, at Lerwick, who on being satisfied that the men applying are so qualified as to be likely to pass the inspection of the Agent of the Marquis of Barbacena, will enrol their names; and they will be allowed one shilling per day subsistence money, until embarked. Should any man be rejected, on examination by the Inspector, from any cause, not arising from deception on the part of the man himself, he will be paid *one guinea* in addition to what subsistence money he may have received, as a compensation for his loss of time.

4. On the men being approved of by the said Inspector, they will sign a contract in the form annexed, and which will be previously signed by the Marquis of Barbacena; and each man will then be paid *two months' wages in advance.*

5. On receiving their two months' advance, they will be required to provide themselves with the following clothing, or so much thereof as they may not have:—
   A hat,
   A blue jacket,
   A waistcoat or Guernsey frock
   Two frocks and two pair thin duck trowsers,
   One pair shoes,
   Six shirts.

This clothing they will have the opportunity of purchasing *at the lowest London prime cost prices,* as an assortment will be sent down in the ship or ships, which will convey them to Brazil, and which will be furnished to them *without any profit whatever* being charged on the original cost in London.

6. A ship or ships, will come to Shetland properly fitted up, by which the men will be conveyed to Brazil, where they will be appointed to the ships in which they are to serve. The men will be provided with Hammocks, Mess utensils, fuel, and will be victualled and have the same allowance of grog, for the voyage out to Brazil. as is customary in the British employ, all free of expense to them. And a medical gentleman will be appointed to attend to them during the voyage.

7. The pay will commence, on the day on which the men sign the contract, and embark on board the ships for their passage to Brazil.

8. Men who may wish to remit a part of their pay home to their families, or friends, will be able to do so.

In addition to the above particulars, it is thought proper to state, that the Brazilian Ships, are commanded almost entirely by English or Scotchmen, most of whom have been brought up in the British Merchant service.—There is no rigorous discipline to be submitted to—*for even in the Brazilian Navy the cat-o-nine-tails is entirely prohibited,*—Brazil is at peace with all the world—And as the object of the patriotic Marquis, is to teach his countrymen seamanship, by placing Brazilian boys and youths gradually under the direction of the British seamen, it naturally follows that, in a service such as this, which is intended to be increased to a considerable extent, steady and deserving men cannot fail to be rapidly advanced, especially if their education should fit them for superior situations.

Form of the Contract between the Seamen and the Marquis of Barbacena.

Contract between the Marquis of Barbacena, on the one part, and the undersigned Men on the other part, viz.

WE The undersigned, agree to enter into the service of the the said Marquis, for the term of three years certain, at the rate of wages set against our names respectively, and under the following conditions, viz.
1. At the end of the three years' service, such men as may desire to quit the employ, to be provided with a passage to England, free of expense to them.
2. The pay to commence on approval, and embarkation, of the men for Brazil.
3. Two months to be paid in advance, the receipt of which as set against our names, is hereby acknowledged.
4. And we hereby agree, and promise faithfully to do our duties in the respective stations, to which we may be appointed and to subject ourselves to all the Laws and Rules which are or shall be established for the Regulation of the service in which we shall be employed.

RATES OF WAGES.
Able Seamen .... £2 5 0 }
Ordinary Seamen .... 2 0 0 } per month.
Landsmen .... 1 12 6 }

The Wages will be paid in the Currency of the Country, at the just equivalent for English Money, every Three Months, the Marquis or his Assigns, retaining Three Months' Pay in hand, which will be paid on the conclusion of the term of service.

TO SHETLANDMEN.

FELLOW COUNTRYMEN,

Although it has been my lot to reside out of my native country from a very early period of life, yet I have never forgotten that I am a Shetlandman, and have ever felt an anxious wish to promote the interest of the poorer classes of my countrymen. Connected with some attempts of that description my name may not perhaps be unknown to some of you. I am sorry that a delay has occurred in carrying these attempts into full effect, on account of circumstances which I could neither control nor foresee. Considering some of these circumstances, it affords me no small pleasure to have it now in my power to promote the interests of a considerable number of Shetlandmen, without having to depend upon either the support or inclinations of any parties in Shetland, except you—the men who are intended to be benefitted by it.

The Brazilian Service offers encouragement for steady, active, and well-conducted men, very far exceeding any other service that I am acquainted with. I need only refer you to the printed "*Terms and Conditions*" above, to convince you of it.

I feel very happy, I can assure you, at having prevailed with the truly enlightened and respectable nobleman from whose patriotic endeavours to improve his native country, the present opportunity of employment proceeds, to permit me to take at least a part of the men from Shetland, which I have accomplished with much difficulty, as there are plenty of men in London who would gladly embrace the offer. I have obtained the Marquis's permission, under a pledge that the Shetlandmen shall be the best, and at the same time the most orderly seamen that have ever yet been in Brazilian employ,—a pledge which, unless my countrymen have very much altered since my youthful days, when I have them more intimately, I have no fear of redeeming.

I have also much gratification in announcing, that there is a still more encouraging prospect of doing good on an extensive scale, for some of the inhabitants of Shetland. The Marquis of Barbacena is possessed of very extensive estates in Brazil. On a part of these estates in the interior, he has already settled a considerable number of families from Germany, who now form an industrious, thriving and happy community—A part of his estates are situated on the sea coast, in a delightful climate and beautiful country, and where an extensive Sperm Whale fishery, was lately carried on by the Brazilian Government. On this spot I have great hopes, he will be induced to settle a Colony of Shetland people. In which case, as their occupations would be pretty much the same as at home, Farming and Fishing, and they would be settled in a sufficient number to form a community of themselves, with their families and friends all around them,—the only difference they would perceive in their change of country would be that of changing a barren and unproductive soil, and a state of miserable dependency, for a splendid and fruitful clime, and a state in which nothing but common industry will be required, to ensure wealth and independence.

I have one remark to make, and that is—that as the opening for promotion in the Brazilian Service is very great, I would recommend that two or three Shetlandmen, capable of instructing the others in Navigation, should be induced to go out with them. There will be a great deal of spare time in the service, to enable those who may wish to improve themselves to do so: and the person who now addresses you can speak from experience of the immense value of a little education, to help a man on in the world, who has little else to start with.

In conclusion, Countrymen, I feel proud, that after a long absence, my first introduction again to you is not in the character of the Head of a Pressgang, in the middle of the night from the midst of their families.—But that I come to propose to, and provide for you, the means of bettering your condition, resting on no authority but that of your own free will.

The term of service is short. Those who remain in it are sure to get forward.—Those who return, if they are careful, may return with from £50 to £100 in their pockets, in a condition to enter into the fisheries, or other branches of industry, in their native Islands, free and independent of the control of any one.

I am
Your sincere well wisher and countryman,
ARTHUR ANDERSON

Terms and Conditions.

in Brazil, but no Orcadians or Shetlanders were ever employed to work under contract to the Marquis of Barbacena.[1]

In the terms and conditions on which the men were to be employed it is mentioned that 'there is no rigorous discipline to be submitted to – for even in the Brazilian Navy the cat-o'-nine-tails is entirely prohibited'. Although over twenty years had passed since his discharge from the Navy, Anderson had not forgotten the horror of impressment, and included a message 'To Shetlandmen', the penultimate paragraph of which reads: 'In conclusion, Countrymen, I feel proud, that after a long absence, my first introduction again to you is not in the character of the Head of a Pressgang, in which some Shetlandmen have appeared, hunting their fellow-countrymen from rock to rock like wild beasts, or dragging them in the dead of night from the midst of their families. But that I come to propose to, and provide for you, the means of bettering your condition, resting on no authority but that of your own free will.'

---

[1] Various references to the matter are made in the third issue of *The Shetland Journal* dated 12 November 1836, the fourth issue of 2 January 1837 and the fifth issue of 1 February 1837.

Caithness

During the long French Wars most Caithness recruits served in the army. The Militia Act required a parish levy in direct proportion to the population, the men being selected by ballot, and those chosen were bound to serve personally or pay money which exempted them for a period of time. Failing this substitutes had to be found.

But impressment for sea service did leave its mark on the county, and armed naval vessels as well as privateers were active in the waters around the north of Scotland. Fearful of the real possibility of enforced recruitment, Caithness fishermen took care before putting to sea. The appearance of a cutter caused consternation in every coastal hamlet, and able-bodied men fled to the hills or hid in caves where they might remain for days. Only the old and disabled remained, and together with women they had to attend to essential work on the croft.

The pilots who plied their trade in the dark surges of the Pentland Firth were particularly skilled seamen. They too were constantly on the alert for lurking cutters. One fine summer morning in 1802 the crew of a Stroma pilot boat were caught off guard when a ship expected to employ them revealed itself as a naval brig. The warship was anxious to obtain seamen and the Stroma men made haste for their island, just short of which they were intercepted by an eight-oared gig and taken for examination as a preliminary to impressment. On the ship's deck, Walter Smith seized hold of the main boom and shouted to his companions 'Boys 'is is lek ma faither's ploch-bame.'[1] Then, sitting astride it he issued the strange order 'Swingle-tree haul.'[2] Such idle, incoherent talk ensured his release.

Another version is that Smith appeared fascinated by the Captain's brass buttons, gazing at them with wonder and amazement. He appeared so foolish that he was summarily returned to the pilot boat. George Smith and George

---

[1] 'Boys, this is like my father's plough-beam.'
[2] The swingle-tree was the bar in a plough – or carriage – draught to which the traces were attached.

Moodie had physical disabilities and they too were rejected but three others, William Sinclair, Andrew Sinclair and James Moodie served in the Navy for nearly four years. It is said that they fought at Trafalgar before being honourably discharged whereupon they returned to Stroma.

There was a clear understanding that a boat at sea could not be left so undermanned that it was put in jeopardy. A story in the Caithness dialect tells how three Freswick men used this safeguard to outwit the gang: 'Weel, there were three Freswick men oot wan day, fan e press gang took wan chiel, but e other chiel hed his wits aboot him: he said at e third chiel wis daft, at he couldna be left alone in e boat wi a daftie. An e naval officer didna believe at crack, so he threw a half croon til e daft chiel, an e daft chiel threw it in e sea. An at at stage they did believe him an they put e first man back on e boat.'[1]

James Mowat from Mey, who later became a Pentland Firth pilot, was on a homeward-bound whaler when a man of war's cutter was sighted. Most of the crew took to the boats, leaving a complement just sufficient to work the vessel. Mowat, delaying his departure to collect personal belongings, was left behind and when the whaler was boarded the skeleton crew were one man over the permitted number. Mowat turned his cap back to front, distorted his face, disarranged his clothing and awaited inspection, open mouthed, drooling and speechless. He was classed as mentally retarded and quite unsuitable for service.

Sailors had to be particularly careful to avoid being pressed from vessels negotiating the Pentland Firth. In a mid-nineteenth century memoir[2] a Dundee man described how whalers approaching the north coast of Scotland took the precaution of landing numbers of sailors:

When a vessel neared the coast, all hands that could be spared took to the boats and made for the nearest land, happy if they could escape the tenders which were continually hovering about. The cases of the poor men employed in the whale fishing were particularly hard: coming from their dreary and hazardous voyages, they dared not openly return to the comforts of home and the caresses of their families; but, on approaching Cape Wrath had to land in that barren country and make the best of their way over desolate mountain, moor and glen to Aberdeen, Montrose, Dundee, Leith, Greenock or Hull, and

---

1 *Tocher No 1*, p. 23.
2 The memoir was begun in 1843 by Alexander Maxwell, Dundee, and was addressed to his eldest son David. In 1851 his youngest son George continued the work, writing from his father's dictation – the break of eight years was due to Alexander's illness. The story gives an excellent impression of how people in Dundee and the surrounding countryside regarded the gang. In 1980 the original manuscript was in the possession of George Maxwell's grand-daughter, Mrs Edith Maxwell Hill, St Andrews.

perchance only to be dragged from their hearths after they had thus reached them, to fight the French and probably be killed in action.

Returning whalers sailing along the north coast of Scotland often had Caithnessians[1] and Orcadians as crew, these experienced seamen being highly desirable recruits. One whaler returning from Davis Strait was intercepted, but sixteen Orcadian crew members escaped and landed at Scartans Geo, Nybster, closely pursued by men from a cutter. After hiding in the hills the islanders stole a boat, sailed across the Pentland Firth and reached home.

A similar story is told about fourteen Orcadians who, late one night, awakened Sannie[2] Begg the miller at Milton, Aukengill. They came from a whaler and had left their vessel west of Strathy Point, Sutherland. Taking turns to row, and hoisting blankets to catch any favourable wind, the men had sailed eastwards, keeping close to land. Begg gave them shelter, they remained undetected and later were able to cross to South Ronaldsay.

The crews of small coastal craft trading out of Orkney were constantly at risk. One summer day a Caithness crofter carting peats saw two men running towards him – Orcadians from a smack intercepted at Dwarwick Head, Dunnet Bay. One seaman jumped on the cart and Nicolson, a sympathetic crofter, quickly covered him with peats, subsequently hiding the fugitive in his home. He stayed there until the naval men left the district. The other Orcadian ran on and was captured eight miles away, near the Shones[3] of Brabster.

Caithness folk feared and detested the gang. A ship was wrecked at Freswick and all the crew perished except a youth who was cast ashore. A woman demanded that he be killed, declaring that he was one of the gang who had stolen her 'coo'. 'Na, na,' cried the survivor, 'A'm juist a puir prentice laddie frae Aberdeen.' Doubtless his age and accent saved him.

At Dunbeath there is a sea cave with a concealed entrance into which a small boat can manoeuvre. Men in danger of being pressed sought safety there and it is said that the laird encouraged them to use this sanctuary.

The following description[4] of the cave dates from about 1783:

Underneath is a large cavern below the foundation of the castle, running up from the sea, and into which the sea enters at a certain height of the tide, and approaches near to a

---

1 Caithness men habitually travelled to Stromness where they joined the Hull whalers which favoured that port.
2 Sandy.
3 Bogs.
4 Calder, *Sketch of the Civil and Traditional History of Caithness*, 1861, p. 152.

dark, dreary vault – the bottom of which is about 50 feet deep from the surface of the rock on which the castle stands. From within the castle, the approach to this dismal place is by steps cut in the rock, formed like a narrow stair, twisting round and round as it descends into the vault ... Most probably it was used as a passage to the sea, in order to escape in boats when the castle was besieged by an enemy.

Bibliography

Adkins, Roy & Lesley, *Jack Tar, Life in Nelson's Navy*, Little, Brown, London, 2008

Anderson, James, *Anderson's Guide to the Orkney Islands*, Kirkwall, 1884

Anderson, Peter D, *Robert Stewart Earl of Orkney Lord of Shetland* 1533–93, Edinburgh, 1982

Anderson, Tom and Swing, Pam, *Haand me doon da fiddle*, 1979

Angus, James Stout, *A Glossary of the Shetland Dialect*, Paisley, 1914

Angus, James Stout, *Echoes from Klingrahool*, 1898

Baynham, Henry, *From the Lower Deck the Old Navy 1780–1840*, 1969

Beattie, Dr Alan M, 'Shetlanders in the Royal Navy 1792–1815', in *Coontin Kin*, No 7, Lerwick, June 1993

Bowes, Rev H R, *The Launching of Methodism in Shetland*, 1822, reproduced by the Wesley History Society, August 1972

Brewer, E Cobham, LLD, *Dictionary of Phrase and Fable*, 1901

Bryant, Arthur, *Years of Victory 1802–1812*, 1944

Burgess, J J Haldane, *Some Shetland Folk*, 1902

Burrows, Edmund H, *The Moodies of Melsetter*, 1954

Burrows, Harold, CBE FRCS, ed., *The Perilous Adventures and Vicissitudes of a Naval Officer 1801–1812*, William Blackwood & Sons, Edinburgh, 1927

The Caledonian Mercury, 1st March 1777

Calder, James T, *Sketch of the Civil and Traditional History of Caithness*, 1861

Catton, Rev James, *The History and Description of the Shetland Islands*, P I Tuxford, Wainfleet, 1838

Chambers Journal, 1 June 1895

Clark, W Fordyce, *Shetland Nights – Tales from the Land of the 'Simmer Dim'*, ND

Clowes, Sir William Laird, *The Royal Navy – A History*, London, 1899.

Cluness, A T, *The Shetland Book*, 1967

Cormack, Maribelle *The Cormacks of Eday, Orkney Islands, Scotland. The families of Black Banks, Red Banks, Heatherbrae, Quoyfaulds and of Breck, 1786 to 1969*, Park Museum, Providence, Rhode Island, USA, 1969

Correspondence of The Right Honourable Sir John Sinclair, Bart, Vol I, 1831

Cowie, L W, 'The Martello Towers' in *History Today*

Dennison, Walter Traill, *The Orcadian Sketch-Book*, 1880

Bibliography

Dictionary of National Biography, Sir Leslie Stephen and Sir Sidney Lee, eds., Volume XVII, London, 1917

Donaldson, Gordon, *Surnames and Ancestry in Scotland,* ND

Duncan, W R, *Zetland Directory and Guide*, Second Edition, 1861

Edinburgh Annual Register, 20 September 1814

Edinburgh Chronicle, 5–7 July 1759

Edmondston, Arthur, MD, *A View of the Ancient and Present State of the Zetland Islands*, Vol II, 1809

Edmondston, Thos, *An Etymological Glossary of the Shetland and Orkney Dialect*, 1866

Eunson, Mrs R, 'Round the Shores of Deerness', *The Orcadian,* 8 and 15 September, 1936.

Fasti Ecclesiae Scoticanae, Vol III, Part 1

Fea, Allan, *The Real Captain Cleveland*, London, 1912

Fea, James, *The Present State of the Orkney Islands Considered*, 1775

Fea, Peggy, *An Orkney Family Saga*, 1976

Fenton, Alexander, *The Northern Isles; Orkney and Shetland*, John Donald Publishers, Edinburgh, 1978

Fereday, Dr R P, 'Exploring Tankerness – Cannons, Caves and a Cairn', *The Orcadian,* 24 July 1969.

Fereday, Dr R P, 'Three Caves in Eynhallow', *The Orcadian,* 7 September 1972

Gardner, James Anthony, *Above and Under Hatches,* London, 1955

Goudie, Gilbert, ed., *The Diary of the Reverend John Mill*, 1889

Gunn, John, ed., *The Orkney Book*, Thomas Nelson & Sons, 1909

Graeme, P N Sutherland, *Orkney and the Last Great War*, Kirkwall, 1915

Graham, John J, *The Shetland Dictionary*, 1979

Grant, Francis J, WS, *The County Families of the Zetland Islands*, 1893

Grant, William and Murison, David D, eds., *The Scottish National Dictionary*, Vol VII, Vol IX, Edinburgh, 1968 and 1974

Greig, P W, *Annals of a Shetland Parish*, Delting, 1892

Griffiths, Captain Anselm John RN, *Impressment Fully Considered*, London, 1826

Groundwater, Henrietta, *Memories of an Orkney Family*, Kirkwall, 1967

Hamilton's Universal Tune-Book, 1844

Harcus, Rev Henry, *The History of The Orkney Baptist Churches*, David Hourston, Ayr, 1898

Hibbert, Samuel, MD FRSE, *Description of the Shetland Islands* Edinburgh, 1822

Hossack, B H, *Kirkwall In The Orkneys*, 1900

Hughes, John Scott, *Kings of the Cocos*, 1950

Hutchinson, J R, *The Press-Gang Afloat and Ashore*, Eveleigh Nash, London, 1913

Irvine, J W, *Lerwick; The Birth and Growth of an Island Town*, Lerwick, 1985

Jakobsen, Jakob, *The Dialect and Place-Names of Shetland*, 2nd edition, Lerwick, 1926

Bibliography

Jakobsen, Jakob, *The Place-names of Shetland*, 1936

Jamieson, Peter, unpublished manuscript on the Press Gang in Shetland

John O' Groat Journal, 7/9/1906, 27/8/1915, 3/9/1915

Johnson, Robert L, *Shetland Life* No 45, July 1984

Johnston, A W, and Johnston, A, eds., *Orkney and Shetland Miscellany*, Vol I, 1907–8

Johnston, A W, and Johnston, A, eds., *Old Lore-Miscellany of Orkney, Shetland, Caithness and Sutherland,* Vol III, 1910, Vol VI, 1913

Johnston, Laurence G, *Laurence Williamson of Mid Yell*, 1971

Kemp, Daniel William, ed., *Tours in Scotland 1749, 1750, 1760*, Edinburgh, 1887

Kemp, Rev Dr, *Observations on the Islands of Shetland*, Edinburgh, 1801

Kemp, Peter, ed., *The Oxford Companion to Ships and the Sea*, Oxford University Press, 1976

Ker's Naval Log, 1778–1782, National Library of Scotland, Ms 1083

The Kirkwallian, December 1924

Laffin, John, *Jack Tar*, London, 1969

Laing, John, Surgeon, *An Account of a Voyage to Spitzbergen*, London, 1815

Leask, J T Smith, *A Peculiar People and Other Orkney Tales*, W R Mackintosh, Kirkwall, 1931

Letters of Sir Walter Scott 1811–1814, H J C Grierson LLD LittD FBA, ed., Constable & Co, London, 1932

Lewis, Michael, *A Social History of the Navy, 1793–1815*, London, 1963

Lockhart, J G, *Memoirs of Sir Walter Scott*. Vols II & III, London, 1900

Lubbock, Basil, *The Arctic Whalers*, Brown, Son & Ferguson, Glasgow, 1937

MacGregor, George, Jun, *Descriptive Notes on Orkney*, 1893

Mackintosh, W R, *Around the Orkney Peat Fires*, Orcadian Office, Kirkwall, 1949

Mackintosh, W R, *Glimpses of Kirkwall and its People in the Olden Time*, 1887, Kirkwall

Manson, Thomas, *Lerwick During the Last Half Century*, 1923

Marwick, Alexander, *Reminiscences*, 1870

Marwick, Ernest W, 'The Nor'Wasters', ND

Marwick, Hugh, *Orkney Farm Names*, W R Mackintosh, Kirkwall, 1952

Marwick, Hugh, *The Place Names of Birsay*, Kirkwall, 1970

Marwick, Hugh, *The Place Names of Rousay*, Kirkwall, 1947

Masefield, John, *Sea Life in Nelson's Time*, 1925

Mooney, John, Eynhallow, *The Holy Island of the Orkneys*, Kirkwall, 1949

Mitchell, J Stirling, *Longhope Lore*, 1932

Neill, Patrick A M, *A Tour through some of the Islands of Orkney and Shetland*, Edinburgh, 1806

Nelson, G M, *The Story of Tingwall Kirk*, 1965

The New Shetlander, 1968 and 1975

Nicolson, James R, *Shetland*, 1972

Bibliography

Nicolson, John, *Restin' Chair Yarns*, 1937

The Orcadian, 9/12/1911, 26/10/1912, 2/11/1912, 9/11/1912, 28/12/1912, 13/11/1924, 4/12/1924, 11/12/1924, 18/12/1924, 8/1/1925, 21/5/1925, 3/9/1972, 3/9/1936, 15/9/1936, 24/7/1969

The Orkney Herald, 8 August 1865

Peterkin, Alexander, *Notes on Orkney and Zetland*, Vol I, Edinburgh, 1822

Robertson, T A, and Graham, John J, eds., *Shetland Folk Book*, Vol IV, 1964,

Robinson, Charles N, RN, *The British Tar in Fact and Fiction*, Harper & Brothers, London, 1909

Roding, J H, *Allgemeines Worterbuch der Marine*, 1793–97

Rogers, Nicholas, *The Press Gang*, London, 2007

Russell, Rev John, MA, *Three Years in Shetland*, Alexander Gardner, 1887

Saxby, Jessie M E, *Shetland Traditional Lore*, Grant & Murray, Edinburgh, 1932

The Shetland Advertiser, 1/9/1862

Shetland Folk Book, Vol IV, ed. T A Robertson and John J Graham, 1964

Shetland Folk Book, Vol VI, ed. John J Graham and Jim Tait, 1976

The Shetland Journal, 11 June 1836, 10 September 1836, 12 November 1836, 2 January 1837, 1 February 1837

The Shetland News, 27 February 1909

The Shetland Times, 5/9/1936, 3/5/1879, 20/2/1892, 15/1/1876, 12-19-26/1/1889

Sinclair, Sir John, Bart, *The Orkney Parishes*, W. R. Mackintosh, Kirkwall,1927

Smith, Rev J A, DD, *Sinclair Thomson: or The Shetland Apostle*, reprinted by *Shetland Times*, 1969

Spence, John, *Shetland Folk-lore*, Johnson and Greig, Lerwick, 1899

Tait, E S Reid, FSA Scot, FRSGS, *The Hjaltland Miscellany*, Lerwick, 1934

Taylor, Alexander Burt, *The Orkneyinga Saga*, Edinburgh, 1938

Thomson, W P L, *The Little General and the Rousay Crofters*, 1981

Tocher No 1, The School of Scottish Studies, Edinburgh University, 1971

Tudor, John R, *The Orkneys and Shetland*, 1883

Tulloch, Peter A, *A Window on North Ronaldsay*, 1974

Vedder, David, *Poems, Lyrics and Sketches*, Kirkwall, ND

Walls and Sandness Kirk Session Register, vol II

Whall, Captain W B, *Sea Songs and Shanties* (6th Edition), Brown, Son & Ferguson, Glasgow, 1930

Willson, Beckles, *The Great Company (1667–1871)*, Vol I, p. 242, 1900.

Wheatley, Henry B, FSA, ed., *The Diary of Samuel Pepys*, Vols IV–VI, 1893

Informants

This list comprises the many people with whom I have communicated either by letter or in person, and who have supplied assistance and information in my research.

R N Abernethy, Kirkwall, 1979 & 1980.
Duncan Alexander, Egilsay, 1978.
A Anderson, Whalsay, 1980.
Fraser Anderson, Stenness, 1977.
L W Anderson, Out Skerries, 1977 & 1974.
Tom Anderson, Lerwick, 1979.
Alex Annal, South Ronaldsay, 1971.
Reuben Appleyard, Kirkwall, 1980.
William Arthur, Weisdale, 1980.

James Bain, Westray, 1972.
Robert M Bairnson, Dunrossness, 1977.
T Balfour, Orkney, 1976.
Alfred A Banks, St Margarets Hope, 1978.
Dr Alan M Beattie, 2009 & 2010.
Miss Mary Borwick, Kirkwall, 1975.
Bill Bews, Kirkwall, 1978.
Mrs Mary Bichan, Harray, 1974.
Steven Bichan, Deerness, 1980.
W J Birnie, Lerwick, 1977.
Patrick Bourne, Edinburgh, 2009.
James Brown, Westray, 1972.
George Bruce, Thurso, 1977.

Erling J P Clausen, Lerwick, 1978.
Dr Joyce Collie, Kirkwall, 1976.
James D Cooper, Stronsay, 1983.

Mrs Margaret Cooper, Stronsay, 1983.
R Copland, North Collafirth, 1981.
Mrs J A Craigie, Rousay, 1978.
Russell Croy, Kirkwall, 1976.
Mrs G Cuthbertson, Edinburgh, 1972.

Rev J J Davidson, Orkney, 1975.
John Dennison, Kirkwall, 1974 & 1983.
Magnus Dennison, Stronsay, recorded by E W Marwick.
Sandy Dennison, Harray, 2010.
Adam Doull, Sullom, 1978 & 1979.
Mrs M Drever, Kirkwall, 1974.
Davis Duncan, Kirkwall, 1981 & 1982.
Magnie Duncan, Collafirth. Recorded by The School of Scottish Studies, 1975.
W Dunnet, Longhope, 1973.

Lt Col L D Edmondston, Unst, 1980.
David Edmondston, Unst, 2009.
Jerry Eunson, Glasgow, 1974.
Margaret Eunson, Harray, 1980.
Mr & Mrs Robert Eunson, Deerness, 1973 & 1977.
Dr George Ewen, Lerwick, 1979.
Mrs Isobel Eyre, 1983.

Alison Fraser, Kirkwall, on many occasions.
Ronald Fea, Weisdale, 1974.
Dr R P Fereday, Kirkwall, 1981 & 1983.
John Flett, Kirkwall, 1983.

D N S Gibson, Rousay, 1983.
John J Graham, Lerwick, 1976.
Gilbert Gray, Shetland, 1980.
Miss Mimie Gray, Shetland, 1980.
Mrs J M Grieve, Harray, 1973.
J Grieve, Harray, 1974.
John A Groat, Lerwick, 1976, 1980 & 2010.
J M F Groat, Longhope, 1980, 1982 & 1983.

Informants

T Gullion, Holm, 1978.
Mrs David Gunn, John O'Groats, 1974, 1977 & 1981.

John George Halcro, St Margarets Hope, 1971.
J Halcro Johnston, Orphir, 1974.
John Firth, Orphir, 1974.
William Clouston, Orphir, 1974.
John Laughton, Orphir, 1974.
R M Hall, Kirkwall, 1980 & 2010.
Harry Harcus, Westray, 1972.
Mrs J Harcus, Kirkwall, 1978.
Mrs K Harcus, Rousay, 1970, 1973 & 1974.
Bruce Henderson, Yell (S). Recorded by The School of Scottish Studies, 1955.
D Henderson, Skerries, 1981.
Tom Henderson, Lerwick, 1981.
Robert Hepburn, Deerness, 1976.
Andrew Hughson, Lerwick, 1976.
Peter Hughson, Whalsay, 1980.
Malcolm Hourie, Evie, 1974.
Andrew Hunter, South Nesting. Recorded by The School of Scottish Studies, 1974.
Dr J A Hunter, Voe, 1974.
John Hutchison, Westray, 1972.

Captain Arthur M Irvine, Spiggie, 1976.
A Irvine, Gulberwick, 1977.
Arthur Irvine, Northmavine, 1974.
Captain J W Irvine, Surrey, 2010.
R W J Irvine, Whalsay, 1979.
James A Isbister, Walls, 1979.
Robert Isbister, Foula, 1979.
Dr W J Isbister, Orphir, 1970.

Peter Jamieson, Lerwick, 1972 & 1975.
Mrs W Jamieson, Burra Isle, 1981.
Angus Johnson, Lerwick, 2009 & 2010.
Bertie Johnson, Kergord, 1978.
James W Johnson, Reawick, 1972.

R Johnson, Skerries, 1974.

J W Johnston, Skeld, 1972.

Tom Johnston, Bridge of Walls, 1977.

Mrs Kathleen Keldie, Tankerness, 2010.

W Laughton, Holm, 1978.

Alex Laurenson, Laxo, 1974 and. 1976.

James J Laurenson, Fetlar, 1973, 1974, 1978.

T Laurenson, Bressay, 1979 & 1980.

Mrs Peter Leisk, Shetland, 1975.

Peter K I Leith, Stenness, 1978 & 2010.

Mrs Johina Leith, Stenness, 1978.

Raul Lima, Director of National Archive, Rio de Janeiro, Brazil, 1971.

T Logie, Westray, 1972 & 1979.

Hugh Louttit, Finstown, 1974.

Captain George MacDonald, Australia, 1971.

John Macrae, Kergord, 1982.

George W Mainland, Burray, 1974.

Mrs Laura Malcolmson, Cunningsburgh, 1974.

Mary Jane Manson, Lerwick, 1975.

Captain R A Manson, Lerwick, 1975.

Thomas Manson, Stenness, 1973.

Dr T M Y Manson, Lerwick, 1971 & 1983.

A B Marwick, Evie, 1971, 1976 & 1980

Ann Marwick, Kirkwall, 1990.

Ernest W Marwick, Kirkwall, 1974, 1975 & 1976.

R W Marwick, Edinburgh, 1974 & 1983.

Charles Matches, Harray, 1983.

Mrs A J Mathers, Stenness, 1972.

J Meadows, Birsay, 1974.

Isaac Moar, Hoy, 1974.

J D Moar, Birsay, 1974 & 1981.

Rev H L Mooney, Deerness, 1972, 1977, 1978, 1980 & 1983.

George Morrison, Weisdale. Recorded by Dr A J Bruford, The School of Scottish Studies, 1970.

Ronald Mowat, Graemsay, 1979.
J Mowat, Eshaness, 1979.
A Mowat, Hillswick, 1979.
J W Muir, Glasgow, 1973.

George Nelson, Tingwall, 1974.
James Nicolson, Egilsay, 1973.

George P S Peterson, Brae, 1974 & 1979.
Charles Poleson, Whalsay. Recorded by The School of Scottish Studies, 1974.
Rena Prentice, Edinburgh, 1978.

J Ratter, Ollaberry, 1981.
Balfour Rendall, Westray, 1972.
Jack Rendall, Rackwick, 1974 & 1978.
Mrs Mina Ridland, Westerskeld, 1979.
A S Robertson, Lerwick, 1976, 1977 & 1978.
David S Robertson, Nairn, 1984.
Ian Robertson, Lerwick, 1974.
Sheila Robertson, Kirkwall, 1979.
Sinclair Robertson, Kirkwall, 2010.
T A Robertson, Lerwick, 1974.
James Rosie, South Ronaldsay, 1981.
John Rousay, Kirkwall, 1978.

William Sabiston, Birsay, 1972 & 1976.
Bruce Sandison, Lerwick, 1972, 1975, 1980, 1982 & 1983.
George Sandison, Westray, 1972.
Mrs E Seatter, Rendall, 1968.
Mrs J R Sclater, Stenness, 1981.
Ian Scott, North Ronaldsay, 2010 & 2011.
John Scott, Westray, 1979 & 1983.
Mrs J Sinclair, Harray, 1983.
Tom Sinclair, South Mainland, Shetland. Recorded by The School of Scottish Studies, 1960.
Tom Sinclair, Stromness, 1980.
Robert Slater, Trondra, 1972. Recorded by Dr A J Bruford, The School of Scottish Studies, 1974.

Brian Smith, Lerwick, 1981, 2010 & 2011.
Mrs I Spence, Sandwick (O), 1973.
Mrs Sheila Spence, Harray, 1974.
George Stevenson, Evie, 1980.
Malcolm Stewart, Hoy, 1974.
W Sutherland, Lerwick, 1978.

J Taylor, Birsay, 1974.
W G Thomson, North Ronaldsay, 1974.
John Tulloch, North Ronaldsay, 1980.
Tom Tulloch, Yell, 1981.

Brian Vale, London, 1971.
Gilbert Voy, Glasgow, 1975.

Dr B Watson, Edinburgh, 1976.
Mrs Margaret Watters, Stenness, 2009.
Dr Jonathan Wills, Lerwick, 2011.
Bryce Wilson, Stromness, 2009.
Alie Windwick, Kirkwall, 1978.

Glossary

AFFRUG: spent wave receding from the shore.

AMAS: deserved.

ANEUCH, ANOUCH: enough.

ANKER: measure of capacity, a third of a barrel, 10 gallons.

BAAKS: beams.

BALLED: threw.

BARBERS: freezing mist rising from the surface of the sea.

BEAL, BEIL: fester, suppurate.

BEESWEEL: anyhow.

BENISON: blessing.

BEN ROOM: parlour/best room.

BERE BANNOCK: barley scone.

BIDDEN: asked.

BILBOES: fetters. The word is a corruption of the Spanish town Bilbao.

BISMAR: traditional wooden weighing-beam.

BLYDE: glad.

BOD: also called a *booth* it contained all necessary items of fishing gear and household goods. The landlord did not permit another shop on his land and tenants were expected to deal only at his booth. There was an annual reckoning between landlord and tenant. Bods or booths are not to be confused with the lodges where fishermen lived. The latter were constructed of stones and turf and thatched with faels and straw. In his *Description of the Shetland Islands* written in 1822, Hibbert depicts a booth as: 'a small ware-room filled with vendible articles, chiefly imported from Scotland. This is after the manner of the Hamburgh and Bremen merchants, who, in their visits to Shetland, above a century ago, for the sake of trafficking with the natives for fish, opened booths in various parts of the country, for the sale of fishing-lines and nets, coarse cloth and linen, spirits, strong beer, and other articles (p. 417)'.

BREUT: brute.

BRUNIE: thick scone or bannock made of flour or oatmeal.

BUDDIE: friend, term of endearment.

Glossary

BURSTIN: bere which has been dried in a pot over a fire (instead of being dried in a kiln) and ground down like meal.

BUT: kitchen/living room.

CABE: single-stemmed rowlock.

CATAWHISSIE: owl.

CEULED: cooled.

COARN: small quantity.

CORBIE: raven.

CRAIGS (at da): rock fishing.

CREUKID: crooked.

CREWALS: tubercular glands or scrofula.

CROOK, CROCK: earthenware vessel.

CRUB: sheep fold; small enclosure.

CRUG, CROOG: couch.

CUBBIE: basket made of straw usually for carrying peats.

CUITHE: saithe or coal fish.

CUPPLE-BACK: cross-beam.

CUTTACK: term of endearment addressed to a pleasant young girl, and perhaps derived from cuttack, a vole. A fine peerie cutto (Evie): a girl with a nice manner, a pleasant, sonsy girl. A cuttie lass (Deerness): an older schoolgirl, usually plump. A young cuttie (Deerness): a mischievous young boy.

DER WAAS: their ways.

EBB MEAT: shellfish.

EELA BOAT: inshore fishing boat.

FAELS: turf.

FAERDIN MEAT: food provided for a journey.

FAIR YIVERS: agitated.

FASH: trouble.

FEUL: fool.

FEYNESS: spirit, ghost.

FILTY LEEAN TAED: filthy lying toad.

FLAALSOOPLES AN HAN'STAFFS: parts of a flail.

GAET: path.

GAVEL: gable.

GIRN: complain.

GIRNEL: chest or barrel for holding meal.

GIRSE: grass.

Glossary

GLAMSE: make a sudden dive; snatch; grab.

GLED, GLEID: glowing, burning.

GLOUP: rock cavern whose roof has collapsed well inland from its mouth, leaving a yawning chasm upon which one comes entirely unawares.

GRAITH: urine.

GROTTIEBUCKIE: small cowrie shell.

GRUP: grasp.

GUDDLE: catch fish by groping under stones or banks.

HAIRST: Autumn.

HALLAN: area of cross-bars below the roof used by hens for roosting.

HALLOW: bundle of straw.

HAUL KEUTHES: fish for saithe.

HECK: crutch.

HECKLER: flax-dresser.

HENCHING STONE: stone thrown by jerking the arm against the thigh.

HERDIE BOY: young lad who kept animals from straying onto crops growing on unfenced land.

HIRDIN: bringing home crops after harvesting; biggin corn was building it into skrus (stacks) in the yard.

HOOSEAGETTAN AN GOSSAPAN: house visiting and gossiping.

IMPRECATE: curse.

JALOOSED: guessed.

JUPE, JUPI, JUPIE: flannel shirt or jacket; woollen shirt; singlet; sleeved pull-on woollen or canvas garment for the torso.

KILN: conical building for drying corn.

KISHIE, KESSI, CASSIE: carrying-basket made of straw or dried dock stocks, used for the transport of peats or manure.

KIST: chest or strong box with a lid.

KLIVVY: cleaving.

KOLLIE: small open lamp usually made of iron with a rush or cloth wick, in which seal or whale oil was burnt.

KOW: tufted stem of heather.

LAAMHUS: lamb house.

LANDWAITER: an officer of the Custom House.

LANGBAND: roof purlin or crossbeam.

LIPPEN: to expect; to look forward to.

LUDER, LOODER: ON ludr, a trumpet.

Glossary

LUM: opening on the roof ridge of a house.

LUPPID: jumped.

MATLO, MATILOT: common house fly, less frequently blue bottle.

MELLISHON: Shetland form of malison; a malediction or curse in archaic English and Scots usage.

MIRK: dark, black, gloomy.

MUCKLE KETTLE: large cooking pot.

MUCKLE PACE: much peace.

MULD: topsoil.

MURMELTED: lamented.

MUTCH: cap, usually of linen, worn by women.

NARLANS: nearly, almost.

NAVE: fist.

PAETIE-NEUK: peat recess usually in the kitchen in which the immediate supply of fuel was kept.

PEERIE TROWIE TING: small sickly thing.

PIVERAN WI GLUFF: trembling with fright.

PLOWT KIRN: butter churn.

PLOY: trick.

POOER O STOOR AN STJUCH: a cloud of dust and fumes.

PRETTY: brave, well-made.

RANT: social celebration; happy gathering with dancing.

RATTAN: short cane or stick used in the naval punishment of Starting.

REKKED: reached.

RIG: strip of cultivated land.

RIGGED: dressed.

ROOM or ROOME: an arable holding.

ROOG: heap, pile.

ROOST, ROST, ROUST: tumultuous waters caused by the meeting of rapid tides; area of rough, irregular and dangerous waves.

SAETREE: pole for carrying water-tub.

SECKAN: such.

SIMMOND(S), SIMMEN(S), SIMMAN(S): plaited rope or band made of straw, floss, coarse grass and sometimes heather, used for various purposes such as securing house-thatching and stack-thatching. In 1920 an old Orcadian recalled using heather simmonds. 'Ye might as weel wind simmonds oot o sand': an impossible task.

SIXAREEN, SIXERN: six-oared open fishing boat.

Glossary

SKAILED: dispersed, scattered.
SKOL: wooden bowl.
SKRU, SKROO: corn stack.
SLOPS: sailors ready-made clothing and other furnishings from the ship's store.
SOE: bait to attract sillocks.
SPEERED: enquired.
SPIK: whale blubber.
SOCK: sink in.
SPOOT EBB: particularly low ebb.
STAIG: stallion.
STAPPID: crammed.
STIGGIE: stile.
STRAITSMAN: man engaged in whaling at Davis Strait.
STREEKIT: laid out on a bier; prepared for burial.
TACKSMAN: tenant.
TECKET HOOSE: thatched house.
TEKK, THECK: dried heather mingled with coarse grass, used for thatching.
TEKKING: thatching.
TEKK-SYE: scythe for cutting coarse thatching.
TENGS: fire-tongs.
THRONG: hectic period of bustle or activity, busy time.
TOILER: troublemaker.
TOWE: thaw.
TRANG: busy.
TRAPPLE: trachea, windpipe.
TRIG: neat and tidy.
TRISTY: thirsty.
TROWIE: sickly.
TULLYA: fracas.
VILD WITCHY JAD: vile witchlike jade.
VILD: vile, portending evil or mischief.
VOAR: Spring.
VOOD: vowed.
WAKE: watch or vigil held over a body during the night before burial.
WARE (O), WAAR (S): large broad-leaved seaweed which grows under water. It was for many years widely used as manure – 'the very backbone of the old husbandry.'
WHALLER: whaler.

Glossary

WHEER LEUKAN CROOD: queer looking crowd.
WITE: blame.
WITHIFO: wicked.

Appendix A

Colloquy of Three Orcadian Sailors in a Spanish Prison
~ Extract from *The Orcadian Sketch Book*
by Walter Traill Dennison, Kirkwall, 1880

These men were novices and had been at sea for only two weeks when their ship was taken. The incident took place during the war of the Spanish Succession, 1702–1714. This story was told often at weddings by a well-known Orkney minister, himself an Orcadian. It was recounted to him by one of the men who lived to return home.

[FIRST MAN]
Oh whan! O whan, boys! An' this is to be the end o'd a'. An' they're stappid is i' this filt'y hol' tae dee like breuts. I wiss I hed luppid i' da sea afore I leut the Spanish ruffians tak' me. Hid wad hae been a short death, an' a clean death, ony wey. Lord luck on is! Tae t'ink that we s'u'd dee i' this heathenish land; an' wha kens bit they'll lay wur feet tae the wast! i'm seur i'll never rest i' me grave, gin they lay me i' this withifo' land.

[SECOND MAN]
I cinno' t'ink th'u wad hae rested muckle better gin th'u luppid i' the sea; for there's no muckle p'ace there aither for deed or livin' folk. An' th'u needs no' t'ink that ony whal' wad hae spued thee on land as he deud wi' Jonah; for Deil 'e t'rou' his t'rapple wad thee heid gong. i'm seur, thee naevs wad chok' the craig o' ony whal' that ever swam, let aleen thee muckle heid. Bit i'me seur, I need no' mak' a sport o' thee; for wur a' gr'und i' 'ee grist. O! De'il swall me auld creukid mooth'd aunty Maggie! Vild witchy jad'! Hid's her I wite for'd a'. Sheu ceust her malison on me for stealin' her darnin' needle. I hed hid stickin i' me co't for luck the day we wur ta'en. Sheu girned an' sheuk her heid at me the day I geed awa'; an' sweur geud wad never come oot o'd. As seur as death, I saw the auld sinner, me aunty, on wur fore tap the day we wur teen. I wad ken her amang a thoosan', by her cockle-mooth an' buckie-nose. I saw her blawin' wind i' the Frenchman's

Appendix A

sails, while sheu sookid every ca'ld ceul oot o' wurs ap under her pettico'ts. The bullets flew around her an thick as matlos, but niver a ane touched her; – for the De'ill's aye geud tae his ain. Lord, gin I hed me fit on Sanday gr'und ance mair! I wad laul keuthes a' me days i' Tammy Sannysen's boat, an never gong a tether lent' frae the Nouster.

[THIRD MAN]
O! boys, hid's a' weel, wi' you, beside me. Ye're baith single men; but there's me bonnie bit o' wife, Babo, i'll never forget me pertin' wi' her. While they boonied the boat, we baith geed oot o' sight under the dyke o' Hangie. We teuk ane anither i' bosams; an' sheu gret till I t'ought her he'rt wad brak'. An' yet, peur t'ing! sheu said, "I deu no' bleem' thee for ga'n tae sea, for hid's only black starvation tae stey." Bit Best kens wha'll win her breid, an' me bairns' breid noo! An' there's me bonnie bit o' burd o' a bairn Jenno. Aye a better bairn niver hed a loo'se i' her heid! Sheu wad no' grutten a word though ye beur her tae Jerusalem i' a heather cubbie.

Dialect words:

aleen	alone
boonied the boat	put the boat in order
breuts	brutes
cald ceul	cool breath of wind
ceust her malison	cursed, cast her spell or curse
co't	coat
craig	throat, gullet
girned	complained
grutten	cried, wept
haul keuthes	fish for saithe
heather cubbie	basket made of heather usually for carrying peats
leut	let
loose	louse
luppid	jumped
malison	malediction or curse
matlo	common house fly, less frequently blue bottle
muckle	large
naevs	fists

Appendix A

seur	sure
sookid	sucked
spued	vomited
stappid	incarcerated
swall	swell
tether lent' frae the Nouster	tether length from the landing place
trapple	throat
vild witchy jad	vile witchlike jade
wite	blame
withifo	wicked, fit to grace the withy or gallows

Appendix B

Will by James Fea, prisoner of war in Valenciennes, 8th March 1806

In the name of God Amen, I James Fea native of the Island of Orkney now a fisherman belonging to London, but at present Prisoner of War in Valenciennes, being very sick and weak of body, but of perfect mind and memory, thanks be given unto God, calling unto mind the mortality of my body, & knowing that it is appointed for all men once to die, do make and ordain this my last will & testament that is to say principally and first of all, I give & recommend my soul into the hand of Almyhty God that gave it, and my body I recommend to the earth, to be buried as may be thought proper – nothing doubting but at the general resurrection I shall riceive the same again by the mighty power of God.

And as touching my wordly affairs I give, demise, & dispose of the same in the following manner.

First I appoint my well beloved friends shipmates, & fellow prisoners, Willm Gun and Peter Sutherland my sole heirs & executors, to act seperately or conjunctly, that is to say whereas my late Masters & Employers Messrs Selby Crosswell & sons of London fishmongers to whom I served a faithfull apprenticeship of six years, have still in their hands fourteen pounds Stg. more or less due from my wages of that apprentice ship, I appointed the said Willm Gun, & Peter Sutherland to draw the same for their own use, if seperate one half each, or if together the whole amount together.

Also I bequeath to my said beloved friends Willm Gun, & Peter Sutherland all such wordly affairs as I am at present possessed of, or may afterwards appear to be possessed of.

And I do hereby utterly disallow, revoke, and disannul all and every other former testaments, wills, lagacies, bequests, and executors by me in any ways before named, willed and bequeathed, ratifying and confirming this, and no other as my last will and testament In witness whereof, I have hereunto set my hand and seal, this eight day of March, in the year of our Lord one thousand eight hundred and six.

Signed, sealed, published, pronounced and declared, by the Said James Fea, as his last will and testament, in his presence, and in the presence of each other, who have hereunto subscribed our names.

James Fea
Peter Perrots
James Robertson

Appendix C

Extract from
A Tour through some of the Islands of Orkney and Shetland
Patrick Neill A.M., 1806

6. *Whale-fishing exaction.*[1] – I formerly stated [...] that for every lad who goes to the Greenland or Davis Straits whale-fishery for the summer, the cottar family to which he belongs must pay to the landlord one guinea of fine or of additional rent. I have been challenged for making this statement without having previously examined all the 'land-mails legers' of the country, (by which I presume, are meant the rental-books), I adhere to my former statement; and yet am ready to believe, that, if the whole land-mails legers of the country were examined, no trace of this exaction might be found. This would not prove that the evil does not exist, but only that, if it does exist, the landlords who practise it are not insensible to its flagrant injustice. These gentlemen may perhaps deny that it is either a *fine**, or an *exaction*, or an *additional rent*. Let it, then be called a *bargain*, to which they surely cannot object. I give them the option of the name; for the name will not alter the spirit of the transaction. As an indubitable proof that it does exist, and that it is not a private bargain with the tenant, but an arbitrary and fluctuating imposition, I have now to state, on the best authority, that *advertisements* were, last spring (1805), affixed to some of the parish church doors of Shetland, informing the poor Shetlanders belonging to particular estates, that no permission would henceforth be granted them to go to the whale-fishery, under *three guineas,* instead of one! This dictatorial method of announcing a rise of price, is quite inconsistent with the notion of a previous fair bargain with a tenant. It proves, on the contrary, the previous existence of the smaller exaction of one guinea, as I had formerly stated. Such an advertisement, pasted on the church-doors, could only be directed to men who were considered as *adscripti glebae*, or, at least, as abjectly and inevitably dependant. – Whether

---
1 pp. 111–13.

Appendix C

this advertisement be engrossed in any of the 'land-mails legers' of Shetland, I know not: but its existence and authenticity will not, I am certain, be called in question. It may be proper here to repeat what I formerly hinted, that several of the Shetland landlords have disdained, at all times, to make the unequal bargain in question with their poor and dependant tenantry.

To conclude: In my former remarks I rather vindicated the landlords of Shetland from the unqualified charges of severity and oppression brought against them by Mr Pennant, in his Introduction to the Arctic Zoology; by Tompson, in Bath Papers, vol. vi.; and by the writer in the 1st volume of the Transactions of the Highland Society. But I cannot certainly agree to that unlimited approbation, to which I understand they lay claim, and which they assume (erroneously perhaps) as having been awarded to them by the Committee of the House of Commons in 1785: For I cannot help remarking, that the act passed next year (1786), for establishing the Society for improving the Scottish fisheries, mentions the *want of public stores*, where the islanders might freely purchase the implements of fishing, as one evil to be remedied; and that it states the essence of the evil to be, that, in whole districts, there were "only a few private stores where some articles are dealt out for the fisheries, *on condition of selling the fish to the owners of the stores at their own prices.*" Is not this the exact state of matters in Shetland at this day, and one principal evil still to be remedied.

EDINBURGH,
1st Nov. 1805

---

* *Fines*, I must observe, appear to be avowedly exacted on other occasions. The tenant is taken bound to deliver all his produce to his landlord at a stipulated low rate; "and has he knows that he cannot obtain the same price from his master for the articles he has to dispose of, that another would give him, he is often tempted to trespass his contract: and when found out (which is most frequently the case) he is *fined at discretion*, or has a summons of removal immediately executed against him. This is subversive of every virtuous principle, and introduces a low cunning and chicanery in the transactions of the people. Stat. Acc. vol. xx. p 116.

Appendix D

Walls Session Records 1759
Request by Robert Lawrenceson to change his name
to Robert Johnstone[1]

W[ALLS] Decr 27th, 1759

This day Compear'd before y^e [the] Session Lawrence Johnson Shoemaker in Gruitquey in this Parioch, and Produc'd a Letter from his Son Robert directed to the Said Lawrence, requesting the Session might cause ye Same to be Insert in their Public register, and that the desire of ye Said Letter might be Intimate from the Pulpit of this Congregation where his Said Son was born, and resided, till ye year 1757. And the Session having read and Considered the Said Letter, and finding per comparationem Literarum that it was the Genuine Holograph of the Said Robert, thought fit to grant ye Petition of the Said Lawrence Johnson by appointing ye Said letter to be Insert in the Register by George Greid Mer^{tt} [merchant] in Papa, and Clerk pro tempore to this Session. And they recommended it to the Min^r to read this Minute and the Said Letter from the Pulpit on the nixt day of the monthly meeting in this Parioch being the 16th day of Jan^{ry} nixt to Come, allowing the Said Lawrence Johnson or any of his Concerns extracts hereof how Soon it shall be Insert in the Register, he or they Satisfying the Clerk for his pains, and the Tenor of ye Said Letter follows. London July 6th 1759. Dear Father and Mother This comes with my Duty to you hoping this few Lines will find you in good health as I am at Present thank God, I am Sorry that I should have writ to Shetland along wth Mr Umphray that I was Coming home. I would Come along wth Mr Layburn but I could not keep Clear of ye press – because Randall inform'd against me and James Henderson which we was obliged to keep our Selves up for four weeks, which we could not Show our faces in the Streets, we have Shipt our Selves both together in a Ship bound for Gibraltar, and from

---

1 His entire family also have their names changed to Johnstone. Walls and Sandness Kirk Session Register, Vol 2, folios 91–2 in The Shetland Archives.

Appendix D

there to Gurie[1] which I do beleive will be a Twelve month before we return back. The Captains name is Webb and the Ships names is ye Ann Galley. I have Three Pound Ten Shillings a month. I have left wth Mrs Torrie my will and power in my Fathers name that whatever is belonging to me that he can receive it all if anything should happen [to] me in my voyage. Now Loving Father and Mother I shall not trouble you with no more at Present but rests your Affectionate and Loving Son till death. Sic Subscribitur Robert Johnstone. P.S. I was obliged to Change my name because of the Information that Randall gave against me to the press gangs. So you must get my name Registrate in the Session books the Same that it is in this Letter, and yours Likewise, and your Sons and Daughters name the Same, for my will and power is made in your name Johnstone, and my name is the Same in the will and power. Direct for me To ye Care of Mrs Torrie Living in the long cellar near the Hermitage bridge London. Directed thus, To Mr Lawrence Johnstone living in Gruitquey in the Parish of Walls, Zetland.

Moreover The Session Appoints the Sirnames of ye Said Lawrence, and the Said Robert his son, and the rest of his Children to be hencefurth converted, The Fathers name from Johnson, and the Childrens from Lawrenceson into Johnstone, conform to ye Desire of the above Roberts Letter, and of the Said Lawrence his Father now Judicially concurring therwith, and Intimation hereof to be made to the Congregation as above, by reading the whole Minute to y^m [them] for that end. And the Session appoints the original Letter above mention'd to be keept in Retentis as the Proper voucher of this their deed.

---

1 Goury on the Cherbourg Peninsula.

Appendix E

Memorial & Defences for And^r Morrison & others against Impress 1809

Memorial in the Case of Andrew Morrison, Thomas Manson and Magnus Anderson – privates in the Corps of Lerwick volunteers. Defenders in the Action before the Court of Session at the Instance of Capt Nicolson Regulating Officer of the Impress in Shetland.

28 March 1809
These three Defenders are Farmers or sons of Farmers in the Island of Bressay, and occasionally Fishermen but no seamen. In the end of last fishing season having gone to attend muster as Volunteer, they were impressed by Capt Nicolson and detained during one of the best fishing weeks this summer: but having brought their case before the Sheriff Substitute of Shetland, and proved to the satisfaction of the Court that from their habits and occupations they were not liable to impress, they were accordingly set at liberty, having however sustained great loss in their fishing by their detention and incurred considerable expence in defending themselves, they applied to the Court for indemnification. The Sheriff Substitute took that point to consideration to a distant day, transmitted the proces to Mr Rae the Sheriff Depute at Edinburgh who returned it with an Interlocutor, confirming his Substitutes decree that these men were not impressible and ordaining their expences which were accordingly paid by Capt Nicolson.

Notwithstanding of all which, and the trouble anxiety thus occasioned to these poor men, Capt Nicolson has thought proper to advocate the Cause, and drag them before the Supreme Court, where on account of their poverty, and the extravagant expence they are unable to defend their just Cause, or preserve that invaluable blessing their liberty, without great assistance & support.

The Cause having come before the Lord Polkimmet he by his Interlocutor of the 3^d March 1809 Ordained "To see and answer within Six weeks, meantime lists procedure and to be intimated." and it was intimated upon the 28th March.

Appendix E

The Islands of Shetland ly in the high northern latitude of betwixt 60 and 61 degrees, a Climate stormy wet and inconstant: the soil of them being comparatively barren, and agriculture imperfectly understood, the produce of the ground alone is insufficient for the mantainance of the Inhabitants; and the defenders with others of their Class, who Cultivate small Farms the greater part of the year, are obliged to have recourse also to fishing Ling Cod and Tusk in small norway skiffs or boats, during nine or Ten Weeks of the Summer, to enable them to live, and pay their Credit and landlords rent. Almost all the Common people are thus imployed in farming and occasional fishing, but they are no seamen, and have not the least knowledge of working Ships. the very few seamen who belong to Shetland are those employed in four or five small Vessels in the Coasting or foreign trade, and a few who go constantly to the Greenland Whale Fishery some young men go occasionally to that business, but they by so doing do not become seamen and are generally spoilt from being good land men: yet they have of late been supposed liable to be impressed and no oppostion has been made in their behalf. But with regard to the defenders the Case is very different: if people of their description Viz Fishing farmers or farmers assistants living at home with their parents should be considered liable to be dragged into his Majestys service, the total ruin of Shetland would be the consequence; almost all the young men in it would stand in that predicament; the fishery of the Country (that valuable and most productive nursery for seamen) would be ruined & the very cultivation of the soil neglected.

Nothing but direful necessity can sanction the depriving men of their freedom, particularly in a land boastful of its envied liberty, and when recourse must be had to that deplorable measure, through the imperfection of political systems the misfortune should fall on those only who come clearly under the description of impressible and ought not to be extended to doubtful cases. The anguish occasioned to British free born subjects by the loss of liberty is not to be conceived by those who are out of the reach of that danger. In the Shetland Islands the necessity for impressing does not exist. The inhabitants are disposed voluntarily to enter into the Naval Service in as great numbers as the Country can spare, or as is consistant with the prosperity of its fishery, and therefore no impressing ought to be resorted to. Whenever the Government made a demand for men from Shetland for the Navy since the French War of 1756 they have been furnished by the Active interference and hearty co-operation of the Landholders, who paid Bounties out of their own pockets and this procured Volunteers before any Regulating Officer was established and since a

Rendezvous was opened in the year 1781, great numbers have entered beside the quotas occasionally demanded by Government, and in consequence of such quotas being supplied, the remaining Inhabitants have been generally protected by the Admiralty. In the course of the present war only, it is computed that above 700 men have gone into the Navy. While the Bulwark of the Nation is so effectually and liberally supported by those poor & neglected Islanders, it is both ungrateful and impolite to molest them, even if the point of law clearly sanctioned it. The surest means of continuing that support is not by ruining but cherishing their fishery, which affords such a constant and liberal supply of Volunteers in the British Navy, a supply unequalled by any other district in the nation of equal population – It is therefore devoutly to be hoped that the Lords of Session will view the case of the Defenders and all others of their description in the same light in which the Sheriff has done, and no sentence will be pronounced by them which may forfeit the liberty of the whole Inhabitants of a Country, on pretence of benefiting the public service, and ruin one part of the Kingdom to advance the interest of another. If impressing must take place in Shetland, the Defenders humbly think it ought to fall on the numerous class who frequent the Greenland fishery in Ships, rather than on them or others in their situation; and that the small Island of Bressay to which they belong, ought not to be singled out in particular and harrassed more than any other part of the Country, as has been the case for some years past. Independent of the great numbers who have entered into the navy, many have during the last & present wars enlisted for the Army, and many gone into the Merchant service, and a great proportion of the last has ultimately come into the Navy, for which Shetland should also have credit. The precise number cannot be ascertained.

Independent of other circumstances the Defencers apprehend that their being engaged in his majestys land service as Volunteers exeems them effectually from impress, and they were alwise taught to think so.

Appendix F

List of Wills

Wills of Orkney and Shetland Seamen held in the National Archives and accessible on their website, www.nationalarchives.gov.uk.

Will of Henry Spence, Mariner late belonging to His Majesty's Ship Leopard of Orkney 03 March 1679; REF = PROB 11/359

Will of David Mason, Mariner of Orkney and Shetland, 13 April 1693; REF = PROB 11/414

Will of Charles Moody, Gentleman at present Purser of His Majesty's Ship Yarmouth of Island of Orkney, Orkney and Shetland, 30 March 1697; REF = PROB 11/437

Will of William Spence, Mariner belonging to Her Majesty's Ship Salisbury of Kirkquhar in the Isle of Orkney, 31 July 1713; REF = PROB 11/534

Will of William Anderson, now belonging to His Majesty's Ship the Pearl of Cross on the Island of Sanday, Orkney, 01 July 1730; REF = PROB 11/638

Will of John Williams, now of His Majesty's Ship Orford of Orkney, Orkney and Shetland, 13 March 1742; REF = PROB 11/717

Will of David Waters, Sailor, formerly belonging to his Majesty's Ship Cumberland but on Board His Majesty's Ship Superb of Catness, Shetland, 28 January 1743; REF = PROB 11/723

Will of Oliver Walter otherwise Waters, Mariner belonging to His Majesty's Ship Dunkirk of Islands of Orkney, Orkney and Shetland, 18 June 1746; REF = PROB 11/748

Will of John Gollaway or Gallaway, Mariner belonging to His Majesty's Ship Berwick of Calder Lerwick, Shetland, 27 October 1746; REF = PROB 11/750

Will of William Moor, Mariner of Islands of Orkneys, Orkney and Shetland, 26 July 1748; REF = PROB 11/763

Will of James Ogilny or Ogilvy, Mariner of Island of Shetland, Orkney and Shetland, 04 August 1749; REF = PROB 11/772

Will of Peter Johnston, now belonging to His Majesty's Ship Exeter of Birsay, Orkney, 13 September 1749; REF = PROB 11/773

Will of William Spence, now Sailor on board His Majesty's Ship Porcupine of Steness, Orkney, 30 September 1756; REF = PROB 11/825

Appendix F

Will of George Hutchen, Mariner of Orphir, Orkney, 22 October 1760; REF = PROB 11/859

Will of John Swan, formerly belonging to His Majesty's Ship Elizabeth but late to the Turkey Merchant of North Ronaldsay, Orkney, 20 May 1758; REF = PROB 11/838

Will of James Orkney, Mariner now belonging to His Majesty's Ship Jersey, 15 August 1760; REF = PROB 11/858

Will of Henry Sinclair, Mariner and now belonging to His Majesty's Ship Sunderland of Island of Orkney, Orkney and Shetland, 15 April 1762; REF = PROB 11/875

Will of Alexander Orkney, Mariner belonging to His Majesty's Ship Prince Frederick, 08 November 1762; REF = PROB 11/881

Will of Samuel Jones, Mariner and now belonging to His Majesty's Ship Sunderland of Island of Orkney, Orkney and Shetland, 07 January 1763; REF = PROB 11/883

Will of Henry Richardson, belonging to His Majesty's Sloop Hound in the Isles of Orkney, 26 May 1763; REF = PROB 11/888

Will of Theodore Donaldson, now belonging to His Majesty's Ship Elizabeth of Island of Shetland, 25 June 1764; REF = PROB 11/899

Will of James Manson otherwise Magnesson otherwise Magnison, Mariner of Shetland Islands, 08 November 1764; REF = PROB 11/903

Will of Magnus Downey, Seaman belonging to His Majesty's Ship Buffalo of Kirkwall, Orkney and Shetland, 09 August 1780; REF = PROB 11/1068

Will of Andrew Mowat, Mariner of Rendell Main Land, Orkney and Shetland; 08 September 1780; REF = PROB 11/1069

Will of William Miller, Mariner late Boatswain of His Majesty's Ship Nautilus of Stronsay, Orkney and Shetland, 08 November 1780; REF = PROB 11/1071

Will of Magnus Johnston, Mariner of Stromness, Orkney & Shetland, 14 November 1781; REF = PROB 11/1084

Will of Peter Sinclear or Sinclair, Mariner belonging to His Majesty's Ship Suffolk of Stromness, Orkney & Shetland, 29 November 1781; REF = PROB 11/1084

Will of John Cragg otherwise Greig, belonging to the Charon Forty Gun Ship at Gloucester in Virginia in North America of Island of Orkney, Orkney and Shetland, 14 April 1783; REF = PROB 11/1102

Will of Thomas Sandison, belonging to His Majesty's Ship Isis, Seaman in the Pay of His Majesty's Navy of Westray, Orkney, 30 September 1784; REF = PROB 11/1122

Will of John Sinclair, Masters Mate of his Majesty's Ship Champion of Lerwick, Orkney and Shetland, 01 September 1785; REF = PROB 11/1134

Will of John Murray, Lieutenant in His Majesty's Navy of Shetland, 19 April 1794; REF = PROB 11/1244

Will of Alexander Gray, Mariner of Breaks Grimness, Orkney and Shetland, 23 August 1808; REF = PROB 11/1484

Appendix F

Will of Nicholas Flatt otherwise Flett, Lieutenant of the Royal Navy of Rendall, Orkney, 08 March 1813; REF = PROB 11/1542

Will of John Moodie, Seaman belonging to his Majesty's Ship Dauntless of South Walls, Orkney, 09 July 1813; REF = PROB 11/1546

Will of Andrew Randall, of His Majesty's Ship Modeste, of Yell, Shetland, 28 September 1813; REF = PROB 11/1548

Will of George Ross, late Seaman on board His Majesty's Ship Traave of Island of South Ronaldshay, Orkney, 28 May 1816; REF = PROB 11/1580

Appendix G

Three Sisters List

This table details the ninety-three Orkney men on the musters[1] of the *Three Sisters* who were taken between March and May 1778. The place of birth and age are not always given: O – Ordinary Seaman; Ab – Able-bodied Seaman.

Appearance	Born	Age	Name	Quality
29 Mar	Eavy	20	William Shurie	O
29 Mar	Isle of Rosey	22	George Flaws (1)	O
29 Mar	Isle of Rosey	22	Rowland Cooper	O
29 Mar	Firth, Pomona Island	30	William Flett	Ab
29 Mar			John Irving	
29 Mar	Eavy	19	Charles Dinnett	O
29 Mar			John Flaws	
29 Mar			George Spence	
29 Mar	Saundey Island	24	John Liddle	Ab
29 Mar			James Marwick	
29 Mar			George Rendall	
29 Mar	Rosey Island	21	William Folsetter	O
29 Mar	Rosey Island	21	George Flaws (2)	O
30 Mar	Rosey Island	26	Thomas Brand	O
30 Mar			John Linay	
30 Mar	Isle of Sheepancey	21	Thomas Heddle	O
30 Mar	Isle of Westray	19	Thomas Harcus (1)	O
30 Mar	Deerness	32	John Mowat	O
30 Mar	Kirkwall	23	George Eunson	O
30 Mar			Patrick Mowat	
30 Mar	St Andrews	20	James Louttit	O
30 Mar	Kirkwall	28	James Linay	O
30 Mar			Archibald Sinclair	
30 Mar	Holm	21	William Mowat	O
30 Mar	Eavy	23	Hugh Hughston	O
30 Mar	Gearsy Island	39	George Flett	Ab
30 Mar			Hugh Rendall (1)	
30 Mar	Saundy Island	19	Robert Cursetter	O
30 Mar	Saundy Island	18	Robert Drummond	O
30 Mar			Thomas Russtland	
30 Mar	Westray Island	19	Thomas Harcus (2)	Ab
30 Mar			Robert Miel	O

1 ADM36/7983.

Appendix G

Appearance	Born	Age	Name	Quality
30 Mar			Robert Gullion	O
30 Mar	Westray Island	34	Thomas Sandison (1)	Ab
30 Mar	Westray Island	31	William Inkster	Ab
30 Mar	Westray Island	20	James Tulloch	O
30 Mar			Henry Logie	
31 Mar	Firth parish	25	Hugh Scleater	O
31 Mar	Saundy Island	25	Robert Hay	O
31 Mar	Stronsey Island	20	John Cooper	O
31 Mar	Sandy Island	22	Thomas Sandison (2)	O
31 Mar			Thomas Fotheringham	
31 Mar	Kirkwall	28	John Coarston	O
31 Mar	Parish Bersey	24	Andrew Harvey	O
31 Mar			Thomas Valiant	
31 Mar			William Spence	
31 Mar			Robert Mowat	
31 Mar	Parish Birsey	17	William Moor	O
31 Mar	Parish Sandwick	20	John Hourston	O
31 Mar			John Sibeston (1)	
31 Mar			William Laughton	
31 Mar	St Andrews	31	John Patrie	Ab
1 Apr	Parish of Hoy	25	William Sands	Ab
1 Apr	Orford	24	Robert Balantine	Ab
1 Apr	Kirkwall	37	John McKay	O
1 Apr			Robert Tulloch	
1 Apr			George Moore	
1 Apr			John Louttit	
1 Apr			Hugh Ross	
3 Apr			William Rendall	
3 Apr			Hugh Rendall (2)	
3 Apr	Staness	21	John Omand	Ab
3 Apr			James Downie	
3 Apr			William Gibson	
3 Apr	Isle Rosey	23	William Leaskes	O
4 Apr	Rendell	22	John Harper	O
4 Apr			William Isbister	
5 Apr			Thomas Smith	
5 Apr			Peter Miller	
5 Apr			David Delder	
5 Apr	Stronsay	30	James Geutarey	O
5 Apr			Edward Duncan	
5 Apr			Robert Sinclair	
5 Apr	South Ronaldsay Island	34	David Fubister	Ab
5 Apr			Gilbert Rosie	
6 Apr	South Ronaldsay Island	38	John Annal	O
6 Apr	South Ronaldsay Island	29	Galloway Rosie	Ab
6 Apr	Eady	21	Henry Murry	O
6 Apr			William Liddle	
6 Apr			Alexander Laughton	
12 Apr			Magnus Tait	
20 Apr			William Captain	
24 Apr			Peter Irving	
28 Apr			Alexander Cromerty	

Appendix G

Appearance	Born	Age	Name	Quality
28 Apr			Hugh Manson	
28 Apr			James Cooper	
28 Apr	Westrey Island	24	Alexander Robinson	O
6 May			Peter Coupland	
6 May			William Windwick	
6 May			John Sibeston (2)	
6 May			Alexander Baikie	
6 May			James Tulloch	
6 May			James Willson	

Index

Note: page numbers in *italics* denote illustrations

Abbs, William 18
Abernethy, Adam J 86–7
Abernethy, Thomas 130–1
Adamson, Charlotte 236
Adamson, John 234–5, 236
Adkins, Roy and Lesley 5
Admiralty
    exemptions 2–3
    levy of men 44–8
    Pepys 4
    Protection 128, 329
    quota from Orkney 53, 111, 273–5, 279–80, 281
    quota from Shetland 202
    releases petitioned 228–9, 228n1, 229
    see also Commissioners of Supply
Aeolus 283
Africa 25
Aglath, Tam 105, 107
Alexander, constable 37
Allan, Catherine 181
Allan brothers of Swona 181
Allen, Andrew 38
American Revolution, War of 2, 27
American War of Independence 1, 2, 26, 56–7, 117, 235, 237
Amiens, Peace of 57–8
Anderson, Arthur 289–93
Anderson, James, of Bressay 80
Anderson, James. of Stromness 75, 77
Anderson, Magnus 60, 327–9
Anderson, Robert 113, 114
Anderson, Theodore 233
Anderson, Thomas 80
Anderson, Tom: *Haand Me Doon Da Fiddle* 234n4
Andrew Ross ballad 245–7
Angus, James Stout 251
Ann Galley 114, 326
Anna Brettie cave 137
Annie Elspeth's Rest 168
apprentices 19, 111

Archibald, of Starlea 72
Archturus 54, 55
The Arctic Whalers (Lubbock) 222
Ardent 285, 289
Armadale, Lord 283
Army service impressment 33, 34, 35, 36
Around the Orkney Peat Fires (Mackintosh) xiv
Arthurson, Magnus 169
assoilyce 112
Augsburg League, War of 1
Austrian Succession, War of 1

Baikie, William 280
Bain, James 234–5
Balfour, Thomas 47, 279
Balfour, William 30, 71–2
ballads 245–54
banishment as punishment 21
The Banks of the Shannon 189
Barbacena, Marquis of 290n2, 293
Barn of Scradda 174
Barnetson, Ben 55
Basque Roads engagement 230
Beattie, Dr Alan M, 26, 54–5
Begg, Sannie 297
Bellerophon 240
    muster books 240n1
bere crop 97, 187, 311
Bermuda 289
betrayal 103–11
    and just retribution 225
    for money 193
    by neighbour 102
    for spurning of love 195–6
    unwitting, by child 135
    by women 139, 190
    see also informers
Bews, John 75, 77, 142, 182
Bichan, George 206–7
Bigton cave 175
Billy Paint-your-Whistle 262–5
Billy Taylor, ballad of 248–9

Index

Birsay
    caves 138–9
    coast 116
    constables 33, 36
bod or booth 193n8, 311
Bolt, Bruce 20
Bolt, Magnus 221–2
Bolt, Thomas, Deputy Vice-Admiral 46, 47, 228
Bolt, Thomas of Cruister 65, 289
Bon Homme Richard 235
Bonaparte: *see* Napoleon Bonaparte
bounty system
    constables 33, 36
    lairds 9–10, 273–4, 275, 276, 278, 280, 282, 283–4, 285–6, 287–8
    recruits 2, 14
    volunteers 26, 33, 36, 48–9, 50, 63, 225–6, 276–7, 280–1, 283–4, 287–8
box beds 94, 133, 178, 238
Brass, John 84
Brazilian Navy scheme 289–93
Bre Brough 88
breaking out holdings 236n2
Breck, Thomas 33, 36
Bremen 290, 311
Bressay
    caves 162–3, *164–5*, 166
    Fencibles 327
    folklore 101
    press gangs 80, 125, 329
    public notice 12, 14
Bressay Sound 20
    Carysfort 63–4, 79
    Catherine 202
    dangers of 80
    Don 127
    Eliza 128, 129
    fiddler 93
    Nyaden 112
    warning signals 82
    Wilson 127
bribery 38–9, 103–4
bronchitis 5
Brough, Tom 94
Brown, Billy 92
Brown, Christie 86–7
Brown, John 80
Bruce, Donald 48
Bruce, John, Collector of Customs 104
Bruce, John of Sumburgh 236
Bruford, Dr Alan 247, 248
Budge, David 247–8
Budge, Magnus 91

Budge, Mrs 247–8
Budge, Thomas 68
Burgar, James 113, 114
Burgi Stacks 175
burials 219–20
Burra Isle cave 158
Burrallie Burn 256, 257
Burray constables 36
Burray Geo caves 137

Caesar o' Haan 138
Caithness
    fishermen 295
    fugitives 297
    impressment 109
    Orkney ferry 277n2, 279
    and Orkneymen 204, 297
    recruitment 295–8
    Sinclair's scheme 61
    volunteers 25
The Caledonian Mercury 14
Campbell, Donald 66
Carr, William 86n1
Carse, Alexander: *The King's Shilling* 74
HMS *Carysfort* 63–9, 79
    muster books 66–8
Cast Books 49
Catherine 202
Catton, Rev James: *The History and Description of the Shetland Islands* 167
Cave of Skrue 138
The Cave of the Bard 162, *163*, *164–5*
caves 133, 136–7
    Orkney 137–58
    Shetland 158–76
Cellar o Himera Geo 153
Chalmers, John (Chambers) 115
Chalmers, William 75
Chamberlain, Captain 20
Chambers, John (Chalmers) 115
The Chammers o Goldie 152
Charity Collection 54, 55
Charles, Duke of Buccleuch 210
Chaser 222
Chatham, Lord 46, 277, 278
HMS *Cherokee* 111
chimneys, hiding in 134
Church Courts 190–1
church support 19, 20, 54–7
Chyne, Katharine 196–7
Clark, Andrew 131
Clark, Peter 54
Clark, Thomas 54–5

Index

Clouston, Andrew 99
Clouston, Harry 88, 260, 261, 264–71
Clouston, John 106, 107
Clouston, Johnnie, fiddler 264, 265
Clowes, William Laird 4
Clumlie men 136
Cluness, Hugh 79
Cluness, John 79–80
Clunies-Ross, John 205–6
Cock, Thomas 68
Cocos Islands 206n1
Cogle, John 55
Collector of Cess 29, 36, 276, 281, 282
Collins: *The Press Gang of Tower Hill* xii
Colloquy of Three Orcadian Sailors in a Spanish Prison (Dennison) 219–20, 317–19
Comloquoy, Kitty 188
Comloquoy, Robert 233
Comloquoy, Sandy 188
Commissioners of Supply 2n3, 29–30, 33, 36, 48, 50, 53–4
community/kinship 9
Constable Holes 152, *154*, 155
constables 31–40
    attacked 37–9, 55, 184
    bounty system 33, 36
    bribery of 38–9
    complaint against 208–9
    sympathetic 39–40
constable's baton *vi*, 39, 40, 73n2
Cooper, of Westray 134
Cooper, on the *Victory* 238
Copland, James 36
Cormack, Hugh 224
corn hook as weapon 184, 186, 187
Corporation of Shoemakers 18
Corrigall, Kate 193
Corrigell, John 38–9
Corrigle, John 48
Corunna, battle of 224
Costa 86, 153
Cottar Hole 139
cottars 40, 199, 225, 323–4
Coupper, John 32
Covenanters Cave, Burra Isle 158, *159*
Covenanters Cave, Rousay 138
Covingtrie, David 30–1
Craigie, Gilbert 68
Craigie, Jessie Alexina 133
Craigie, William 108–11
Crimean War 232n2
criminals, impressment 21–3
crimps 5

Crocodile 20
Crofters Commission, Cunningsburgh 236
Crofts, Ernest 241
Cromarty, David, Constable 36
Cromarty, David, of Deerness 135
Crukshank, Hary 184
Cumbrian 212
Cumminess, Nether and Over 264–7
curses 92, 194, 195–6, 220
Customs House 6
Customs Officer 230

Dacres, Admiral 285
Dass, Jock 248
The David 47, 48
Davidson, George 77
Davidson, Robert 126
Davis Strait whalers 7, 88, 102, 126, 199, 201, 212, 285–6, 297, 323
    see also Straitsmen
Dearness: *see* Deerness
Dearness, William 18
death, feigned 100–1
debt bondage 10
decoys 103, 109
Deerness
    caves 137
    complaint by Covingtrie 30–1
    constables 36
    Cromarty 135
    Delday 219
    fishermen 182
    Paplay 91, 190
    quota 46
    warrants for arrest 48
Deerness, Arthur 222
defence subscription 51, 52
Delday, Andrew 88
Delday, George 97
Delday, William 219
Delting cave *170, 171*, 174
Delting Kirk Session 54
Da Den a Crudel 159–60
Dennison, Walter Traill: *The Orcadian Sketch Book* 219–20, 317–19
deprivation, domestic 71
Description of the Shetland Islands (Hibbert) 311
Descriptive Notes on Orkney (MacGregor) 144–5
deserters 4, 5, 111–15, 196
    see also fugitives
Dick, Magnus 30–1
Dinneson, James 30
Dinnie, Barbara 182n1

disease 5, 71, 97–8, 179, 180, 218, 219, 232
    see also specific illnesses
disguise, as women 101–3
district conflict, quota system 104–8
doctors, sympathetic 97
Dogger Bank battle 273
Don (brig) 127, 226
Donaldson, James 79
Donaldson, Joseph 80
Donaldson, Robert 79
Da Doos Holl 175
dreams of fish 185–6
Dunbeath sea cave 297–8
HMS *Duncan* 287
Duncan, Andrew, Procurator Fiscal 208, 210
Duncan, James, Constable 128
Duncan, James, disturber of peace 127–8
Duncan, Rev 190
Duncan, W R 10–11
Dundas, Sir Thomas 44–5, 46, 47, 274, 277, 283
Dundee man 296
Dundee whaling vessels 97–8
Dunrossness caves 175
Dutch Wars 1, 4

Eagle 25
The Earls Palace celebrations 188
Easson, James 48
Eday, Hidey Hole *132*, 146
Eday constables 36
Edinburgh Annual Register 226
Edinburgh Chronicle 23, 25
Edinburgh Evening Courant 25
Edmondston, Dr Arthur 25, 26, 27, 41, 72, 81
Edmondston, Dr Laurence 124
Egilsay pilots 108–11
Egyptian imprisonment 219, 260, 261
Eliza 128, 129
English language 61
English Primitive School: *The Press Gang* 76
enlisting money 21, 28
    see also bounty system
epilepsy 21, 48
Erasmuson, John 207–8
Erskine, William 211
Eshaness cave 174
Esson, Arthur 36
Eunson, Peter 274
Eunson, William, Andrew and James 97
Eunson of Quarff 220–1
Eunson's cave 137
ewe-shooting incident 88
exemptions from impressment 2, 4, 12–19, 26, 47, 127, 129, 200,
    cottars 40
    farmers 40
    Fencibles 60, 329
    fishermen 31, 64
    temporary 117
    see also Protection
expenses, liability for 52–4
Experiment 122
Eynhallow, Holy Island of The Orkneys (Mooney) 152
Eynhallow caves 146–7

factor's Account Book 287–8
Fair Isle caves 168–9
Da Fairies Hoose 163, *166*
Fanshawe, Captain Robert 64, 65–6
Fara 82
'Farewell to Stromness' 212
farmers 15, 40
    see also cottars
Fea, Barbara 156, 158
Fea, Helena 156, 158
Fea, James 7–8, 43
    will of 218, 321–2
Fea, John (Fraser) 115
Fea, Patrick 156
Fencibles 57–60
    Bressay 327
    deserter 111
    exemption from impressment 60, 329
    Kirkwall 58
    Orkney 276, 277, 279
    paid off 283
    Robertson, Wiilliam 43
    Shetland 279
    Stromnes 58
Fenton, Alexander 27
Fereday, Dr R P, 142n5, 147
Ferry Inn, St Mary's 277n2
Fetlar caves 158–9
Fetlar impressment 79–80
fiddlers 84–5, 180n1, 93–4, 218, 228–9, 233–4, 264, 265
Firth, David 36
Firth, George 102
Firth, Thomas 39–40
Firth constables 36
fishermen
    Caithness 295
    captured by privateers 218
    Deerness 183
    early impressment 23

Index

exemptions from recruitment 31, 64
farming duties 15
impressment 7–12, 115–16
Protection 14–15, 200, 201
skills 8
see also Davis Straits whalers; Greenland whalers; whaling crews
Flatpund, Walls 95
flax 40n3
Fleece cliff 146
Da Flegman's Hoose 160, *161*
Fleming, John 20
Flett, Ann 143
Flett, James 38, 134
Flett, Jocky 145–6
Flett, John, of Bea 37, 38
Flett, John, of Mirbuster 37
Flett, Magnus 20–1
Flett, Robert 143
Flottay constables 36
folk memory xiii, 10, 101, 237
Fordyce, Laurence 92
Fordyce, William 92
Foreign Enlistment Act 290
Foreign Office 290n2
Fort Charlotte 126, 183, 207, 208
Forth, Firth of 23
Fortitude 126–7
Fotheringame, Buchanon 38–9
Fotheringham, Jas 48
Fotheringham, Mr 283–4
Foula 19
Foula cave 174
Fraasa Cave 138
France
  imprisonment 221, 226
  prisoners of war 215, 216, 217
Fraser, Abraham 218
Fraser, Alexander 36
Fraser, John (Fea) 115
Fraser, Laurence 124
Fraser, Lieutenant 125
Fraser, Walter 128, 129
French Revolutionary War 2, 221
  veterans from 232
French Wars 26, 79, 143, 146, 295–8
  Marwick on 238
  veterans from 237–43
French words 220–1
Freswick men 296
fugitives
  Caithness 297
  food for 132, 133, 180–1

Jacobite Rebellion 153
local knowledge 94–5
see also caves; deserters; hiding places
Fullerton, Samuel 20

Gaddie, James 216
Galvao, Ambassador 290n2
Garioch, William 287
Garrick, Charles 215, 216, 217
Garrick, Christiana 215
Garrick, John 215–16
Garrioch, Constable 237
Garrioch, John 188, 275
Garrioch, William 142
Gaudie, George 239
Gaudie, John 239
Gentlemen's Cave 153
Gerawin, fugitive 142
Gibson, Joseph, Captain 202
Gifford, Gideon 65
Ginsty, Lieutenant 202
Glasgow Orkney and Shetland Literary and Scientific Association: tales of press gang 255–71
Glory 273, 277–8, 279, 281
Goar, Charles 156, 158
Goldie, Tom 104, 152
Goodlad, John 60
Gordon, John 278
Gorie, Sibbie 266, 267
Gossawater Loch 116
Goudie, Magnus 97
Goudie brothers 136, 175
Gourly, Captain John, Regulating Officer 37, 54, 80, 93, 133, 184, 201–2, 286
Graeme, Alexander of Graemeshall 51, 133, 201–2, 215, 240, 273–88
Graeme, Jean 280–1
Graeme, Mungo 273
Graemsay cave 152
Graemsay impressment 187–8
Graham, Robert 283
graith bucket 263n1, 312
gravits 68n2
Gray, Annie 228–9
Gray, Catherine 225
Gray, David 228–9
Gray, Gilbert 228–9
Gray, Robbie 223
Green Skerry 153
Greenland whalers
  annual visits 15, 26, 200, 201, 285, 286
  armed resistance 207–10

bears *203*, 212
catch of 202
Dunrossness brothers 206
fines for 199, 323–4
gravits 68n2
homecoming 12, 60, 206–7, 220, 222, 229
in Lerwick Tolbooth 201
protection for 126–7
Shetland fishermen 4, 27, 199, 207, 211, 328–9
Shetland lairds 199–200, 285
statistics 81
Greig, Alexander 223
Greig, David 128, 129
Greig, James, Procurator Fiscal 123, 126, 190, 191, 210
Grierson, Andrew 64–5, 211–12
Grierson, Christopher 19
Groat, Dr Robert 97
Groat, Malcolm 55
Groundwater, Edward 223–4
Groundwater, Henrietta: *Memories of an Orkney Family* 143
Groundwater, William 205
Gullion, George 87
Gun, Will 218, 321
Guthrie, Solomon 103

Haa of Our Ness 153
Haand Me Doon Da Fiddle (Anderson and Swing) 234n4
Hagart, Patrick 45, 46
Halcrew, Elizabeth 191
Halcrew, Elspeth 190–1
Halcrow, Laurence 127–8
Halkland, James 32
The Hall 144–5
Halliday, Captain 286
Halls of Garth 156, *157*
Hamburg 290, 311
hamesuckin 38
Hamilton, Emma 239, 240
Hanson, Ertie 92
Harcus, of Lochend 225–6
Harcus, of Tankerness 86
Harcus, sweetheart of 197–8
Harper, Andrew 125
Harper, William 88
Harray constables 37
Harray of Castlehill 221
harvest time 82, 115, 183, 186–8
Hawick, Gilbert 20
Hawn Skerry 138

Hay, James 131, 202
Hay, Robert 42
haystacks, as hiding holes 180
Head of Houton 139–40, *141*, 256, 257
health issues 4–5
see also disease
Hebe 169
Hectorson, Laurence 111–12
Heddle, William 135
Hellier Hol 163
Henderson, James 114
Henderson, James, ballad singer 248
Henderson, James of Lea, Whalsay 233
Henderson, John 119–20
Henderson, Lang Willie 233n1
Hercus, William 217
heritors: *see* lairds
Herston, Hall of 146
Hervie, William 36
Da Heylor a Jonaberg 169
Hibbert, Samuel: *Description of the Shetland Islands* 311
Hidey Hole, Eday *132*, 146
Da Hidey Holl, Skaw Taing 169, *172*, *173*
hiding places 105, 115, 133–76, 180, 256, 257
Hill, Edith Maxwell 296n2
The History and Description of the Shetland Islands (Catton) 167
Hoiden-Holl, Unst 176
Hol of Bugars 163
Hole in the Brough 137
Hole o Houton 139, 142
Hole o the Head 139, *141*, 152
Hole o the Ness 152
Holes o the Horn 137
Holes of Cupsermung 256, 257
Da Holl a Eastermuir 169
Da Holl a Leeans 169
Da Holl a Sneugans 169
Da Holl o da Gowans 169
Holm cave 152
Holms 256, 257
Home, Sir George 274, 278, 280
Honyman, Captain 285
Da Hoose a Heylor *170*, *171*, 174
Da Hoose o Hirdie Geo 174–5
Da Hoose o Sholmack 174–5
Hoseason, Lang Willie 232–3
Hoseason, of Bressay 117
Hossack, B H, *Kirkwall in the Orkneys* 43n3, 49–50
Hotchkis, Captain 282
Hourston, Alexander 38

Index

Hourston, George 36
Hourston, Hugh 108–11
Hourston, John 186
Hourston, William 33, 36
Howarcroft, Evie 185–6
Hoy affray 55
Hoy man 84
Hubie woman, of Fetlar 194
Hudson Bay Company 5n1, 7, 29
Hull, W V 224
Hull men 212
Hull whaling vessels 97–8
Hunter, Agnes 130
Hunter, John 211–12
Hunter, Joseph 94–5
Hunter, Lieutenant 25
Hunter, Murray 79
Huntlins, Ket 193
Huntly, Kate 192–3
Hutchinson, J R: *The Press Gang Afloat and Ashore* 2n2, 2n4, 5, 73n4
Hutchison, Lieutenant 54
Huxter, Clemmie o 184–5

HMS *Illustrious* 230, 232
Impress Act 37
Impress Service 4–5, 47, 48
impressment 1
    Army service 33, 34, 35, 36
    conditions on board ship 25, 26, 71, 119
    of criminals 21–3
    discontinued 1–2, 61
    early 23, 25–6
    of fishermen 7–12, 115–16
    folk memory 10
    Graemsay 187–8
    homecoming 223–43
    Kirkwall records 27–8
    naval engagements 71
    navy expansion 2
    poverty 186
    revenge 237
    of schoolboys 125
    statistics 12, 26–7, 29
    wedding celebrations 7, 72, 93, 182, 188, 250
    see also exemptions from impressment; press gangs
impressment avoidance 71–2
    alarms 81–3
    arguments by law 73, 75, 77
    melancholy endings 77–80
    name changes 114–15, 325–6
    narrow escapes 83–5

    strength and athleticism 85–7
    subterfuge and disguise 94–103
    violence 88, 91–2
    see also fugitives; weapons
imprisonment
    on Continent 215–22
    in Egypt 219, 260, 261
    in France 221, 226
    in Spain 219–20, 317–19
incest charge 190
Incorporation of Hammermen 18
ineligibility 19–21
informers 103–11
    because of jilting 190
    just retribution 225
    on Kate Huntly and son 192
    Spence 152
    uncle on nephew 145
Ingoe 139
Ingsa, Constable 178
Ipswich 112, 113
Ireland and Stenness men 104–8, 262, 263, 264, 265
Irvine, J W 26
Irvine, James 175
Irvine, John 87
Irvine, Robert 130
Isbister, Magnus 186
Isbister, William 205
Isbuster, James Jr 119–20
Izat, Rev James 180n10, 226n1

Jack, Margaret 120–1
Jack in the Bilboes (1804) 90
'Jack is Yet Alive' 234
'Jack's Alive!' 234
Jack Tar, Life in Nelsons Navy 5n3, 16n1
Jackson, George Vernon: *Perilous Adventures and Vicissitudes of a Naval Officer* 63–4
Jacobite Rebellion 153
Jakobsen, Jakob: *The Place-names of Shetland* 163n2
Jameson, James (drowned) 79
Jameson, James, of Olnafirth 121–3
Jameson, Magnus 207
Jameson, Marion 193–4
Jamesson, James, of Fetlar 193, 194
Jamesson, Jerome 193, 194
Jamieson, James 73, 75
Jarmson, John 224
jaundice, French cure for 218
Jeanette 221
Jeemson, Walter 115–16

Jenkin's Ear, War of 1
Jeromsdaughter, Marion 193–4
jilting of girl 190
Jocky Flett's Hole 145–6
John, the fiddler 94
Johnson, Angus 202n1, 228
Johnson, John 84
Johnson, Laurence G: *Laurence Williamson of Mid Yell* 79
Johnson, Lawrence 114–15
Johnson, Samuel 4
Johnson, Smithy 80
Johnson, William 224
Johnson brothers of Quarff 220–1
Johnston, David 48
Johnston, James 146
Johnston, John 188
Johnston, Magnus, Constable 36
Johnston, Magnus, of West Burrafirth 95n2
Johnston, Mary 134
Johnston, Tom 95n2
Johnston of Outbreaks 105, 107
Johnstone, Alexander: *Seizing a Waterman at Tower Hill* ii
Johnstone, James 283
Johnstone, Robert (Lawrenceson) 114–15, 325–6
Jones, John Paul 234–6
Justices of the Peace 2n1, 29–40, 50, 53, 55, 73n2, 125

kelp harvest 16, 18, 277, 279, 285
Kemp, Rev Dr 8, 27
Kent, James 225
   Nelson's cabin-boy 239–40
Ker, naval surgeon 8, 201
Kettlebaak 175
King's shilling 73–7
The King's Shilling (Carse) 74
kinship/community 9
Kirkcaldy's Sword story 77–8
Kirkwall
   contributors 25, 49–50
   Customs House 6
   Fencibles 58
   impressment records 27–8
   Justices of Peace 30
   Lammas Market 71n1
   levy 48, 49
   Napoleonic Wars recruitment drive 50–1
   postal services 43n1
   press gang at wedding 182
   The Ship Inn 73
   Tolbooth 24, 29, 32
Kirkwall Volunteers 57
Kirn of Gula 92
Da Kist a Muckle Birriers Geo 159
Klifts cave 160
Da Klist a Klonger 160
Klivvie of Heshiber 138
knitting skills 102

Da Lad at wis ta'en in Voar ballad 251–2
Lady Kirk graveyard 135
Laing, M. 285
Laing, Robert 280n1
lairds
   bounty system 9–10, 273–4, 275, 276, 278, 280, 282, 283–4, 285–6, 287–8
   Fanshawe's request 64–5
   quotas 9–10, 273, 275
   recruitment 7, 40
   releases from impressment 18–19
   role of 40
   tenants 8, 225, 226
   whaling 199–200
   see also specific landowners
Lamb, Grizel 100–1
Lamb, James 100–1, 163
Lamb, Jeannie 101
Lammas Market, Kirkwall 71n1
land-mails leger 323
landman/landsman 5, 50
landmen/landsmen, protection from impressment 75, 77
landowners: *see* lairds
Lang Geo caves 137
Langskaill, Janet 42
Laughton, John 217, 287
Laughton, William 287
Laurence Williamson of Mid Yell (Johnson) 79
Laurenceson, John 59–60
Laurenceson, Tammie 166
Laurenson, Arthur 11, 220n6
Laurenson, of Fetlar 84
Laurenson, Tammie 101
Lawburrows 22, 120
Lawrenceson, Robert (Johnstone) 114–15, 325–6
Leask, Andrew 125
Leask, Henry 36
Leask, J T Smith
   'An Orcadian Battle' 106n4
   A Peculiar People and Other Orkney Tales 142, 177n1, 219, 255–71
Leask, Oliver 36

Index

Leith 14, 25, 47, 48, 235
Leith, Charles 232
Leith, James 232, 238–9
Leith, Nicol 230, 232
Leith, Peter 230
Leith, William 230
Leith brothers, Stenness 229–32
HMS *Lenox* 54, 55
Lerwick
    Carysfort 66, 68, 69
    Customs House 6
    farmers, impressment 119–20
    Fencibles advertisement 58, 59
    Impress Service 119, 123
    and the Mousa Men 234–6
    Regulating Officers 10
    Rendezvous 10, 72, 103, 128, 129, 130
    Sheriff Court cases 119
    Tolbooth 24, 72n3, 201
    volunteers 60, 81
    whaling crews ashore 4, 210, 211
Leydn 232
The Liberty of the Subject. Women opposing the Press Gang (1799) 179
Linak, John 217
linen industry 40
Linklater, James 37, 38
Linklater, Jane 97
Linklater, Thomas 86
literacy levels 7, 223, 230
The Little General and the Rousay Crofters (Thomson) 225
Little John o Mirky 137
living conditions 7–8
Lobb, Captain 25
Lochend curse 195–6
Longhope Lore (Mitchell) 206
Longie Geo 160
look-out points 83
Loutit, George 75
Louttit, Ann 178, 180
Lubbock, Basil: *The Arctic Whalers* 222
luder horns, as fog horns 82
Lunnasting cave 160–1
HMS *Lynx* 230

Maa Water 95
McCra, James 121–3
McDonald, John 104
MacGregor, George: *Descriptive Notes on Orkney* 144–5
Mackintosh, W R: *Around the Orkney Peat Fires* xiv

McKay, Janet 130–1
Maggie Cuttie's Cave 137
maiming of hands 98
Mainland, Henry 85n1, 112–14, 123–4
Mainland, William 32
Maitland, Captain 241
Manson, Robert 169
Manson, Skipper 221
Manson, Dr T M Y 251–2
Manson, Thomas 60, 327–9
Margaret 16, 18
Martha Jane 245–6
Marwick, Alexander: *Reminiscences* 134
Marwick, Ernest W 238, 5n1
Marwick, Hugh 32
Marwick, Robert W 109
Marwick brothers, David, William and Roland 31
Marwick cave 138, *139*
Marwick's Hole, St Magnus Cathedral 198
Mary 22, 75, 77, 207, 209
Mary Ann 249
Matches, James 204
Mathewson, Andrew Dishington 12, 78–9
Mathewson, Thomas 11
Maxwell, Alexander 296n2
Maxwell, George 296n2
Meadows and Taylor, Messrs *139*
Meason, Gilbert 279, 281
medical unfitness 97, 98, 187, 224, 295–6
Melsetter 18–19
Melvin, William 16, *17*
Memorial & Defences (Morrison *et al*) 60, 327–9
Memorial to Earl of Morton 200–1
Memories of an Orkney Family (Groundwater) 143
mental illness 99–100, 192, 295–6
    see also simple-mindedness, feigned
Merriman, William 37–8
Methodism 207
Michall, William 217
Militia Act 295
Mill, Rev John 56–7
Millar, Isobel 43
Miller, Elizabeth 42
Miller, Peter 36
Miller, Robert 102–3
miracles 195
Mirk Holes 137, 146
Mirki Geo 163
miscreants apprehended 127–8
Mitchel, Captain 283

Index

Mitchell, Sir Andrew 78
Mitchell, J. 286
Mitchell, J Stirling: *Longhope Lore* 206
Mitchell, John 55
Mitchell, Sir John 194
Mitchell, John, Writer at Kirkwall 183
Mitchell, William 221
Moad, Merran 177
Moar, Hugh 36
Moar, Laurence 99–100
Moar, Thomas 218
HMS *Modeste* 44
Moncrieff, Hackie 169
Money Box 152–3
Moodie, George 295–6
Moodie, James 18–19, 296
Moodie, William 98
Mooney, John: *Eynhallow, The Holy Island of The Orkneys* 152
Moore, Sir John 224
Morley, Robert: *The Press Gang* 13
Morrison, Andrew 60, 327–9
Morrison, James (Richard) 20
Morrison, Matthew 77–8
Morton, Earl of 200–1
Mouat, Alexander 125
Mouat, Rev Hugh 56
Mouat, John 80
Mouat, Thomas 111–12
Mouat, William 54, 60, 117
Moul Head, Deerness 182
Mousa Men 234–6
Mowat, George 178
Mowat, James, of Graemsay 104
Mowat, James, of Mey 295, 296
Mowat, Robert 111
Mowat, Walter 32
Muckle John o Mirky 137
Muckle Roe cave 160
Muckle Roe men 177–8
Mudie, Lieutenant Donald 20, 21
Muir, John 153
Muir, Margaret 42
Mure, Robert 32
Murray, Andrew 80
Murray, Laurence 80
muster books
    Bellerophon 240n1
    Carysfort 66–8
    Three Sisters 335–7

name-changing 114–15, 325–6
Napean, Captain Evan 18

Napier, Captain Charles 14
Napoleon Bonaparte 11n5, 224, 226, 240–2
    as threat 11, 182
Napoleonic Wars
    end of 1, 6
    Leith brothers 229–32
    need for men 2, 50–1
    Orkney 238–9
    start of 50
    Tait 240–1
    veterans of 221, 225, 232
National Service 6
Nautical Reminiscences (Vedder) 204–5
naval service 2, 10–11, 53, 71, 81
Neill, Patrick: *A Tour through some of the Islands of Orkney and Shetland* 9, 199, 323–4
Nelson, George 93
Nelson, Horatio 2n1, 5, 238–40
nettle rash 97, 258, 259
Newlands, Willie 232n2
Nicol, Mrs 130
Nicolson, Captain James 10, 58–9, 60, 73, 75, 112, 113, 117, 119, 126, 327–9
Nicolson, John 207
Nightingale 20
The Nightingale ballad 247–8
Nine Men Hole 147, *150*
Ninianson, Magnus 68–9
Ninianson, Robert 68–9
Nisbet, Magnus 120
Norfolk 54
North Ronaldsay 134, 153
Northern Lights Commissioners 169
Northmavine cave 160
The Nor'Wasters 7n1
Notes on Orkney and Zetland (Peterkin) 212
Nyaden 112, 113

oars as weapons 91, 187
oat stack hiding hole 134
oatmeal kist hiding hole 134
Oddie, Constable 39
Ogilvy, Thomas 126
Ogilvy, William 75
Ollison, Magnus 55
Oman, John 75
Omand, of Bigswell 105, 107, 108
oral tradition xiii, 71, 245–54
The Orcadian 245
The Orcadian Sketch Book (Dennison) 317–19
Orkney
    caves 137–58
    Commissioners of Supply 46–7

Index

Fencibles 276, 277, 279
ferry 204, 297
impressment 27–8, 29, 57
living conditions 7–8
poverty 220
protections 16, 18
see also specific islands
The Orkney Herald 221
Orkney men/Orkneymen
    Caithness 204, 297
    HMS *Carysfort* 68
    press gangs xiii
    remittances 41, 49
    in Spanish prison 317–19
The Orkney Parishes (Sinclair) 61, 226n1
The Orkneying Saga (Taylor) 147
Orkneyman's Cave 162, 163, *164*–5
Orphir caves 139, 140, 142
Orphir constables 36
Osnaburgh 202
Ottar Holes 137
Otway, Rear Admiral 131
Oughton 25

Da Paeds Hoose 167
Paets Hole 156
Palmerston, Lord 290n2
Papa Stour
    caves 174–5
    grandfather/grandson story 88, 91
Paplay, Andrew 91, 190
Paplay's Hole 142–3, *144*
Park, George 36
patronymic system 68, 115n1, 193n7, 224n3
Peace's Orkney and Shetland Almanac and County Directory 109–11
peat stacks 133, 134, 158
A Peculiar People and Other Orkney Tales (Leask) 142, 177n1, 219, 255–71
peep-holes 83
Penant, James 120
Peninsular & Oriental Shipping Company 289
Pennant, Mr 324
pensions 229, 230, *231*, 239
Pentland Firth 86, 97, 156, 204, 295, 296
Pepys, Samuel 4
Perilous Adventures and Vicissitudes of a Naval Officer (Jackson) 63–4
Perrots, Peter 322
Peterkin, Alexander: *Notes on Orkney and Zetland* 212
Peterson, Andrew 208
Peterson, Henry 208–10

petitions for release 32–3, 75, 119–23
Petrie, Archibald 285
Petrie, David 133, 201–2, 215, 273–88
Petrie, David Jr 216
Pharos 210
Da Picts Hoose 163
pipers 93, 280
Pirie, Lieutenant 25
Pitt, William, the Younger 2
The Place-names of Shetland (Jakobsen) 163n2
Polyphemus 232
Porteous, Arthur 181
Porteous, Mrs 181
Portsmouth 5, 223, 229, 239, 277–9, 282
Post Office Acts 237n1
postal services, Kirkwall 43n1
poverty
    Brazilian scheme 290
    Memorial 60, 327
    Orkney and Shetland 7–8, 9, 220
    whaling crews 207
    women left behind 186
pregnancy by incest 190–1
The Press Gang (19th Century) 89
The Press Gang (English Primitive School) 76
The Press Gang (Morley) 13
The Press-Gang, or English Liberty Displayed 3
The Press Gang Afloat and Ashore (Hutchinson) 2n2, 2n4, 5, 73n4
The Press Gang of Tower Hill (Collins) xii
Da Press-gang Sang 253–4
press gangs xiii
    Bressay 80, 125, 329
    overcome with drink 192
    prevalence of 1
    Scalloway 207, 208, 209
    The Shetland Times 182–3
    tales of 255–71
    at wedding 7, 72, 93, 182–3, 188, 250
    and whalers 206
    wife of leader 186
    see also impressment
Da Press Hole 162
Da Pressgengs Point 78
prisoners of war 215, 216, 217, 321–2
    see also imprisonment
privateers 9, 204, 218, 221, 295
protected men as decoy 103
Protection 12–19
    compromised 75
    disputed 128–9
    document *17*
    for fishermen 14–15, 200, 201

Index

Greenland whalers 126–7
landmen 75, 77
public notices on church doors 12–13, 199, 323
Pygmy 54

HMS *Quebec* 228
Quota Acts 2, 48–54
quota system
    advertisement 14
    deficiencies 53
    district conflict 104–8
    Government-demanded 328–9
    lairds 9–10, 273, 275
    volunteers 18

Rae, Sheriff Depute 327
Raith 222
Randall, Andrew 44
Randall, Barbara 44
Randall, Catharine 44
Randall, Elizabeth 44
Ratter, of Northmavine 224
recapture 22, 111, 215, 222
Recruiting Act 32
recruitment 2
    avoidance 206–7
    Brazilian Navy 291
    Caithness 295–8
    foreknowledge of 71–2
    French Wars 295–8
    lairds 7
    whaling skippers 206
Regulating Officer 4, 10, 27, 47, 53, 102
release from impressment 18–19, 54–5
Reminiscences (Marwick) 134
remittances
    accredited collection 6
    from Orkney men 49
    receipts for 42
    from Shetlanders 41–4
Rendal, James 16, 36
Rendall, Catherine 227
Rendall, James 43
Rendall, of Halbreck 180
Rendezvous 4
    Kirkwall 29, 73, 75
    Leith 14, 85, 97, 129, 142
    Lerwick 10, 25–6, 66, 72, 103, 120–2, 128, 129, 130, 328
Repenting Stool cave 137
HMS *Resistance* 22
Resolution 48
revenge, belated 237

rewards
    for catching deserters 111, *113*
    for impressment 14, 30, 33, 36
    informers 103
    of rent-free land 236
rheumatism 5
Richan, Mr 277, 279, 280, 283
Richan, William 281
Riddoch, James 217
Riddoch, Mr 278
Ridland, Robbie 169
Ridland, William 169
Ritch, Edward 55
Ritch, George 36
Ritch, Mrs 186
Ritch, William 186
Rivick o the Moul 137
Robertson, Arthur Scott 234n1
Robertson, J D M 133, *155*
Robertson, James 218, 322
Robertson, Peter 21–3
Robertson, Robert 229
Robertson, William 43
The Rocky Shop 83
Rodgers, Captain Henry 245–7
room/roome 30
Rosamund 37
Rose 232
Rosie, nephew of Tomison 185
Ross, Collector of Customs 126
Ross, Jamie 221, 222
Rossie, Walter 99
Rousay
    caves 138
    constables 31
    warning signs 82
Rowland's Cave 152
rum 4–5n3, 239n2
Rusland, William 240n1

St Magnus Cathedral, Marwick's Hole 198
Sally and Becky 25
Salvador del Munor 224
San Francisco Examiner 242–3
Sandcroma geo *139*
Sandison, James 42
Sandison, Thomas 42
Sandness district 55, 82
Sands, Mrs Jean 55
Sands, Rev Robert 55
Sandsting cave 175
Sandwick
    caves 152

Sinclair family 123–5
substitute sailor 116–17
women 183–4
Saxby, Jessie M E: *Shetland Traditional Lore* 136, 176
Scalloway press gang 207, 208, 209
Scapa Flow defence system 139
Scarborough 235
Scatsta Session Minutes 54
School of Scottish Studies 228
schoolboys, impressment of 125
Sclater, Thomas 36
Scots money 49
Scott, Andrew 18
Scott, Christina 178
Scott, George 125
Scott, James 47
Scott, John 128
Scott, Lieutenant Keith 85, 279
Scott, of Rendall 81–2
Scott, 'Old Melby' 19
Scott, Thomas 40
Scott, Sir Walter 20n3, 163, 169, 199n1, 210–11
Scott, Walter, Justice of Peace 207–8, 209
Scott, Walter, Regulating Officer 10, 27, 80, 104
Scottish Society for Propagating Christian Knowledge (SSPCK) 8, 27
scurvy 5, 97–8, 219, 232
sea caves 136–7
Sea Fencibles: *see* Fencibles
Seagull 221
Sea Songs and Shanties (Whall) 212–14
seals 91, 146n2, 163, 202
Seizing a Waterman at Tower Hill (Johnstone) ii
self-abnegation 115–17
self harm 98
Serapis 235, 236
Seven Years War 1, 26, 29–30, 200n3
shape-shifting 195–6
Shapinsay kirkyard 135
Shark 29
Shearer, Ann 186
Shearer, James, Bailie 186
Shearer, James, Constable 36
Shearer, Ned 227
sheep's head, burning 178
Shetland
and Admiralty 47
agriculture 9
Brazilian Navy 289–90
caves 158–76
Fencibles 58–9, 279
fiddlers 93–4

Greenland whalers 199–201, 328–9
impressment xiii, 12, 57
living conditions 7–8
parliamentary representation 10n2
poverty 220
quota for Napoleonic Wars 54
remittances from men pressed 41–4
Scottish Society for Propagating Christian Knowledge 8, 27
see also specific islands
The Shetland Advertiser 11–12, 102, 137, 229
The Shetland Journal 290, 293n1
The Shetland News 226, 236
The Shetland Times 56, 182–3, 224–5
Shetland Traditional Lore (Saxby) 136, 176
The Ship Inn 73
shoemaker imprisoned 221
Shoordie and his fiddle 93–4
Shurie, John 82
simple-mindedness, feigned 48, 99–100, 295, 296
Simpson, of Skaw 100
Sinclair, Andrew 296
Sinclair, Catherine 123
Sinclair, David 58
Sinclair, Edward 32
Sinclair, Hary 38–9
Sinclair, James 117
Sinclair, Sir John: *The Orkney Parishes* 61, 226n1
Sinclair, Kirsty 187
Sinclair, Laurence 126–7
Sinclair, Margaret 117
Sinclair, Peter 93
Sinclair, Robert 127–8
Sinclair, Thomas 187
Sinclair, William 142, 296
Sinclair family, of Sandwick 123–5
skaithless 120
Skaw village 100n3
Skeld cave 169
Skerries 82, 116, 167–8, 233
Skerry Firth 160
skin disorder 97
slop, drawing 5
slops, charges for 202
smallpox 178, 180
smart money 21
Smith, Adam 191
Smith, George 116–17, 295–6
Smith, James, of Fetlar 92, 193, 194–5
Smith, James, of Mousa 234–5
Smith, James, of Sandwick 123
Smith, James, of Westray 43

Index

Smith, John, of Sandwick 123, 124
Smith, Laurence 190
Smith, Lieutenant Laurence 77
Smith, Lieutenant 36, 207–8
Smith, Malcolm, of Hillswick 20
Smith, Malcolm, of Sandwick 123, 124
Smith, Malcolm, 85n1
Smith, Mark 209
Smith, midshipman 37
Smith, Olla 21–3
Smith, Ursula 123–4
Smith, Walter 295–6
Smith, William 19
The Smuggler's Cave 137
Snody, James 93
song and verse, oral tradition 245–54
South Ronaldsay caves 145–6
South Walls caves 156
Spain, imprisonment 219–20, 317–19
Spanish Succession, War of 1, 29, 219
    veterans returning 237
Spence, David 152
Spence, James 125
Spence, John 36
Spence, Thomas 43
Spence of Gorn 225
Stenchwater 92
Stenness men 75, 104–8, 262–3, 264–5
Stephens, of the Admiralty 46
Stewart, James, of Brough and Cleat 225–6
Stews Head cave 146
Stickle, of Vealie croft 180
Stickle family 180n1, 228
Store House of Howar 153
story-telling, returning veterans 232–4
Stout, William 55, 125
Stove, William 91
Straitsmen 204, 230, 262–5, 314
Strenuous 131
Stromness
    constables 37, 38–9
    enlisting Orkney men 29
    Fencibles 58
    harbour 212
    impressment 19
    narrow escape 83
    protection for men 75
    sea shanties 212–14
Strong, Thomas 112–13, 113–14
Stronsay
    caves 156–7
    constables 36
    man breaking own leg 98

old man 82
subscriptions for prisoners of war 217
substitute sailor 116–17
Sutherland, Donald 20, 21
Sutherland, Dr J 32
Sutherland, Captain Eupham 275–6, 278, 280, 281
Sutherland, James 55
Sutherland, Peter 218, 321
Sutherland coast 109, 204
Swan 25
Swanney, Quartermaster William 237–8, 238n1, 242
Swanson, William 55
Sweyn's Cave 147, *151*, 152
Swing, Pam: *Haand Me Doon Da Fiddle* 234n4
swingle-tree haul 295
Swona 146, 181

Taederson, Annie 188
Tait, James 240–1
Tait, John 77–8
Tait, John, of Holm 97
Tait, Joseph 187
Tait, Lawrie 130
Tait, Magnus 48
Tait, Peter 182
Tait, Robert 32
Tait, William 99
Tammie Tyrie's Hidey Holl 116, 168
Tankerness caves 142–5
Taylor, A B: *The Orkneying Saga* 147
Taylor, George 36
Taylor, Peter 145
Taylor, Thomas (Tulloch) 156
Teddy and Patty *189*
tenants
    and Andrew Grierson 211
    booth 193n8, 311
    and lairds 8, 225, 226
    of Moodie 98
    petitions for 117
    and Dr Robert Groat 97
    Skaw 100n3
    and whalers 199–200
    see also cottars
Da Thieves Holl, Eshaness 174
Thomson, Grizel 180–1
Thomson, Magnus 180–1
Thomson, of Silwick 169
Thomson, Sinclair 84–5, 175
Thomson, W P L: *The Little General and the Rousay Crofters* 225

350

Index

Three Sisters 41, 42
    muster books 335–7
Tiefs Holls, Fair Isle 168–9
Da Tieves Cave 160
Da Tieves Holl, Foula 174
Tilloch, John 217
Tilloch, William 217
Tolbooth
    Kirkwall *24*, 29, 32
    Lerwick *24*, 72n3, 201
    Rendezvous 25–6
Tomison, Donald 145–6, 185
Tompson, Bath Papers 324
Tormiston farm house, Stenness 94
A Tour through some of the Islands of Orkney and Shetland (Neill) 9, 199, 323–4
Towie, Tammy 168
Trafalgar, Battle of 26, 232, 238–9, 240
    veterans of 229, 296
Traill, George William 225
Traill, Jean 276
Traill, John 32
Traill, Thomas 30
Transactions of the Highland Society 324
Troall, North Unst 83
Trondra caves 175
truck system 10n1
True Lovers ballad 250–1
tuberculosis 5, 230, 239
Tudor, John R. 163, 236
Tulloch, Bobby 253–4
Tulloch, John of Senness 237
Tulloch, Malcolm 125
Tulloch, Thomas 30, 153
Tulloch, Rev William 72
Turfus, Peter 153
Turnbull, John 20n3
Turnbull, Rev John 56, 85
Twatt district 134
Twenty Men Hole 146–7, *148*, *149*
typhus 5
Tyrie, James 30
Tytler, queen of Rackwick 178

Uillcox & Anderson 290
Umphry, Elizabeth 104
Da Un 136, 175
underage impressment 19, 20
underfloor holes 133
Unst
    bartering in harbour 223
    caves 176
    impressment of farmers 120–1

An Unwelcome Visit from the Press Gang 96
Urquhart, Thomas 43, 49
Uyea cave 175

Valenciennes 321–2
Vat of Kirbister cave 156
Vedder, David: *Nautical Reminiscences* 204–5
Vedder, Gilbert 48
Velzian of Hoosewhee 105–6, 107–8
HMS *Vengeance* 43
veterans returning
    as decoy 103
    disabled/self-harm 98
    of French Wars 232, 237–43
    of Napoleonic Wars 221, 225, 232–3, 237
    pensions 239
    of Spanish Succession War 237
    story-telling 232–4
    as substitute 117
    from Trafalgar 229, 296
    from Waterloo 232
Victory 2n1, 238
Vienna, Congress of 12
A View of the Whale-Fishery 203
Volunteer 121
volunteers 2, 115–17
    bounty system 26, 33, 36, 48–9, 50, 63, 225–6, 276–7, 280, 283–4, 287–8
    Caithness 25
    criminals 21
    enlisting money 28, 29, 63
    lairds 7, 40
    Lerwick 60, 81
    Navy 11
    Orkney 16–17, 18, 25, 41, 48, 49–51
    see also Fencibles; quota system
Voy, Gilbert 250n1
Voy, James 282

Walls, warnings by minister 83
Walls Kirk Session 55, 196–7
Walls Session Records 114–15, 325–6
Walterson, of Isbister 87
Walty Reid's Hole 138
Da War Hooses 174
warning signals 82–3, 160, 167, 188, 258, 259
Warrender, Crown Agent 48
Wasbister 134
watch tower, Weisdale 174
Waterloo, battle of 207, 224, 241–2
    veterans from 232
Watson, Robert 120
Watt, William 56

Watt, William, of Skaill 19, 183, 184
weapons
   arquebuse 112-113
   clubs 91
   corn hook 184, 186, 187
   gun 88
   knives 79, 84, 88, 207, 258, 259
      blubber 88, 205
      sheath 84
   oars 91, 187
   rifle 235
Webb, Captain 114
wedding celebrations 7, 72, 93, 182, 188, 250
Weisdale 56, 82, 174, 207
Wellington, Duke of 232, 238
Westness, Rousay 225
Westray 31, 85, 152–3, 197–8
'The Whale' 212, *213*
whaling
   lairds 199–200
whaling crews 7, 199–213
   fines 199, 323–4
   homecoming 10, 15, 102, 201–2, 204–6, 297
   nature of 210–12
   poverty 207
   press gang 4, 206
   sea shanties 212–14
   see also Davis Strait whalers; Hudson Bay Company; Greenland whalers
whaling vessels 97–8
Whall, Captain W B, *Sea Songs and Shanties* 212n4
Whalsay caves 169
Whitby men 212
White, Thomas 54
White Breast, of Hoy 256, 257
Wick, Barbara 182
Wick, Peter 187
Widewall Bay 178
William Henry, Prince 169
William III 27–8
William IV 290
Williamson, John 20
Williamson, John, ship's master 120–1
Williamson, Laurence 79
wills 43–4, 218, 321–2, 331–3
Wills, Dr Jonathan 101
Wilson, deserter 111–12
Wilson, John 205
Wilson, Lieutenant William 10, 119–31
   apprehension of apprentice 19

apprehension of miscreants 127–8
character of 129–31
commissioned 119
disputed Protection 129
Impress Service 119
Petitions against 119–23
removed from post 131
Sandwick violence 123–5
threats by 126
Winwick, James 120
Wishart, John 18
Wishart, Nicol 36
witchcraft 92
   and curses 193–8, 194, 220
   shape-shifting 195–6
women's roles
   disguise for men 101–3
   food for fugitives 133, 142, 180–1
   guile 177–8, 180–1, 191–2
   harvest time 186–8
   love, loyalty and betrayal 139, 188, 190–2
   Mrs Clouston 266, 267
   poverty 186
   as sentinels 185–6
   strength and determination 181–5
   witchcraft and curses 193–8
Wood, John 240n1
Wood, Magnus 240n1
Wood, William 276
Work, James 226–7
Work, John 104
Work, Laurence 226–7
Work, Magnus 32–3
Work brothers, of Shetland 226–7
Wrath, Cape 109, 204, 205, 296
Wylie, Harry 103

Yell
   caves 162
   impressment of farmers 120–1
   press gang stories 181n3
   thatch, hiding in 134–5
   woman against press gang 181
yellow fever 5, 66, 69
Yenstay Head 144–5
Yetts, Lieutenant 47, 48, 274, 275–6, 279
Yorston, James 32

Zealand 283
Zetland: *see* Shetland

ORCADVM et SCHET[LANDIÆ]
INSVLARVM accuratissima [descriptio]

EST NOBILIS IRA LEONIS.

ORCADES

The Faire Yle

MARE GERMANICVM.

OCEANVS DEVCALEDONIVS

North Ranals Øy
Ouskerrie
Streoms Øy
Stronsa
Linga
Papa
Wester Øy
Heth Øy or Eda
Sekskherry
Fara
Siapins Øy
Roous Øy
Wyer
Eglis Øy
Kirkwale
POMONIA or MAINLAND
Coupins Øy
Burra
South Ranals Øy, or South Ronas Øy
HOY
Flotta
Pentland, or Pichtland Skerries
Southa
Sonna
Pichtland Fyrth
Dungsby head

SCOTIÆ PARS OF CATNES. PARS.

Thurso

Milliaria Scotica
Milliaria Anglica
Milliaria Germanica